INTRODUCTORY ADA®

PACKAGES FOR PROGRAMMING

WADSWORTH SERIES IN COMPUTER SCIENCE

Ageloff and Mojena, *Applied FORTRAN 77*

Amsbury, *Data Structures: From Arrays to Priority Queues*

Brown, *From Pascal to C: An Introduction to the C Programming Language*

Lewis and Birjandi, *Macintosh Hands-On Pascal*

Merchant, *FORTRAN 77: Language and Style*

Reynolds, *Program Design and Data Structures in Pascal*

Texel, *Introductory Ada: Packages for Programming*

Walker, *Modula-2: Programming with Data Structures*

INTRODUCTORY ADA®

PACKAGES FOR PROGRAMMING

PUTNAM P. TEXEL

Wadsworth Publishing Company
Belmont, California
A Division of Wadsworth, Inc.

Computer Science Editor: Frank Ruggirello
Editorial Assistant: Serina Beauparlant
Production: Julia Chitwood, Bookman Productions
Designer: MaryEllen Podgorski
Illustrator: Marilyn Hill
Print Buyer: Ruth Cole
Cover: Hal Lockwood, Bookman Productions
Signing Representative: Jeff Wilhelms

Printed in the United States of America

1 2 3 4 5 6 7 8 9 10—90 89 88 87 86

ISBN 0-534-06348-9

Library of Congress Cataloging-in-Publication Data

Texel, Putnam P.
Introductory Ada.

Includes index.
1. Ada (Computer program language) I. Title.
QA76.73.A35T49 1986 005.13'3 85-29418
ISBN 0-534-06348-9

To Nico Lomuto

"If he is indeed wise he does not bid you enter the house of his wisdom, but rather leads you to the threshold of your own mind."

Kahlil Gibran, *The Prophet* (treatise on teaching)

FOREWORD

Ada is a high-order programming language developed by the U.S. Department of Defense to help defray the rising costs of software, specifically the rising costs associated with software maintenance. It is a well-known fact that errors that are detected early in the development process are less costly to fix than errors that are detected after the system has been deployed. Because of that fact, it is extremely important to spend time understanding the problem being solved and to spend time making sure that the representation of the solution to the problem is simple, clear, and easy to understand. Why? Because the software will be maintained either by someone who did not work on the original solution at all or by the *original* problem solver who may have temporarily migrated to another project and returned to the original project a year or two later.

Ada is a language that permits us to represent our solution in a clear, simple, and easily understood fashion. This text will show how that can be done.

CONTENTS

PREFACE

Many individuals say that Ada is a complex language and that it can only be taught to those with a very sophisticated computer science background. I challenge that statement. Because Ada is a powerful language it gives the user tools that make life simple for him or her. An analogy is Einstein's theory of relativity. The science of relativity is complex, but the formula for the user is quite simple. The science of software engineering is complex, but the tool for the user, Ada, is quite simple. Why? Ada is simple because it permits us to represent our problem-solving thought process directly in the code.

This text is designed for the student who perhaps has had one introductory high-school or college course in BASIC, Pascal, or FORTRAN. Therefore I do not explain I/O, variables, and so forth. This text is equally appropriate for those individuals well versed in another language who wish to learn the new concepts of this increasingly important language. Finally, this text will serve as an excellent introduction to Ada for those individuals who have heard about Ada and are curious to know what makes Ada different from other languages.

Ada is the ideal candidate for a teaching language because:

1. Ada supports software engineering. We can teach software engineering early without giving it that "label."
2. We do not have to teach all of Ada at once. There are degrees of Ada that support a natural career path.

3. The features of Ada that support the development of large systems can be introduced early, thus providing a mechanism for prototyping the commercial software development process in the academic world.
4. Many features of Ada support a software components industry. For true productivity gains, we will have to grow in that direction.
5. The Ada package provides a natural mechanism for presenting Ada itself.
6. By using Ada as a teaching language, we are giving the students an opportunity to be on the leading edge of software technology.

Pedagogical Approach

The order of presentation of topics is a top-down approach. Packages are presented first and used as a basis for the entire book. Basic control constructs are presented second, types third, and finally packages are revisited to show how package bodies are constructed.

Packages are introduced first because packages provide one kind of reusable software. Packages (and generics) are the basic software components that, once coded, can be reused in other application areas. In the near future corporations will have an internal "package store" where staff can go and retrieve existing software components that can be *reused,* not *rewritten.* Because of that fact, most constructs in this introductory text are presented within the context of a package to show the student how to *use* existing packages. Progressing through the text, the student is gradually transitioned from *using* packages to *designing* elementary packages.

Finally, paragraph numbers from the *Reference Manual for the Ada Programming Language* [© U.S. Government (OUSDRE) 22 Jan. 1983] are provided after appropriate section titles as an additional source of information for the reader.

How Much Ada?

Because it is important to learn to solve problems with Ada, not to learn every feature of Ada, the entire language is not presented in this one text. Once we learn how to solve problems using Ada, additional features of the language can be introduced and used within a proper framework. A second text, *Advanced Ada: Programming with Packages,* will address those features of Ada that are not covered in this text, for example, discriminated records, access types, generics, and tasks.

Exercises

Each chapter contains exercises to be completed by the student. Solutions to the odd-numbered exercises are found in the back of the text, and solutions to the even-numbered exercises are in the accompanying Instructor's Guide. Many of the exercises require the student to select and use previous packages. In the later chapters there are a number of exercises that either modify existing code or can be done as team projects. Because of the design of the exercises and the order of presentation of topics, this text can be used as an introduction to the industrial world of software development.

Acknowledgments

Writing a text is not an easy task. No book happens without the efforts of many people. First, this book is dedicated to Nico Lomuto who, in a car on the way to Mexico, said "Think graphics" and who answered my incessant questions. Second, thank you to the U.S. Army and SofTech, Inc. for conceiving the idea of the U.S. Army Model Ada Training Curriculum that I was fortunate enough to participate in. A large part of this text is an expansion of part of *An Ada Primer,* a book developed as part of that curriculum while I was an employee of SofTech, under contract to the U.S. Army (Contract #DAAB07-83-C-K514). The individuals who participated in the review of *An Ada Primer* and therefore have contributed to this text in an indirect way are as follows: Christine Ausnit, Andrea Cappelini, Norman Cohen, John Goodenough, Frank Laslo, Nico Lomuto, Karen Sather, and Suzanne Seminski Ruegsegger.

Thank you to the following reviewers of *Introductory Ada* for their many valuable suggestions: Richard Bolz, U.S. Air Force Academy (Retired); Grady Booch; John Buoni, Youngstown University; Genevieve Knight, Hampton Institute; Frank Laslo; Patricia Lawlis, Wright Patterson AFB; Lavonne Manning, University of District of Columbia; Stuart Regis, Stanford University; M. Susan Richman, Penn State University, Capitol Campus; G. Boyd Swartz, Monmouth College; Peter Wegner, Brown University; and Tom Wheeler, Stevens Institute of Technology.

Thank you to Frank Ruggirello, senior editor at Wadsworth, for having faith in me; to Julia Chitwood of Bookman Productions, the production editor, for her tolerance level; and to Penny Dalto for her ideas for the illustrations.

A special thank-you is due two employees of AAI Corporation in Baltimore, Md., Pat Smeton and John Cannella, for the code that they checked, the code that they produced, and for the exercises that they completed for both the text and the accompanying Instructor's Guide.

Another thank-you goes to Frank Laslo for his second pair of eyes that proved so invaluable throughout the galley and page proof process. A special thank-you to George Sumrall, U.S. Army, for his not-so-gentle nudges. And, finally, another special thank-you to Dick Bolz for spending one day in Tinton Falls, N.J. that changed my life.

Thank you to my two Rays, husband and son, who, in the face of adversity, unselfishly survived on their own.

P. P. T.

1

PACKAGES AND THEIR USE

CHAPTER OBJECTIVES

- State the two parts of a package.
- State how the two parts of a package support abstraction and information hiding.
- Read a package specification.
- Import packages via a **with** clause.
- Access package resources with and without **use** clauses.
- State that **with**ing is not transitive.
- Understand that ambiguous references can occur as a result of using the **use** clause.
- Define a context clause.
- Write a simple procedure.
- Define a program library.
- Write a comment.

In English a package is defined as "any finished product which has been made ready for immediate operation . . . or use by preassembling all essential elements into a self-contained, compact unit."* This is also a fairly good definition of an Ada package.

Instead of dealing with system libraries, FORTRAN COMMONs, or JOVIAL COMPOOLs, Ada provides the package. A *package* in Ada is a mechanism that groups logically related resources into one "box." Just as attic storage boxes may be labeled with names appropriate to their contents, such as Photographs, Cooking Utensils, or Old Clothes, Ada packages must be labeled or named. Simple_Graphics is an example of an Ada name or identifier. (Generally an underscore is a replacement for the spaces between words, in order to make the names easier to read.) The rules for writing names in Ada will be presented in Chapter 2. We need to learn some concepts before we learn how to write names.

1.1 Package Specifications (LRM 7.2)

A label on a box in the attic tells you what is inside the box. For example, the label in the foreground of Figure 1-1 states that the box contains cooking

FIGURE 1-1 Labeled attic storage boxes

* *Webster's New Collegiate Dictionary* (G. & C. Merriam Company, 1961)

utensils, specifically an egg beater, knives, spatula, and mixing bowls. However, the label does not tell everything about the contents of the box. The label does not state whether the egg beater is a wire whisk or the hand-cranked kind, or whether the mixing bowls are stainless steel, ceramic, or wooden. The label doesn't need to tell us that information. If we need an egg beater, or the mixing bowls, we know which box contains them and all we need to do is go get the box. Like this kind of label, an Ada *package specification* states *what* an Ada package contains.

Let us look at a specific example. Suppose we have an Ada package that provides the following resources:

- a means to write points in Cartesian coordinates;
- the ability to draw a line, given the starting and terminating points of the line in Cartesian coordinates;
- the ability to draw a circle, given the center in Cartesian coordinates and the radius;
- the ability to express coordinates of all points and the radius as whole numbers.

These resources can be stated in an Ada package specification as follows:

```
package Simple_Graphics is
   type Point_Type is array (1..2) of Integer;
   procedure Draw_Line (From, To : Point_Type);
   procedure Draw_Circle (Center : Point_Type;
                          Radius : Integer);
end Simple_Graphics;
```

Figure 1-2 shows this specification as a label on an Ada "box."

Understanding a Package Specification

Now let's look at each of the lines of the package specification for Simple_Graphics in more detail.

Line 1: **package** Simple_Graphics **is**

FIGURE 1-2 Package specification for Simple_Graphics

This line states that the specification is for a package named Simple_Graphics. The word **is** indicates that a list of the package contents follows. Any items appearing between this line and the line

```
end Simple_Graphics;
```

will specify what is in the package.

Line 2: **type** Point_Type **is array** (1..2) **of** Integer;

This line introduces a *data type* called Point_Type. We will cover Ada's data types in more detail in later chapters, but let us briefly review the concept of a data type here and compare Ada's handling of data types with that of other languages.

In FORTRAN, a type statement indicates the kind of value that can be associated with a variable. For example,

```
INTEGER COUNT, X
```

states that the variables COUNT and X may assume only integer values (values that do not contain decimal points). The type statement

```
REAL TIME, DISTANCE, RATE
```

states that the three variables TIME, DISTANCE, and RATE may assume only real values (values containing a decimal point).

In most versions of BASIC, a data type symbol follows the variable name.

For example, a variable name followed by a $, such as A$, indicates a string variable. Therefore, the only allowed values for this variable will be sequences of characters.

In Pascal, the programmer must explicitly state in the variable declaration section that a variable belongs to a certain type, for example:

```
VAR
   counter : integer;
```

This declaration states that "counter" is a variable that may assume only integer values.

Floating, Fixed, Real, Integer, and Character are all common names for data types. These names specify what kinds of values can be associated with variables of that type. Any attempt to assign an incorrect value to a variable may cause a compile-time or run-time error. Ada, like the other languages just described, includes the concept of a data type as being a set of values that variables of the type may acquire. Additionally, like Pascal, Ada's typing mechanism defines the set of operations that can be performed on variables and constants of the type. Indeed, Ada extends the data type concept even further than Pascal, as we shall see in future chapters.

FORTRAN and BASIC supply their data types as part of the language. Pascal supplies some types as part of the language and allows the programmer to define additional ones. Ada is like Pascal in this respect. Defining your own data types allows you to more closely model the real world.

Returning to our line of Ada code, we see that Point_Type is a programmer-defined data type that is declared to be a one-dimensional array with integer indices and two components of type Integer. Integer is a predefined data type in Ada. A value of type Integer must always be written as a whole number, without any decimal point. The type Point_Type allows us to write values that define points in Cartesian coordinates, such as (1, 3).

Line 3: **procedure** `Draw_Line (From, To : Point_Type);`

This line declares that within package Simple_Graphics there is a *procedure* named Draw_Line. An Ada procedure is similar to a FORTRAN subroutine or a Pascal procedure. Procedures are used to divide large programs into smaller modules that are easy to write and understand.

The identifying word **procedure** in our line of code is directly followed by the name of the procedure, Draw_Line. The procedure's *formal parameter list*, "From, To : Point_Type," follows within parentheses. A formal parameter list indicates data required and/or produced by a procedure (that is, inputs and outputs). Draw_Line requires two data items of type Point_Type. Note that names of parameters of the same type are separated from each other by a comma and are separated from the type name by a colon. The rules for writing and using formal parameter lists are given in Chapter 2.

To summarize, this line of code states that package Simple_Graphics has as one of its resources a procedure, Draw_Line, which requires two values of type Point_Type (that is, two points) and which, upon execution, draws a line connecting the two points.

```
Line 4: procedure Draw_Circle (Center : Point_Type;
                               Radius : Integer);
```

This line describes another resource supplied by package Simple_Graphics. This resource is also a procedure and is named Draw_Circle. Like Draw_Line, Draw_Circle requires two data items. The first is a value of type Point_Type that is the center of the circle, and the second is the circle's radius, which is of type Integer. Note that parameters of different data types are separated by a semicolon. Upon execution, this procedure draws a circle centered at Center, with a radius equivalent to the value passed for Radius.

```
Line 5: end Simple_Graphics;
```

This line terminates the package specification for Simple_Graphics. The use of the package name here is optional but strongly recommended. Throughout this text, we will place the package name after the word **end** when we indicate the end of a package specification. The final semicolon in this line is mandatory.

In summary, a package specification states *what* resources the package makes available to a user, just as the label on a storage box indicates *what* resources the box makes available to whoever drags the box out of the attic—which brings us to the next section.

1.2 How to Get the Package (LRM 10.1.1)

Gaining access to the resources in a storage box is fairly simple. We bring the box from the attic, open it, and remove the needed items from the box. The mechanism for gaining access to and using the resources of an Ada package is also relatively simple.

The *with* Clause

The following code uses the resources of Simple_Graphics to draw a line connecting the two points (1, 5) and (2, 7).

```
with Simple_Graphics;
procedure Draw_Specific_Line is
  --
  -- Two hyphens indicate a comment line in Ada.
  -- They have the same function
  -- as a REM statement in BASIC,
  -- a C in column 1 in FORTRAN,
  -- and braces, { }, in Pascal.
  --
begin -- Draw_Specific_Line
  --
  -- This procedure draws a line
  -- from the point (1, 5)
  -- to the point (2, 7).
  --
  Simple_Graphics.Draw_Line( (1, 5), (2, 7) );
end Draw_Specific_Line;
```

The clause "**with** Simple_Graphics;" must be placed prior to procedure Draw_Specific_Line. This clause imports package Simple_Graphics to procedure Draw_Specific_Line and makes all resources provided by Simple_Graphics available to Draw_Specific_Line. Thus, just as we get a box from the attic, the **with** clause gets an Ada package for us (see Figure 1-3).

Notice how the Simple_Graphics resource desired, procedure Draw_Line, is obtained. The name of the procedure is prefixed by the package name and a dot (.), that is, Simple_Graphics.Draw_Line.* The value (1, 5) is used for the parameter named From, and (2, 7) is used for the parameter named To. Both values are enclosed within a single set of parentheses. A semicolon is required to terminate the line.

Multiple **with** clauses may be written to access several packages simultaneously. For example, suppose we want to place the following text:

Figure 6. A Straight Line.

underneath the line that was just drawn. Assume that there is a package named Text_IO that provides Input/Output (I/O) services and includes a proce-

* When a package resource is referenced by prefixing the resource name with the package name and a dot (.), this notation is called *expanded name* notation.

FIGURE 1-3 The **with** clause

dure named Put, which expects a sequence of characters enclosed within quotation marks as a parameter and prints out that same sequence of characters. To perform the operation described, we would write the following code:

```
with Simple_Graphics;
with Text_IO;
procedure Draw_Specific_Line is
begin -- Draw_Specific_Line
  --
  -- This procedure draws a line
  -- from the point (1, 5) to the point (2, 7).
  --
   Simple_Graphics.Draw_Line( (1, 5), (2, 7) );
   Text_IO.Put ("Figure 6. A Straight Line.");
end Draw_Specific_Line;
```

When importing (using the resources of) more than one package, you may write each **with** clause on a separate line, as in

```
with Simple_Graphics;
with Text_IO;
```

or you may write them on one line, as in

```
with Simple_Graphics; with Text_IO;
```

In either case, each **with** clause must be terminated by a semicolon.

As a shorthand notation, you may write the word **with** once, followed by the names of the packages to be imported, separated by commas:

```
with Simple_Graphics, Text_IO;
```

When you use this notation, you must follow the final package name with a terminating semicolon.

The *use* Clause (LRM 8.4)

The code that accesses Draw_Line can be abbreviated by adding a **use** clause as follows. The boxes indicate changes made to the code shown earlier in this section.

```
with Simple_Graphics; use Simple_Graphics;
procedure Draw_Specific_Line is
   --
   -- Illustrating use of the use clause.
   --
begin -- Draw_Specific_Line
   --
   -- This procedure draws a line from
   -- the point (1, 5) to the point (2, 7).
   --
   Draw_Line( (1, 5), (2, 7) );
end Draw_Specific_Line;
```

When the **use** clause is added, the prefix "Simple_Graphics." is no longer required to access the resource Draw_Line. The **use** clause is placed after the **with** clause. A **use** clause may be followed only by a package name, for reasons that will become apparent in Chapter 2.

Multiple **use** clauses are permissible. The following code presents an alternative way of producing the desired figure title.

```
with Simple_Graphics; use Simple_Graphics;
with Text_IO;         use Text_IO;
procedure Draw_Specific_Line is
   --
   -- Illustrating use of the use clause.
   --
begin -- Draw_Specific_Line
   --
   -- This procedure draws a line from
   -- the point(1, 5) to the point (2, 7).
   --
   Draw_Line( (1, 5), (2, 7) );
   Put ("Figure 6. A Straight Line.");
end Draw_Specific_Line;
```

The following are also legal ways of writing multiple **with** and **use** clauses:

```
with Simple_Graphics; with Text_IO;
use Simple_Graphics; use Text_IO;
```

or

```
with Simple_Graphics, Text_IO;
use Simple_Graphics, Text_IO;
```

All of the preceding are examples of *context clauses.* A context clause in Ada is any mixture of **with** and **use** clauses that together define a run-time environment. Within a context clause, a **use** clause may not appear until *after* a **with** clause that imports the specified package.

Let us complete our analogy of the attic storage box. The **with** clause obtains a package for us. The **use** clause provides a shorthand notation for selecting a specific resource from the package. Neither the **with** clause nor the **use** clause actually opens Simple_Graphics. We *cannot* see how Draw_Line is coded. We must open the storage box in order to use the egg beater, but Ada permits use of package contents without "opening" the package.

A Word of Caution (LRM 8.3)

Although a **use** clause is a convenient way to refer to the resources of a package, multiple **use** clauses can sometimes lead to trouble. Consider the following package specification:

```
package Page_Headings is
  type Margin_Type is array ( 1..2 ) of Integer;
  procedure Print_Header_Text;
  procedure Draw_Line
            (Left_Margin, Right_Margin : Margin_Type);
  procedure Print_Blank_Lines (Number : Integer);
end Page_Headings;
```

Assume that Print_Header_Text prints a header at the top of a page, Draw_Line in this package underlines the header text, and Print_Blank_Lines prints the number of blank lines specified.

Assume also that the following procedure is coded:

```
with Page_Headings;    use Page_Headings;
with Simple_Graphics; use Simple_Graphics;
procedure Draw_Graph is
  --
  -- This procedure will not
  -- compile successfully.
  --
begin -- Draw_Graph
  Print_Header_Text;                       --Page heading
  Draw_Line ( (0, 10), (60, 10) );         --Underline it
  Print_Blank_Lines (10);                  --10 blank lines
  Draw_Line ( (1, 5), (2, 7) );            --Draw the line
end Draw_Graph;
```

Procedure Draw_Graph is supposed to place a page heading at the top of the page, underline the heading, and then insert ten blank lines before drawing a line connecting the points (1, 5) and (2, 7).

But there is a major problem here. Draw_Graph imports two packages, Simple_Graphics and Page_Headings. Both packages contain a procedure named Draw_Line with identical parameter requirements: two points whose coordinates are written as integers. Does Draw_Line ((0, 10), (60, 10)); refer to Simple_Graphics.Draw_Line, or Page_Headings.Draw_Line? *We* know that Draw_Line from Simple_Graphics is used to draw a line between two points on a Cartesian coordinate system, while Draw_Line from package Page_Headings underlines header text at the top of a page—but unfortunately, the compiler does not have that same understanding. The compiler simply looks at both Draw_Lines as procedures with the same name that require identical data to execute. We view the points for Draw_Line in package Simple_Graphics as being in a plane and the two points in Draw_Line from package Page_Headings as being left and right margin boundaries on a page, but the compiler views ((0, 10), (60, 10)) as a legal value of either type Point_Type or type Margin_Type. The compiler therefore issues a diagnostic stating that it cannot determine which Draw_Line to use.

As this example shows, identical names appearing in different packages can cause problems when those packages are simultaneously imported. One solution to this problem is easy: simply refer to the resource by its expanded name. The resource's expanded name, you may recall, is the resource name prefixed by the name of the package and a dot. Revised code for our example, using expanded names, would look like this:

```
with Page_Headings;    use Page_Headings;
with Simple_Graphics; use Simple_Graphics;
procedure Draw_Graph is
  --
  -- No more confusion.
  -- The ambiguity is removed.
  --
begin -- Draw_Graph
  Print_Header_Text;
  Page_Headings.Draw_Line ( (0, 10), (60, 10) );
  Print_Blank_Lines (10);
  Simple_Graphics.Draw_Line ( (1, 5), (2, 7) );
end Draw_Graph;
```

Another solution would be to disallow use of the **use** clause for most packages, thus requiring the majority of resources to be specified in their expanded form. However, the entire problem could have been avoided if the writer of the package specification for Page_Headings had chosen a more appropriate name for the procedure that underlines the header text, such as Underline_Header_Text.

A Chain of Packages

The following package specification imports Text_IO.

```
with Text_IO; use Text_IO;
package Simple_Graphics is
  --
  -- The specification as previously supplied.
  --
end Simple_Graphics;
```

The following procedure imports Simple_Graphics.

```
with Simple_Graphics; use Simple_Graphics;
procedure Draw_Specific_Line is
  --
  -- This code will not compile.
  -- It is in error.
  --
begin -- Draw_Specific_Line
  --
  -- This procedure draws a line from
  -- the point (1, 5) to the point (2, 7).
  --
  Draw_Line ( (1, 5), (2, 7) );
  Put ("Figure 6. A Straight Line"); -- **ILLEGAL**
end Draw_Specific_Line;
```

Is Text_IO also imported to Draw_Specific_Line? Does Text_IO come along with Simple_Graphics to draw Specific_Line? The answer is no. Text_IO does *not* come along with Simple_Graphics when it is imported to Draw_Specific_Line. The above code is incorrect, and a diagnostic will be issued by the compiler indicating that it does not recognize Put. For the same reason, the compiler will not recognize the expanded name Text_IO.Put. The "chaining" doesn't work: the fact that package A is imported to package B and package B is imported to another unit, C, does *not* mean that package A is available to C. To output the desired figure title, Text_IO must be *explicitly* imported to Draw_Specific_Line by writing a **with** clause, in the manner shown earlier.

But Where Is the Code? (LRM 7.3)

As stated previously, the code in a package specification simply declares what resources the package provides. A package specification does not state *how* the resources are implemented. This information is contained in the *package body* [see Figure 1-4(a)].

The package specification for Simple_Graphics states that this package contains a procedure called Draw_Line, which, when we call it, will draw a line between two points. This information does not tell us how Draw_Line is coded or how it operates—for example, whether it draws from left to right or right to left. The code for Draw_Line contained within the package body does indicate how the line is drawn [see Figure 1-4(b)]. But is it really necessary to know this information? As a user, isn't it enough to know that Simple_Graphics provides this resource and that once we import the package, we can draw lines and circles at will? The answer to this question is usually *yes.*

Simple_Graphics is an example of both *abstraction* and *information hiding,* two software engineering concepts that will be stressed in this text. Abstraction allows one to focus on the most essential elements of a problem, temporarily ignoring details in order to reduce the complexity of the problem and provide an easier path to its solution.† Here, we just need Simple_Graphics to provide services, specifically the ability to draw lines and circles. The details of its method for drawing a line or a circle are usually irrelevant to us. The package specification focuses only on the package's essential elements.

FIGURE 1-4(a) Package structure

Specification

```
package Package_Name is
   --
   -- What is provided
   --
end [Package_Name]*;
```

* Brackets [. . .] indicate optional items.

Body

```
package body Package_Name is
   --
   -- How it is implemented
   --
end [Package_Name];
```

† D. T. Ross, J. B. Goodenough, and C. A. Irvine, "Software Engineering Process, Principles, and Goals," *Computer* (May 1975): 65.

The package also provides an example of information hiding. Whereas abstraction reveals the details essential at a given level, information hiding makes inaccessible the details nonessential at that level so that other parts of the system will not be affected.* A procedure that uses Simple_Graphics cannot access the executable code for the resources provided by Simple_Graphics and therefore cannot inadvertently modify it.

In summary, an Ada package provides resources to be used and consists of a package specification and a package body. The package specification tells exactly what the package's resources are, while the package body contains the implementation of those resources. Figure 1-5 reminds us that the user of the package has access only to the package specification.

FIGURE 1-4(b) Simple_Graphics package structure

Specification

```
package Simple_Graphics is
   type Point_Type is array (1..2) of Integer;
   procedure Draw_Line (From, To : Point_Type);
   procedure Draw_Circle (Center : Point_Type;
                          Radius : Integer);
end Simple_Graphics;
```

Body

```
package body Simple_Graphics is
   --
   -- Code for the two procedures placed here
   --
end Simple_Graphics;
```

* D. T. Ross, J. B. Goodenough, and C. A. Irvine, "Software Engineering Process, Principles, and Goals," *Computer* (May 1975): 65.

FIGURE 1-5 The user's view of a package

Specification

```
package Simple_Graphics is
   type Point_Type is array (1..2) of Integer;
   procedure Draw_Line (From, To : Point_Type);
   procedure Draw_Circle (Center : Point_Type;
                          Radius : Integer);
end Simple_Graphics;
```

Body

```
package body Simple_Graphics is
   --
   -- Code for the two procedures placed here
   --
end Simple_Graphics;
```

1.3 Compiling Programs into Program Libraries (LRM 10.1)

Just as a jigsaw puzzle is made up of pieces that fit together to form a finished product, an Ada program is comprised of pieces that also fit together. We now have a package specification, a package body, and a procedure: three pieces of an Ada *program*. The **with** clause links procedure Draw_Specific_Line to the package specification for Simple_Graphics, and there is an automatic tie between the package specification and the package body for Simple_Graphics (see Figure 1-6).

A jigsaw puzzle normally comes in a distinct container, such as a cardboard box or canister. In attempting to complete a jigsaw puzzle, you wouldn't try to incorporate pieces from another puzzle located in a different container. An Ada *program library* is similar to a jigsaw puzzle container. Basically, an Ada

FIGURE 1-6 Parts of an Ada program

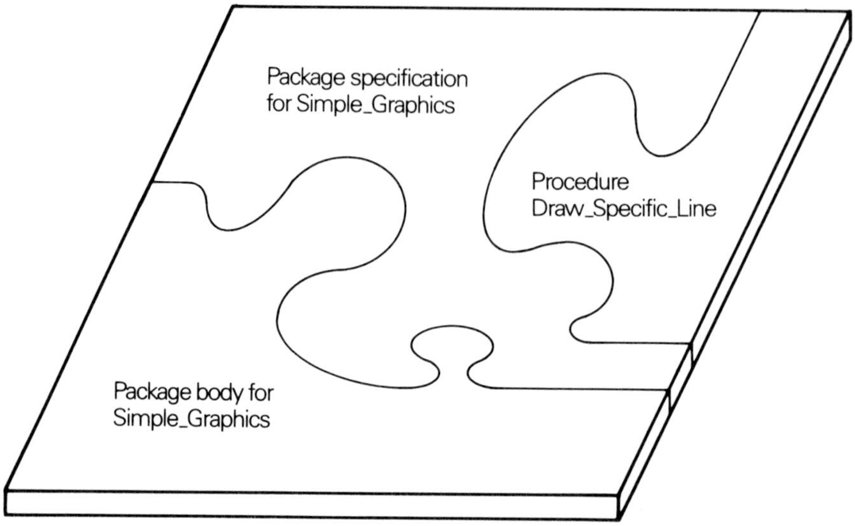

program library is a container for the pieces of an Ada program or programs. Each program library has its own name and contains all the pieces required for an Ada program or programs (see Figure 1-7).

Dependency and Compilation Order

All the components of an Ada program must be compiled into a program library before the main program is executed. There is a specific compilation order

FIGURE 1-7 An Ada program library named Graphics

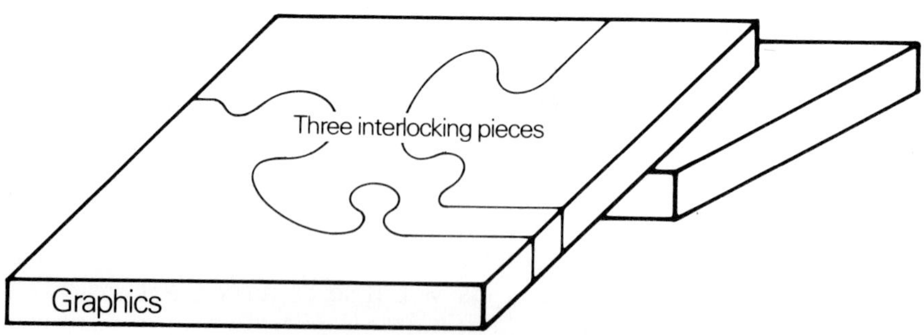

required by the language. Pieces that have other pieces depending on them must be compiled first. This compilation order can be shown in a *dependency diagram.*

Figure 1-8 depicts a dependency diagram for Draw_Specific_Line and consequently specifies the order in which the "pieces" of this program are to be compiled into the program library called Graphics. The arrows indicate dependency. The package body for Simple_Graphics depends on the package specification for Simple_Graphics, so the specification must be compiled before the body. Package specifications must always be compiled before package bodies. Procedure Draw_Specific_Line also depends upon the package specification for Simple_Graphics. Thus the package specification for Simple_Graphics must be compiled into the library before procedure Draw_Specific_Line. Whether the package body or the procedure is compiled second is immaterial. What is important is that the package specification is compiled into the library first because both the package body and the procedure depend upon it.

A Multiprogram Library

A jigsaw puzzle container holds pieces that make up a single picture, but an Ada program library may contain several different Ada programs. Consider the pro-

FIGURE 1-8 Dependency diagram for Draw_Specific_Line

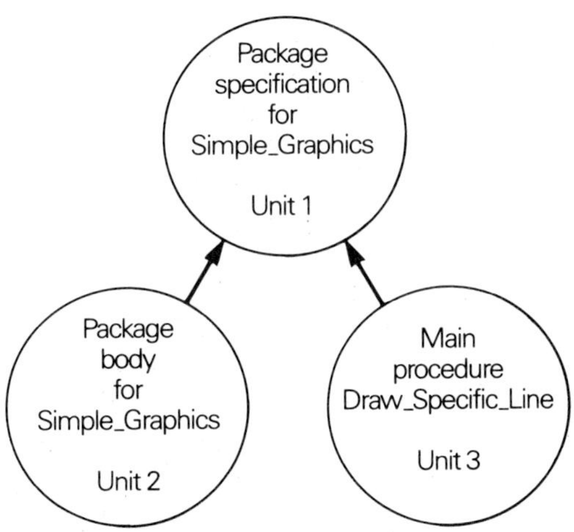

Legal Compilation Orders

Compilation order 1: Unit 1, Unit 2, Unit 3

Compilation order 2: Unit 1, Unit 3, Unit 2

cedure Draw_Specific_Circle, which draws a circle centered at (0, 0) with a radius of 2.

```
with Simple_Graphics;
procedure Draw_Specific_Circle is
  --
  -- This code draws a circle centered
  -- at (0, 0) with a radius of 2.
  --
begin -- Draw_Specific_Circle
  Simple_Graphics.Draw_Circle( (0, 0), 2 );
end Draw_Specific_Circle;
```

To access the resources of Simple_Graphics, Draw_Specific_Circle must be compiled into Graphics, the same library that contains Draw_Specific_Line. Graphics now contains two Ada programs (see Figure 1-9). One program consists of the package specification and body for Simple_Graphics and the procedure Draw_Specific_Line. The second program consists of the package specification and body for Simple_Graphics and procedure Draw_Specific_Circle. Even though the two procedures are completely independent, they are compiled into the same library so that they can access a single copy of Simple_Graphics. Because they are different programs, however, the programmer must specify in the execute command *which* Ada program is to be executed.

1.4 An Ada Procedure (LRM 6.3)

You probably noticed that all the procedures you have seen so far are similar in structure. Each started with the word **procedure,** followed by a user-supplied name for the procedure and the word **is.** The word **begin** indicated the beginning of the executable code. In our example, **begin** was followed by a comment indicating the name of the procedure. Although it is not required by the language, writing the name of the procedure as a comment after **begin** provides more maintainable code. The word **end,** followed by the name of the procedure and a terminating semicolon, indicates the end of the procedure. Just as with package specifications, placing the procedure name after the word **end** is optional but strongly recommended, and we will do so throughout this text. The basic structure of an Ada procedure is shown in Figure 1-10.

FIGURE 1-9 Multiple Ada Programs within Graphics Program Library

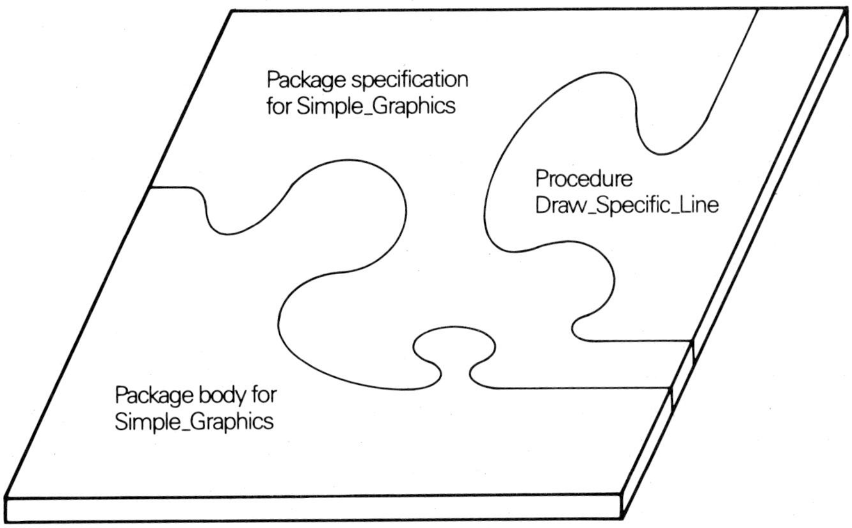

Program 1. Draw_Specific_Line

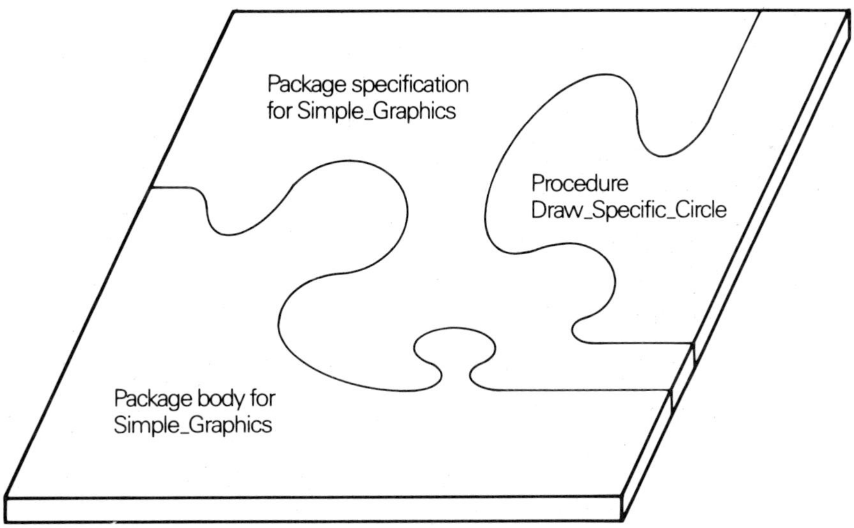

Program 2. Draw_Specific_Circle

```
procedure Procedure_Name is
begin -- Procedure_Name
   statements
end Procedure_Name;
```

FIGURE 1-10 Basic Structure of a Simple Ada Procedure

You have now been introduced to Ada packages, procedures, programs, and program libraries. A procedure is one kind of Ada *subprogram.* In the next chapter you will learn more about procedures, and you will also meet another kind of subprogram. You will learn how to construct subprograms, call them, and combine them in useful ways.

EXERCISES

Although procedures have not yet been treated formally, the examples in this chapter should provide enough information for you to code the following exercises.

For Exercises 1.1 through 1.3, refer to the package specification for Simple_Graphics. Assume that the package specification and body for Simple_Graphics have been compiled into a program library named Graphics.

1.1 Write an Ada procedure called Draw_Square to draw the square shown below. Do not label the corners of the square. Include only **with** clause(s) in the context clause.

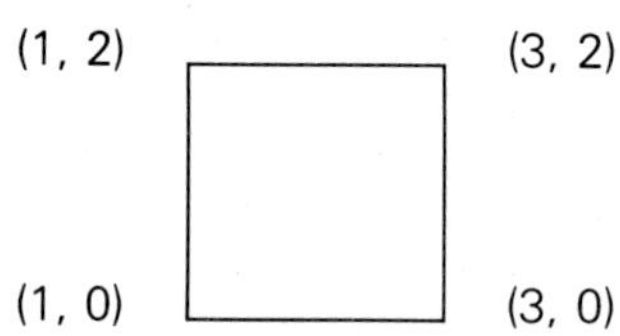

1.2 Rewrite Exercise 1.1 using both **with** clause(s) and **use** clause(s) in the context clause.

1.3 Write a procedure called Draw_Flag that draws the following flag. Again, do not label the diagram.

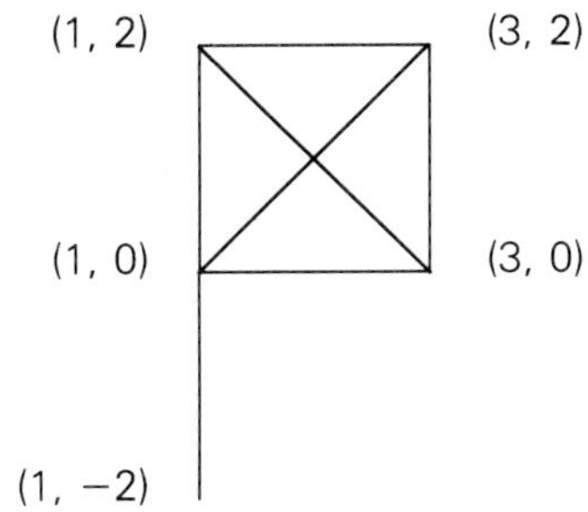

Use the following package specification for Exercises 1.4 and 1.5.

```
package Math_Library is
  procedure Print_Square_Root (Number : Integer);
  procedure Print_Cube_Root   (Number : Integer);
  package Trigonometric_Functions is
    procedure Print_Sine_of (Angle_in_Degrees: Integer);
    procedure Print_Cosine_of
              (Angle_in_Degrees : Integer);
  end Trigonometric_Functions;
end Math_Library;
```

1.4 Write a procedure named Roots_of_64 to print out the square root and cube root of 64. Write it first using only the **with** clause; then write it using both the **with** and the **use** clause. Assume that the specification and body for package Math_Library have been compiled into a program library named Math.

1.5 Write a procedure named Sine_of_30 that prints the sine of 30 degrees. (Hint: Consider what

Math_Library.Trigonometric_Functions.Print_Sine_of(...)

references.) Again assume that this package has been compiled into the program library called Math of Exercise 1.4.

1.6 State one advantage and one disadvantage of writing a **use** clause in conjunction with a **with** clause when accessing the resources of a package.

1.7 Discuss the main advantages of referencing a package using only a **with** clause.

1.8 Draw stars, polygons, and pictures at will. Let your imagination be your guide.

2

SUBPROGRAMS

CHAPTER OBJECTIVES

- Write identifiers.
- Read procedure and function specifications.
- Write procedure and function calls using positional or named notation.
- Write procedure and function bodies.
- Declare local data.
- Nest procedures and functions.
- Define the three parameter modes.
- Stub out subprogram bodies.
- Write subunits.
- Import subprograms.
- Overload subprograms.
- Write recursive subprograms.
- Define a compilation unit.
- Define the order of compilation of program units into a program library.
- State how subprograms support abstraction, information hiding, and modularity.

Subprograms are used to develop Ada programs in a hierarchical, or top-down, fashion. Subprograms allow us to break up a large problem into smaller subproblems that can be more readily solved.

An Ada subprogram may be either a procedure or a function. The differences between procedures and functions, and the rules for calling them, will be presented in this chapter. Additionally, subprograms occurring as a package resource (like procedure Draw_Line) and subprograms occurring as a main program (like procedure Draw_Specific_Line) will be discussed. Let us begin, however, by learning the rules for writing Ada names.

2.1 Naming Things (LRM 2.3)

An *identifier* is a sequence of characters used to name data types, variables, packages, procedures, and the like. In Chapter 1 you met a package named Simple_Graphics. Simple_Graphics is an identifier consisting of 15 characters. Ada specifies rules for creating identifiers. Identifiers not conforming to the rules will be detected at compile time.

The following characters may be used to create identifiers:

- the 26 letters of the alphabet (upper and lower case)
- the digits 0 through 9
- underscore(s).

The rules for creating an identifier are as follows: An identifier

- must start with a letter
- is optionally followed by any sequence of letters, digits, and isolated, embedded underscores
- may be as long as a line
- may use upper or lower case
- may not include spaces

Note that underscores, which are often used to substitute for spaces between words, must be isolated and embedded. *Isolated* means that underscores may not appear next to each other in an identifier. *Embedded* means that an underscore must always occur between two characters, neither of which is an underscore. In other words, an underscore may never be the first or last character of an identifier. Use of an underscore in an identifier creates a distinct identifier; that is, Simple_Graphics is not the same identifier as SimpleGraphics. If the compiler sees SimpleGraphics when it expects Simple_Graphics, the compilation will not be successful and the compiler will issue a diagnostic stating that SimpleGraphics is an unknown identifier.

Identifiers in Ada are not case sensitive; that is, use of different cases in an identifier does not create distinct identifiers. The identifiers Simple_Graphics and SIMPLE_GRAPHICS are identical. The folllowing are all legal Ada identifiers:

```
Simple_Graphics
SIMPLE_GRAPHICS
SIMPLEGRAPHICS
Simplegraphics
SimpleGraphics
```

The first of these most nearly conforms to the English language. Proper use of underscores and case creates identifiers that seem natural to the eyes and are easy to read. A good convention for user-supplied identifiers is to write the first letter of each word in the identifier in upper case and the remaining characters in lower case. Prepositions should occur entirely in lower case, as should special words such as **procedure, function,** and **end.** While these words are legal identifiers, they have specific meanings in Ada. They are called *reserved*

TABLE 2-1 Reserved Words of the Language

abort	declare	generic	of	select
abs	delay	goto	or	separate
accept	delta	if	others	subtype
access	digits	in	out	task
all	do	is	package	terminate
and	else	limited	pragma	then
array	elsif	loop	private	type
at	end	mod	procedure	use
begin	entry	new	raise	when
body	exception	not	range	while
case	exit	null	record	with
constant	for		rem	xor
	function		renames	
			return	
			reverse	

words because their use is "reserved" or "saved" to denote specific information about an Ada program. Reserved words may not be used as user-supplied identifiers. The reserved words in Ada are listed in Table 2-1 and appear in boldface type throughout this text.

Recall procedure Draw_Line contained within package Page_Headings? The procedure deserved a far more appropriate name, such as Underline_Header_Text. Choose your identifiers carefully. Try to make them specific and easy to understand. Remember, Ada was designed to help the maintenance process.

EXERCISES

2.1 State whether each of the following is a legal or illegal identifier. If an identifier is illegal, state the reason(s) why.

a. Altitude
b. Front_40
c. Front_40_
d. Range_of_Values
e. Amount_in_$
f. Accept
g. Stop_the_Clock
h. First__Value
i. Simple Graphics
j. _Silly_Name
k. 1_to_1
l. Range

2.2 Write identifiers to represent the following:

a. A checking account opening balance
b. A checking account closing balance
c. A checking account deposit
d. A check written but not cleared
e. An overdraft charge
f. A charge for purchased checks
g. A monthly service charge
h. A procedure that balances a checkbook

2.2 Procedures (LRM 6.1)

Just as Ada packages have a specification and a body, so do Ada procedures. We'll look at procedure specifications now and discuss procedure bodies later in this section.

Procedure Specification (LRM 6.1)

A *procedure specification* states what needs to be known in order to use the procedure. To be more precise, a procedure specification

- states that the item specified is a procedure
- names the procedure
- lists the procedure's formal parameters, if any

Formal parameters, as you may recall, are the data items required by a procedure to execute or are produced by the procedure as a result of execution.

The syntax for a procedure specification is as follows:

```
procedure Procedure_Name [(formal parameter list)]
```

Here, as in the last chapter, brackets indicate optional items: that is, a procedure need not have parameters.

The reserved word **procedure** states that this is a subprogram procedure. The procedure name follows the rules for Ada names and conventionally begins with an imperative verb. The names of parameters are separated from their type by a colon in the formal parameter list. Names of parameters of the same type may be separated by a comma, as in

```
                           ↓
procedure Draw_Line (From, To : Point_Type)
```

while parameters of different types are separated by semicolons, like this:

```
                                              ↓
procedure Draw_Circle (Center : Point_Type; Radius : Float)
```

The entire parameter list is enclosed in parentheses.

Each of the above procedure specifications contains

- the word **procedure**
  — to state that it is a procedure
- the name of the procedure
  — here either Draw_Line or Draw_Circle
- a formal parameter list
  — here either (From, To : Point_Type)
  or (Center : Point_Type; Radius : Float)

Recall that in the specification for package Simple_Graphics, each procedure specification was followed by a terminating semicolon. When a procedure specification is followed by a semicolon, the resulting construct is called a *procedure declaration.* A procedure declaration can appear in a package specification to indicate that the procedure is a resource supplied by the package.

As indicated by the brackets in the syntax for the procedure specification, a procedure need not have parameters. Procedures that print a page heading, print the date, and so on are examples of parameterless procedures. Additionally, most main programs, like Draw_Specific_Line, are written as parameterless procedures.

Main programs are invoked by the programming support environment within which Ada programs are developed and executed. How does the environment know which program to execute if multiple parameterless procedures reside in the same program library? Recall from Chapter 1 that when multiple programs reside in the same program library, the command to execute must specify *which* main program to execute.

Procedure Call (LRM 6.4)

A procedure specification provides all the information required to use the procedure. You use a procedure by issuing a *procedure call.* A procedure call is a statement in Ada that has the following syntax:

```
Procedure_Name [(actual parameter list)];
```

where the *actual parameter list* consists of values (and/or variables), separated by commas, that are to be associated with the parameters named in the formal parameter list. The terminating semicolon is required for a procedure call.

The following:

```
Draw_Line ( (1, 5), (2, 7) );
```

is an example of a legal procedure call. Here the name of the procedure, Draw_Line, is followed by the actual parameters—the points (1, 5) and (2, 7)—enclosed in parentheses. The closing parenthesis is followed by the required terminating semicolon. The first actual parameter in the call, "(1, 5)," is associated with the first formal parameter in the specification, "From." Similarly the second actual parameter in the call, "(2, 7)," is associated with the second formal parameter in the specification, "To."

Positional and Named Notation (LRM 6.4)

All the procedure calls that you have seen so far use *positional notation.* With positional notation, actual parameters supplied by the call are associated with the formal parameters appearing in the specification by their order of appearance in the call: that is, the first actual parameter listed in the call is associated with the first formal parameter in the specification, the second actual parameter is associated with the second formal parameter, and so on.

As another example of positional notation, consider the call

```
Draw_Circle ( (2, 3), 4);
```

which calls the Draw_Circle procedure introduced in Chapter 1. This call draws a circle centered at (2, 3) with a radius of 4. The value (2, 3) is associated with the procedure's first formal parameter, Center, and 4 is associated with the second formal parameter, Radius.

With positional notation, the order of appearance of the actual parameters is *significant.* Thus, the call

```
Draw_Circle (4, (2, 3) ); -- **ILLEGAL**
```

is illegal, because procedure Draw_Circle expects the first value in the parameter list to be of type Point_Type and the second value to be of type Integer, and here the first actual parameter in the call is of type Integer. As a result of this *type mismatch,* the association cannot be made (see Figure 2-1). The compiler will detect this error and issue an appropriate diagnostic.

An alternative way to represent the desired association of actual to formal parameters is called *named notation.* In named notation, the formal parameter

FIGURE 2-1 An illegal association

with which an actual parameter is to be associated is *explicitly* named. The following procedure call illustrates named notation:

```
Draw_Line (From => (1, 5), To => (2, 7) );
```

The name of the formal parameter is written in the call, followed by an arrow (=>) and then by the value of the actual parameter to be associated with that formal parameter.

With named notation, the order of the parameters is *not significant.* For example, the following two calls achieve the same result:

```
Draw_Line ( From => (1, 5),     To => (2, 7) );
Draw_Line (   To => (2, 7), From => (1, 5) );
```

This call is also legal:

```
Draw_Circle (Radius => 4, Center => (2, 3) );
```

Positional and named notation may be used in the same call, as long as all actual parameters to be associated using positional notation are listed first and in their correct order. Once named notation is introduced in a call, this form of notation must be used for the remainder of the call. To see why, suppose package Simple_Graphics contained the following procedure declaration:

```
procedure Draw_Rectangle
 (Horizontal_Side_Length, Vertical_Side_Length : Integer;
  Top_Left : Point_Type);
```

The following:

```
-- **ILLEGAL**
Draw_Rectangle ( Vertical_Side_Length => 1, 4, (2, 3) );
```

represents an illegal call to Draw_Rectangle to draw the following rectangle:

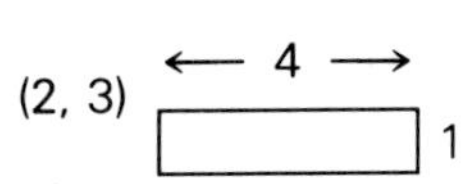

The call is illegal because once the actual parameter 1 is associated with the formal parameter Vertical_Side_Length, the compiler does not know what to do with the remaining actuals.

This call may be corrected in many ways, of which the following are examples:

```
Draw_Rectangle (4, 1, (2, 3) );
Draw_Rectangle (Top_Left                => (2, 3),
                Horizontal_Side_Length => 4,
                Vertical_Side_Length   => 1);

Draw_Rectangle (4, 1, Top_Left => (2, 3) );

Draw_Rectangle (4, Vertical_Side_Length => 1,
                          Top_Left => (2, 3) );
```

The first call uses positional notation. The second call uses named notation. The third and fourth calls use a mixture of positional and named notation.

In general, calls written in named notation enhance readability and reduce errors. Additionally, named parameter associations are easier to read when aligned vertically, as in the second call above.

Procedure Body (LRM 6.3)

As we have noted, a procedure specification provides only the information needed to call the procedure. Knowledge of the way a procedure implements its algorithm is not required to call it. To call Draw_Line, all that you need to know is that it is a procedure, its name, and what actuals to supply [see Figure 2-2(a)]. Just as a package body contains the *how* of the package resources, a procedure body contains the *how* of a procedure. A procedure body includes both the procedure specification and the executable code for the procedure.

To be more precise, a procedure body

- states that the item specified is a procedure
- names the procedure
- lists the formal parameters in parentheses
- lists local data required by the procedure
- contains the code to be executed

The syntax for a procedure body is as follows:

```
procedure Procedure_Name [(formal parameter list)] is
  --
  -- Local data, if any, placed here.
  --
begin [-- Procedure_Name]
  --
  -- Statements to be executed
  -- placed here.
  --
end [Procedure_Name];
```

A procedure body begins with a procedure specification followed by the reserved word **is.** Next comes *local data,* the meaning of which we will discuss shortly. Notice that a procedure body is structurally divided by the word **begin.** Local data is placed prior to the **begin,** while the executable statements are placed after the **begin.** It is a good idea to always follow the **begin** with the name of the procedure, given as a comment. The word **end** indicates the end of the procedure. The use of the procedure name after **end** is optional but strongly recommended. The terminating semicolon is required.

FIGURE 2-2(a) Draw_Line specification

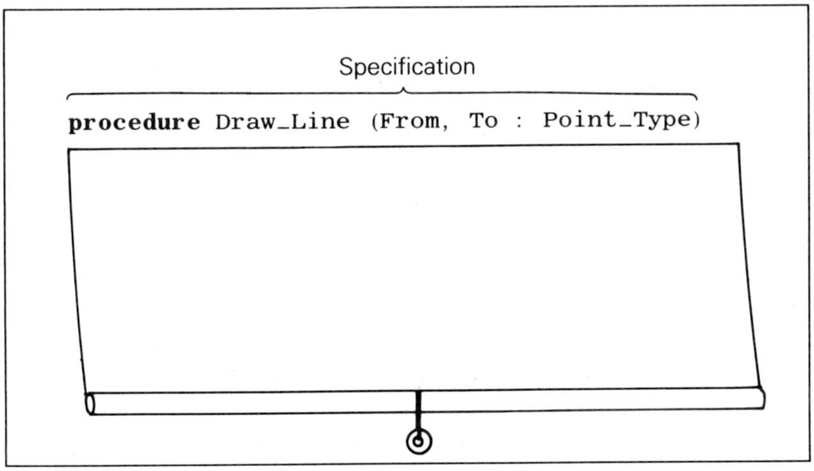

FIGURE 2-2(b) Draw_Line body

Body: Specification

```
procedure Draw_Line (From, To : Point_Type) is
   --
   -- Local data specified here.
   --
begin -- Draw_Line
   --
   -- Executable statements placed here.
   --
end Draw_Line;
```

FIGURE 2-3 Structure of main procedure Draw_Specific_Line

Body: Specification

```
procedure Draw_Specific_Line is
   --
   -- This is the I/O Version.
   --
begin -- Draw_Specific_line
   Draw_Line ( (1,5), (2,7) );
   Put ("Figure 6. A Straight Line");
end Draw_Specific_line;
```

Figure 2-2(b) shows a procedure body that is the implementation of a package resource. Figure 2-3 is a procedure body of a main procedure. The structure of the two is identical, except that the main procedure has no formal parameter list. As previously stated, this is true of most main procedures.

Another procedure, named Draw_Square, is shown in Figure 2-4. The procedure's specification is as follows:

FIGURE 2-4 Procedure Draw_Square

Declarative part:

```
procedure Draw_Square (Top_Left     : Point_Type;
                       Side_Length : Integer) is
   --
   -- Local data specified here. This local data
   -- may not be accessed outside this procedure.
   --
   -- Three data items are introduced to represent
   -- the three other corners of the square. This is
   -- done to improve the readability of the
   -- executable code.
   --
   Top_Right    : Point_Type
                := (Top_Left(1) + Side_Length,
                    Top_Left(2));
   Bottom_Right : Point_Type
                := (Top_Left(1) + Side_Length,
                    Top_Left(2) - Side_Length);
   Bottom_Left  : Point_Type
                := (Top_Left(1),
                    Top_Left(2) - Side_Length);
```

Executable part:

```
begin -- Draw_Square
   Draw_Line ( Top_Left, Top_Right );       --top
   Draw_Line ( Top_Right, Bottom_Right);    --right side
   Draw_Line ( Bottom_Right, Bottom_Left);--bottom
   Draw_Line ( Bottom_Left, Top_Left);      --left side
end Draw_Square;
```

```
procedure Draw_Square (Top_Left    : Point_Type ;
                       Side_Length : Integer)
```

The specification states that we have a procedure named Draw_Square, with two formal parameters; the first, named Top_Left, is of type Point_Type, and the second, named Side_Length, is of type Integer. The body of Draw_Square has three data items—Top_Right, Bottom_Right, and Bottom_Left, all of type Point_Type—which appear prior to the **begin** and represent the remaining three corners of the square. These three data items are introduced to make the executable code more readable and are known only to Draw_Square. They are therefore *local data.* Notice that Ada permits assigning initial values to local data. For example, the variable Top_Right, of type Point_Type, is assigned an initial value. The x-component of Top_Right is the value of the x-component of Top_Left plus the Side_Length. The y-component of Top_Right is the same as the y-component of Top_Left. Following the word **begin** are the statements that will be executed when the procedure is executed. Here the executable code consists of four procedure calls to Draw_Line, which draw the four sides of the square.

As stated earlier, the word **begin** structurally divides a procedure into two parts. Prior to **begin** is the declarative part, and following **begin** is the executable part. The declarative part of a procedure body may contain any number of local declarations (other variables, procedures, packages, and so on), that is, data that is not needed for calling the procedure but is either logically required for execution of the procedure or introduced to improve readability.

In Chapter 1 you were exposed to the concept of a procedure body contained in a package body, specifically Draw_Line, and a main procedure, specifically Draw_Specific_Line. If a procedure is a resource supplied by a package, this fact is stated by having its procedure declaration inside the package specification and its implementation (the procedure body) in the package body. You can access this resource by first importing the package containing it, via an appropriate context clause, and then calling it, following the rules you have just learned. Alternatively, a procedure body may appear by itself as a main procedure, as was the case with Draw_Specific_Line. Such a procedure is not called, but rather is compiled into a program library and then executed. (A procedure may also be a compilation unit, as we will see in Section 2.8.)

Nested Procedures (LRM 6.3)

Procedures may be nested within the declarative part of other procedures. (The word *procedure* here means a procedure body.) Nested procedures are *local* to the enclosing procedure; in other words, a nested procedure is recognized only by the enclosing procedure. Because the enclosing procedure's specification is the only interface to any potential caller, a caller can never "see" a nested procedure and therefore can never call it.

Recall procedure Draw_Square that draws a square, given the top left corner of the square and the length of a side (see Figure 2-4). Figure 2-5 shows a procedure named Draw_Flag that uses Draw_Square to draw the flag requested in Exercise 1.3 and shown again here.

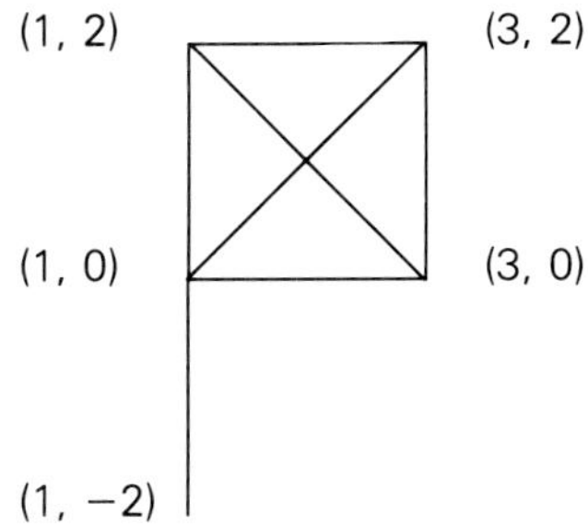

FIGURE 2-5 Draw_Square nested within Draw_Flag

```
with Simple_Graphics; use Simple_Graphics;
procedure Draw_Flag is
   --
   -- This procedure draws the flag by first drawing
   -- the square. Then it draws the two diagonal lines,
   -- and finally draws the remainder of the pole.
   --
   -- This procedure does not label the points.
   --
   procedure Draw_Square (Top_Left    : Point_Type;
                          Side_Length : Integer) is
      --
      -- Local data specified here. This local data
      -- may not be accessed outside this procedure.
      --
      -- Three data items are introduced to represent the
      -- three other corners of the square. This is done
      -- to improve the readability of the executable code.
      --
```
(*continued*)

FIGURE 2-5 *(continued)*

```
Top_Right     : Point_Type
              := (Top_Left(1) + Side_Length,
                  Top_Left(2));
Bottom_Right  : Point_Type
              := (Top_Left(1) + Side_Length,
                  Top_Left(2) - Side_Length);
Bottom_Left   : Point_Type
              := (Top_Left(1),
                  Top_Left(2) - Side_Length);
   begin -- Draw_Square
      Draw_Line ( Top_Left, Top_Right );        -- top
      Draw_Line ( Top_Right, Bottom_Right);     -- right side
      Draw_Line ( Bottom_Right, Bottom_Left);-- bottom
      Draw_Line ( Bottom_Left, Top_Left);       -- left side
   end Draw_Square;
begin -- Draw_Flag
   Draw_Square ( (1,2), 2 );          -- draw the square
   Draw_Line ( (1, 2), (3, 0) );      -- draw diagonal \
   Draw_Line ( (3, 2), (1, 0) );      -- draw diagonal /
   Draw_Line ( (1, 0), (1, -2));      -- draw rest of pole
end Draw_Flag;
```

You will note that procedure Draw_Square is nested in the declarative part of Draw_Flag. Notice, too, that the executable code for Draw_Flag is more readable than the code in the solution shown in Figure 2-6. Draw_Square operates at a much higher level of abstraction than does Draw_Line. Remember, however, that Draw_Square is now known only within the procedure Draw_Flag. Any attempt to call Draw_Square from outside Draw_Flag will result in an error that will be detected at compile time.

FIGURE 2-6 A less abstract solution for Draw_Flag

```
with Simple_Graphics; use Simple_Graphics;
procedure Draw_Flag is
   --
   -- This procedure draws the flag by first drawing
   -- the entire flag pole, then completing the square,
   -- and finally drawing the diagonals.
   --
   -- This procedure does not label the coordinates of
   -- the points.
   --
begin -- Draw_Flag
   Draw_Line ( (1, 2), (1, -2));   -- draw entire pole
   Draw_Line ( (1, 2), (3, 2) );   -- top of square
   Draw_Line ( (3, 2), (3, 0) );   -- right side of square
   Draw_Line ( (3, 0), (1, 0) );   -- bottom of square
   Draw_Line ( (1, 2), (3, 0) );   -- diagonal \
   Draw_Line ( (3, 2), (1, 0) );   -- diagonal /
end Draw_Flag;
```

EXERCISES

2.3 List the three parts of a procedure specification. Does every procedure specification have to contain all three parts?

Use the following specification for Exercises 2.4 through 2.7. Assume that it has been compiled into a program library named Bank. (A value of type Float is written with a decimal point. Ada requires that a digit both precede and follow the decimal point. Ada functions are discussed in the next section.)

```
package Teller_1 is
   function Balance_of (Account_Number : Integer)
                       return Float;
   procedure Accept_Deposit
                 (Account_Number  : Integer;
                  Amount          : Float);
   procedure Accept_Withdrawal
                 (Account_Number  : Integer;
                  Amount          : Float);
   procedure Accept_Order_for_New_Checks
                 (Account_Number  : Integer;
                  Quantity        : Integer);
end Teller_1;
```

2.4 The following

```
procedure Accept_Withdrawal
              (Account_Number  : Integer;
               Amount          : Float);
```

is called a procedure ____________________. This procedure ______________________________ states this procedure is a ____________________ in a package.

2.5 For each of the procedures in package Teller_1, list the formal parameters and their respective types.

2.6 Write a procedure to represent a trip to the bank to perform the following functions related to your checking account, which has the account number 12369: (1) deposit $50.00 and (2) order 300 new checks. Use positional notation in all calls.

2.7 List the actual parameters in Exercise 2.6.

2.8 Rewrite Exercise 2.6 using named notation in all calls.

2.9 Rewrite procedure Draw_Flag of Figure 2-5 by adding another nested procedure, called Draw_Diagonals, to draw the two diagonals.

2.10 State the main advantage of using named notation.

2.3 Functions (LRM 6.1)

The second kind of Ada subprogram is called a *function.* Just as packages and procedures have a specification and a body, so do functions. A function specification states what must be known in order to call the function, while the implementation of the function is contained in the function body (see Figure 2-7). This should sound *very* familiar by now! We'll look at function specifications first, then at function bodies.

Function Specification (LRM 6.1)

A function specification

- states that the item specified is a function
- names the function
- lists the function's formal parameters, if any, in parentheses
- includes the word **return**
- specifies the type of the value to be returned

FIGURE 2-7 Structure of function Mean_of

Specification

Body

```
function Mean_of (Class_Grades : List_of_Grades)
        return Float                                is
   --
   -- Local data placed here.
   --
begin -- Mean_of
   --
   -- Executable statements placed here.
   --
end Mean_of;
```

If you compare this list with the list provided for a procedure specification in Section 2.2, you will note that there are two new items here: the word **return** and a specification for the type of the value to be returned. Every function *must* return a value of some type.

The syntax for a function specification is as follows:

```
function Function_Name [(formal parameter list)]
        return Type_Name
```

Whereas imperative clauses are usually used for procedure names, function names should be nouns; procedures name actions, while functions name values or conditions. As with procedures, functions may have a formal parameter list. Here, too, formal parameters of the same type may be separated by a comma, while formal parameters of differing types must be separated by a semicolon. The type of the value to be returned by the function follows the word **return** in the function specification. The following is an example of a function specification:

```
function Mean_of (Class_Grades : List_of_Grades)
        return Float
```

The function specification for Mean_of contains

- the word **function**
  — to state that it is a function
- the name of the function
  — Mean_of
- the formal parameter list
  — (Class_Grades : List_of_Grades)
- the word **return**
- the type of the value to be returned upon execution of the function
  — Float

Consider the following specification for a package named Statistics, which includes Mean_of as a resource.

```
package Statistics is
  type List_of_Grades is array (1..10) of Integer;
  function Mean_of     (Class_Grades : List_of_Grades)
                        return Float;
  function Highest_of (Class_Grades : List_of_Grades)
                        return Integer;
  function Lowest_of   (Class_Grades : List_of_Grades)
                        return Integer;
end Statistics;
```

Statistics contains a data type named List_of_Grades. Type List_of_Grades is defined as an array of ten Integer values, specifically ten class grades. Additionally, this package provides the capability to determine the average (mean) grade, the highest grade, and the lowest grade for the list of ten grades. These resources are implemented as functions, not procedures. The function Mean_Of, when we pass it a list of ten grades, will return a value of type Float that represents the mean. (As mentioned in the exercises of the preceding section, a value of type Float is written with a decimal point, with a digit both before and after the point.)

Recall that when a package specifies that it contains a procedure as a resource, the construct consisting of the procedure specification followed by a terminating semicolon is called a procedure declaration. Similarly, functions have function declarations. There are three function declarations in the package specification for Statistics. Each function returns one value, as indicated by Table 2-2.

Function Call (LRM 6.4)

Functions and procedures are called differently. Why? Because functions *must* return a value, and the procedures we have seen so far have not returned any

TABLE 2-2 Statistics Resources

Function Name	*Type Returned*	*Execution Results*
Mean_of	Float	Returns average grade to caller
Highest_of	Integer	Returns highest grade to caller
Lowest_of	Integer	Returns lowest grade to caller

values. (Procedures *can* return results, however; we will see how to accomplish that soon.) The value returned by the function must be captured by the caller. Consider the following example:

```
with Statistics; use Statistics;
procedure Statistics_for_Ada101 is
  Mean_Ada101              : Float;
  Highest_Grade_Ada101,
  Lowest_Grade_Ada101      : Integer;
  Ada101_Grades            : List_of_Grades
        := (75,60,80,85,95,78,88,30,88,100);
begin -- Statistics_for_Ada101
  Mean_Ada101              := Mean_of (Ada101_Grades);
  Highest_Grade_Ada101     := Highest_of (Ada101_Grades);
  Lowest_Grade_Ada101      := Lowest_of (Ada101_Grades);
end Statistics_for_Ada101;
```

The main procedure, Statistics_for_Ada101, has a **with** clause to import package Statistics, followed by a **use** clause that allows us to refer to the resources supplied by Statistics without using the prefix "Statistics.". Because functions must return a value, the declarative part of Statistics_for_Ada101 specifies three local variables to hold the results returned by the three functions. These three variables are known only to procedure Statistics_for_Ada101. As stated previously, the word **begin** indicates the end of the declarative part of the main procedure and the beginning of the executable part. Here there are three executable statements, all of them assignment statements. In each, the value of the variable on the left side of the assignment symbol (:=) is replaced by the value of the expression on the right side of the symbol. The expression on the right side of each of these assignment statements is a function call.

The function Mean_of is called first. The actual parameter passed to the formal parameter Class_Grades is the list of ten grades, Ada101_Grades, which is a value of type List_of_Grades. The value of the average grade is calculated, returned to the point of call, and assigned to the variable Mean_Ada101. (The number of digits in a value of type Float depends on the implementation, so one implementation might return, say, 77.900, while another might return 77.9003.) An identical process occurs in the execution of the remaining two assignment statements.

The syntax of a function call is

```
Function_Name [(actual parameter list)]
```

Simply write the name of the function, followed by the list of actual parameters enclosed in parentheses. Note that there is no terminating semicolon in a function call; whereas a procedure call in Ada is a statement and therefore requires a semicolon, a function call is not a statement. A function call appears as part of an expression, for example on the right side of an assignment statement. (We will see other uses of function calls later.)

A function call may be written using either named or positional notation, following the rules specified in Section 2.2.

Function Body (LRM 6.3)

As with procedures, a function specification provides only the information required to call the function. The function body contains the actual code that is executed when the function is called.

Specifically, a function body

- states that the specified item is a function
- names the function
- lists the formal parameters in parentheses
- specifies the type of the value to be returned
- lists local data required by the function
- contains the code to be executed

The syntax for a function body is as follows:

```
function Function_Name [(formal parameter list)]
                        return Type_Name is
  --
  -- Local data placed here.
  --
begin [-- Function_Name]
  --
  -- Statements to be executed
  -- placed here. At least one
  -- return statement must appear.
  --
  return Some_Value;  -- a return statement
                      -- where Some_Value is
                      -- of type Type_Name
end [Function_Name];
```

A function body begins with a function specification followed by the word **is.** Like procedure bodies, function bodies are structurally divided by the word **begin:** local data is placed prior to the **begin,** while executable code is placed after the **begin.** As with procedures, it is wise to follow **begin** with the name of the function as a comment. The word **end** indicates the end of the function. Use of the function name after the word **end** is optional but strongly recommended. The terminating semicolon is required.

Note that function bodies *must* contain at least one **return** statement. Execution of the **return** statement terminates execution of the function and passes the result back to the caller. The **return** statement is of the form

```
return Expression;
```

where Expression represents the result to be returned to the caller and is of the type specified after the word **return** in the function specification.

The following is an example of a function body. This function calculates the area of a square, given the length of a side.

```
function Area_of_Square (Length_of_Side : Integer)
                         return Integer is
  --
  -- One local data item in this implementation.
  --
  Area : Integer;
begin -- Area_of_Square
  Area := Length_of_Side ** 2;
  return Area;
end Area_of_Square;
```

Here is an alternative, and probably better, way of coding the same function:

```
function Area_of_Square (Length_of_Side : Integer)
                         return Integer is
  --
  -- No local data in this implementation.
  --
begin -- Area_of_Square
   return Length_of_Side ** 2;
end Area_of_Square;
```

Both Area and Length_of_Side ** 2 are legal Integer expressions, and either one may appear in the **return** statement.

Nested Functions (LRM 6.3)

As with procedures, functions may be nested in the declarative parts of other procedures or functions. For example, examine the code in Figure 2-8, which draws the pictured square and computes its area.

FIGURE 2-8 Area_of_Square nested within Display_Square

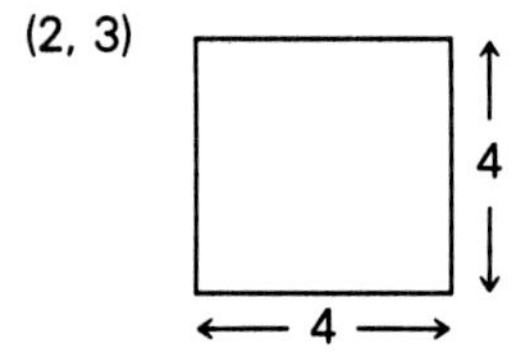


```
with Simple_Graphics; use Simple_Graphics;
procedure Display_Square is
  Area : Integer;
  function Area_of_Square (Length_of_Side : Integer)
                          return Integer is
  begin -- Area_of_Square
     return Length_of_Side ** 2;
  end Area_of_Square;
  procedure Draw_Square (Top_Left    : Point_Type;
                         Side_Length : Integer) is
    --
    -- See Figure 2-4 for the code.
    --
  end Draw_Square;
begin -- Display_Square
  Draw_Square ( (2, 3), 4);     -- Draw the square
  Area := Area_of_Square (4);  -- Compute area
  --
  -- We will learn how to print Area shortly.
  --
end Display_Square;
```

EXERCISES

2.11 List the five parts of a function specification. Must every function specification have five parts?

Use the following package specification for Exercises 2.12 through 2.15. Assume it has been compiled into a program library named Bank.

```
package Teller_2 is
  function Balance_of (Account_Number : Integer)
                      return Float;
  function Deposit_into (Account_Number : Integer;
                         Amount         : Float)
                      return Float;
  function Withdrawal_from (Account_Number : Integer;
                            Amount         : Float)
                      return Float;
  procedure Accept_Order_for_New_Checks
                     (Account_Number : Integer;
                            Quantity : Integer);
end Teller_2;
```

This package is a modification of package Teller_1 used in Exercises 2.4 through 2.7. Deposit_into and Withdrawal_from have been recoded as functions and now return the balance of the account at the completion of the transaction.

2.12 The following:

```
function Withdrawal_from (Account_Number : Integer;
                          Amount         : Float)
                 return Float;
```

is called a function ______________________. This function ______________ states that this is a package ______________________.

2.13 List the formal parameters for each of the three function declarations of Teller_2. Then list the type of result returned by each function.

2.14 Recode Exercise 2.6 using package Teller_2.

2.15 List the actual parameters for each call.

2.16 Write a function to compute the area of a rectangle. The function is to have two formal parameters, the length and width of the rectangle, of type Integer. The function should return the area as a value of type Integer and have only one executable statement.

2.17 Using the results of Exercise 2.16, write a procedure to draw and compute the area of the following rectangle:

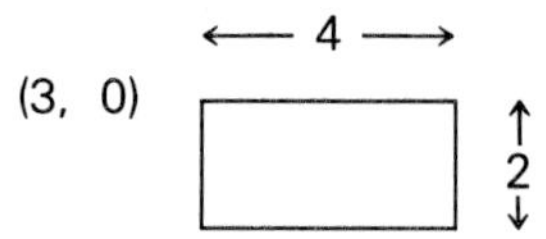

2.4 Parameter Modes (LRM 6.2)

So far you have seen only one kind or *mode* of parameter. All the parameters that you have studied in this book are parameters of mode **in.** An **in** parameter specifies that a value for this formal parameter is to be supplied to the subprogram in the call.

Ada provides three parameter modes: **in**, **out**, and **in out**. The mode of each parameter is specified in the formal parameter list, following the colon and preceding the type of the formal parameter. If no mode is specified, mode **in** is assumed. In other words, the *default* mode for Ada parameters is **in**.

You can think of parameter modes as a way of specifying the flow of data with respect to the subprogram (see Figure 2-9). A value for a parameter of mode **in** flows *in* to the called subprogram as part of the call. The caller supplies the value. A value for a parameter of mode **out** flows *out* of the called subprograms to the caller as a result of the execution of the procedure. A value for a parameter of mode **in out** flows both *in and out* of the called procedure. (Can you guess how procedures return results?)

FIGURE 2-9 Parameter modes as data flow

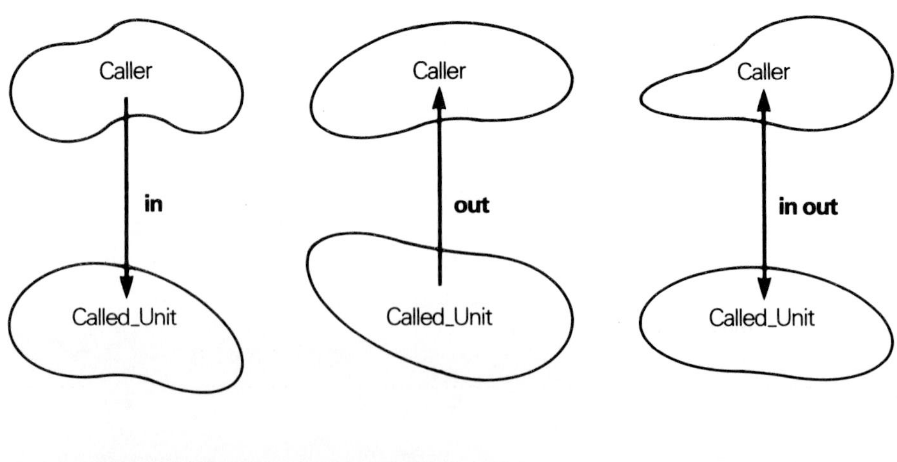

The rules applicable to each of the three parameter modes are addressed in the next three subsections and are summarized in Table 2-3. Any violation of the rules will be detected at compile time.

Parameter Mode *in*

As coded in Chapter 1, the parameters for the Simple_Graphics resources Draw_Line and Draw_Circle are of mode **in** by default. The specification for Simple_Graphics could also be written with the mode **in** stated explicitly, as follows.

```
package Simple_Graphics is
   type Point_Type is array (1..2) of Integer;
   procedure Draw_Line (From, To : in Point_Type);
   procedure Draw_Circle (Center : in Point_Type;
                          Radius : in Integer);
end Simple_Graphics;
```

An **in** parameter acts as a local constant. Because constants may not have their values changed, a parameter of mode **in** may not be modified. In procedure Draw_Line, the parameters From and To are **in** parameters and therefore may not be modified with Draw_Line. This means that the names

TABLE 2-3 Parameter Modes Summary

	Mode		
Feature	*in*	*out*	*in out*
Acts as	Local constant	Local variable	Local variable
Value	Supplied by actual parameter	Assigned as a result of execution	Provided by actual parameter
Allowed Operations	Read only	Write only	Read and write
	Cannot be modified by the subprogram	Value assigned by the procedure	May be read and modified by the procedure

From and To may not occur on the left side of any assignment statement within procedure Draw_Line. The values may be "read"—that is, used—but they may not be written to. Similarly, the formal parameter Length_of_Side in the function Area_of_Square may not be modified. It may be "read," as in the statement

```
return Length_of_Side ** 2;
```

but it may never be modified.

Two final notes. First, functions may have parameters *only* of mode **in,** because a function returns a single value, as specified in the **return** statement. Second, it is a good idea to always explicitly state the mode of an **in** parameter in a procedure specification. Do not state it in a function specification, because Ada specifies that the only allowed parameter mode for a function is **in**.

Default values may be specified for parameters of mode **in.** When a default value is specified, a call in which an actual parameter for that formal parameter is omitted will cause the formal parameter to assume the default value supplied in the specification. A default value is inserted in the subprogram specification between the name of the type and a separating semicolon or between the name of the type and the terminating closing parenthesis. To specify a default value, write the assignment symbol (:=) followed by a legal value for the type of the parameter.

The following package specification for Simple_Graphics contains a default value of (0, 0) for the formal parameter Center.

```
package Simple_Graphics is
   type Point_Type is array ( 1 . . 2 ) of Integer;
   procedure Draw_Line (From, To : in Point_Type);
   procedure Draw_Circle (Center : in Point_Type := (0, 0);
                          Radius : in Integer);
end Simple_Graphics
```

The call

```
Draw_Circle (Radius => 6);
```

draws a circle centered at the origin, (0, 0), with a radius of 6.

Be careful in calling subprograms with default values; keep in mind the rules for positional and named notation. The call

```
Draw_Circle(6);  --**ILLEGAL**
```

is illegal because Draw_Circle expects the first actual parameter in positional notation to be of type Point_Type, not of type Integer. If a parameter is omitted in a call, named notation must be used to associate the remainder of the actuals, unless of course the default value is supplied for the last parameter in the formal list.

Values other than the default may be supplied in a call, in which case the actual values supplied in the call override the default values. For example, the call

```
Draw_Circle ( (2, 3), 6);
```

causes the circle to be centered at (2, 3), not (0, 0).

Parameter Mode *out*

Another approach to obtaining the area of a square is to code the algorithm as a procedure with an **out** parameter, like this:

```
procedure Calculate_Area_of_Square
                (Length_of_Side : in Integer;
                           Area : out Integer) is
   --
   -- No local data required here.
   --
begin -- Calculate_Area_of_Square
   Area := Length_of_Side**2;
end Calculate_Area_of_Square;
```

Upon execution, Calculate_Area_of_Square uses the actual parameter supplied for Length_of_Side to calculate the value for Area. Upon termination of the procedure, the value in Area is supplied to the actual parameter in the calling statement.

Recall procedure Display_Square, introduced in Section 2.3, that draws the following square and computes its area using the function Area_Of_Square.

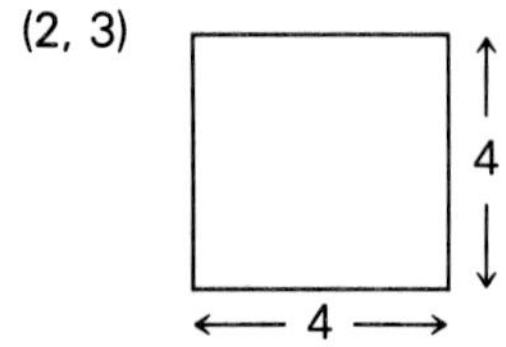

Figure 2-10 shows Display_Square recoded, using the procedure Calculate_Area_of_Square.

Notice that:

- A local variable, The_Area, is required to accept the value of Area supplied by Calculate_Area_of_Square.
- The call to Calculate_Area_of_Square is now written as a procedure call.
- The variable The_Area now contains the desired area of the square.

An **out** parameter acts as a local variable within the called procedure. The value of this variable is assigned as a result of the execution of the procedure. Here, Area is assigned the value of the area of the square, Length_of_Side **2. Upon termination of the procedure, the result is returned to The_Area.

Default values may not be specified for parameters of mode **out.**

Calculate_Area_of_Square contains only one **out** parameter. Procedures may contain multiple **out** parameters to return multiple results.

Parameter Mode *in out*

A parameter of mode **in out** permits data to be modified. Consider the following package specification, which provides resources for binary operations.

```
package Binary_Operations is
   procedure Interchange (First, Second : in out Integer);
   . . .
end Binary_Operations;
```

The three dots indicate that there are additional resources in the package but they are not listed here. Right now we are concerned only with the procedure Interchange, which exchanges two values. After its execution, the values passed to First and Second are reversed.

To exchange or reverse two values, Interchange needs to read *and* modify the values before returning them. Use of parameter mode **in** would not allow Interchange to modify the values. If parameter mode **out** were used, Interchange could not read the values in order to interchange them. Clearly the use of the parameter mode **in out** is required.

FIGURE 2-10 Returning results via parameter of mode **out**

```
with Simple_Graphics; use Simple_Graphics;
procedure Display_Square is
   The_Area : Integer;      --required to obtain area from
                            --procedure Area_of_Square
   procedure Calculate_Area_of_Square
                (Length_of_Side : in Integer;
                           Area : out Integer) is
      --
      -- No local data required.
      --
   begin -- Calculate_Area_of_Square
      Area := Length_of_Side**2;
   end Calculate_Area_of_Square;
   procedure Draw_Square (Top_Left    : in Point_Type;
                          Side_Length : in Integer) is
      --
      -- See Figure 2-4 for the code.
      --
   end Draw_Square;
begin -- Display_Square
   Draw_Square ( (2, 3), 4);       -- Draw the square
   Calculate_Area_of_Square (4, The_Area); --Find the area
   --
   --The_Area will be printed soon.
   --
end Display_Square;
```

Look at the procedure body for Interchange (which, remember, is located in the package body for Binary_Operations).

```
procedure Interchange (First, Second : in out Integer) is
   Temp : Integer := First;
begin -- Interchange
   First  := Second;
   Second := Temp;
end Interchange;
```

If parameter mode **in** had been used in the procedure specification, the statement

```
First  := Second;
```

would be in error, because **in** parameters are read only and may not be written to. Values for parameters of mode **in** are supplied by the caller and may not be modified within the called procedure. The assignment statement modifies First. An error message would be generated by the compiler.

If parameter mode **out** had been used in the procedure specification, the initialization of Temp to First and the statement

```
First := Second;
```

would be in error. The calling procedure does not supply values for **out** parameters, so there would not be any value for First to use in initializing Temp, and similarly there wouldn't be any value for Second to assign to First. The value for an **out** parameter is provided as a result of execution of the procedure and returned to the caller.

It should now be clear why parameter mode **in out** is the only logical choice for the parameters of Interchange.

To summarize, values for parameters of mode **in out**

- are provided by the caller
- can be read by the called procedure
- can be written to as a result of execution of the procedure
- are returned, most frequently in a changed state, to the caller

Consider the following:

```
with Binary_Operations; use Binary_Operations;
procedure Exchange_4_and_5 is
   Value_1 : Integer := 4;
   Value_2 : Integer := 5;
begin -- Exchange_4_and_5
   Interchange (Value_1, Value_2);
   --We will learn to output results soon
end Exchange_4_and_5;
```

Before the call, Value_1 is 4 and Value_2 is 5. After the call, Value_1 is 5 and Value_2 is 4. Values for First and Second are

- provided by the caller: Value_1 and Value_2 are provided for First and Second by Exchange_4_and_5.
- read by the called procedure: First and Second are read by Interchange in order to save the value for First in Temp and then use the value for Second to redefine First.
- written to as a result of execution of the procedure: First and Second are both modified within Interchange.
- returned, in their changed state, to the caller: Once modified, First and Second are passed back to Value_1 and Value_2 as 5 and 4, respectively.

A natural question to ask is, "Why go through all that just to interchange 4 and 5? Can't the call simply be coded as Interchange (4, 5)?" The answer is that this call *cannot* be written as Interchange (4, 5); the compiler will issue a diagnostic stating that the actual parameter in the call is not a variable. Interchange expects a parameter that it can read and modify, and a number, like 4, cannot be modified.

Default values may not be specified for parameters of mode **in out.**

2.5 Modularity

Chapter 1 introduced two principles of software engineering, abstraction and information hiding. A third principle is that of *modularity*. Recall package

Statistics. We could have had one long piece of sequential code that found the mean, the lowest value, and the highest value of a list of grades. If during the testing process an incorrect result were obtained for the lowest value, the programmer would have had to trudge through line after line of code just to find the *area* of the code that dealt with calculating the lowest value. Next, to figure out what was wrong with the logic, the programmer would have had to deal with every variable used in the code. What a horrendous way to do business!

It is far better to modularize. Make each subprogram perform *one activity.** In our package Statistics, one subprogram calculates the mean, one obtains the highest grade, and one evaluates the lowest grade. The only data available to all three subprograms—and all that needs to be available—is the list of grades. Any data required for execution of an individual subprogram is included as local data within that subprogram and is modifiable only by that subprogram. If, in a test run, the lowest grade value is found to be in error, only two areas need to be checked: the list of grades, to make sure that the individual grades are correct, and the logic of function Lowest_of in package Statistics. It is not necessary to wade through pages of code to find the area that deals with determining the lowest grade, and the programmer is not concerned with data required by the other subprograms for their algorithms. Properly modularized programs greatly simplify the process of finding errors.

EXERCISES

2.18 Write a procedure called Draw_Rectangle, that has three formal parameters: Top_Left, of type Point_Type, and Length and Width, of type Integer. Draw_Rectangle is to draw a rectangle with the origin, (0, 0), as the top left point if no other actual parameter is supplied.

2.19 Write a single procedure that uses the results of Exercise 2.18 and draws the following two rectangles:

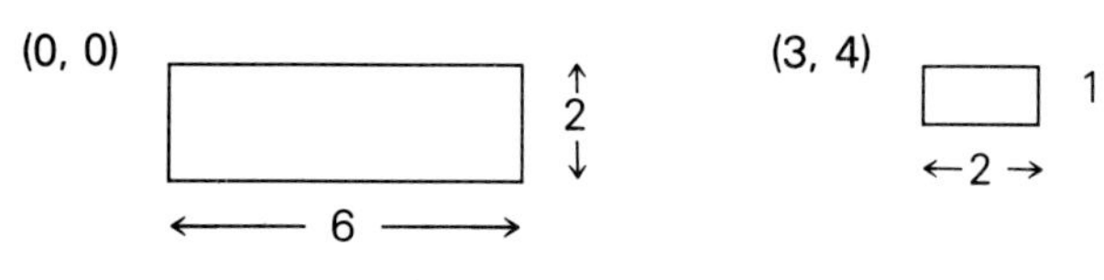

---

* D. L. Parnas, "On the Criteria To Be Used in Decomposing Systems into Modules." *Communications of the ACM* 15 (December 1972): 1053-1058.

2.20 Modify Exercise 2.19 so that the areas of the two rectangles are calculated.

2.6 Stubbing and Subunits (LRM 10.2)

Recall Display_Square, from Section 2.3, that draws a square and computes its area. Suppose you start coding Display_Square on a Friday afternoon. You first determine which packages are required (here only Simple_Graphics). You then realize that if you had a function, Area_of_Square, to return the area of a square and a procedure, Draw_Square, to draw the square, the main line of code could be written as

```
Draw_Square ( (2, 3), 4);      -- Draw the square.
Area := Area_of_Square (4);  -- Calculate the area.
```

which is very readable. You write the following:

```
with Simple_Graphics; use Simple_Graphics;
procedure Display_Square is
   Area : Integer;
   function Area_of_Square (Length_of_Side : Integer)
                           return Integer is
        -- MUST FILL THIS IN LATER
   procedure Draw_Square (Top_Left    : in Point_Type;
                          Side_Length : in Integer) is
        -- MUST FILL THIS IN LATER
begin -- Display_Square
   Draw_Square ( (2, 3), 4);      -- Draw the square.
   Area := Area_of_Square (4);  -- Calculate the area.
end Display_Square;
```

The comments are notes to yourself to fill in the bodies.

You realize that basically the problem is solved, because the first level of the solution is completed. The main line of code represents the conceptual view of the problem: first the square is drawn, then the area of the square is calculated. All that remains is to code the details of the two subprograms.

You are just settling back to work on Area_of_Square when a friend arrives and says, "Hey, it's 5:30. Let's go for a burger!" You think it would be nice to check the work completed so far by submitting your top-level solution to the compiler to work on while you're out. A partial check by the compiler at this point could test that the calls to the resources of Simple_Graphics are correct, that the calls to Area_of_Square and Draw_Square are correct, that all local data have been declared, that all identifiers are legal, and so on.

A partial check *can* be done in Ada. Here's how. Instead of writing the comment

```
-- MUST FILL THIS IN LATER
```

declare the two subprograms as **separate,** as follows:

```
with Simple_Graphics; use Simple_Graphics;
procedure Display_Square is
   Area : Integer;
   function Area_of_Square (Length_of_Side : Integer)
                           return Integer is separate;
   procedure Draw_Square (Top_Left    : in Point_Type;
                          Side_Length : in Integer)
                             is separate;
begin -- Display_Square
   Draw_Square ( (2, 3), 4);      -- Draw the square.
   Area := Area_of_Square (4); -- Calculate the area.
end Display_Square;
```

Note that each subprogram specification is now followed by the words **is separate.** A subprogram specification followed by the words **is separate** is called a *stub,* and the process of deferring the coding of a body is called *stubbing out* the body. A stub states that the body is physically separate from its "parent" unit and, in all probability, is contained in a separate text file. A subprogram stub is written as follows:

```
subprogram specification is separate;
```

Now that you have stubbed out the two subprograms, you can submit the file containing Display_Square to the compiler and go off to enjoy your burger!

You return to find that you have a successful compilation. Now you code function Area_of_Square as a *subunit.* Subunits are bodies, preceded by a **separate** clause, that have been previously declared as **separate** in another unit. Both procedure bodies and function bodies may be stubbed out and written as subunits.

Code the subunit for Area_of_Square as follows:

```
separate (Display_Square)
function Area_of_Square (Length_of_Side : Integer)
                         return Integer is
begin -- Area_of_Square
  return Length_of_Side ** 2;
end Area_of_Square;
```

Compile it into the program library. Code Draw_Square as another subunit, as follows:

```
separate (Display_Square)
procedure Draw_Square (Top_Left    : in Point_Type;
                       Side_Length : in Integer) is
    --
    -- See Figure 2-4 for the code.
    --
end Draw_Square;
```

and compile it into the same program library. The solution to your problem is now complete.

The solution was completed in two steps. First you concentrated on the highest level of abstraction of the solution and coded and compiled this abstraction. The details of the solution were not filled in, nor did they need to be. Next, after a successful compilation of the abstract solution, you proceeded to the next level of abstraction and coded and compiled the details that you previously had rightfully ignored. What an easy way to go about solving problems! Each level of abstraction in the solution can be represented in Ada and checked.

The syntax for a subprogram coded as a subunit is

```
separate (Parent_Unit_Name)
subprogram body
```

where Parent_Unit_Name represents the subunit's parent. Write the word **separate**, followed by the parent's name enclosed in parentheses. A terminating semicolon is not required and in fact is illegal. This line is then directly followed by the subprogram body.

Subunits themselves may contain stubs. Consider Figure 2-11.

The subunit for Sort_Both_Ways is coded with two stubs, as in Figure 2-12.

FIGURE 2-11 A stub: Sort_Both_Ways

```
with Statistics; use Statistics;
procedure A_Contrived_Example is
   Grades,
   Grades_in_Ascending_Order,
   Grades_in_Descending_Order : List_of_Grades;
   procedure Sort_Both_Ways
       (Array_to_be_Sorted : in List_of_Grades;
        Ascending_Array,
        Descending_Array   : out List_of_Grades)
        is separate;
begin -- A_Contrived_Example
   -- Statements to input the list
   Sort_Both_Ways
       (Array_to_be_Sorted => Grades,
        Ascending_Array    => Grades_in_Ascending_Order,
        Descending_Array   => Grades_in_Descending_Order);
   -- Statements to output the two lists
end A_Contrived_Example;
```

The first subunit within Sort_Both_Ways is coded as follows:

```
separate (A_Contrived_Example.Sort_Both_Ways)
procedure Sort_Ascending ( . . . ) is
      . . .
end Sort_Ascending;
```

The second subunit, Sort_Descending, would have a similar structure.

When the parent unit of a subunit is not itself a subunit, as is the case for Display_Square (the parent of Area_of_Square and Draw_Square) and A_Contrived_Example (the parent of Sort_Both_Ways), the naming of the parent unit does not present a problem. When the parent of a subunit is itself a

FIGURE 2-12 Two stubs of Sort_Both_Ways

```
separate (A_Contrived_Example)
procedure Sort_Both_Ways
      (Array_to_be_Sorted : in List_of_Grades;
       Ascending_Array,
       Descending_Array   : out List_of_Grades) is
procedure Sort_Ascending              -- stub 1
      (Array_In  : in List_of_Grades;
       Array_Out : out List_of_Grades) is separate;
   procedure Sort_Descending  -- stub 2
      (Array_In  : in List_of_Grades;
       Array_Out : out List_of_Grades) is separate;
begin -- Sort_Both_Ways
   Sort_Ascending  (Array_In  => Array_to_be_Sorted,
                    Array_Out => Ascending_Array);
   Sort_Descending (Array_In  => Array_to_be_Sorted,
                    Array_Out => Descending_Array);
end Sort_Both_Ways;
```

subunit, the Parent_Unit_Name is the unit containing the first stub in the chain, and is written using its expanded name, as in

```
separate (A_Contrived_Example.Sort_Both_Ways)
```

There are limitations to coding subunits. The effect of a subunit is *exactly* the same as if the body for the subunit had been written in place of the stub. Because a stub is written in the declarative part, the unit stubbed out is not callable from outside that unit. In other words, subunits are not callable by any other units in a library. Thus, Sort_Both_Ways is not callable outside of A_Contrived_Example, and Sort_Ascending and Sort_Descending are not callable outside of Sort_Both_Ways.

One of the goals of Ada is to provide reusable code so that we do not have to continually reinvent the wheel. Subunits may *import* required resources, but subunits may not be *imported.* Because subunits are not reusable, you might think that Ada has not achieved this goal. Not so!

2.7 Reusable Subprograms (LRM 10.1.1)

How can procedures such as Draw_Square and Area_of_Square, which are neither package resources nor main subprograms, be made reusable? Very easily. Just as you can **with** packages, you can **with** subprograms. However, subunits may *not* be **with**ed. This means that the two subprograms required by Display_Square must be coded and compiled into the program library as units in their own right, not as subunits that belong to a parent. To do this, remove the **separate** prefix and code Area_of_Square as follows:

```
function Area_of_Square (Length_of_Side : Integer)
                        return Integer is
begin -- Area_of_Square
   return Length_of_Side ** 2;
end Area_of_Square;
```

For Draw_Square, again remove the **separate** prefix and import Simple_Graphics.

```
with Simple_Graphics; use Simple_Graphics;
procedure Draw_Square (Top_Left    : in Point_Type;
                       Side_Length : in Integer) is
   --
   -- See Figure 2-4 for the code.
   --
end Draw_Square;
```

Draw_Square and Area_of_Square may now be imported to any other units in the library that need them. Let's see how.

Modify Display_Square by (1) adding the required **with** clauses for the two subprograms to the context clause, (2) removing the stubs, and (3) removing the **with** and **use** clauses for Simple_Graphics.

```
with Area_of_Square;
with Draw_Square;
procedure Display_Square is
   Area : Integer;
   --
   -- The stubs are removed.
   --
begin -- Display_Square
   Draw_Square ( (2, 3), 4);      -- Draw the square
   Area := Area_of_Square (4);  -- Calculate the area
end Display_Square;
```

The context clause here consists of two **with** clauses that import two different units to Display_Square. The two subprograms are not referenced by **use** clauses. (As you learned in Chapter 1, the **use** clause may name only packages.) Packages supply resources to be used, all of which are listed in the package specification. When a package is **with**ed, the **with** clause imports the named package. The **use** clause provides an easy way to refer to the package's resources. But remember that the only visible portion of a subprogram is the specification. The subprogram specification provides the necessary interface information. A subprogram's local data and executable code are not resources to be made available to any other unit. Therefore a **use** clause referencing a subprogram is meaningless.

2.8 Compilation Units (LRM 10.1)

As stated in Chapter 1, an Ada program consists of combinations of program units that are compiled in a specific order into a program library. How is this done? Does one text file contain all the pieces of the program listed sequentially in the correct order, or is it possible to have several text files, each representing a portion of the program, compiled separately? Multiple possibilities exist, as you will see. But first, a definition: A *compilation unit* is any unit that can be compiled as a *distinct text file.* The following are all legal compilation units:

- package specification
- package body
- procedure declaration
- procedure body
- function declaration
- function body
- subunit

All these compilation units may be developed as distinct text files and compiled separately, may be developed as one text file and submitted to the compiler as a single compilation, or may be developed as several text files, where each file consists of one or more compilation units appearing sequentially. The order in which separate files are submitted to the compiler is imposed by the language. This compilation order is the same for multiple compilation units appearing in a single text file.

The compilation units for Draw_Specific_Line (from Chapter 1) are:

1. package specification for Simple_Graphics
2. package body for Simple_Graphics
3. procedure body Draw_Specific_Line

The compilation units for Display_Square (from Section 2.7) are:

1. package specification for Simple_Graphics
2. package body for Simple_Graphics
3. function body Area_of_Square
4. procedure body Draw_Square
5. procedure body Display_Square

Order of Compilation (LRM 10.3)

In general, units that have dependent units must be compiled into a program library first. The following list summarizes the more specific rules that define the order in which compilation units may be compiled into a program library.

- A unit cannot be compiled into a library until after all units mentioned in its context clause have been compiled.
- A subunit cannot be compiled until after its immediate parent.
- A specification must be compiled before its body.

In Chapter 1, Simple_Graphics was already compiled into the library named Graphics, so you needed only to compile Draw_Specific_Line into Graphics. Ada specifies that the package specification must be compiled prior to the package body and the main procedure, because both the package body and the main procedure depend on the package specification. Once the package specification is compiled, however, you will recall that it does not matter whether the package body or the main procedure is compiled next because they do not depend on each other.

Revisiting Display_Square of Section 2.6, we see that it cannot be compiled into the library Graphics until all units named by its context clause have been compiled. Here the context clause names one unit, Simple_Graphics. Again it is assumed that Simple_Graphics has already been compiled into the library. Display_Square's two subunits, in turn, may not be compiled into Graphics until after their parent, Display_Square. After Display_Square is compiled, it does not matter which subunit is compiled next. The dependency

FIGURE 2-13 Subunit dependency structure

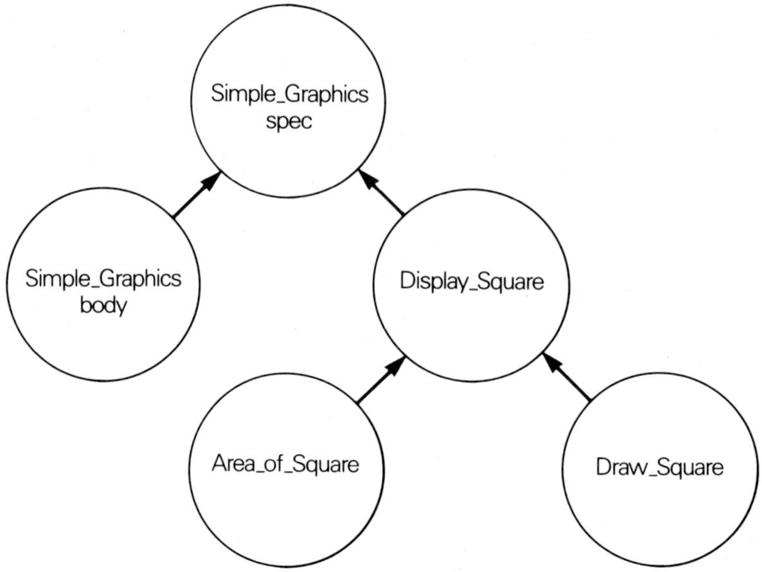

FIGURE 2-14 Reusable subprogram dependency structure

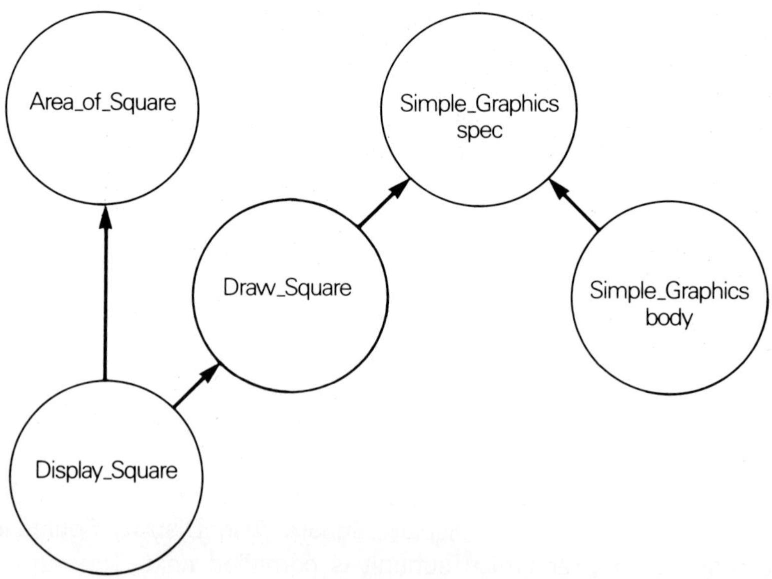

structure of Display_Square of Section 2.6 with Area_of_Square and Draw_Square coded as subunits is shown in Figure 2-13, while the dependency structure of Display_Square (Section 2.7) with the two subprograms coded as reusable subprograms is illustrated in Figure 2-14.

The advantage to developing programs in distinct pieces is that when a change is required, only the unit requiring the change, along with any other compilation units depending on it, needs to be recompiled. When a program is developed as a single text file, on the other hand, the entire program must be recompiled whenever any modification is made. For example, a modification to the specification for Simple_Graphics requires recompilation of the package specification and body for Simple_Graphics, as well as the procedure Draw_Specific_Line, but a change in procedure Draw_Specific_Line requires only Draw_Specific_Line to be recompiled.

EXERCISES

2.21 Recode A_Contrived_Example. Leave Sort_Both_Ways coded as a subunit, but code Sort_Ascending and Sort_Descending so they may be used by other units within the program library. (Do not code the implementation of Sort_Ascending or Sort_Descending.)

2.22 Name the compilation units of A_Contrived_Example as coded in the text. Then name the compilation units as coded in Exercise 2.21.

2.23 Draw a dependency diagram and list ten possible legal orders of compilation for A_Contrived_Example as coded in Section 2.6.

2.24 Draw a dependency diagram and list ten possible legal orders of compilation for A_Contrived_Example as coded in Exercise 2.21.

2.25 Name one illegal order of compilation for each version of A_Contrived_Example. State why the order is illegal.

2.26 If a modification is made to Sort_Ascending, which units, in addition to Sort_Ascending, need to be recompiled? Answer the question with respect to the coding in the text and the coding in Exercise 2.21.

2.27 If a modification is made to Sort_Both_Ways, which units, in addition to Sort_Both_Ways, need to be recompiled? Again, answer the question with respect to A_Contrived_Example as coded both in the text and in Exercise 2.21.

2.28 In Section 2.7, Draw_Square and Area_of_Square are recoded as reusable subprograms. Why is Simple_Graphics imported to Draw_Square and not to Display_Square?

3

WRITING PROGRAMS

CHAPTER OBJECTIVES

- Input data using package Text_IO.
- Output data using Text_IO.
- Define an **exception.**
- Write handlers for exceptions.
- Localize exception handlers using a block statement.
- Code simple **loop** and **for loop.**
- Name loops and blocks.
- Nest loops.
- Code **exit** statements.

The basic structure of Ada programs was the focus of Chapters 1 and 2. Packages, and how to use their resources, were discussed in Chapter 1. Subprograms, and how to use them, were discussed in Chapter 2. In this chapter we will begin to look at writing useful Ada programs. First, two practical topics are introduced: input/output and a brief introduction to error handling in Ada. Finally, we will present some statements and control constructs used to build Ada programs.

3.1 Input-Output (LRM 14.3)

Section 2.3 showed a procedure named Display_Square that used a nested function named Area_of_Square and a nested procedure named Draw_Square to draw the following square.

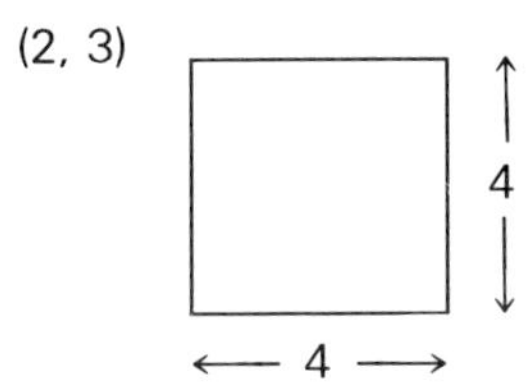

Display_Square computed, but did not print, the area of the square. Let us now add to this procedure the capability to print the area.

Text I/O facilities (as opposed to binary I/O) are provided as part of the Ada language in a package named Text_IO. As you know, to use the resources of a package you need to have the package specification. Unfortunately, Text_IO is a very complex package, and showing its specification at this point would be counterproductive and confusing. For now, therefore, simply do the following:

Step 1: When I/O is required, include a **with** and a **use** clause for Text_IO in the context clause for the unit doing the I/O, as follows:

```
with Text_IO; use Text_IO;
```

Step 2: If performing I/O on type *Integer*, write the following two lines of code in the declarative part:

```
package Int_IO is new Integer_IO (Integer);
use Int_IO;
```

If performing I/O on type *Float*, write the following two lines of code in the declarative part:

```
package Flt_IO is new Float_IO (Float);
use Flt_IO;
```

If performing I/O on *both* types in the same unit, write all four lines of code in the declarative part.

You may now Get and Put values of type Integer or type Float interactively or from a file by writing procedure calls. Get is a procedure that inputs a single value, and Put is a procedure that outputs a single value. Elementary interactive I/O will be covered now, and file I/O will be covered in Chapter 9.

How to Display Results (LRM 14.3.10)

Figure 3-1 shows how Text_IO is used to print the area of the square in Display_Square. The boxes indicate changes made to the code of Section 2.3.

The Put procedure outputs the value of the actual parameter passed, here Area. The actual parameter may be a variable, a value, or a function call that returns a value of the required type. The cursor is not positioned at the beginning of the next line, but remains ready to print in the next column on the same line. Unfortunately, Put is limited and outputs only one value at a time. To output *n* values requires *n* calls to Put.

When you want to output text, perhaps to label a result, write a procedure call to Put or Put_Line, both procedures in Text_IO, with the desired text enclosed in quotes. After outputting the text, Put leaves the cursor positioned at the next available column on the same line. For example, the two statements

```
Put ( "The area of the square is: ");
Put (Area);
```

produce

```
The area of the square is: 16
```

If the last character in a call to Put is printed in the last column of a line, Put advances the cursor to the first column in the next line.

A call to Put_Line outputs the text and then positions the cursor at the beginning of the next line. The two statements

```
Put_Line ( "The area of the square is: ");
Put (Area);
```

produce

```
The area of the square is :
16
```

The characters that may be used to form printed text are listed in Table 3-1. The

FIGURE 3-1 Displaying results

```
with Simple_Graphics; use Simple_Graphics;
--
-- STEP 1
--
with Text_IO;  use Text_IO;
procedure Display_Square is
   Area : Integer;
   function Area_of_Square (Length_of_Side : Integer)
                             return Integer is
   begin -- Area_of_Square
      return Length_of_Side**2;
   end Area_of_Square;
   procedure Draw_Square (Top_Left    : in Point_Type;
                          Side_Length : in Integer) is
      --
      -- See Figure 2-4 for the code.
      --
   end Draw_Square;
  --
  -- STEP 2
  --
  package Int_IO is new Integer_IO (Integer);
  use Int_IO;
begin -- Display_Square
   Draw_Square ( (2, 3), 4);     --Draw the square
   Area  := Area_of_Square (4); --Calculate the area
   Put (Area);                   --Output results
end Display_Square;
```

TABLE 3-1 Printable Characters

Upper Case Letters

A B C D E F G H I J K L M N O P Q R S T U V W X Y Z

Lower Case Letters

a b c d e f g h i j k l m n o p q r s t u v w x y z

Digits

0 1 2 3 4 5 6 7 8 9

Special Characters (Printer/Terminal Dependent)

" # & ' ( ) * + , - . / : ; < = > _ | ! $ % ? @ [\ ] ^ ` { } ~ space character

length of text may not exceed the length of a line. Use the catenation operator, &, to output text that exceeds the length of a line, as in

```
Put_Line ("This is a very long line of text," &
          "which cannot be placed on one line. But it" &
          "can be printed using one call to Put_Line" &
          "when coded using the catenation operator.");
```

The procedure Put_Line is *only* defined for outputting text enclosed in quotation marks. Another way to state this is that the only legal actual parameter for a call to Put_Line is a sequence of printable characters enclosed in quotes. The following attempt to print the value of Area and position the cursor at the beginning of the next line is illegal:

```
Put_Line (Area); --**ILLEGAL**--
```

The desired effect can be obtained by a call to Put to output the value of Area, followed by a call to another procedure in Text_IO named New_Line, like this:

```
Put (Area);
New_Line;
```

When an actual parameter is not supplied, New_Line advances to the beginning of the next line. Otherwise, New_Line advances the number of lines indicated by the actual parameter, which must be a positive integer value, as in

```
New_Line(3);
```

This will advance three lines, leaving two blank lines between lines of output. The maximum number of lines that may be advanced will depend on the implementation, that is, it depends on the Ada compiler you are using and may vary from compiler to compiler.

How to Enter Data (LRM 14.3.10)

Suppose Display_Square were to draw a square starting at the same point as it presently does but obtain the value of the length of the side from the terminal. The code for this procedure would then appear as in Figure 3-2, with the boxes highlighting changes from the previous section.

Upon execution of the Get statement, an implementation-dependent prompt may appear. Like the Put procedure, the Get procedure is limited; it can obtain only one value at a time. After the prompt, enter one value to be associated with the variable Side_Length. Remember to enter a value written without decimal points because Side_Length is of type Integer. If you attempt to enter a value with a decimal point, the program will crash. In the next section we will describe ways to keep this from happening.

Note that the declarative part of Display_Square now contains two local data items: Area and Side_Length. Ada requires all local data to be explicitly declared in the declarative part of the unit. Had the declaration

```
Side_Length : Integer;
```

been omitted from the code, the compiler would have flagged the Get statement as being in error, citing Side_Length as an undeclared identifier.

An Example: Exchange_Two_Values

The code in Figure 3-3 produces the following output, assuming that the "greater than" symbol (>) is the prompt used by the implementation:

```
Enter first value:
>4
Enter second value:
>5
The first value is now: 5
The second value is now: 4
```

The first call to Put_Line outputs the prompt "Enter first value:" and positions the cursor at the beginning of the next line. The first call to Get causes the prompt to be displayed and a value for Value_1 to be obtained from user

FIGURE 3-2 Entering data

```
with Simple_Graphics; use Simple_Graphics;
--
-- STEP 1
--
with Text_IO; use Text_IO;
procedure Display_Square is
  Area        : Integer;
  Side_Length : Integer;
  function Area_of_Square (Length_of_Side : Integer)
                             return Integer is
  begin -- Area_of_Square
     return Length_of_Side**2
  end Area_of_Square;
  procedure Draw_Square (Top_Left     : in Point ;
                         Side_Length  : in Integer) is
     --
     -- See Figure 2-4 for the code.
     --
  end Draw_Square;
  --
  -- STEP 2
  --
  package INT_IO is new Integer_IO (Integer);
  use Int_IO;
begin -- Display_Square
  Get (Side_Length);       -- Obtain the length.
  Draw_Square ( (2, 3), Side_Length ); -- Draw the
                                       -- square.
  Area  := Area_of_Square (Side_Length);  -- Calculate
                                          -- the area.
   Put (Area);             -- Output results.
end Display_Square;
```

input. The process is similar for the next two statements. The call to Interchange interchanges the two values. The first call to Put outputs the text "The first value is now:" and positions the cursor at the column after the last character displayed, here a blank space. The second call to Put outputs the current value of Value_1 immediately following the blank space. The use of two Put calls keeps the text and the results on the same line. The call to New_Line, after Put(Value_1);, causes the text "The second value is now:" to start on a new line. Table 3-2 summarizes these I/O procedures.

There are two problems with this code. The first, already mentioned, is that the program will crash if a value with a decimal point is entered for either Value_1 or Value_2. The second is that this program can be used only once: there is no mechanism in the code to allow the user to enter a second set of values to be interchanged. In the next section you will find out how to remedy these inadequacies.

FIGURE 3-3 Exchange_Two_Values

```
-- using Binary_Operations from Section 2.4
with Binary_Operations; use Binary_Operations;
with Text_IO;           use Text_IO;
procedure Exchange_Two_Values is
   Value_1, Value_2 : Integer;
   package Int_IO is new Integer_IO (Integer);
   use Int_IO;
begin -- Exchange_Two_Values
   Put_Line ("Enter first value: ");
   Get (Value_1);
   Put_Line ("Enter second value: ");
   Get (Value_2);
   Interchange (Value_1, Value_2);
   Put ("The first value is now: ");
   Put (Value_1);
   New_Line;
   Put ("The second value is now: ");
   Put (Value_2);
end Exchange_Two_Values;
```

TABLE 3-2 A Few Text_IO Procedures

Procedure Name	*Actual Expected*	*Execution Result*
Put	Variable Expression Function call	Outputs current value of the actual parameter. Cursor set to next column on same line.*
Put	Sequence of printable characters enclosed in quotation marks	Outputs text. Cursor set to next column on same line.*
Put_Line	Sequence of printable characters enclosed in quotation marks	Outputs text. Positions cursor at beginning of next line.
Get	Variable	Obtains a value for the actual parameter.
New_Line	None	Advances cursor to beginning of next line.
New_Line	1 < N < Max**	Advances cursor to column 1, N lines ahead.

* If the last character is output to the last column in the line, the cursor is set to the first column of the next line.

** where Max is implementation defined

EXERCISES

3.1 Modify Exercise 2.20 so that the areas of the two rectangles are printed out in the following form:

```
The area of the first rectangle is:
XXX
The area of the second rectangle is:
XXX
```

3.2 Modify 3.1 to display one rectangle with Top_Left at the origin, (0, 0), and with a length and width that are obtained as inputs.

Use the following package specification for Exercises 3.3–3.6.

```
package Metric_Conversions is
   function Inches_to_Centimeters (Inches : Float)
                                  return Float;
   function Centimeters_to_Inches (Centimeters : Float)
                                  return Float;
   . . .
   procedure Convert_Inches (Inches : in Float;
      Centimeters, Meters, Kilometers : out Float);
   procedure Convert_Centimeters (Centimeters : in Float;
      Inches, Feet, Miles : out Float);

   function Quarts_to_Liters  (Quarts : Integer)
                              return Float;
   function Gallons_to_Liters (Gallons : Integer)
                              return Float;
   function Liters_to_Gallons (Liters : Float)
                              return Float;
   function Liters_to_Quarts  (Liters : Float)
                              return Float;
   . . .
end Metric Conversions;
```

3.3 Write a program that inputs a value for inches and outputs the corresponding value in centimeters. The following should prompt the user for a value:

```
Enter the inches to be converted:
```

The following should precede the desired output:

```
The value in centimeters is:
```

3.4 Write a program that inputs a value for inches and outputs the corresponding value in centimeters, meters, and kilometers. The following should prompt the user for a value:

```
Enter the inches to be converted:
```

The following layout should be used for the output:

```
XXX inches is XXX centimeters.
XXX inches is XXX meters.
XXX inches is XXX kilometers.
```

3.5 Write a program that inputs a number to be interpreted as gallons and outputs the equivalent number of liters. Include a prompt for the input and explanatory text preceding the output.

3.6 Write a program to convert quantities such as two gallons and 1 quart, or three gallons and 2 quarts to liters. Include prompts for inputs and text preceding results.

3.2 Exceptions (LRM 11)

Obviously, it is not desirable to have a program crash when an incorrect value is entered for a variable. Entering 3.5 for Value_1 in Exchange_Two_Values could not have been detected as an error during compilation because the association occurs during program execution. This is therefore an example of a *run-time error.* A run-time error in Ada is called an *exception*. Other examples of run-time errors include evaluation of a value too large for the machine, an attempt to open a file that is already open, and evaluation of an index of 11 for an array of length 10. When exceptions such as these occur, normal processing cannot continue.

Most programming languages do not provide a mechanism to cope with run-time errors, and traditionally it has been left to the programmer to tediously debug the code in an attempt to locate the cause of a crash. Ada, however, does provide a mechanism for handling such errors. When a run-time error occurs, the language points it out; we say that *an exception is raised.* We tell the computer how to deal with the problem by writing an *exception handler*, a sequence of statements to be performed when the exception is raised. The exception handler's purpose is to give the system a chance to respond to the error in a way that allows the program to continue executing and, indeed, to regard the error as nothing more than a minor hiccup.

There are exceptions that are provided as part of Text_IO, and exceptions that are provided as part of the language. Tables 3-3 and 3-4 list the exceptions that will be dealt with in this text and some conditions that will cause the exceptions to be raised. These exceptions are already named, and the system raises them automatically at run time if they arise. You may also see exceptions declared in package specifications, as in Figure 3-4. For now assume that the

TABLE 3-3 A Frequently Used Text_IO Exception

Exception Name	*Raised By*	*Error Condition*
Data_Error	Get	An attempt to input a value that is not a legal value for the type of the formal parameter.

TABLE 3-4 Frequently Used Predefined Language Exceptions

Exception Name	*Possible Error Condition*
Constraint_Error	An attempt to access an undefined index value for an array
Numeric_Error	An attempt to calculate a value that is not defined for the hardware
Program_Error	An attempt to leave a function other than by a **return** statement

Note: Additional conditions that cause these exceptions to be raised will be addressed throughout the text.

FIGURE 3-4 An exception provided by a package

```
package Breathing_Operations is
   procedure Inhale;
   procedure Exhale;
   procedure Receive_Heimlich_Maneuver; -- raises Choking
   procedure Get_Back_Slapped;
   Choking : exception;
end Breathing_Operations;
```

package raises the exception. Our concern now becomes how to write exception handlers.

Exception Handlers (LRM 11.2)

An exception handler is written as follows:

```
when Exception_Name => sequence of statements
```

The exception handler may occur only inside a *frame,* that is, between a **begin** and an **end.** Specifically, it must appear as the *last* part of the frame. The only frames we have met so far are subprogram bodies. A frame containing one or more exception handlers looks like this:

```
begin
   -- executable statement(s)
exception
   -- exception handler(s)
   when Exception_Name => sequence of statements
  {when Exception_Name => sequence of statements}
end;
```

The reserved word **exception** indicates that handlers appear next. Only handlers may appear between the words **exception** and **end** in the frame.

The code in Figure 3-5 attempts to keep Exchange_Two_Values from crashing when an incorrect value for Value_1 is entered.

The rules for writing exception handlers have been observed. The handler for Data_Error appears after the reserved word **exception**, all of which appears between the **begin** and **end** in the subprogram body. The handler is coded by writing the reserved word **when** followed by the name of the exception, here Data_Error. The arrow (=>) precedes the sequence of statements to be executed when Data_Error is raised. Well and good. But now suppose you enter 3.5 for Value_1. What actually happens?

When the inappropriate value is perceived, Text_IO raises Data_Error. The run-time system then looks for a handler, searching within the innermost enclosing frame (the only frame available, in this case), and finds one. The statements in the Data_Error handler are executed—and control passes to the first statement after the **end.** In other words, the execution of a handler *completes the frame.* Control does *not* return to the statement that caused the exception to be raised, as is the case in some other languages. If the **end** of the frame is the end of a subprogram, the subprogram terminates—which is what happens here.

You now may well be wondering, "What good does the handler do, then?" You're right in this case: it really doesn't do much, since the frame here is the subprogram body. Because the procedure terminates, the statements after the Get statement are never executed, and there is no opportunity to input another value. The same thing would have happened if an incorrect value had been entered for Value_2.

In many instances, termination of the procedure after a handler has been executed is appropriate, but obviously it is not desirable here. What

FIGURE 3-5 Adding an exception handler

```
with Binary_Operations; use Binary_Operations;
with Text_IO;           use Text_IO;
procedure Exchange_Two_Values is
   Value_1, Value_2 : Integer;
   package Int_IO is new Integer_IO (Integer);
   use Int_IO;
begin -- Exchange_Two_Values
   Put_Line ("Enter first value: ");
   Get (Value_1);
   Put_Line ("Enter second value: ");
   Get (Value_2);
   Interchange (Value_1, Value_2);
   Put ("The first value is now: ");
   Put (Value_1);
   New_Line;
   Put ("The second value is now: ");
   Put (Value_2);
exception
   when Data_Error =>
      Put_Line("Invalid entry.");
      Put_Line("Enter integer value.");
end Exchange_Two_Values;
```

Exchange_Two_Values needs is a mechanism to associate a handler with just the Get statement that actually raises Data Error. That way, corrective action could be taken and the remaining statements of the procedure could then be executed. A *block statement* is part of such a mechanism.

Blocks for Localization (LRM 5.6)

A block statement in Ada takes the following form:

```
[declare
    -- local declarations]
begin
    -- sequence of executable statements
end;
```

A block statement acts as a single statement. When the block statement is executed, local data declared in the optional declarative part become available to the sequence of statements in the executable part of the block. These local data are not known outside the block. After the sequence of statements within the block is executed, control passes to the first statement after the block, and the local data are no longer accessible.

A block statement can help to solve our problem because the run-time system looks for an exception handler within the *innermost* frame. A block, you will note, has the **begin** and **end** structure required of a frame and therefore may contain exception handlers. Now recode Exchange_Two_Values as shown in Figure 3-6.

Let's walk through this code. The prompt "Enter first value:" is output, the block is entered, and the Get statement is executed. If the user enters an invalid value for Value_1, Data_Error is raised. A handler for Data_Error is found within the innermost enclosing frame, which here is the block. Control then passes to that handler, and the two lines of text are output. The block terminates, and control passes to the first statement after the block. Exchange_Two_Values does not terminate. Instead, the second prompt is output, and the process is repeated for the second value.

Enclosing each Get statement in a block is a step in the right direction. First, the statements output as a result of execution of the exception handlers will indicate which Get raised the exception. Second, since the exception handlers are embedded within a block, the main procedure will not terminate prematurely. But there are still problems with this code. If an illegal value is

FIGURE 3-6 Adding a block around the exception handler

```
with Binary_Operations; use Binary_Operations;
with Text_IO;           use Text_IO;
procedure Exchange_Two_Values is
   --
   -- Declarations as before.
   --
begin -- Exchange_Two_Values
   Put_Line ("Enter first value: ");
   --
   -- Localize the exception by placing
   -- the Get within a block that contains
   -- the exception handler.
   --
   begin
      Get (Value_1);
   exception
      when Data_Error =>
         Put_Line("Invalid entry for 1st value.");
         Put_Line("Enter integer value.");
   end;
   Put_Line ("Enter second value: ");
   --
   -- Again, localize the exception by placing
   -- the Get within a block that contains the
   -- exception handler.
   --
   begin
      Get (Value_2);
   exception
      when Data_Error =>
         Put_Line("Invalid entry for 2nd value.");
         Put_Line("Enter integer value.");
   end;
   Interchange (Value_1, Value_2);
   Put ("The first value is now: ");
   Put (Value_1);
   New_Line;
   Put ("The second value is now: ");
   Put (Value_2);
   -- First exception handler removed.
end Exchange_Two_Values;
```

entered for Value_1, the procedure will simply continue to execute without a value for Value_1: there is no way for the user to try again to enter a legal value. Control needs to be returned to the Get statement where the exception was raised, so it will be executed again, allowing the user to re-enter the data. Next, let us see how.

Simple *loop* (LRM 5.5)

We can return control to the Get statement by placing the block inside a *loop statement*. A loop statement is used to cause a sequence of statements to be executed repeatedly, zero or more times. A *simple loop* has the following structure:

```
loop
   --
   -- Sequence of statements to
   -- be executed repeatedly
   --
end loop;
```

A simple loop statement is executed by executing the first statement in the loop, then the second, and so on until **end loop** is reached. Control then returns to the first statement in the loop, and the process is repeated ad infinitum.

Recall the package specification shown in Figure 3-4 and in the following subprogram:

```
with Breathing_Operations;
procedure Mortality is
   --
   -- No local data necessary.
   --
begin -- Mortality
   loop
      Breathing_Operations.Inhale;
      Breathing_Operations.Exhale;
   end loop;
end Mortality;
```

Note that procedure Mortality makes repeated calls to Inhale, then Exhale, with no provision for choking.

The package specification for Breathing_Operations identifies an exception named Choking, shown in Figure 3-4. In other words, the package recognizes that while inhaling, a person may choke. Assume that the package indicates that choking is occurring by raising Choking. Assume also that the package does not perform any corrective action when Choking is raised, so that the user of the package is left to decide whether to be slapped on the back, receive the Heimlich maneuver, or supply another solution. (An Ada package does not have to supply options for corrective action, nor, if a package supplies options, does one of them have to be chosen by the using unit.)

Let's now code a handler for Choking and change the name of the procedure to Immortality.

```
with Breathing_Operations;
procedure Immortality is
   --
   -- No local data necessary.
   --
begin -- Immortality
   loop
      begin
         Breathing_Operations.Inhale;
         Breathing_Operations.Exhale;
      exception
         when Breathing_Operations.Choking =>
Breathing_Operations.Receive_Heimlich_Maneuver;
      end;
   end loop;
end Immortality;
```

Our program now requests the Heimlich maneuver in the event of choking. When a choking incident occurs, the exception Choking is raised by the procedure Inhale. Assuming there is no handler for Choking within procedure Inhale, the exception is *propagated,* or reraised, at the point of call to Inhale, and the Choking handler is found within the frame enclosing the call to Inhale. Control passes to the exception handler for Choking, the Heimlich maneuver is performed, and the block terminates. Control then passes to the **end loop,** which returns control to the beginning of the loop so that normal breathing resumes.

Stated more generally, when an exception is raised within a subprogram and there is no handler for it, the exception is propagated to, or reraised at, the point of call of the subprogram. If a handler exists within the frame containing the call, it is executed. If no handler exists in that frame, the exception is again propagated to the subprogram that called it, and so on. If a handler exists somewhere along this chain of subprogram calls, the handler is executed. If the exception is propagated all the way back to the main subprogram, and there is no handler, the main subprogram terminates.

Figure 3-7 shows Exchange_Two_Values recoded, with a simple loop added around each of the two blocks. Enclosing each block in a loop is another step in the right direction. If an invalid entry is input for Value_1, Data_Error is raised, a handler is found, the two calls to Put_Line are performed, the block statement terminates, and control passes to the **end loop.** Since this is a simple loop, control passes back to the beginning of the loop, the block is entered, and the Get call is executed again, providing another opportunity to input a correct integer value. This code now properly handles an incorrect input. But what happens when a correct value is input for Value_1? In this case the handler is not invoked, the block terminates, and we are again at the **end loop.** Control passes back to the block, and the Get is executed again. We have created an endless loop! This is clearly *not* what is wanted.

The solution to the problem is the **exit** statement, which Ada provides to complete a loop statement.

The *exit* Statement (LRM 5.7)

One form of an exit statement is simply

```
exit;
```

Additional forms will be introduced later. Execution of an **exit** statement completes the *innermost* loop.

Consider Figure 3-8. The exception-handling mechanism executes just as in the previous version of the code. But now, when a correct value is entered for Value_1 or Value_2, control passes to the next statement, which is the **exit** statement. The loop is then exited, and processing continues. You can see that

FIGURE 3-7 Adding a **loop** around the block

```
with Binary_Operations; use Binary_Operations;
with Text_IO;           use Text_IO;
procedure Exchange_Two_Values is
   Value_1, Value_2 : Integer;
   package Int_IO is new Integer_IO (Integer);
   use Int_IO;
begin -- Exchange_Two_Values
   Put_Line ("Enter first value: ");
   --
   -- Now place the block within a loop.
   --
   loop
      begin
         Get (Value_1);
      exception
         when Data_Error =>
            Put_Line("Invalid entry for 1st value.");
            Put_Line("Enter integer value: ");
      end;
   end loop;
   Put_Line ("Enter second value: ");
   --
   -- Again, place the block within a loop.
   --
   loop
      begin
         Get (Value_2);
      exception
         when Data_Error =>
            Put_Line("Invalid entry for 2nd value.");
            Put_Line("Enter integer value: ");
      end;
   end loop;
   Interchange (Value_1, Value_2);
   Put ("The first value is now: ");
   Put (Value_1);
   New_Line;
   Put ("The second value is now: ");
   Put (Value_2);
end Exchange_Two_Values;
```

FIGURE 3-8 Adding an **exit** statement to the **loop**

```
with Binary_Operations; use Binary_Operations;
with Text_IO;           use Text_IO;
procedure Exchange_Two_Values is
   Value_1, Value_2 : Integer;
   package Int_IO is new Integer_IO (Integer);
   use Int_IO;
begin -- Exchange_Two_Values
   Put_Line ("Enter first value: ");
   -- Now add an exit after the Get.
   -- Upon successful input, the loop terminates.
   loop
      begin
         Get (Value_1);
  exit;
      exception
         when Data_Error =>
            Put_Line("Invalid entry for 1st value.");
            Put_Line("Enter integer value: ");
      end;
   end loop;
   Put_Line ("Enter second value: ");
   -- Again, place an exit after the Get.
   loop
      begin
         Get (Value_2);
  exit;
      exception
         when Data_Error =>
            Put_Line("Invalid entry for 2nd value.");
            Put_Line("Enter integer value: ");
      end;
   end loop;
   Interchange (Value_1, Value_2);
   Put ("The first value is now: ");
   Put (Value_1);
   New_Line;
   Put ("The second value is now: ");
   Put (Value_2);
end Exchange_Two_Values;
```

exception handlers often need to be used in conjunction with other constructs such as blocks, loops, and exit statements in order for the code to model the desired solution. Align the **exit** statement to signal the fact that this is an abnormal exit from the loop.

Nested Loops (LRM 5.5)

At present, Exchange_Two_Values allows us to interchange only two values. To permit multiple interchanges we must use nested loops. Loops may be nested in Ada, as in other languages, and the order of completion is like that in other languages; that is, inner loops are completed before outer loops.

The code in Figure 3-9 is a revision of the code in Figure 3-8 and allows multiple interchanges to occur. A call to New_Line has been added to ensure that the first prompt starts on a new line for subsequent executions of the outer loop.

Currently our exception handlers allow the user to try to enter correct values as often as necessary. If correct values are entered, the values will be interchanged, and the outer loop will be executed again—and again and again. How can we make this program stop? We will discuss that little problem in the final section of this chapter and also in Chapter 4, Decision Making.

Naming Blocks and Loops (LRM 5.5, 5.6)

Loops and blocks may be named. Doing so helps to create code that is self-explanatory. The name must be a legal Ada identifier and must be directly followed by a colon. When a loop or block is named, the name *must* be repeated after the corresponding **end**. Writing the name entirely in capital letters makes it easier to locate the loop or block within the code.

Figure 3-10 shows Exchange_Two_Values with the loops named.

When loops are named, the **exit** statement may be written as

```
exit Loop_Name;
```

as in

```
exit OBTAIN_FIRST_VALUE;
```

Use of an **exit** statement within a nested loop causes completion of the inner loop unless the outer loop is explicitly named in the **exit** statement (see

FIGURE 3-9 Nested loops

```
with Binary_Operations; use Binary_Operations;
with Text_IO;           use Text_IO;
procedure Exchange_Two_Values is
   Value_1, Value_2 : Integer;
   package Int_IO is new Integer_IO (Integer);
   use Int_IO;
begin -- Exchange_Two_Values
   -- Now adding outer loop
   loop
   Put_Line ("Enter first value: ");
      loop
         begin
            Get (Value_1);
      exit;
         exception
            when Data_Error =>
               Put_Line("Invalid entry for 1st value.");
               Put_Line("Enter integer value: ");
         end;
      end loop;
      Put_Line ("Enter second value: ");
      -- Again, place an exit after the Get.
      loop
         begin
            Get (Value_2);
      exit;
         exception
            when Data_Error =>
               Put_Line("Invalid entry for 2nd value.");
               Put_Line("Enter integer value: ");
         end;
      end loop;
      Interchange (Value_1, Value_2);
      Put ("The first value is now: ");
      Put (Value_1);
      New_Line;
      Put ("The second value is now: ");
      Put (Value_2);
      New_Line;
   end loop;
end Exchange_Two_Values;
```

FIGURE 3-10 Named loops

```
with Binary_Operations; use Binary_Operations;
with Text_IO;           use Text_IO;
procedure Exchange_Two_Values is
   -- Declarations as before.
begin -- Exchange_Two_Values
      --
      -- Now name all three loops.
      --
MAIN:
   loop
   Put_Line ("Enter first value: ");
   OBTAIN_FIRST_VALUE:
      loop
         begin
            Get (Value_1);
      exit;
         exception
           when Data_Error =>
              Put_Line("Invalid entry for 1st value.");
              Put_Line("Enter integer value: ");
         end;
      end loop OBTAIN_FIRST_VALUE;
      Put_Line ("Enter second value: ");
   OBTAIN_SECOND_VALUE:
      loop
         begin
            Get (Value_2);
      exit;
         exception
            when Data_Error =>
               Put_Line("Invalid entry for 2nd value.");
               Put_Line("Enter integer value: ");
         end;
      end loop OBTAIN_SECOND_VALUE;
      Interchange (Value_1, Value_2);
      Put ("The first value is now: ");
      Put (Value_1);
      New_Line;
      Put ("The second value is now: ");
      Put (Value_2);
      New_Line;
end loop MAIN;
end Exchange_Two_Values;
```

FIGURE 3-11 Exiting nested loops

```
OUTER:
   loop
      --
      -- Initial outer loop statements.
      --
      INNER:
         loop
            --
            -- Inner loop statements which
            -- may include an exit.
            --
         exit;
         end loop INNER;
      -- <-
      -- Final outer loop statements.

   end loop OUTER;
```

UPON EXECUTION OF exit STATEMENT CONTROL RESUMES HERE. [callout arrow points to the line following end loop INNER]

3-11 (a) Exiting an inner loop

```
OUTER:
   loop
      --
      -- Initial outer loop statements.
      --
      INNER:
         loop
            --
            -- Inner loop statements which
            -- may include an exit.
            --
         exit OUTER;
         end loop INNER;
      --
      -- Final outer loop statements.
      --
   end loop OUTER;
   <-
```

UPON EXECUTION OF exit STATEMENT CONTROL RESUMES HERE. [callout arrow points to the line following end loop OUTER]

3-11 (b) Exiting an outer loop

Figure 3-11). Using a single **exit** statement to exit through several layers of nested loops is possible but not recommended because it violates the single entry-single exit principle of structured programming.

EXERCISES

3.7 State whether each of the following represents a compile-time or a run-time error. For a compile-time error, state the error and correct the code. For a run-time error, state the exception raised.

a.
```
OBTAIN_FIRST_VALUE:
  loop
    .
    .
    .
  end loop;
```
b. An attempt to use a 16-bit machine to calculate 8164 squared. (Assume type Integer is the only predefined integer type for the implementation. See LRM Appendix C paragraph 7.)

c. Value := Value/0.0; where the slash, (/), represents division and Value is of type Integer.

d. Value := Value/0.0; where the slash, (/), represents division and Value is of type Float.

e. An attempt to reference Center(3) where Center is of type Point_Type provided by package Simple_Graphics.

f. An attempt to reference Center(I) where Center is of type Point_Type and I evaluates to 3.

3.8 State the three parts of Ada's exception-handling mechanism.

3.9 The ________________________ construct can be used to localize an exception handler.

3.10 Recode Exercise 3.2 with appropriate handler(s).

3.11 The following package specification is given:

```
package Factorial_Operations is
   function Factorial_of (Number : Integer)
               return Integer;
   function Number_Whose_Factorial_Is
               (Value : Integer) return Integer;
   -- Negative_Number is raised by Factorial_of
   Negative_Number : exception;
   -- Not_Factorial is raised
   -- by Number_Whose_Factorial_Is
   Not_Factorial   : exception;
end Factorial_Operations;
```

a. Write a procedure that inputs a value and computes its factorial. Include an exception handler for Data_Error.
b. What exception is raised if the input value results in a factorial whose value is larger than the hardware can support?
   (Hint: Enter 300 and see what happens. Modify 3.11(a) to include a handler for this exception. The handler should output a message that says "The factorial of XXX is too large for the system to handle.")
c. Modify 3.11(b) by adding an exception handler for Negative_Number.
d. Write a procedure that inputs a value and determines whether or not that value represents a factorial. Include an exception handler for Not_Factorial.

3.3 The *for* Loop (LRM 5.5)

Currently the code for Exchange_Two_Values permits an infinite number of attempts to enter a value. This is slightly unrealistic. After several, let's say three, unsuccessful tries at entering an Integer value, the user should be told that enough is enough. To do this we need a mechanism to iterate (repeat) each block, as in the previous section, but only for a specified number of times. Iteration for a specific number of times is handled in Ada by the **for** loop. The syntax of a **for** loop is as follows:

```
for Loop_Parameter in [reverse] Iteration_Range
   loop
      --
      -- Sequence of statements
      --
   end loop;
```

where Loop_Parameter is a legal Ada identifier and Iteration_Range is, for now, written as

```
Lower_Bound .. Upper_Bound
```

where Lower_Bound and Upper_Bound can be either values or expressions of type Integer. The statements within the loop are executed once for each value of the loop parameter within the specified range.

For example, the OBTAIN_FIRST_VALUE loop can be recoded with a **for** loop to permit three attempts at inputting a correct value.

```
OBTAIN_FIRST_VALUE:
   for Counter in 1 .. 3
   loop
      begin
         Get (Value_1);
   exit;
      exception
         when Data_Error =>
            Put_Line("Invalid entry for 1st value.");
            Put_Line("Enter integer value: ");
      end;
   end loop OBTAIN_FIRST_VALUE;
```

The block is executed three times—once for each of the three permissible values of Counter, which are 1, 2, and 3. If a correct value has not been input after three attempts, the loop terminates. The loop also terminates when a correct value is input. Thus the loop statement can be exited two ways: via the **exit** statement when a correct value is entered, and via completion of the **for** loop when an incorrect value is entered on the third try. Some mechanism is thus required to determine whether we have completed the loop with or without a legitimate value for Value_1. We need to be able to provide alternate paths of control; the code needs to make decisions based on information within the program. That will be the focus of Chapter 4, Making Decisions.

Loop Parameter (LRM 5.5)

The entire set of values for a loop parameter is defined by the corresponding Iteration_Range. The loop parameter Counter has as its entire set of possible values the integer values 1, 2, and 3. As a consequence, the loop parameter may not be modified (written to) within the loop. To write

```
for Counter in 1 .. 3
loop
   --
   -- some statements
   --
   Counter := Counter + 1; --**ILLEGAL**--
end loop;
```

is illegal. In this sense a loop parameter acts like a parameter of mode **in**. A loop parameter may never be passed as an actual parameter to a subprogram whose formal parameter is of mode **out** or mode **in out.**

The loop parameter is not accessible outside the loop. Any attempt to investigate or assign to Component *outside* the following **for** loop,

```
for Component in 1 .. 2
loop
   --
   -- Statements that investigate
   -- a variable of type Point_Type
   -- to determine if one component is 0
   --
end loop;
```

to determine which component, if any, was 0, is illegal. This is similar to local data declared in subprograms and blocks. Local data "goes away" when the subprogram or block terminates. The loop parameter also "goes away" at the completion of the loop. To retain a value of a loop parameter outside the loop, a local variable must be declared outside the loop and used within the loop to hold the desired value.

Until now, every variable you have seen has been declared, except for formal parameters, which are implicitly declared by their appearance in a formal parameter list. A loop parameter should not be declared either. Its appearance in the loop statement is all that is necessary. A loop parameter is implicitly declared by its appearance in the loop statement.

Expressing the Iteration Range (LRM 5.5)

Variables or function calls can be used to express the lower and upper bounds of Iteration_Range. Figure 3-12 shows code allowing the iteration range to be dynamically determined, as does Figure 3-13.

FIGURE 3-12 Obtaining iteration range dynamically

```
with Binary_Operations; use Binary_Operations;
with Text_IO; use Text_IO;
procedure Exchange_Two_Values is
   Lower, Upper : Integer;
   Value_1, Value_2 : Integer;
   package Int_IO is new Integer_IO (Integer);
   use Int_IO;
   procedure Obtain_Iteration_Range
      (Lower_Bound, Upper_Bound : out Integer) is
   begin -- Obtain_Iteration_Range
      --
      -- Get statements that obtain values for
      -- Lower_Bound and Upper_Bound. Appropriate
      -- exception handlers exist.
      --
   end Obtain_Iteration_Range;
begin -- Exchange_Two_Values
   Put_Line ("Enter first value: ");
   Obtain_Iteration_Range (Lower, Upper);
OBTAIN_FIRST_VALUE:
   --
   -- Illustrating use of variable to
   -- express the desired Iteration_Range.
   --
   for Counter in Lower .. Upper -- Uses a variable
   loop
      begin
         Get (Value_1);
   exit;
      exception
         when Data_Error =>
            Put_Line("Invalid entry for 1st value.");
            Put_Line("Enter integer value: ");
      end;
   end loop OBTAIN_FIRST_VALUE; -- Repeated loop name.
   --
   -- Etc.
   --
end Exchange_Two_Values;
```

FIGURE 3-13 Obtaining Upper_Bound dynamically

```
with Binary_Operations; use Binary_Operations;
with Text_IO; use Text_IO;
procedure Exchange_Two_Values is
   Value_1, Value_2 : Integer;
   package Int_IO is new Integer_IO (Integer);
   use Int_IO;
   function Upper_Bound return Integer is
      A_Bound : Integer;
   begin -- Upper_Bound
      --
      -- Get statement that obtains a value
      -- for A_Bound. Appropriate exception handler
      -- exists.
      --
      return A_Bound;
   end Upper_Bound;
begin -- Exchange_Two_Values
   Put_Line ("Enter first value: ");
OBTAIN_FIRST_VALUE:
   --
   -- Illustrating use of a function call
   -- to express the desired bounds of the
   -- Iteration_Range.
   --
   for Counter in 1 .. Upper_Bound
   loop
      begin
         Get (Value_1);
   exit;
      exception
         when Data_Error =>
            Put_Line("Invalid entry for 1st value.");
            Put_Line("Enter integer value: ");
      end;
   end loop OBTAIN_FIRST_VALUE; -- Repeated loop name.
   --
   -- Etc.
   --
end Exchange_Two_Values;
```

TABLE 3-5 For Loop Execution

Relationship of Bounds	*Number of Times Loop Executed*
Lower_Bound < Upper_Bound	Upper_Bound − Lower_Bound + 1
Lower_Bound = Upper_Bound	Once
Lower_Bound > Upper_Bound	0 (Loop not executed)

Table 3-5 shows how a **for** loop is executed for various evaluations of the bounds of the iteration range.

The loop parameter in a **for** loop is always incremented in steps of 1. There is no construct in Ada, such as STEP 2 in BASIC or the "step" portion of a FORTRAN DO statement, that increments in steps other than 1. In Ada the bounds may, however, be negative or 0, as in

```
for Temperature in -50 .. +50
loop
   --
   -- Statements that calculate the
   -- number of locations reporting
   -- a specific temperature.
   -- Decision making is required.
   --
end loop;
```

that executes one hundred one times or

```
for X_Coordinates in -10 .. 0
loop
   --
   -- Search a portion of the
   -- negative X-axis from
   -- left to right.
   -- Decision making is required.
   --
end loop;
```

that executes eleven times.

Later we will see how data types other than Integer can be used to control loop processing.

The *reverse* Option (LRM 5.5)

If you want to search the same portion of the negative X-axis from right to left, starting at the origin, write

```
for X_Coordinate in reverse -10 .. 0
loop
   --
   -- Search a portion of the
   -- negative X-axis from
   -- right to left.
   --
end loop;
```

This code causes the loop parameter to start at 0 and end at −10, decrementing in steps of 1. The iteration range should *always* be *written* in ascending order. Use of the word **reverse** causes the values to be assigned to the loop parameter in descending order.

EXERCISES

Use package Factorial_Operations of Exercise 3.11 for Exercises 3.12 through 3.14.

3.12 Write a program to print out the factorials of 1 to 10 inclusive. Output both the number and its factorial.

3.13 Write a program to compute the factorials of the numbers 1 to *n*, where *n* is obtained as an input. Output each number and its corresponding factorial. Include an exception handler for Data_Error. Include an exception handler for Numeric_Error that outputs a message indicating overflow and terminates the program. Include any other appropriate exception handlers.

3.14 Write a program to accumulate the sum of whole numbers from 1 to *n,* where *n* is obtained as input. Include exception handlers for Data_Error and Numeric_Error. Output the sum and the last whole number included in the sum.

4

DECISION MAKING

CHAPTER OBJECTIVES

- Declare Boolean objects.
- Perform I/O on Boolean objects.
- Write Boolean expressions.
- Code **if** statements.
- Nest **if** statements.
- Write short-circuit control forms.
- Code **while** loops.

There were several instances in Chapter 3 where some sort of decision-making capability was needed. Such capability is provided by Ada's **if** statement, which is the focus of this chapter. Before we discuss the **if** statement, however, we need to introduce a third predefined data type in Ada, type Boolean.

4.1 Type Boolean (LRM 3.5.3)

Until now we have worked exclusively with the predefined data types Integer and Float. Values of type Boolean, a third predefined type in the language, are False and True.

Variables of type Boolean are declared in the same way as variables of type Integer or Float. For example, the following declares Successful to be a Boolean variable.

```
Successful : Boolean;
```

Initial values may be supplied at declaration time, as in

```
Successful : Boolean := False;
```

and Boolean variables may be assigned to, as in

```
Successful := True;
```

Boolean Expressions

Boolean expressions may be formed using the following operators:

Relational	*Logical*
= /= < <= > >=	**not and or xor**

We will see in this chapter how Boolean expressions can be used to control processing.

Relational operators are used to determine relationships between two operands of the same type and return a value of type Boolean, either True or False. For example, given a variable Account_Balance of type Float, the Boolean expression

```
Account_Balance = 0.00
```

compares the left operand, Account_Balance, to the right operand, the value 0.00. The result of the expression is True if the current balance is 0.00, False otherwise. Similarly, the expression

```
Account_Balance /= 0.0
```

returns False when the account is empty, True otherwise.

The operands on either side of a relational operator must be of the same type. To write

```
Account_Balance = 0   --**ILLEGAL**--
```

is illegal because 0 has no decimal point and therefore is not of type Float. This error will be detected at compile time.

As another example, suppose a sensor is declared to be a variable of type Boolean, with an initial value of False, as in

```
Sensor_1 : Boolean := False;
```

The value of Sensor_1 can be examined to determine the current state of the sensor, as in

```
Sensor_1 = True    --a test for equality (=)
```

Table 4-1 defines the *logical operators.* The following Boolean expression

TABLE 4-1 Logical Operators

and	True	False
True	True	False
False	False	False

and: True only if both operands True

or	True	False
True	True	True
False	True	False

or: True if any operand True

xor	True	False
True	False	True
False	True	False

xor: True only if one operand True

not	True	False
	False	True

not: Negation, reverses value

results in True only if *both* sensors are enabled (have the value True).

```
Sensor_1 and Sensor_2
```

If either sensor is not enabled, or if both sensors are not enabled, the expression is False. The expression

```
Sensor_1 or Sensor_2
```

results in True if either sensor is enabled or if both sensors are enabled, while

```
Sensor_1 xor Sensor_2
```

results in True only when just one sensor is enabled.

All these expressions look like good candidates for controlling program execution. For instance, suppose we have multiple seismometers placed throughout a region to register movement during earthquakes. By examining various Boolean expressions, we can determine which seismometers are enabled and which are not. We can then perform different activities depending upon the specific seismometers enabled.

Recall from Section 3.2 that the Get statement for obtaining a value to be interchanged with another value was placed in a **for** loop to restrict the user to three input attempts. The code for the input loop was as follows:

```
OBTAIN_FIRST_VALUE:
   for Counter in 1 .. 3
   loop
      begin
         Get (Value_1);
   exit;
      exception
         when Data_Error =>
            Put_Line("Invalid entry for 1st value.");
            Put_Line("Enter integer value: ");
      end;
   end loop OBTAIN_FIRST_VALUE;
```

As previously stated, this loop terminates either when a correct input is received or when the user has made three unsuccessful attempts at inputting a correct value. After the loop, we need to know which of these two situations transpired, because it makes sense to obtain a value for Value_2 only if there is a valid value for Value_1.

One way to determine how the loop was exited is to use something called a program flag. Declare a Boolean variable, Successful, and initialize it to False. The variable Successful is a program flag. Successful is set to True only after a successful execution of the Get statement. The code in Figure 4-1 includes this capability. The boxes indicate modifications to the code of Section 3.3.

When the OBTAIN_FIRST_VALUE loop terminates, the value of Successful will indicate whether a successful input has been achieved. The value of Successful can be examined to determine whether procedure Exchange_Two_Values should terminate or continue processing and attempt to accept a value for Value_2.

Boolean I/O (LRM 14.2.10)

I/O for type Boolean is similar to I/O for the predefined types Integer and Float, as described in Section 3.1. Step 1 is identical. For type Boolean, step 2 becomes

```
package Bool_IO is new Enumeration_IO (Boolean);
use Bool_IO;
```

The code on page 113 illustrates the steps.

FIGURE 4-1 Boolean variable as program flag

```
with Binary_Operations; use Binary_Operations;
with Text_IO; use Text_IO;
procedure Exchange_Two_Values is
   --
   -- Declarations as before
   --
   Successful : Boolean := False;
begin -- Exchange_Two_Values
MAIN:
   loop
   Put_Line ("Enter first value: ");
   OBTAIN_FIRST_VALUE:
      for Counter in 1 .. 3
      loop
         begin
            Get (Value_1);
            Successful := True;
      exit;
         exception
            when Data_Error =>
               Put_Line("Invalid entry.");
               Put_Line("Enter integer value: ");
         end;
      end loop OBTAIN_FIRST_VALUE;
   --
   -- Examine Successful here.
   -- If the value of Successful is True, a valid value
   -- exists for Value_1. If the value of Successful is
   -- False, Value_1 does not have a valid value.
   -- How to do this is covered in the next section.
   --
   -- Remaining code goes here.
   --
   end loop MAIN;
end Exchange_Two_Values;
```

```
--STEP 1
with Text_IO; use Text_IO;
procedure Illustrate_Boolean_IO is
   Sensor_1 : Boolean := False;
   -- Enables a sensor by setting its value to True.
   procedure Enable_Sensor (A_Sensor : in out Boolean)
      is separate;
   -- STEP 2
   package Bool_IO is new Enumeration_IO (Boolean);
   use Bool_IO;
begin -- Illustrate_Boolean_IO
   Get (Sensor_1);
   New_Line;
   Enable_Sensor (Sensor_1);
   Put (Sensor_1);
end Illustrate_Boolean_IO;
```

This code displays the values False and True (the values of Sensor_1 before and after the sensor is enabled) on separate lines as shown below.*

```
FALSE
TRUE
```

EXERCISES

4.1 Write a program to input a Boolean value and display the opposite value. Code for any exceptions that may be raised.

4.2 Write a program that generates the **and** table.

4.3 Write a program that generates Table 4-1.

---

* Most compilers print these values either all in upper case or all in lower case.

4.2 The *if* Statement (LRM 5.3)

Consider the following:

```
MAIN:
   loop
   -- as before
   OBTAIN_FIRST_VALUE:
      for Counter in 1 .. 3
      loop
          -- as before
      end loop OBTAIN_FIRST_VALUE;
      if not Successful then
   exit;     -- exits MAIN
      end if;
   -- processing as before
   end loop MAIN;
```

Notice how readable the code is. If the input attempt is not successful, the outer loop, MAIN, is exited and Exchange_Two_Values terminates. If the input attempt is successful, the **exit** statement is ignored and the **if** statement terminates. Note that before the program attempts to obtain a value for Value_2, Successful needs to be reassigned the value False. The final version of the code is shown in Figure 4-2.

As you can see, the **if** statement allows selection of a sequence of statements depending on the value of a Boolean expression. There are two basic forms of the **if** statement in Ada. Each is described in the following pages.

The Simple *if* (LRM 5.3)

The following shows the form of a simple **if** statement where Condition is any Boolean expression.

```
if Condition then
   statement(s)
end if;
```

FIGURE 4-2 Exchange_Two_Values

```
with Binary_Operations; use Binary_Operations;
with Text_IO; use Text_IO;
procedure Exchange_Two_Values is
   Value_1 : Integer;
   Value_2 : Integer;
   Successful : Boolean := False;
   package Int_IO is new Integer_IO (Integer);
   use Int_IO;
begin -- Exchange_Two_Values
MAIN:
   loop
        Put_Line ("Enter first number: ");
      OBTAIN_FIRST_VALUE:
        for Counter in 1 .. 3
        loop
           begin
              Get (Value_1);
              Successful := True;
        exit;    -- exit OBTAIN_FIRST_VALUE
           exception
              when Data_Error =>
                 Put_Line("Invalid Entry for Value_1.");
                 Put_Line("Enter Integer Value.");
           end;
        end loop OBTAIN_FIRST_VALUE;
        if not Successful then
   exit;     -- exit MAIN
        end if;
        Successful := False;    -- reinitialize Successful
        Put_Line ("Enter second value: ");
      OBTAIN_SECOND_VALUE:
        for Counter in 1 .. 3
        loop
           begin
              Get (Value_2);
              Successful := True;
        exit;    -- exit OBTAIN_SECOND_VALUE
           exception
              when Data_Error =>
                 Put_Line("Invalid Entry for Value_2.");
```

(continued)

FIGURE 4-2 *(continued)*

```
            Put_Line("Enter Integer Value.");
         end;
      end loop OBTAIN_SECOND_VALUE;
      if not Successful then
   exit;    -- exit MAIN
      end if;
      Interchange (Value_1, Value_2);
      Put ("The first value is now : ");
      Put (Value_1);
      New_Line;
      Put ("The second value is now : ");
      Put (Value_2);
      New_Line;
   end loop MAIN;
end Exchange_Two_Values;
```

When Condition evaluates to True, the statement(s) enclosed by the **if** statement are executed, the **if** statement terminates and control passes to the first statement after the **if** statement. If Condition evaluates to False, the statement(s) enclosed within the **if** statement are not executed and control passes to the first statement after the **end if.**

In Figure 4-2, Successful is initialized to False. If a valid input is obtained in the OBTAIN_FIRST_VALUE loop, Successful is set to True. The value of the expression "**not** Successful" therefore becomes False. As a result, the **exit** statement enclosed within the **if** statement is not executed, the **if** statement terminates, and control passes to the first statement after the **end if,** which is

```
Successful := False;
```

This statement reassigns the value False to Successful prior to entering the OBTAIN_SECOND_VALUE loop.

As another example, assume that Sensor_1 has been declared to be of type Boolean. Assume Enable_Sensor has been imported, converts its parameter to True, and has the following specification:

```
procedure Enable_Sensor (A_Sensor : in out Boolean)
```

Then

```
if Sensor_1 = False then
   Enable_Sensor(Sensor_1);
end if;
```

ensures that Sensor_1 is enabled before any statements after the **if** statement are executed.

The *elsif* Alternative (LRM 5.3)

Additional alternatives may appear in an **if** statement. They are coded as **elsif** alternatives. The basic form for this code is

```
if Condition_1 then
   statements_1
elsif Condition_2 then
   statements_2
{elsif Condition_n then
   statements_n}
end if;
```

If Condition_1 evaluates to True, statements_1 are executed, the **if** statement terminates, and control passes to the first statement after the **end if**. If Condition_1 evaluates to False, then Condition_2 is evaluated. If Condition_2 evaluates to True, statements_2 are executed, the **if** statement terminates, and control passes to the first statement after the **end if.** If Condition_2 evaluates to False, the next condition is evaluated, and so on. If none of the conditions evaluates to True, the **if** statement terminates without executing any of the subordinate statements, and control passes to the first statement after the **end if.**

As an example, consider the code in Figure 4-3. This program prints a message if the two numbers are equal; otherwise it calls Display_Results with the larger value.

There is no limit to the number of **elsif** alternatives that may be contained within an Ada **if** statement.

An *else* Alternative (LRM 5.3)

The code in Figure 4-3 requires Number_1 to be compared against Number_2 three times. The third comparison is unnecessary, however, because if

Number_1 is neither greater than nor less than Number_2, it must be equal to Number_2. To deal with this kind of situation, Ada allows for the inclusion of an **else** alternative within an **if** statement. An **else** alternative allows a sequence of statements to be executed when none of the preceding conditions evaluates to True. The following code uses an **else** alternative to avoid a third comparison.

```
if Number_1 > Number_2 then
   Display_Results (Number_1);
elsif Number_1 < Number_2 then
   Display_Results (Number_2);
else
   Put_Line ("The numbers are equal.");
end if;
```

FIGURE 4-3 The **if** statement with **elsif** alternatives

```
with Text_IO; use Text_IO;
procedure Compare_Values is
   Number_1, Number_2 : Integer;
   package Int_IO is new Integer_IO (Integer);
   use Int_IO;
   procedure Get_A_Value_For (Value : out Integer)
      is separate;
   procedure Display_Results (Value : in Integer)
      is separate;
begin -- Compare_Values
   Get_A_Value_For (Number_1);
   Get_A_Value_For (Number_2);
   if Number_1 > Number_2 then
      Display_Results (Number_1);
   elsif Number_1 < Number_2 then
      Display_Results (Number_2);
   elsif Number_1 = Number_2 then
      Put_Line ("The numbers are equal.");
   end if;
end Compare_Value;
```

If Number_1 is neither greater than nor less than Number_2, procedure Put_Line is called.

The following indicates that an **else** alternative may be included within a simple **if** statement or within an **if** statement with **elsif** alternatives.

```
if Condition then
   statement(s)
else
   else_statement(s)
end if;
```

```
if Condition_1 then
   statement(s)_1
elsif Condition_2 then
   statement(s)_2
-- possibly other elsifs
else
     else_statement(s)
end if;
```

There may be only one **else** alternative within an **if** statement, and when appearing, it must be the last alternative.

As a final example, recall from Chapter 3 the **for** loop:

```
for Component in 1 .. 2
loop
   --
   -- Statements that investigate
   -- a variable of type Point_Type
   -- to determine if one component is 0
   --
end loop;
```

The key word in the comment is the word *if.* If the X-coordinate is 0, the point lies on the X-axis. If the Y-coordinate is 0, the point lies on the Y-axis. If neither coordinate is 0, the point does not lie on any axis. In any event, we want to know *if* there is a zero component.

Consider Figure 4-4. An **if** statement has been coded here instead of a loop. (Can you figure out why?) If either the X-coordinate or the Y-coordinate of the point is 0, or if the point is on the origin, then Zero_Component_Present is set to True, a message indicating the presence of a zero component is displayed, and the **if** statement terminates. If neither of the coordinates is zero, a

```
with Text_IO; use Text_IO;
with Simple_Graphics; use Simple_Graphics;
procedure Determine_Zero_Component is
   Point : Point_Type;
   Zero_Component_Present : Boolean := False;
   procedure Display_0_Present is separate;
   procedure Display_0_Not_Present is separate;
   procedure Get_A_Point
      (A_Point : out Point_Type) is separate;
begin -- Determine_Zero_Component
   Get_A_Point (Point);
   if Point(1) = 0 or Point(2) = 0 then
      Zero_Component_Present := True;
      Display_0_Present;
   else
      Display_0_Not_Present;
   end if;
      --
      -- further processing driven by
      -- the value of Zero_Component_Present
      --
end Determine_Zero_Component;
```

FIGURE 4-4 **If** statement with **else** alternative

message indicating absence of a zero component is displayed and the **if** statement terminates. At the completion of the **if** statement, the variable Zero_Component_Present indicates whether or not the point lies on an axis. Of course we don't know which axis. This is left to the reader to code as an exercise.

Nested *ifs* (LRM 5.3)

If statements may be nested, but proper use of the **elsif** alternative may eliminate the need for nested **if**s in certain circumstances. For example, the following algorithm calculates the monthly service charge for a hypothetical bank. The service charge is $10.00 a month for an account with a 0.0 or negative balance. For an account with a positive balance, the service charge is $3.00 a month for a balance less than $300.00 and $1.00 a month for a balance of $300.00 or more.

```
-- Outer if selects positive balances
if Balance > 0.0 then
   if Balance < 300.00 then  -- Positive balance
      Service_Charge := 3.00;
   else
      Service_Charge := 1.00;
   end if;
else                          -- 0 or negative balance
   Service_Charge := 10.00;
end if;
```

Notice how much easier the code is to read when coded using **elsif** alternatives.

```
if Balance <= 0.0 then
   Service_Charge := 10.00;
elsif Balance < 300.00 then
   Service_Charge := 3.00;
else
   Service_Charge := 1.00;
end if;
```

Short-Circuit Control Form (LRM 4.5.1)

In the expression

```
Statement_Balance = Current_Balance
```

both operands are evaluated and Ada does not specify which of the operands of an expression is evaluated first. The language does not specify whether

Statement_Balance or Current_Balance is obtained first. Ordinarily it does not matter. However, consider the following code segment, which prompts a depositor to deposit money into his or her account if the current balance of the account dips 50 percent or more below an average daily balance.

```
if Balance > 0.0 and
      Daily_Average/Balance <= 0.50 then
   --
   -- Statements that calculate the
   -- amount to be deposited to bring the
   -- account up to the average balance
   --
   Put ("Please deposit ");
   Put (Amount);
   Put (" into your account.");
   New_Line;
end if;
```

The expressions Balance > 0.0 and Daily_Average/Balance <= 0.50 are evaluated. Again, the language does not specify which expression is evaluated first. Suppose the Balance *is* 0.0, and the expression Daily_Average/Balance <= 0.50 is evaluated *first.* In this case the exception Numeric_Error will be raised because division by 0.0 is attempted, and, unless an exception handler is provided, the program will abort.

One way to ensure that division by 0.0 does not occur is to use nested **if**s, as follows.

```
if Balance > 0.0 then
   if Daily_Average/Balance <= 0.50 then
      --
      -- Statements that calculate the
      -- amount to be deposited to bring the
      -- account up to the monthly average balance
      --
      Put ("Please deposit ");
      Put (Amount);
      Put (" into your account.");
      New_Line;
   end if;
end if;
```

This form of the code ensures that Daily_Average/Balance will be evaluated only if Balance is greater than 0.0. But again, nested **if**s clutter the code and are generally less readable than a non-nested **if** statement.

To deal with this kind of situation, Ada provides additional logical operators, called the *short-circuit* operators. These operators are used to force the left operand of a Boolean expression to be evaluated first. If that result is sufficient to determine the value of the *entire* expression, the right operand is not evaluated. If the result of evaluating the left operand is not sufficient to determine the result of the expression, the right operand is evaluated and the result of the final expression is then determined.

Two short-circuit operators are provided by the language. They are:

and then and **or else**

The result returned by these operators is exactly the same as that for their respective counterparts, **and** and **or.** Using short circuit operators simply forces the left operand to be evaluated first. For example, use of the operator **and then** in the following forces the left operand, Balance > 0.0, to be evaluated first.

```
if Balance > 0.0 and then
      Daily_Average/Balance <= 0.50 then
   --
   -- Statements that calculate the
   -- amount to be deposited to bring the
   -- account up to the monthly average balance
   --
   Put ("Please deposit ");
   Put (Amount);
   Put (" into your account.");
   New_Line;
end if;
```

If there is no money in the account, the result of Balance > 0.0 is False. That value alone is sufficient to determine the result of the entire expression

```
Balance > 0.0 and then Daily_Average/Balance < 0.50
```

which represents the condition of the **if** statement. The **and** operator returns True only if both operands are true, and here one operand is false. If there is no money in the account, the left operand is False; therefore the entire expression is False, and Daily_Average/Balance is *not* evaluated. If there is money in the account, the result of the expression Balance > 0.0 is True. This first True is not sufficient to determine the outcome of the condition of the **if** statement; therefore the right operand, Daily_Average/Balance <= 0.50, is evaluated. If the result is True, we have

```
True and then True
```

which results in True, causing the appropriate calculations and output to be performed. If Daily_Average/Balance <= 0.50 resulted in False, we would have

```
True and then False
```

which results in False, causing the **if** statement to terminate.

Whatever the outcome, the point is that Daily_Average/Balance is evaluated only when there is a legitimate balance in the account. Use of the short circuit operator **and then** ensured a well-defined result for the right operand.

Similarly, suppose we have a system that consists of two sensors. The following displays appropriate messages depending upon the state of the system.

```
if Sensor_1 or else Sensor_2 then
   Put_Line ("At least one sensor enabled.");
else
   Put_Line ("Both sensors disabled.");
end if;
```

If Sensor_1 is True, that is sufficient to determine the result of the entire condition, which is True, and the message that at least one sensor is working is output. Time need not be wasted evaluating Sensor_2. If Sensor_1 is False, however, that is not sufficient to determine the result, because the **or** operator returns True if either one or both of the operands are True. Therefore Sensor_2 is evaluated, the result of the condition is determined, and the appropriate message is displayed.

Short circuit operators reduce the need for nested **if**s, as does the **elsif** alternative. In general, nested **if**s should be avoided when another, less complicated method can be used. The short circuit operators should always be used when evaluating the right operand of a Boolean expression first might cause an exception to be raised.

EXERCISES

4.4 Write a program to input two values of type Float and output True if the first value is larger than the second, False otherwise.

4.5 Modify Determine_Zero_Component of Section 4.2 to indicate whether the point lies on the X-axis, lies on the Y-axis, or is the origin. (Remember that Point(1) accesses the X-coordinate of the point and Point(2) accesses the Y-coordinate of the point.)

4.6 Determine whether a triangle can be constructed from three line segments whose integer lengths are input from the terminal. Output an appropriate message. (The sum of the lengths of any two sides must be greater than the length of the third side for a triangle to be constructed.)

4.7 Modify Exercise 4.6 to additionally calculate the area of those triangles that can be constructed. Use the formula

$$\text{Area} = \sqrt{s(s - a)\,(s - b)\,(s - c)}$$

where

$$s = (a + b + c)/2$$

and a, b, and c represent the lengths of the three sides. (Hint: Ada does not provide primitive functions like SQRT. Do you need another package?) (Hint: To convert an Integer expression to an expression of type Float, write the following:

```
Float (expression)
```

Conversion is covered in Chapter 5.)

4.8 Modify 4.7 to additionally determine if the triangle is a right and/or isosceles triangle.

4.9 Given the following specification:

```
function Quadrant_of (Point : Point_Type) return Integer
```

write the body to determine to which quadrant the point belongs. If the point lies on an axis, state which axis.

4.3 The *while* Loop (LRM 5.5)

Two loops were presented in Chapter 3, the simple loop and the **for** loop. There is a third loop in Ada, the **while** loop. A **while** loop uses a Boolean expression to control iteration.

Consider the following function, which expects a value of type Integer and returns the largest integer whose factorial is less than or equal to that value. The function returns −1 if a negative value or zero is passed as an actual parameter.

```
function Largest_Factorial (Value_to_be_Matched : Integer)
           return Integer is
   function The_Answer return Integer is separate;
begin -- Largest_Factorial
   if Value_to_be_Matched <=0 then -- Filter negatives
      return -1;                   -- and 0
   elsif Value_to_be_Matched = 1 then -- Filter value 1
      return 1;
   else -- the normal case
      return The_Answer;
   end if;
end Largest_Factorial;
```

The code for the subunit The_Answer is as follows:

```
separate (Largest_Factorial)
function The_Answer return Integer is
   Next_Integer, Factorial : Integer := 1;
begin -- The_Answer
   while Factorial <= Value_to_be_Matched
   loop
      Next_Integer := Next_Integer + 1;
      Factorial := Factorial * Next_Integer;
   end loop;
   return Next_Integer - 1;
end The_Answer;
```

In the function The_Answer, the Boolean expression Factorial <= Value_to_be_Matched controls whether or not the next factorial is calculated. The current value of the factorial (Factorial) is compared with the value passed in Value_to_be_Matched. If Factorial is less than or equal to the value, the value of the expression Factorial <= Value_to_be_Matched is True and the next factorial is calculated. If the current value is not less than or equal to the value to be matched, we have exceeded the value passed in and the value of Factorial <= Value_to_be_Matched is False. The statements within the loop therefore are not executed, control resumes at the first statement after the loop, and Next_Integer is decremented by 1 to return its value to the correct result.

The syntax of a **while** loop is as follows:

```
while Condition
loop
   Statement(s)
end loop;
```

where Condition is a Boolean expression.

The **while** loop tests the condition at the *top* of the loop. If the value of the condition is True, the loop is entered and the statement(s) within it are executed. If the value of the Condition is False, control passes to the first statement after the **end loop** and the statements within the loop are not executed.

A final question: Would Value_to_be_Matched be known to The_Answer if The_Answer had been coded as a reusable subprogram rather than as a subunit? Exercise 4.12 will help you answer this question.

EXERCISES

4.10 Find the greatest common divisor (gcd) of two positive integers using Euclid's algorithm. Euclid's algorithm repeatedly replaces the larger of the two values by their difference until the difference between the two values is 0. When the values are the same, that value represents the gcd of the two values. (Consider the numbers 8 and 6. They are not equal. Replace the larger value 8 by 8 − 6 or 2. Now examine 2 and 6. They are not equal. Replace 6 by the difference of the 2 values, 4. Consider 2 and 4. Replace 4 by the difference of 4 and 2, or 2. Now 2 = 2. The gcd of 8 and 6 is 2.)

4.11 Write a program to calculate the square roots of the numbers from 1.0 to 10.0 inclusive in steps of .1. Output each number and its square root. Use Newton's method, which states that if Root is a good approximation to the square root of X, then

(X/Root + Root)/2.0

is a better one. Stop when the difference between two successive approximations is less than some predefined small value, such as .000001.

4.12 Recode Largest_Factorial of Section 4.3 with The_Answer coded as a reusable subprogram. What modification needs to be made?

5

INTEGER TYPES

CHAPTER OBJECTIVES

- Define the classes of Ada types.
- State the kinds of Scalar Types.
- Declare Integer objects.
- Declare Integer objects with a range constraint.
- Perform I/O on Integer objects.
- Declare user-defined integer types.
- Perform I/O on user-defined integer objects.
- Define attribute.
- Use the attributes applicable to the class of integer types.
- Declare a named number.
- Write integer literals.

Ada's typing mechanism is one of its most powerful features. An Ada data type defines the set of possible values that variables and constants (both called *objects*) may take on and the set of allowable operations that may be applied to objects of the type.

Several classes of types exist in Ada, as shown in Figure 5-1. *Scalar* types consist of one component; they are the subject of the next three chapters. An example of a scalar type is the predefined type Integer. *Composite* types usually have more than one component; they are treated in Chapters 8–11. An example of a composite type is Point_Type, introduced in Chapter 1. Each object of type Point_Type has two components, the X- and Y-coordinate of a

FIGURE 5-1 Classes of Ada Types

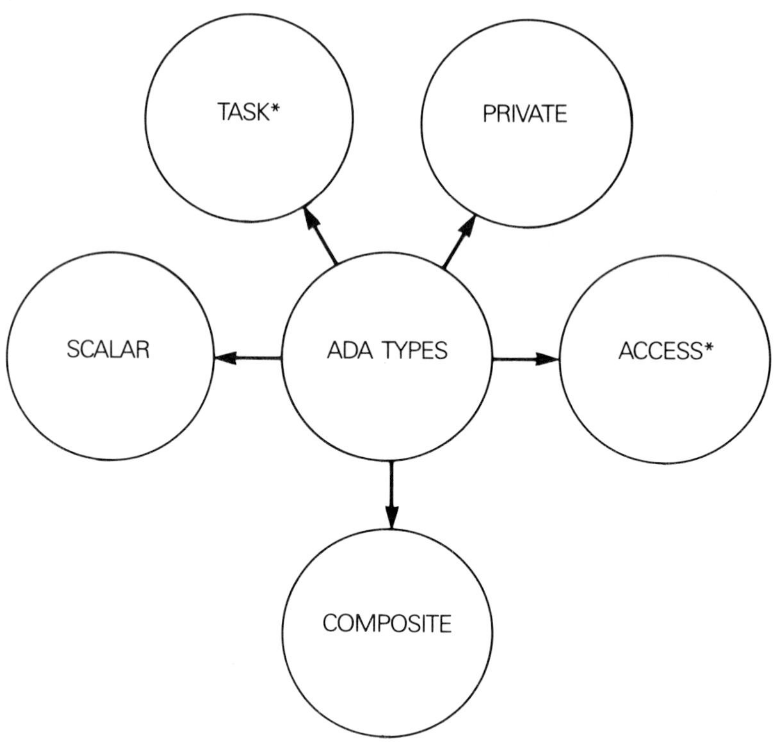

* Not covered in this text

point. *Private* types are covered in Chapter 12. *Access* types and *task* types are beyond the scope of this text.

Scalar types in Ada are divided into *discrete* and *real* types (see Figure 5-2). Values of a discrete type are ordered and distinct, while values of a real type are approximations to real numbers. Integer and Enumeration are examples of Discrete Scalar types, while Floating and Fixed are examples of real scalar types. (Fixed real types will not be discussed in this text.)

FIGURE 5-2 Scalar Types

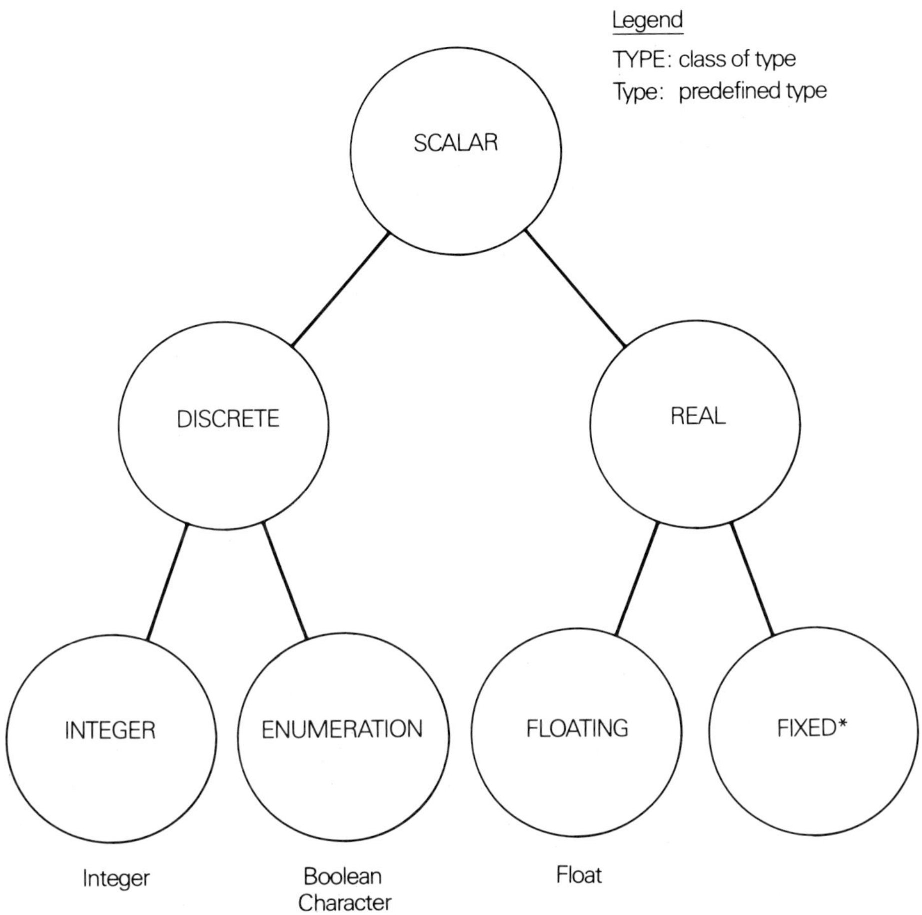

* Not covered in this text

5.1 Predefined Type Integer (LRM 3.5.4)

As you know, type *Integer* is predefined by the Ada language. The set of values for objects of type Integer, however, is implementation defined: the value of the smallest allowable value of type Integer (lowest negative) and the largest allowable value of type Integer (highest positive) depend on the underlying hardware. The values may differ for 16-bit and 32-bit machines. The specific values for a given system may be obtained using *attributes*. An attribute is an operation that allows access to properties or characteristics of types (and in some cases objects).

To obtain the value of the smallest value of type Integer in your system, simply write the expression

```
Integer'First
```

To obtain the value of the largest value of type Integer, write

```
Integer'Last
```

First and Last are attributes predefined by the language and may be applied to any scalar type. Alternative procedures to determine the smallest value of type Integer are shown in Figure 5-3(a,b).

Note that an attribute is preceded by an apostrophe ('), read as *tic* or *prime,* and in most cases follows a type name. For the remainder of this text, the most commonly used attributes for a specific type will be introduced when the type is introduced.*

Variable Object Declarations (LRM 3.2)

Variable objects in Ada may have their values changed. Variable objects are declared in the declarative part of a subprogram or block. Additionally, some packages may provide objects as a resource to be used. Objects declared in package specifications, however, are *global objects*—that is, objects that can be accessed by many users at once. Making variable objects global is generally not a good practice, because if you modify a global value at one point in the code, then read the value 20 statements later, you may find it is no longer the

---

* Appendix A of the LRM contains a list of all attributes predefined by Ada. An implementation may supply additional attributes. If an implementation contains additional attributes, those additional attributes must be described in Appendix F of the LRM.

value you intended. While the 20 statements were executing, the global variable may have been modified by another user!

One way to declare a variable object of the predefined type Integer is to write an *object declaration*, as follows:

```
Variable_Name : Integer;
```

where Variable_Name is a legal Ada identifier.

FIGURE 5-3 Procedure Calculate_Smallest_Integer_Value

```
with Text_IO; use Text_IO;
procedure Calculate_Smallest_Integer_Value is
   Smallest : Integer := Integer'First;
   package Int_IO is new Integer_IO (Integer);
   use Int_IO;
begin -- Calculate_Smallest_Integer_Value
   Put ("The smallest Integer value is : ");
   Put (Smallest);
   New_Line;
end Calculate_Smallest_Integer_Value;
```

FIGURE 5-3(a) Local Variable

```
with Text_IO; use Text_IO;
procedure Calculate_Smallest_Integer_Value is
   package Int_IO is new Integer_IO (Integer);
   use Int_IO;
begin -- Calculate_Smallest_Integer_Value
   Put ("The smallest Integer value is : ");
   Put (Integer'First);
   New_Line;
end Calculate_Smallest_Integer_Value;
```

FIGURE 5-3(b) No Local Variable

The name of the variable you wish to create, Variable_Name, is followed by a colon, which in turn is directly followed by the word Integer to indicate that Variable_Name is of type Integer. The declaration is terminated by a semicolon. By declaring Variable_Name to be of type Integer, we restrict the set of values that Variable_Name can acquire to all whole numbers within the range specified for our machine. For example, in Section 2.4, the following object declaration

```
The_Area : Integer;
```

declared a variable named The_Area to be of type Integer.

Multiple objects of the same type may be declared in one object declaration when separated by commas. The following declaration declares two objects of type Integer:

```
Value_1, Value_2 : Integer;
```

and is equivalent to writing

```
Value_1 : Integer;
Value_2 : Integer;
```

Do not assume that an implicit initial value of 0 is given to Integer objects when they are created. Any program that makes this assumption is erroneous, and its behavior will be unpredictable.

Initial values may be assigned at object declaration time. The syntax for declaring an integer variable with an initial value is as follows:

```
Variable_Name : Integer := Initial_Value;
```

where Initial_Value is any legal expression that yields a value of type Integer. For example, the declaration

```
Value_1 : Integer := 4;
```

assigns the initial value 4 to Value_1.

Remember that a call to a function that returns a value of type Integer is a legal expression of type Integer. Therefore, the declaration

```
Value_1 : Integer := Some_Integer_Value;
```

where Some_Integer_Value is a function with the specification

```
function Some_Integer_Value return Integer
```

is legal in Ada.

Multiple objects may be initialized to the same value, as in

```
Value_1, Value_2, Value_3 : Integer := 0;
```

but they may *not* be initialized to different values, as in

```
                --**ILLEGAL**--
Value_1, Value_2, Value_3 : Integer := 1,2,3;
```

Constant Object Declarations (LRM 3.2)

As you have seen, the declaration

```
Value_1 : Integer := 4;
```

declares a *variable* object and initializes its value to 4. The value of Value_1 may be changed during the execution of the program. Constants are declared differently and do not change their values during program execution.

To represent a constant in FORTRAN, we simply write the number desired, as in

```
CENTI = 100*METER
```

In Ada, as in Pascal, a number written into the code, like 100, is called a numeric *literal.* The specific rules for writing Integer literals in Ada are discussed later in this section. In Pascal, these literals can be named and declared in the constant declaration section of the program. Ada also allows naming of constants. For example, we might declare a constant object, from now on called a *constant*, of type Integer by writing this statement:

```
Max_Lines_per_Page : constant Integer := 60;
```

There is a distinct advantage to naming literals rather than just writing them into the code. For example, if the maximum number of lines per page changes, only the constant declaration will need to be modified. Had the literal 60 appeared throughout the code, however, it would have had to be changed in each instance, and the programmer would have run the risk of 1) missing an occurrence and/or 2) mistakenly changing an occurrence of 60 to the new number when that particular occurrence represented, say, the maximum number of characters per line rather than the maximum number of lines per page.

The general syntax for declaring a constant of type Integer is as follows:

```
Constant_Name : constant Integer := Constant_Value;
```

where Constant_Name is a user-supplied identifier, followed by a colon and then by the reserved word **constant.** The type to be associated with the constant follows this reserved word. Constant_Value, the value to be associated with the identifier, *must* appear after the assignment symbol. This value can be any expression of type Integer. A constant declaration is terminated by a semicolon.

Operators (LRM 4.5)

As previously stated, a type defines both a set of values and a set of operations on those values. The operations applicable to objects of the predefined type Integer are given in Table 5-1.

Expressions can be formed using operators, objects, and function calls. As in other languages, operators in Ada are assigned a precedence. The hierarchy of all operators in Ada is shown in Table 5-2. Operators of higher precedence are associated with their operands first. Parentheses may be used to override the normal precedence. Association of operators to operands in expressions containing operators of equal precedence proceeds from left to right. As a general rule, it is preferable to parenthesize expressions to avoid potential confusion.*

Range Constraint (LRM 3.2.1,3.5)

The declaration

```
Cruising_Altitude : Integer;
```

permits the variable Cruising_Altitude to take on any value of type Integer within the implementation-defined range. In practical terms, however, many of

* Kernighan, Brian W. and Plauger, P. J., *The Elements of Programming Style* (New York: McGraw-Hill, 1974).

TABLE 5-1 Integer Operators

Binary Numeric Operators (LRM 4.5.3, 4.5.5)

Symbol	*Operation*	*Result Type*
+	Addition	Integer
−	Subtraction	Integer
*	Multiplication	Integer
/	Division	Integer
**	Exponentiation	Integer
mod	Modulo arithmetic	Integer
rem	Remainder on division	Integer

Binary Relational Operators (LRM 4.5.2)

Symbol	*Operation*	*Result Type*
=	Equality	Boolean
/=	Inequality	Boolean
<	Less than	Boolean
<=	Less than or equal to	Boolean
>	Greater than	Boolean
>=	Greater than or equal to	Boolean

Membership Operators (LRM 4.5.2)

Symbol	*Operation*	*Result Type*
in	Member of	Boolean
not in	Not member of	Boolean

Unary Operators (LRM 4.5.4)

Symbol	*Operation*	*Result Type*
+	Plus sign	Integer
−	Minus sign	Integer
abs	Absolute value	Integer

TABLE 5-2 Hierarchy of Ada Operators

Highest Precedence	parentheses	( )
↓	highest precedence	** **abs** **not**
	multiplying	* / **mod** **rem**
	unary	+ −
	binary	+ − &
	relational/membership	= /= < <= > >= **in** **not in**
Lowest Precedence	logical	**and** **or** **xor** **and then** **or else**

these values—for example, −10, 10, or 75,000—will be meaningless: commercial planes do not cruise at either 10 or 75,000 feet. This is an example where it is desirable to limit the range of acceptable values for a specific integer variable. To perform this function, Ada allows the programmer to add a *range constraint* to the variable's declaration. A range constraint has the following form:

```
range L .. U
```

where **range** is a reserved word, L is an integer expression for the lower bound of the range, and U is an integer expression for the upper bound of the range. If an operation attempts to assign a value that is < L or > U to a variable with this range constraint, the exception Constraint_Error is raised at run time. In other words, range constraints allow the constraints imposed by the problem domain to be represented in Ada. Additionally the run time system will inform us when the constraints of the problem domain have been violated by raising the appropriate exception. Finally, writing a handler allows us to specify the corrective action to be taken in such cases.

To declare an object of type Integer with a range constraint, write

```
Variable_Name : Integer range L .. U;
            or
Variable_Name : Integer range L .. U := Initial_Value;
```

For example, the declaration

```
Cruising_Altitude : Integer range 15000 .. 40000;
```

declares Cruising_Altitude to be a variable of type Integer and restricts the values that can be assigned to Cruising_Altitude to between 15,000 and 40,000 inclusive. At run time, any attempt to assign to Cruising_Altitude a value outside the range constraint, say 50,000, raises Constraint_Error. An exception handler for Constraint_Error could flash a message to the navigator, indicating the aircraft is not at the required altitude and provide a plan to return to an acceptable altitude.

As another example, consider a text formatter. One function of a text formatter is pagination. The number of lines printed per page are counted. When the maximum number of lines per page has been printed, a new page number is assigned, top of form is executed, and the counter for the number of lines printed is reset to 0. Assuming one page can accomodate 60 lines, the following declares an object of type Integer to maintain the line count and initializes it to zero (0).

```
Line_Count : Integer range 0 .. Max_Lines_per_Page := 0;
```

The object desired is appropriately named Line_Count.

After a line is printed, Line_Count may be incremented, as in

```
Line_Count := Line_Count + 1;
```

Line_Count may also be compared to 60 to determine if there is still a free line on the current page, as in

```
if Line_Count = 60 then
   Start_New_Page;
else
   Print_Line;
   Line_Count := Line_Count + 1;
end if;
```

The range constraint applied to Line_Count makes it impossible for Line_Count to take on any value outside the range 0 to 60. Thus a line number such as 72 or 567 cannot be inadvertently assigned to Line_Count, which would produce incorrect pagination. Range constraints do not forbid the computation Line_Count + 1 when Line_Count equals 60, but they do forbid the assignment of the resulting value to Line_Count, because Constraint_Error would be raised. This form of coding allows us to represent the real-world constraint of 60 lines per page in Ada in a more readable fashion than

```
Line_Count := (Line_Count + 1) mod 61;
```

Integer Literals (LRM 2.4.1)

In the following object declaration for Line_Count,

```
Line_Count : Integer range 0 .. 60 := 0;
```

there are two *integer literals*: 0 and 60. Integer literals in Ada are assumed to be of base 10. (Ada does allow literals to be specified in a base other than 10. See Appendix B.)

According to Ada's rules, a base 10 integer literal

- is written without a decimal point
- uses the digits 0 through 9
- may contain isolated embedded underscores between consecutive digits
- may be written in exponential notation
- may not include commas or embedded spaces

Use of an underscore in an integer literal does not create a distinct value. Simple_Graphics and SimpleGraphics are two distinct identifiers, but 40000 and 40_000 represent the same literal.

In exponential notation, the exponent indicates the power of ten that the value of the literal without the exponent (the mantissa) is to be multiplied by to obtain the value of the literal. In Ada one writes the integer literal directly followed by the letter E (or e), in turn directly followed by the positive power of 10 desired. An optional plus sign may be inserted between the E and the power of 10. A minus sign may not.

The following are all legal integer literals:

1	represents one (1)
100	represents one hundred (100)
1E2	represents one hundred (100) (exponential notation allows capital E)
1e2	represents one hundred (100) (exponential notation allows lower-case e)
1e+2	represents one hundred (100) (exponential notation allows + sign)
10E1	represents one hundred (100)
123456	hard to read

123_456	easier to read (represents same literal as 123456)
12E1_0	underscore legal within exponent

5.2 User-Defined Integer Types (LRM 3.5.4)

Given these object declarations

```
Character_Count   : Integer range 0 .. 60;
Line_Count  : Integer range 0 .. Max_Lines_per_Page := 0;
```

in the declarative part of some subprogram, the following statement is perfectly legal in the executable part of the same subprogram, because the objects are of the same type:

```
Character_Count := Character_Count + Line_Count;
```

Furthermore, as long as the computed value for the expression Character_Count + Line_Count is within the range constraint specified for Character_Count, the assignment will take place. However, this statement makes absolutely no logical sense. Adding the number of characters in the current word to line count is beyond the comprehension of this author.

We need a mechanism that recognizes that Character_Count and Line_Count, although both objects that require integer values, are different and therefore should not be added, compared, or otherwise operated on together. Happily, Ada provides such a mechanism. Ada allows programmers to define their own integer types by writing an *integer type declaration*. An integer type declaration

- creates a distinct type
- specifies the range of allowable integer values that are applicable to objects of the type
- specifies that the operations applicable to objects of the type are the same as those that can be applied to objects of the predefined type Integer.

An integer type declaration is written as follows:

```
type Type_Name is range L .. U;
```

where Type_Name is a user-supplied identifier naming the type. The range constraint is mandatory in user-defined integer type declarations and is written as previously stated, with one additional requirement: when a range constraint is written within a type declaration, L and U must be *static* expressions.

A static expression is an expression that can be evaluated at compile time. When a range constraint appears in an object declaration, L and U may be any legal integer expression, including a function call. L and U may not be function calls in a range constraint that is part of a type declaration, however.

The following:

```
type Line_Count_Type is range 0 .. 60;
```

is an integer type declaration defining Line_Count_Type. An alternative way to declare Line_Count_Type is

```
Max_Lines_per_Page : constant Integer := 60;
type Line_Count_Type is range 1 .. Max_Lines_per_Page;
```

Both approaches use a static expression to represent the upper bound.

Each of the two alternatives just described

- defines a *new* integer type named Line_Count_Type
- specifies that all objects of type Line_Count_Type will have integer values between 0 and 60 inclusive
- specifies that all objects of Line_Count_Type may be operated on by the set of operators listed for type Integer

Objects of user-defined integer types are declared, as usual, in the declarative part. The following:

```
Line_Count : Line_Count_Type := 0;
```

declares a variable Line_Count to be of type Line_Count_Type and initializes Line_Count to 0. Line_Count may be incremented each time a new line is printed, as in

```
Line_Count := Line_Count + 1;
```

The attributes First and Last may be applied to Line_Count_Type in order to determine the smallest and largest value of this type. The expression Line_Count_Type' First yields 0, while Line_Count_Type' Last yields 60.

It is important to understand that the declaration of Line_Count_Type creates a *new, distinct type.* Line_Count_Type is *not* the same as type Integer. Assuming that the following object declaration existed,

```
Increment : constant Integer := 1;
```

the following statement

```
Line_Count := Line_Count + Increment; --**ILLEGAL**--
```

is illegal because Line_Count_Type and Integer are two distinct types. Line_Count may *not* be added to Increment, because Ada does not permit expressions that mix types. However, the declaration

```
Increment : constant Line_Count_Type := 1;
```

would permit

```
Line_Count := Line_Count + Increment;
```

because the two objects are now of the same type.

Create your own integer types whenever possible to take advantage of Ada's type checking.* Let the compiler check all your expressions, assignment statements, and subprogram calls!

Here are some more examples of integer type declarations:

```
type Days_in_Month_Type is range 1 .. 31;
type Celsius_Scale_Type is range -50 .. 50;
type Fahrenheit_Scale_Type is range -60 .. 120;
type Television_Channels_Type is range 2 .. 83;
type Word_Length_Type is range 0 .. 30;
type Age_Type is range 0 .. 110;
```

---

* Use of user-defined types also permits the compiler to choose the most appropriate representation for the type. See Appendix C of the LRM, page C-2, and discussions of implementation options to provide additional predefined Integer types such as Short_Integer and Long_Integer.

Each of the type names ends in _Type because this makes it easier to distinguish types from objects when reading code. Adding _Type to a type name is not a requirement of the language, however.

Simple_Formatter

Now let's pull all these pieces together and use them to model a very simple text formatter. In this formatter, a page consists of 60 lines of text, and each line consists of a maximum of 60 characters. The formatter prints the page number, maximum 999, in the center of the 58th line. The left margin may be set anywhere between columns 1 and 10 inclusive and has a default setting of 5. The right margin may be set anywhere between columns 51 and 60 inclusive and has a default setting of 55. The package specification in Figure 5-4 includes the requirements we have just specified.

FIGURE 5-4 Package specification for a simple text formatter

```
package Formatter_Specifications is
   Max_Lines_per_Page : constant Integer := 60;
   type Line_Count_Type
        is range 1 .. Max_Lines_per_Page;
   Page_Number_Line : constant Line_Count_Type := 58;
   Maximum_Lines_of_Text :
        constant Line_Count_Type := 55;
   Max_Page_Number  : constant Integer := 999;
   type Page_Number_Type is range 1 .. Max_Page_Number;
   type Left_Margin_Type is range 1 .. 10;
   type Right_Margin_Type is range 51 .. 60;
   procedure Top_of_Form
            (Line_Number : in Line_Count_Type := 2);
   procedure Set_Margins
            (Left : in Left_Margin_Type := 5;
            Right : in Right_Margin_Type:= 55);
   -- Out_of_Paper is raised by Top_of_Form
   Out_of_Paper : exception;
   . . .
end Formatter_Specifications;
```

The main program shown in Figure 5-5 models the text formatter.

Observe that the Line_Count and Page_Count are both incremented by 1. Would Figure 5-6 be correct? (As usual, boxes indicate changes from the preceding version.)

The answer to the question is no. The preceding code is incorrect. Increment may be added to Line_Count because Increment is an object of type

FIGURE 5-5 Main program for a simple text formatter

```
with Text_IO; use Text_IO;
with Formatter_Specifications;
use Formatter_Specifications;
procedure Simple_Formatter is
   Line_Count    : Line_Count_Type := 1;
   Page_Number   : Page_Number_Type := 1;
   -- Gets characters and prints one line of text.
   procedure Print_Line is separate;
   -- Prints the page number
   procedure Print(Number : in Page_Number_Type) is
                              separate;
begin -- Simple_Formatter
   Set_Margins;  -- Uses default setting.
   Top_of_Form;  -- Uses default setting.
PAGE:  -- Main loop handles one page.
   loop
   LINE:  -- Inner loop prints lines per page.
      for Line_Number in 1 .. Maximum_Lines_of_Text
      loop
         Print_Line;
         Line_Count := Line_Count + 1;
      end loop LINE;
      Print (Page_Number); -- Prints page number.
      -- Increments page number.
      Page_Number := Page_Number + 1;
      Top_of_Form;
      Line_Count := 1;    -- Resets Line_Count to 1.
   end loop PAGE;
end Simple_Formatter;
```

Line_Count_Type, but Increment may *not* be added to Page_Count because Increment and Page_Count are of two different types. To declare Increment to be of type Page_Number_Type does not solve the problem either. (Can you figure out why?) It would be nice to have one constant to be used with both types. As it happens, Ada provides such a capability.

FIGURE 5-6 Increment as constant of Line_Count_Type

```
with Text_IO; use Text_IO;
with Formatter_Specifications;
use Formatter_Specifications;
procedure Simple_Formatter is
   Line_Count  : Line_Count_Type := 1;
   Page_Number : Page_Number_Type := 1;
   Increment   : constant Line_Count_Type := 1;
   -- Gets characters and prints one line of text.
   procedure Print_Line is separate;
   -- Prints the page number.
   procedure Print(Number : in Page_Number_Type) is
                            separate;
begin -- Simple_Formatter
   Set_Margins;  -- Uses default setting.
   Top_of_Form;  -- Uses default setting.
PAGE:  -- Main loop handles one page.
   loop
   LINE:  -- Inner loop prints lines per page.
      for Line_Number in 1 . . Maximum_Lines_of_Text
      loop
         Print_Line;
         Line_Count := Line_Count + Increment;
      end loop LINE;
      Print (Page_Number); -- Prints page number.
      -- Increments page number.
      --**ILLEGAL**--
      Page_Number := Page_Number + Increment;
      Top_of_Form;
      Line_Count := 1;    -- Resets Line_Count to 1.
   end loop PAGE;
end Simple_Formatter;
```

5.3 Named Numbers (LRM 3.2.2)

Ada provides a mechanism whereby a constant can be declared so that it may be used within an entire class of numeric types. Such a constant is called a *named number.*

A named number to be used within the class of integer types is declared by writing

```
Name_of_Number : constant := Static_Integer_Expression;
```

where Name_of_Number is a legal Ada identifier. Note that a type name does not appear after the reserved word **constant**. As you may recall from the last section, a static integer expression is an expression whose value is determinable at compile time.

The following are both valid named number declarations:

```
   Tens   : constant := 10;
Hundreds  : constant := 10*Tens;
```

because both 10 and 10*Tens are determinable at compile time. The following are illegal named number declarations:

```
    X : Integer;                       -- variable declaration

Value : Integer := Get_a_Value(X);
Unit  : constant := Value;             -- not static
```

Value is not determinable at compile time. Rather, it is determined at run time.

We can correct the problem we had with Simple_Formatter by declaring Increment to be a named number with a value of 1. Because Increment is now a named number, it may be used in an expression of type Integer, Line_Count_Type, Page_Count_Type, or any other type that belongs to the class of Integer types. The corrected code is shown in Figure 5-7.

FIGURE 5-7 Increment as a named number

```
with Text_IO; use Text_IO;
with Formatter_Specifications;
use Formatter_Specifications;
procedure Simple_Formatter is
   Line_Count  : Line_Count_Type := 1;
   Page_Number : Page_Number_Type := 1;
   Increment   : constant  := 1;    -- a named number
   -- Gets characters and prints one line of text.
   procedure Print_Line is separate;
   -- Prints the page number.
   procedure Print(Number : in Page_Number_Type) is
                            separate;
begin -- Simple_Formatter
   Set_Margins; -- Uses default setting.
   Top_of_Form; -- Uses default setting.
PAGE:  -- Main loop handles one page.
   loop
   LINE: -- Inner loop prints lines per page.
      for Line_Number in 1 .. Maximum_Lines_of_Text
      loop
         Print_Line;
         Line_Count := Line_Count + Increment;
      end loop LINE;
      Print (Page_Number); -- Prints page number.
      -- Increments page number, now legal.
      Page_Number := Page_Number + Increment;
      Top_of_Form;
      Line_Count := 1;   -- reset Line_Count to 1.
   end loop PAGE;
end Simple_Formatter;
```

5.4 I/O For User-Defined Integer Types (LRM 14.3.10)

I/O for user-defined integer types is basically the same as I/O for the predefined type Integer, which we examined in Section 3.1. Step 1 remains the same:

import Text_IO. There is a modification in step 2, however. To perform I/O on the predefined type Integer, you wrote

```
package Int_IO is new Integer_IO(Integer);
use Int_IO;
```

To perform I/O on Line_Count_Type, write

```
package Line_Count_IO is new Integer_IO(Line_Count_Type);
use Line_Count_IO;
```

The basic syntax for I/O for user-defined integer types is as follows:

```
package Type_to_IO is new Integer_IO(Type_Name);
use Type_to_IO;
```

where Type_to_IO is a user-supplied identifier. A good convention is to use the type name with the suffix _Type replaced by the suffix _IO. The type name itself must appear in parentheses after Integer_IO.

Compute_Factorials

Consider the following package specification:

```
package A_Small_Factorial_Package is
   type Argument_Type is range 1 .. Integer'Last;
   type Result_Type is range 1 .. Integer'Last;
   function Factorial_of (Value : Argument_Type)
               return Result_Type;
end A_Small_Factorial_Package;
```

The following main procedure uses this package to compute and print the factorials from 1 to 10.

```
with A_Small_Factorial_Package;
use A_Small_Factorial_Package;
with Text_IO; use Text_IO;
procedure Compute_Factorials_1_to_10 is
   package Argument_IO is new
           Integer_IO(Argument_Type);
   package Result_IO is new Integer_IO(Result_Type);
   use Argument_IO;
   use Result_IO;
begin -- Compute_Factorials_1_to_10
   for Number in Argument_Type range 1 .. 10
   loop
      Put ("The factorial of ");   -- Text_IO.Put
      Put (Number); -- Argument_IO. Put
      Put (" is ");
      Put (Factorial_of(Number)); -- Result_IO.Put
      New_Line;
   end loop;
end Compute_Factorials_1_to_10;
```

Notice that step 2 must be performed for *each* type that needs I/O services.

EXERCISES

5.1 State why each of the following is an illegal integer literal.

a. 1.2	e. 123 456
b. 1e-6	f. 123_456_
c. 123__456	g. 123,456
d. 1e 6	

5.2 State why an integer literal may not have a negative exponent.

5.3 Find and correct the error(s) in the following package specification:

```
package Some_Conversion_Constants is
   Meter_to_Decimeter  : constant Integer := 100e-1;
   Meter_to_Centimeter : constant Integer := 100.;
   Meter_to_Kilometer  : constant Integer := 1,000;
end Some_Conversion_Constants;
```

5.4 Write a program to determine the smallest and largest value of type Integer on your system.

5.5 Write a program to determine which of the years from 1850 to 2500 are leap years. Output the leap years. The program should take into account that the only century years that are leap years are those century years divisible by 400. The year 1200 is a leap year while the year 1100 is not a leap year.

5.6 Modify Simple_Formatter to accomodate double spacing. Is the modification difficult or easy? Why?

5.7 Recode Compute_Factorials_1_to_10 to compute the factorials of as many values as possible. (Will this be implementation dependent? If so, code the solution so that it will be portable, that is so that the solution will run on all Ada implementations.)

6

ENUMERATION TYPES

CHAPTER OBJECTIVES

- Declare user-defined enumeration types.
- Perform I/O on user-defined enumeration objects.
- Use the attributes applicable to enumeration types.
- Write **case** statements.
- Use enumeration types to control **for loop**s.

The alternatives in many situations can be represented as toggles on a control panel. For example, the toggle for an air conditioner in a motel room might look like this:

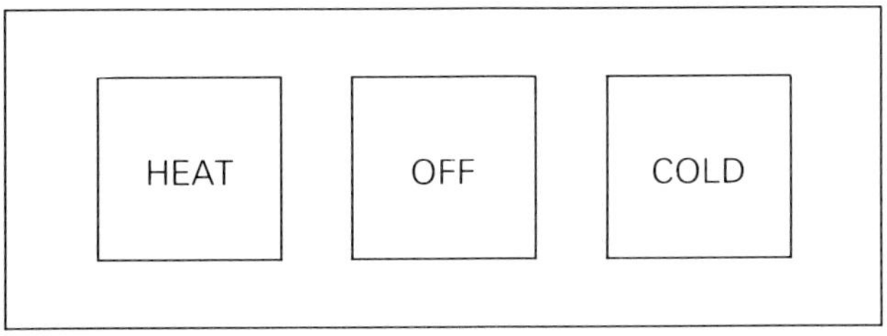

In most computer languages, these states are traditionally implemented as numeric codes. Code for our air conditioner, for example, might be −1 for Heat, 0 for Off, 1 for Cold. The maintainer of such a program must remember the code and its meanings. Of course, this is not very difficult when there are only three values—but what happens when you are representing, say, the days of the week? The real values are Sunday, Monday, Tuesday, Wednesday, and so on. We can give these numeric equivalents, but what a headache it can become to remember which code number represents which value! Adding to the complexity, many value series of this type have an implied order: an enlisted person is a Private before becoming a Sergeant, Tuesday comes before Wednesday, and so on.

Enumeration types in Ada permit the programmer to represent a series of values by using their actual names. They also allow the implied order in the series to be kept.

6.1 Enumeration Type Declarations (LRM 3.5.1)

An enumeration type declaration allows the programmer to list or enumerate the legal set of values for the type in a specific order. Except for type Boolean and type Character (discussed in Chapter 10), which are predefined, enumeration types are user defined. An enumeration type is declared as follows:

```
type Type_Name is (Value_1, Value_2, ..., Value_n);
```

where

- Type_Name is a user-supplied identifier for the type being introduced
- Value_i is either an identifier or a character literal*
- the list of allowed values for the type is enclosed in parentheses and has an order associated with the order of occurrence in the list. The *ith* value is less than the *ith + 1* value.

Enumeration type declarations, like all type declarations, are terminated by a semicolon.

The following are all legal enumeration type declarations:

```
type Control_Unit_Type is (Heat, Off, Cold);
type Enlisted_Rank_Type is (Recruit, Private, PFC,
      Corporal, Sergeant, Staff_Sergeant, Sergeant_FC,
      Master_Sergeant, First_Sergeant, Sergeant_Major);
type Day_Type is (Sun, Mon, Tue, Wed, Thu, Fri, Sat);
type Link_Status_Type is (Up, Down, Busy);
type Traffic_Signal_Type is (Red, Amber, Green);
```

Different enumeration type declarations may contain the same value. The two type declarations

```
type Soda_Type is (Cola, Creme, Orange, Grape);
type Fruit_Type is (Apple, Grape, Orange, Banana);
```

are both perfectly legal. The values Orange and Grape are said to be *overloaded.* In most cases, overloading does not cause a problem. If a problem does exist, just precede the value, enclosed in parentheses, with its type followed by an apostrophe, as in Fruit_Type' (Orange) or Soda_Type' (Orange). This expression is called a *qualified* expression because the value, here Orange, has been qualified by its type.

In general, an enumeration type declaration

---

* A *character literal* is written by enclosing one member of the ASCII character set within single apostrophes, for example, *'R'*.

- names the type
- defines the set of legal values for the type
- establishes an order of values
- defines the set of operators applicable to objects of the type.

For example, the type declaration

```
type Control_Unit_Type is (Heat, Off, Cold);
```

- names the type as Control_Unit_Type
- defines the set of legal values to be Heat, Off, Cold
- establishes a relationship among the values, Heat < Off < Cold, based on the order of their appearance in the type declaration
- defines a set of operations on the type.

6.2 Object Declarations (LRM 3.2.1)

Enumeration objects (variables and constants) are declared in the declarative part of a subprogram or block. Additionally, some package specifications may contain enumeration objects as a resource. Recall that objects declared in package specifications are global.

Enumeration variables are declared by writing

```
Variable_Name : Enumeration_Type_Name;
```

The user-supplied identifier, Variable_Name, is followed by a colon, which is directly followed by the type name. As with all declarations, an enumeration object declaration is terminated by a semicolon. The following are legal object declarations for variables:

```
Room_202         : Control_Unit_Type;
Today            : Day_Type;
TSQ_73_Link      : Link_Status_Type;
Traffic_Signal   : Traffic_Signal_Type;
```

Multiple objects may be declared in one declaration, as in

```
Tomorrow, Yesterday : Day_Type;
```

To supply an initial value at object declaration time, write

```
Variable_Name : Type_Name := Initial_Value;
```

where Initial_Value is a legal expression of Type_Name. Multiple objects may be initialized to the same value, as in

```
Room_202, Room_204, Room_206 : Control_Unit_Type := Off;
```

but multiple objects may not be initialized to distinct values, as in

```
                  --**ILLEGAL**--
Room_202, Room_204, Room_206 : Control_Unit_Type
                             := Heat,Heat,Off;
```

Enumeration constants may be declared much the same as numeric constants are declared. Like any other constant, the value of a constant object of an enumeration type may not change. A constant is declared by writing

```
Constant_Name : constant Type_Name := Constant_Value;
```

where, again, Constant_Value is a legal expression of the type.

Consider

```
First_Day : constant Day_Type := Sun;
```

which declares the identifier First_Day to be a constant of type Day_Type and sets its value to Sun. Similarly, the following

```
Entry_Level : constant Enlisted_Rank_Type := Recruit;
Highest_Enlisted : constant Enlisted_Rank_Type
                   := Sergeant_Major;
```

declare two constants to represent respectively the lowest and highest ranks of an enlisted person in the U. S. Army.

Finally,

```
Church_Day : constant Day_Type := Sun;
Sabbath    : constant Day_Type := Sat;
```

declare two constants to represent church days for two different religions.

6.3 Operators (LRM 3.5.5)

The allowed operators on objects of an enumeration type, as well as the result type of each operation performed, are listed in Table 6-1. You might compare this table with the similar one for numeric types in Section 5.1.

The relational operators are a consequence of the fact that the values specified in the type declaration are ordered. Mon < Tue yields True, while Mon > Tue yields False. Recruit < Sergeant and Sergeant < Sergeant_Major yield True.

The membership operators test whether a value is a member of some range. For example, assuming Today has been declared as an object of type Day_Type, the following expression

```
Today in Mon .. Fri
```

TABLE 6-1 Enumeration Operators

Operators	*Result Type*
Relational	
= /= < <= > >=	Boolean
Membership	
in not in	Boolean

returns True if the value of Today is Mon, Tue, Wed, Thu, or Fri. If the value of Today is Sat or Sun, the expression returns False.

6.4 Attributes (LRM 3.5.5)

Attributes defined for enumeration types are as follows:

```
First
Last
Pred
Succ
Pos
Val
```

The first two attributes, First and Last, do not take any argument. The remaining four attributes require an argument. Table 6-1 describes each attribute.

To use attributes on enumeration types, write

```
Enumeration_Type_Name'Attribute_Name[applicable_argument]
```

For example, given the type declaration

```
type Day_Type is (Sun, Mon, Tue, Wed, Thu, Fri, Sat);
```

the following expressions yield the indicated results:

```
Day_Type'First      yields Sun
Day_Type'Last       yields Sat
Day_Type'Pred(Tue)  yields Mon
Day_Type'Succ(Tue)  yields Wed
Day_Type'Pos(Tue)   yields 2
Day_Type'Val(2)     yields Tue
```

TABLE 6-1 Some Enumeration Type Attributes

First	This attribute returns the first enumeration value in the type declaration.
Last	This attribute returns the last value in the enumeration type declaration.
Pred (enumeration_value)	This attribute returns the predecessor in the enumeration type declaration of the argument. The predecessor of the first value in the list is not defined, and any attempt to access the predecessor of the first value raises Constraint_Error.
Succ (enumeration_value)	This attribute returns the successor in the enumeration type declaration of the argument. The successor of the last value in the list is not defined, and any attempt to access the successor of the last value in the list raises Constraint_Error.
Pos (enumeration_value)	This attribute returns the position in the enumeration type declaration of the specified value. Positioning starts at 0. Any attempt to access the position of an illegal value raises Constraint_Error.
Val (integer_expression)	The final attribute returns the value in the enumeration type declaration in the position indicated by the argument. Any attempt to reference a position not applicable for the type raises Constraint_Error.

while the following expressions

```
Day_Type'Pred(Sun)
Day_Type'Succ(Sat)
Day_Type'Val (7)
```

all raise Constraint_Error.

Similarly, given the type declaration

```
type Traffic_Signal_Type is (Red, Amber, Green);
```

the expression Traffic_Signal_Type'First yields Red, while Traffic_Signal_Type'Pred (Red) raises Constraint_Error.

6.5 Enumeration I/O (LRM 14.3.10)

Performing I/O on enumeration values is very similar to performing I/O on the types you have already studied. Step 1 is identical. For step 2, write the following:

```
package Type_Name_IO is new Enumeration_IO (Type_Name);
use Type_Name_IO;
```

where Type_Name is the name of the type whose values you wish to input or output. Type_Name_IO is a user-supplied identifier. We recommend that this identifier consist of the name of the type with the suffix _Type replaced by the suffix _IO.

6.6 List_Months

The following program prints each value of Month_Type followed by its respective position in the enumeration type declaration.

```
package Calendar_Info is
   type Month_Type is (Jan, Feb, Mar, Apr, May, Jun,
                       Jul, Aug, Sep, Oct, Nov, Dec);
   type Day_Type is range 1 .. 31;
   type Year_Type is range 1980 .. 2500;
   function Leap_Year (Year : Year_Type)
            return Boolean;
   function Last_Day_of (Month: Month_Type)
            return Day_Type;
end Calendar_Info;
```

```
with Text_IO; use Text_IO;
with Calendar_Info; use Calendar_Info;
procedure List_Months_and_Position is
   package Month_IO is new Enumeration_IO(Month_Type);
   package Int_IO is new Integer_IO (Integer);
   use Month_IO; use Int_IO;
begin -- List_Months_and_Position
   for Month in Month_Type'First .. Month_Type'Last
   loop
      Put (Month);       -- output the month using
                         -- Month_IO.Put
      Put ("    ");      -- output some spaces using
                         -- Text_IO.Put
      Put (Month_Type'Pos(Month)); -- output position
                                   -- using Int_IO.Put
      New_Line;
   end loop;
end List_Months_and_Position;
```

Use of Month_Type'First . . Month_Type'Last to express the iteration range in the **for** loop is legal. Any *discrete* range may be used to express the iteration range in a **for** loop. As a matter of fact, any discrete type name may be used to represent the iteration range. When a discrete type name is used to express the iteration range, the loop is executed once for each value in the type.

The following code uses the type name Month_Type to control the loop.

```
with Text_IO; use Text_IO;
with Calendar_Info; use Calendar_Info;
procedure List_Months_and_Position is
   package Month_IO is new Enumeration_IO(Month_Type);
   package Int_IO is new Integer_IO (Integer);
   use Month_IO; use Int_IO;
begin -- List_Months_and_Position
   for Month in Month_Type
   loop
      Put (Month);   -- output the month using
                     -- Month_IO.Put
      Put ("     "); -- output some spaces using
                     -- Text_IO.Put
      Put (Month_Type'Pos(Month)); -- output position
                                   -- using Int_IO.Put
      New_Line;
   end loop;
end List_Months_and_Position;
```

In either case, Integer I/O is required to output the position because the attribute Pos returns the *position* of a value in an enumeration list.

6.7 Calculate_Next_Day

The program in Figure 6-1(a,b) prompts the user for a date—that is, a month, a day, and a year—and then outputs the date of the next day.

FIGURE 6-1(a) The declarative part of Calculate_Next_Day

```
with Text_IO; use Text_IO;
with Calendar_Info; use Calendar_Info;
procedure Calculate_Next_Day is
   -- the declarations
   Month : Month_Type;
   Day   : Day_Type;
   Year  : Year_Type;
   -- STEP 2 for each type
   package Month_IO is new Enumeration_IO (Month_Type);
   package Day_IO is new Integer_IO (Day_Type);
   package Year_IO is new Integer_IO (Year_Type);
   use Month_IO, Day_IO, Year_IO;
   -- I/O procedures stubbed out
   procedure Get_a_Month (Month : out Month_Type)
             is separate;
   procedure Get_a_Day (Day: out Day_Type) is separate;
   procedure Get_a_Year (Year: out Year_Type)
             is separate;
   procedure Put_a_Month (Month : in Month_Type)
             is separate;
   procedure Put_a_Day (Day : in Day_Type) is separate;
   procedure Put_a_Year (Year : in Year_Type)
             is separate;
begin -- Calculate_Next_Day
   -- The executable part is in Figure 6-1(b).
end Calculate_Next_Day;
```

FIGURE 6-1(b) The executable part of Calculate_Next_Day

```
begin -- Calculate_Next_Day
   loop
      Get_a_Month (Month);
      Get_a_Day   (Day);
      Get_a_Year  (Year);
      if Month = Jan or Month in Mar .. Nov then
         if Day = Last_Day_of (Month) then
            Day := 1;
            Month := Month_Type'Succ (Month);
            -- Year stays the same.
         else
            Day := Day + 1;
            -- Month, Year stay the same.
         end if;
      elsif Month = Feb then
         if Day<28 or (Day=28 and Leap_Year(Year)) then
            Day := Day + 1;
         else
            Day := 1;
            Month := Mar;
            -- Year stays the same.
         end if;
      else -- Month is Dec
         if Day = Last_Day_of (Month) then -- Dec 31st
            Day := 1;
            Month := Jan;
            Year := Year + 1;
         else
            Day := Day + 1;
            -- Month, Year stay the same.
         end if;
      end if;
      Put ("The new date is: ");
      Put_a_Month (Month);
      Put (' ');
      Put_a_Day (Day);
      Put (','); -- enclose character in apostrophes
      Put_a_Year (Year);
      New_Line;
   end loop;
end Calculate_Next_Day;
```

The sub unit Get_A_Month is coded as follows:

```
separate (Calculate_Next_Day)
procedure Get_a_Month (Month : out Month_Type) is
begin -- Get_a_Month
   loop
      begin
         Get (Month);
         exit;
      exception
         when Data_Error =>
         -- whatever needs to be done
      end;
   end loop;
end Get_a_Month;
```

The remaining subunits are not shown here but are coded similarly.

6.8 The *case* Statement (LRM 5.4)

As you no doubt noticed, nested **if**s clutter the code of Calculate_Next_Day. Ada provides another statement for conditional control, the *case statement,* which can reduce the clutter and make the code easier to follow.

The **case** statement selects statements for execution from alternative sequences of statements based on the value of a *discrete expression*. A discrete expression evaluates to a discrete value—that is, a value that is either an integer or an enumeration value.

The syntax for a **case** statement is as follows:

```
case Discrete_Expression is
   when Value_1 => Statements_1;
   when Value_2 => Statements_2;
   when Value_3 => Statements_3;
            . . .
   when Value_n => Statements_n;
  [when others  => Statements_o;]
end case;
```

where

- Discrete_Expression is any legal expression of an enumeration type or an integer type.
- Value_1 through Value_n represent mutually exclusive and collectively exhaustive values of the type of the expression.
- If Value_1 through Value_n is not exhaustive, the **when others** alternative must be present.
- The optional alternative, **when others**, represents the choice for those values of the expression not specifically covered in previous values.
- If the alternative **when others** is used, it must appear last.

The execution of the **case** statement chooses one, and only one, sequence of statements depending on the value of the discrete expression. If the value of the discrete expression is Value_2, then Statements_2 are executed and the **case** statement terminates. If the value of the discrete expression does not match any of the explicitly listed values, then the sequence of statements in the **when others** alternative is selected.

As an example of the case statement in action, consider a message switch that handles various transmissions on different channels. Each transmission type is either asynchronous or synchronous. Our switch must support the following:

Channel	*Transmission Type*
1	Synchronous
2	Asynchronous
3	Synchronous
4	Asynchronous
5	Asynchronous
6	Asynchronous
7	Asynchronous

Assume Channel_Type has been declared as an enumeration type, as follows:*

```
type Channel_Type is (Channel_1, Channel_2, Channel_3,
                      Channel_4, Channel_5, Channel_6,
                      Channel_7);
```

The following procedure selects the correct routine to process a message, given the channel number.

```
procedure Select_Correct_Processor
      (Channel : in Channel_Type) is
   procedure Process_Synch is separate;
   procedure Process_Asynch is separate;
begin -- Select_Correct_Processor
   case Channel is
      when Channel_1 => Process_Synch;
      when Channel_2 => Process_Asynch;
      when Channel_3 => Process_Synch;
      when Channel_4 => Process_Asynch;
      when Channel_5 => Process_Asynch;
      when Channel_6 => Process_Asynch;
      when Channel_7 => Process_Asynch;
   end case;
end Select_Correct_Processor;
```

The expression Channel is a discrete expression of type Channel_Type. The choices listed in the case statement are mutually exclusive; that is, only one choice is possible for each value of type Channel_Type. The choices are also exhaustive, since all possible values of Channel_Type are represented. Because all values of Channel_Type are represented, use of the **when others** alternative is not required.

The preceding code is obviously repetitious. For the alternatives for Channels 4 through 7, the code is the same. There are more efficient ways of

---

* Channel_Type was *not* declared as a user-defined integer type,

```
type Channel_Type is range 1 .. 7;
```

because arithmetic operations are *not* performed on channels.

expressing the fact that the same sequence of statements is to be executed for each one of multiple values.

Bar (|) Notation

Choices may be separated by a bar, as follows:

```
when Value_1 | Value_2 => Statement(s);
```

When the discrete expression evaluates to either Value_1 or Value_2, the specified statements are executed.

Using this bar notation, Select_Correct_Processor can be coded as

```
procedure Select_Correct_Processor
          (Channel : in Channel_Type) is
   procedure Process_Synch is separate;
   procedure Process_Asynch is separate;
begin -- Select_Correct_Processor
   case Channel is
      when Channel_1 | Channel_3 => Process_Synch;
      when Channel_2 | Channel_4 | Channel_5 |
               Channel_6 | Channel_7 => Process_Asynch;
   end case;
end Select_Correct_Processor;
```

Process_Synch is called when Channel evaluates to either Channel_1 or Channel_3. Otherwise Process_Asynch is called.

Discrete Range Notation

The previous code is still clumsy in stating when Process_Asynch is called. In searching for an improvement, we note that the values Channel_4 through Channel_7 are consecutive. Consecutive values may be specified in a *discrete range* that has the form

```
when Value_i .. Value_j => Statement(s);
```

When the discrete expression evaluates to any of the values in the range Value_i through Value_j, the specified statement(s) are executed.

Select_Correct_Processor can now be coded as

```
procedure Select_Correct_Processor
          (Channel : in Channel_Type) is
   procedure Process_Synch is separate;
   procedure Process_Asynch is separate;
begin -- Select_Correct_Processor
   case Channel is
      when Channel_1 | Channel_3 =>
            Process_Synch;
      when Channel_2 | Channel_4 .. Channel_7 =>
            Process_Asynch;
   end case;
end Select_Correct_Processor;
```

when others Alternative

Select_Correct_Processor could also be coded using the **when others** alternative, as follows:

```
procedure Select_Correct_Processor
          (Channel : in Channel_Type) is
   procedure Process_Synch is separate;
   procedure Process_Asynch is separate;
begin -- Select_Correct_Processor
   case Channel is
      when Channel_1 | Channel_3 => Process_Synch;
      when others => Process_Asynch;
   end case;
end Select_Correct_Processor;
```

The **when others** alternative appears last and represents all possible values of Channel_Type not specified explicitly in previous choices.

Each of the examples we have just studied contains a single procedure call as the sequence of statements to be executed for a specific choice. This is not a requirement, however. Any legitimate sequence of statements may be specified.

6.9 Calculate_Next_Day Revisited

The example in Figure 6-2 shows our earlier program, Calculate_Next_Day, recoded using a **case** statement.

FIGURE 6-2 Calculate_Next_Day using **case** statement

```
with Text_IO; use Text_IO;
with Calendar_Info; use Calendar_Info;
procedure Calculate_Next_Day is
   -- declarations as before
begin -- Calculate_Next_Day
   loop
      -- get values as before
      case Month is
         when Jan | Mar .. Nov =>
            if Day = Last_Day_of (Month) then
               Day := 1;
               Month := Month_Type'Succ (Month);
                 -- Year stays the same.
            else
               Day := Day + 1;
               -- Month, Year stay the same.
            end if;
         when Feb =>
            if Day<28 or (Day=28 and Leap_Year (Year)) then
               Day := Day + 1;
            else
               Day := 1;
               Month := Mar;
               -- Year stays the same.
            end if;
```

(continued)

FIGURE 6-2 *(continued)*

```
            when Dec =>
               if Day = Last_Day_of (Month) then -- Dec 31st
                  Day := 1;
                  Month := Jan;
                  Year := Year + 1;
               else
                  Day := Day + 1;
                  -- Month, Year stay the same.
               end if;
         end case;
         Put ("The new date is: "); -- Text_IO.Put
         Put_a_Month (Month);
         Put (' ');
         Put_a_Day (Day);
         Put (',');
         Put_a_Year (Year);
         New_Line;
      end loop;
   end Calculate_Next_Day;
```

Figure 6-3 is a version of Calculate_Next_Day that uses the **when others** alternative.

FIGURE 6-3 Calculate_Next_Day using **when others** alternative

```
with Text_IO; use Text_IO;
with Calendar_Info; use Calendar_Info;
procedure Calculate_Next_Day is
   -- declarations as before
begin -- Calculate_Next_Day
   loop
      -- get values as before
      Get_a_Year  (Year);
```

(continued)

FIGURE 6-3 *(continued)*

```
        case Month is
           when Feb =>
              if Day<28 or (Day=28 and Leap_Year(Year)) then
                 Day := Day + 1;
              else
                 Day := 1;
                 Month := Mar;
                 -- Year stays the same.
              end if;
           when Dec =>
              if Day = Last_Day_of (Month) then -- Dec 31st
                 Day := 1;
                 Month := Jan;
                 Year := Year + 1;
              else
                 Day := Day + 1;
                 -- Month, Year stay the same.
              end if;
           when others =>
              if Day = Last_Day_of (Month) then
                 Day := 1;
                 Month := Month_Type'Succ(Month);
                 -- Year stays the same.
              else
                 Day := Day + 1;
                 -- Month, Year stay the same.
              end if;
        end case;
        Put ("The new date is: "); -- Text_IO.Put
        Put_a_Month (Month);
        Put (' ');
        Put_a_Day (Day);
        Put (',');
        Put_a_Year (Year);
        New_Line;
     end loop;
  end Calculate_Next_Day;
```

EXERCISES

6.1 Write a program to input a letter that represents the first letter of a command. Output the expanded form of the command. The possible entries and their expanded form are as follows:

Input	*Output*
D	Debug
E	Edit
H	Help
L	List
P	Print
Q	Quit

Use an **if** statement in your code.

6.2 Recode Exercise 6.1 using a **case** statement.

6.3 Recode 6.1 using only attributes. Do not use an **if** or a **case** statement.

6.4 Discuss the advantages and disadvantages of the different approaches demonstrated in Exercises 6.1, 6.2, and 6.3.

6.5 Given the following package specification:

```
package Toll_Structure is
   type Vehicle_Type is (Car, Car_and_Trailer,
        Motorcycle, Truck, Bus);
   type Weight_in_Tons_Type is range 0 .. 50;
end Toll_Structure;
```

write a procedure to calculate the toll for a vehicle at a parkway toll plaza if the toll charged is

$.25 car	1.00 truck under 5 tons
.50 car with trailer	1.50 truck 5 tons or over
.20 motorcycle	2.00 bus

6.6 A life insurance company bases its premiums on two criteria, weight and smoking habits. The actions taken by the company are as follows:

Doesn't smoke Weight–N or U	Doesn't smoke Weight–O	Smokes Weight–N or U	Smokes Weight–O
Regular rate	Hold for further analysis	Higher rate	Do not insure

where N, U, and O stand for Normal weight, Underweight, and Overweight respectively.

Using the following package specification, write a procedure that prompts the user for the two criteria and prints out the action taken by the insurance company.

```
with Text_IO; use Text_IO;
package Insurance_Criteria is
   type Weight_Type is (Under_Weight, Normal_Weight,
                        Over_Weight);
   type Smoker_Type is (Smoker, Non_Smoker);
   package Weight_IO is new Enumeration_IO (Weight_Type);
   package Smoker_IO is new Enumeration_IO (Smoker_Type);
   use Weight_IO;
   use Smoker_IO;
end Insurance_Criteria;
```

6.7 Recode Exercise 4.9 with Location_Type declared as

```
type Location_Type is (Quadrant_1, Quadrant_2,
     Quadrant_3, Quadrant_4, Positive_X,
     Negative_X, Positive_Y, Negative_Y, Origin);
```

7

FLOATING POINT TYPES

CHAPTER OBJECTIVES

- Declare Float objects.
- Declare Float objects with a range constraint.
- Perform I/O on Float objects.
- Declare user-defined floating point types.
- Perform I/O on user-defined floating point types.
- Declare a named number.
- Write real literals.
- Perform numeric type conversion between the class of Integer types and the class of floating point types.
- Define subtype.
- Declare subtypes of type Float.
- State two predefined subtypes of type Integer.

You were exposed to type Float in Chapter 2, but it is now time to treat this type more formally. Type Float is predefined in Ada. Its purpose is to enable us to work with values that contain decimal points. Because each type is categorized by a set of values and a set of operations on those values, we need to look at these aspects of type Float.

7.1 Predefined Type Float (LRM 3.5.7)

The set of values for objects of type Float is implementation dependent. The attributes 'First and 'Last, when applied to Float (for example Float'Last), will yield the smallest and largest values of the type for any implementation.

Object Declarations (LRM 3.2)

Objects (variables and constants) of type Float are declared in the same manner as objects of other types. The declarations may appear in blocks or declarative regions of subprograms or in package specifications. An object declared in a package specification is global data.

Variables of type Float are declared by writing

```
Variable_Name : Float [:= Initial_Value];
```

where Variable_Name is any legal identifier.

The following are legal object declarations for variables of type Float.

```
    Celsius_Temp : Float;
Fahrenheit_Temp : Float := 32.0;
```

The latter declaration includes a *real literal* value. We will learn the rules for writing real literals shortly. For now, write a real literal with a decimal point and at least one digit before and after the decimal point.

Multiple objects may be declared in one declaration, as in

```
Celsius_Temp, Fahrenheit_Temp : Float;
```

Multiple objects may be initialized to the same value, as in

```
Celsius_Temp, Fahrenheit_Temp : Float := 0.0;
```

However, multiple objects may not be initialized to different values, as in

```
            --**ILLEGAL**--
Celsius_Temp, Fahrenheit_Temp : Float := 0.0, 32.0;
```

Constants of type Float are declared by writing

```
Constant_Name : constant Float := Initial_Value;
```

The following is a legal constant declaration:

```
Pi : constant Float := 3.14;
```

This statement declares Pi to be a constant of type Float with a value of 3.14. The identifier Pi may now be used in expressions of type Float, instead of the literal 3.14.

When declaring objects (variables or constants) of type Float with an initial value, Initial_Value may be any legal expression of type Float. Remember that an initial value is mandatory when declaring a constant, optional when declaring a variable.

Operators (LRM 3.5.8)

The operators that can be used with objects of type Float are listed in Table 7-1. They are subject to the hierarchy specified in Table 5-2. The right operand for exponentiation must belong to the class of Integer types. Thus, to write

```
            --**ILLEGAL**--
Hypotenuse := (Side_1**2 + Side_2**2)**0.5;
```

TABLE 7-1 Floating Point Operators

Operators	*Result Type*
Numeric	
+ − * / **	Float
Relational	
= /= < <= > >=	Boolean
Unary	
+ − abs	Float

is illegal because the 0.5 is a real literal and is not permitted as an exponent. Both occurrences of 2 as an exponent are legal, however.

Real Literals (LRM 2.4.1)

You were exposed briefly to real literals earlier in this section. Real literals such as 3.3 represent approximations and always include a decimal point. As with integer literals, real literals are assumed to be of base 10. (However, as with integer literals, real literals may be written in a base other than 10. See Appendix B.)

The rules for writing a real literal state that a real literal

- contains a decimal point
- uses the digits 0 through 9
- must have at least one digit on each side of the decimal point
- may contain an embedded underscore between consecutive digits
- may be written in exponential notation with either positive or negative integer exponents.

Exponential notation for real literals is essentially identical to exponential notation for integer literals. However, real literals may have negative exponents, whereas integer literals are restricted to positive exponents.

All of the following are legal real literals:

300.0	represents 300
3.0E2	represents 300
3.0e2	represents 300
3.0E-2	represents .03
1000000.0	represents one million (hard to read)
1_000_000.0	represents one million (easy to read)
1.0E6	represents one million
1.0e6	represents one million

As with integer literals, use of an underscore in writing a real literal does not create a distinct value. 1000000.0 and 1_000_000.0 represent the same value.

Readability is the main point to keep in mind when choosing a representation for a value. One million expressed as 10.0e5 is not as immediately recognizable as 1.0E6. 1.0E6 is also far more compact than 1_000_000.0 and is less prone to being changed by a typing error. The value 1_000_00.0 will compile successfully, but it certainly could cause a guided missile to go astray if the value intended was one million! Use common sense when expressing large values.

Use underscores intelligently as well. Place them where you would normally write commas. For example, the literal 1_000.0 is a more appropriate representation for the number 1,000 than the literal 10_00.0.

7.2 User-Defined Floating Point Types (LRM 3.5.7)

Consider the following function, which converts Celsius degrees to Fahrenheit degrees.

```
function Conversion_to_Fahrenheit (C_Degrees : Float)
   return Float is
begin -- Conversion_to_Fahrenheit
   return ( (9.0/5.0)*C_Degrees + 32.0);
end Conversion_to_Fahrenheit;
```

This function deals with quantities that require real values to accurately represent the problem. By working in type Float, however, it is possible to inadvertently mix these quantities in an expression in a way that the compiler will readily accept but that will produce nonsensical results. The situation is similar to adding character counts and line counts. Given the following:

```
Celsius_Temp, Fahrenheit_Temp : Float;
```

in the declarative part of a subprogram, we could have this perfectly legal, yet illogical, assignment statement:

```
Celsius_Temp := Celsius_Temp + Fahrenheit_Temp;
```

Fortunately, just as we were able to declare user-defined integer types, we can declare user-defined floating point types in Ada. To declare a user-defined floating point type, write

```
type Type_Name is digits N [range L .. U];
```

where Type_Name is a user-supplied identifier; N is the number of significant digits desired; and **range** is as previously described.

A user-defined floating point type declaration

- creates a distinct type
- specifies that values for the type must contain a decimal point
- defines the set of values for the type
- specifies the minimum number of significant digits to be associated with values of the type
- defines the set of operations applicable to objects of the type to be the same as those operations allowed for the predefined type Float.

The following declarations:

```
type Celsius_Type is digits 3 range -50.0 .. 50.0;
type Fahrenheit_Type is digits 4 range -60.0 .. 120.0;
```

define two distinct Floating point types, Celsius_Type and Fahrenheit_Type. Both types have, as a set of values, real values that contain decimal points. Objects of type Celsius_Type are restricted to values between −50.0 and 50.0 inclusive. Values of type Fahrenheit_Type are restricted to values between −60.0 and 120.0 inclusive. Objects of both types may be operated on by the operators listed in Table 7-1.

Now, given the following object declarations:

```
Celsius_Temp    : Celsius_Type;
Fahrenheit_Temp : Fahrenheit_Type;
```

this assignment statement

```
        --**ILLEGAL**--
Celsius_Temp := Celsius_Temp + Fahrenheit_Temp;
```

will not compile because the expression on the right side of the assignment symbol contains objects of two distinct types.

As before, use user-defined types to express the logical properties and constraints imposed by the real world. It does not make any sense to add Celsius and Fahrenheit temperatures. Write Ada code to express that constraint and let the compiler and the run-time system do the checking for you!

7.3 Named Numbers (LRM 3.2.2)

Just as you can declare named numbers that belong to the class of integer types, you can declare named numbers that belong to the class of real types.

Consider the following:

```
package Trig_Package is
   Pi : constant := 3.14159;
   type Degrees_Type is digits 4 range 0.0 .. 360.0;
   type Radians_Type is digits 6 range 0.0 .. 2.0*Pi;
   type Answer_Type is digits 5 range -1.0 .. 1.0;
   function Sin (Angle : Radians_Type) return Answer_Type;
   function Cos (Angle : Radians_Type) return Answer_Type;
   function Tan (Angle : Radians_Type) return Float;
   function Csc (Angle : Radians_Type) return Float;
   function Sec (Angle : Radians_Type) return Float;
   function Cot (Angle : Radians_Type) return Float;
end Trig_Package;
```

The named number Pi may be used in any expression of type Float, Degrees_Type, Radians_Type, or any other predefined or user-defined real data type. By declaring Pi to be a named number rather than a constant of type Degrees_Type or Radians_Type, Pi may be used in subprograms that convert between the two units of measure. For example, the following function uses Pi in an expression of type Radians_Type before it is converted to Degrees_Type.

```
with Trig_Package; use Trig_Package;
function Conversion_Radians_to_Degrees
   (Angle : Radians_Type) return Degrees_Type is
begin -- Conversion_Radians_to_Degrees
   return Degrees_Type (Angle*180.0/Pi);
end Conversion_Radians_to_Degrees;
```

The following function uses Pi in an expression of type Degrees_Type before it is converted to Radians_Type.

```
with Trig_Package; use Trig_Package;
function Conversion_Degrees_to_Radians
   (Angle : Degrees_Type) return Radians_Type is
begin -- Conversion_Degrees_to_Radians
   return Radians_Type(Angle*Pi/180.0) ;
end Conversion_Degrees_to_Radians;
```

Normally these kinds of conversion routines would be supplied as resources of a package.

7.4 Floating Point I/O (LRM 14.3.10)

To perform I/O on objects of a user-defined floating point type, use step 1 to import Text_IO as usual. For step 2, write

```
package Type_Name_IO is new Float_IO (Type_Name);
use Type_Name_IO;
```

where Type_Name_IO is the name of the type that requires I/O services (the floating point type whose values are to be input or output) with the suffix _Type replaced by the suffix _IO.

7.5 Convert_Temperature

Consider the following package specification:

```
package Outdoor_Thermometer is
    type Temperature_Type is (Fahrenheit, Celsius);
    type Celsius_Type is digits 3 range -50.0 .. 50.0;
    type Fahrenheit_Type is digits 4 range -60.0 .. 120.0;
    Freezing_Pt_Water_Fahren :
          constant Fahrenheit_Type := 32.0;
    Freezing_Pt_Water_Celsius :
          constant Celsius_Type := 0.0;
    function Conversion_to_Celsius
          (Temp : Fahrenheit_Type) return Celsius_Type;
    function Conversion_to_Fahrenheit (Temp : Celsius_Type)
          return Fahrenheit_Type;
end Outdoor_Thermometer;
```

In addition to the enumeration type Temperature_Type, this package provides two user-defined floating point types, one for Fahrenheit temperatures and one for Celsius temperatures. The two types prevent Fahrenheit and Celsius temperatures from being mixed in one expression. Two constants are declared, representing the freezing point of water in Fahrenheit and in Celsius degrees respectively. Finally, two functions are provided to allow conversion between the different temperature scales.

The procedure in Figure 7-1 prompts the user for the type of temperature to be converted, gets the temperature, calls the conversion routine, and displays the results.

FIGURE 7-1 Convert_Temperature

```
with Outdoor_Thermometer; use Outdoor_Thermometer;
with Text_IO; use Text_IO;
procedure Convert_Temperature is
   Temp   : Temperature_Type;
   F_Temp : Fahrenheit_Type;
   C_Temp : Celsius_Type;
   package Temperature_IO is new Enumeration_IO
      (Temperature_Type);
   package Fahrenheit_IO is new Float_IO
      (Fahrenheit_Type);
   package Celsius_IO is new Float_IO (Celsius_Type);
   use Temperature_IO;
   use Fahrenheit_IO;
   use Celsius_IO;
   -- These three procedures include exception handlers
   -- for Data_Error.
   procedure Get_Choice_of_Temperature
      (Choice : out Temperature_Type) is separate;
   procedure Get_Fahrenheit_Temp
      (Temp : out Fahrenheit_Type) is separate;
   procedure Get_Celsius_Temp (Temp : out Celsius_Type)
      is separate;
begin -- Convert_Temperature
   loop
      Put_Line ("Converting a Celsius or a Fahrenheit" &
                "temperature?");
      Get_Choice_of_Temperature (Temp);
      if Temp = Fahrenheit then
         Get_Fahrenheit_Temp (F_Temp);
         Put (Conversion_to_Celsius(F_Temp));
      else
         Get_Celsius_Temp (C_Temp);
         Put (Conversion_to_Fahrenheit(C_Temp));
      end if;
   end loop;
end Convert_Temperature;
```

7.6 Numeric Type Conversion (LRM 4.6)

Ada is a strongly typed language. Operations on objects of different types are prohibited. Thus, floating point and integer objects may not be mixed in one expression. An object of a user-defined floating point type may not be mixed with an object of another floating point type. An object of a user-defined integer type may not be mixed with an object of another user-defined integer type.

Actually, Ada does allow mixing of these objects—but in a structured and controlled fashion. *An expression of any numeric type may be converted to any other numeric type,* but the conversion must be very explicit. By requiring the conversion to be explicit, Ada makes the maintainer of a program aware that the value being converted is being used in an unusual way.

The syntax for a type conversion is as follows:

```
Target_Type_Name (Expression_To_Convert)
```

where conversion from a floating point value to an integer value is obtained by rounding to the nearest integer.*

The following was used in the Exercises of Chapter 4.

```
package Math_Library is
   function Square_Root (Number : Float) return Float;
   . . .
end Math_Library;
```

The following program is incorrect. Can you tell why?

---

* The value 2.3 is rounded to 2, and the value 2.6 is rounded to 3. Ada does not specify what happens to a value like 2.5; the implementation will determine whether such a value is rounded up or down.

```
with Math_Library; use Math_Library;
with Text_IO; use Text_IO;
procedure Compute_Square_Root_Table is
   package Number_IO is new Integer_IO (Integer);
   package Square_Root_IO is new Float_IO (Float);
   use Number_IO;
   use Square_Root_IO;
begin -- Calculate_Square_Root_Table
   for Value in 1 .. 100
   loop
      Put (Value);
      Put ("                    "); -- some blanks
      Put (Square_Root(Value)); -- **ILLEGAL**--
      New_Line;
   end loop;
end Compute_Square_Root_Table;
```

The function call Square_Root(Value) is illegal because the function Square_Root expects a value of type Float, and Value is an expression belonging to the class of integer types.

Type conversion corrects the error as follows:

```
with Math_Library; use Math_Library;
with Text_IO; use Text_IO;
procedure Compute_Square_Root_Table is
   package Number_IO is new Integer_IO (Integer);
   package Square_Root_IO is new Float_IO;
   use Number_IO;
   use Square_Root_IO;
begin -- Calculate_Square_Root_Table
   for Value in 1 .. 100
   loop
      Put (Value);
      Put ("                    "); -- some blanks
      -- Value converted to Float
      Put (Square_Root ( Float(Value) );
      New_Line;
   end loop;
end Compute_Square_Root_Table;
```

Value is now converted to a floating point value before being passed to the function Square_Root.

Here is the function Conversion_to_Fahrenheit from Section 7.2 recoded with user-defined types.

```
function Conversion_to_Fahrenheit
   (C_Degrees : Celsius_Type) return Fahrenheit_Type is
begin -- Conversion_to_Fahrenheit
   return (9.0/5.0) * Fahrenheit_Type(C_Degrees) + 32.0;
end Conversion_to_Fahrenheit;
```

The parameter C_Degrees must be converted to Fahrenheit_Type. Without this conversion, the statement

```
return (9.0/5.0) * C_Degrees + 32.0; --*ILLEGAL**--
```

is in error because the type of the expression is Celsius_Type and the function is supposed to return a value of Fahrenheit_Type. C_Degrees can be converted to Fahrenheit_Type because the legal range of values for Celsius_Type is a subset of Fahrenheit_Type. F_Degrees (of type Fahrenheit_Type) cannot be converted to Celsius_Type quite so easily. Why?

Finally, in Section 7.3 the functions Conversion_Radians_to_Degrees and Conversion_Degrees_to_Radians required explicit type conversion.

EXERCISES

7.1 State why each of the following is an illegal real literal.

a. 1,000,000.0

b. 1 000 000.0

c. 1_000__000.0

d. 2_5000.0_

e. 300

f. .333

g. 33.

h. 1_.0

i. 1.0E2.3

7.2 Write the number 1,000 as a real literal, base 10, in as many ways as possible without an underscore.

7.3 The law of the sines states that the three ratios obtained by dividing a side of a triangle by the sine of the opposite angle are equal. The formula is

a/Sin A = b/Sin B = c/ Sin C

where a, b, and c represent the three sides of the triangle and A, B, and C represent the angles opposite those sides, as shown below.

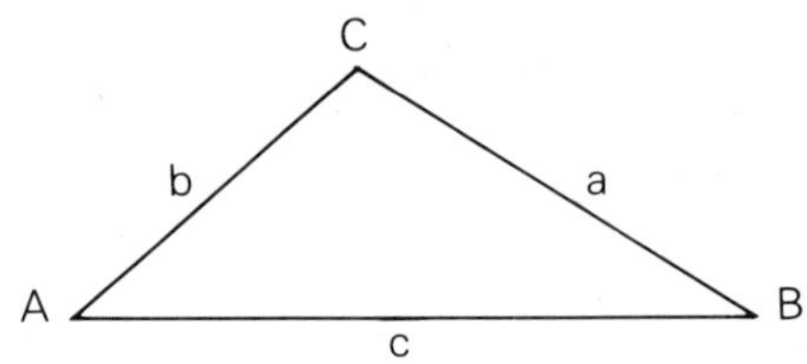

In a Class A signal area there are two transmitting antennas for two television broadcast stations. A receiving antenna for both stations is located as shown in the following diagram.

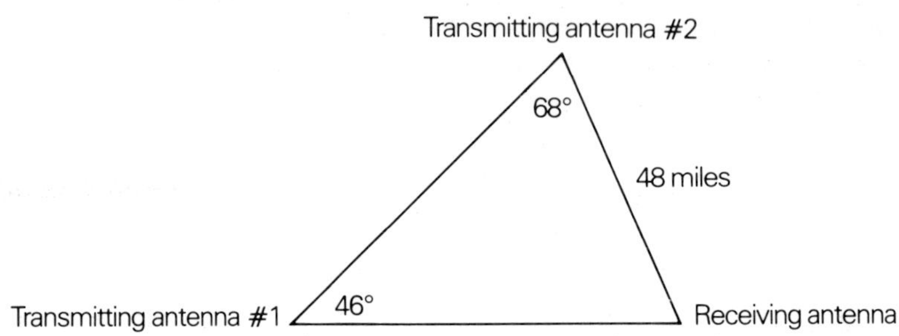

Find the distance, in miles, between transmitting antenna #1 and the receiving antenna.

7.4 Write a program to compute the sine of all angles between 0 and 360 degrees. Output each angle in degrees and the sine of each angle in some appropriate form.

7.5 Write a program that converts from Cartesian coordinates to polar coordinates and vice versa. Refer to the following review of coordinates.

Given a point in a plane, that point is represented in Cartesian coordinates as (x,y)

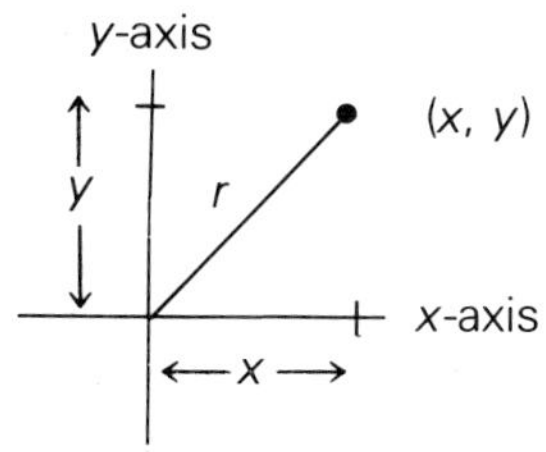

where x is the distance along the x axis and y is the distance along the y axis. Alternatively, the same point may be represented in polar coordinates as (ρ, θ) (rho and theta), where ρ is the distance from the origin, (0,0), and θ is the angle made with the x axis.

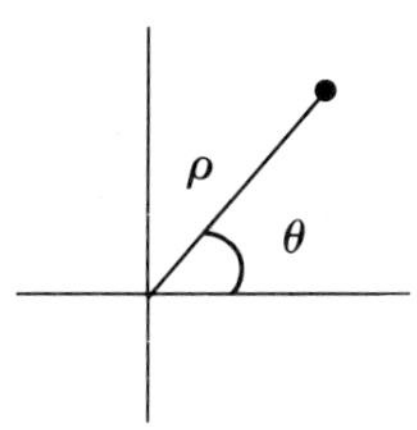

To convert from Cartesian coordinates to polar coordinates, use the following equations.

$$\rho = \sqrt{x^2 + y^2} \qquad \theta = \sin^{-1}(y/r)$$

To convert from polar coordinates to Cartesian coordinates, use the following equations.

$$x = \rho \cos \theta \qquad y = \rho \sin \theta$$

Then

$$r = \sqrt{x^2 + y^2} = \rho$$

7.7 Subtypes

There are times when declaring different types can lead to problems. For example, consider the following:

```
package Television is
   type VHF_Channel_Type is range 2 .. 13;
   type UHF_Channel_Type is range 14 .. 83;
   type Frequency_Type is digits 5 range 50.0 .. 900.0;
      ...
end Television;
```

How can a subprogram be constructed that, when passed a television channel, will select the correct video frequency? Is the following specification adequate?

```
procedure Select_Frequency
                (Channel : in UHF_Channel_Type;
         Video_Frequency : out Frequency_Type)
```

Certainly not. The procedure does not permit a VHF channel to be passed as an actual parameter. For similar reasons, the specification

```
procedure Select_Frequency
                (Channel : in VHF_Channel_Type;
         Video_Frequency : out Frequency_Type)
```

is inadequate because it provides a frequency selection mechanism only for VHF channels.

Now consider

```
procedure Select_Frequency
              (Channel_1 : in VHF_Channel_Type;
               Channel_2 : in UHF_Channel_Type;
         Video_Frequency : out Frequency_Type)
```

This procedure, with a formal parameter of each type, is an excellent example of overkill!

Ada provides a construct that will help a great deal in situations like this. Basically we have two distinct types, VHF_Type and UHF_Type, but we need to consider them as one type with constraints placed on the set of values that objects of each type can obtain. That is, we want to have one parameter that represents a channel, like this:

```
procedure Select_Frequency
                 (Channel : in Channel_Type;
         Video_Frequency : out Frequency_Type)
```

and we want to place limits on the set of values that UHF and VHF channels can obtain.

The construct to implement this concept is called the *subtype*.

Subtype Declarations

The following package specification

```
package Television is
  type Channel_Type is range 2 .. 83;
  subtype VHF_Channel_Subtype is
          Channel_Type range 2 .. 13;
  subtype UHF_Channel_Subtype is
          Channel_Type range 14 .. 83;
  type Frequency_Type is digits 5 range 50.0 .. 900.0;
     ...
end Television;
```

declares Channel_Type as a user-defined integer type. Objects of Channel_Type have values between 2 and 83. VHF_Channel_Subtype and UHF_Channel_Subtype are declared as two *subtypes* of Channel_Type. An object of type VHF_Channel_Subtype is restricted to values between 2 and 13 inclusive, while an object of type UHF_Channel_Subtype is restricted to values between 14 and 83 inclusive. The operations that can be performed on objects of the two subtypes are the same as those that can be performed on Channel_Type, specifically the operations listed in Table 5-1. Channel_Type is called the *base type* of the two subtypes.

Write a subtype declaration as follows:

```
subtype Subtype_Name is Base_Type_Name [range L .. U];
```

Here is another example.

```
type Day_Type is (Sun, Mon, Tue, Wed, Thu, Fri, Sat);
subtype Work_Week_Subtype is Day_Type range Mon .. Fri;
```

The base type of Work_Week_Subtype is Day_Type. The set of values for objects of Work_Week_Subtype is Mon, Tue, Wed, Thu, and Fri. The set of operations that can be performed on objects of Work_Week_Subtype is the same as the set applicable to enumeration types, listed in Table 5-3.

More than one subtype may be constructed from a base type, as in

```
type Month_Type is (Jan, Feb, Mar, Apr, May, Jun,
                    Jul, Aug, Sep, Oct, Nov, Dec);
subtype Spring_Subtype is Month_Type range Mar .. May;
subtype Summer_Subtype is Month_Type range Jun .. Aug;
subtype First_Quarter_Subtype is
        Month_Type range Jan .. Mar;
```

A subtype may be constructed from another subtype, as in

```
subtype First_Half_Subtype is Month_Type range Jan .. Jun;
subtype First_Quarter_Subtype  is
           First_Half_Subtype range Jan .. Mar;
```

The base type of a subtype of a subtype is the base type of the first subtype. Thus, the base type of First_Quarter_Subtype in our example is Month_Type.

Two subtypes are predefined by the Ada language. They are:

```
subtype Natural is Integer range 0 .. Integer'Last;
subtype Positive is Integer range 1 .. Integer'Last;
```

The range of values specified in a subtype declaration must be consecutive values of the base type. Thus the following

```
                    --**ILLEGAL**--
subtype Weekend_Subtype is Day_Type range Sat .. Sun;
```

is an illegal subtype declaration because the values Sat and Sun are not consecutive values of Day_Type.

Object Declarations

Objects of a subtype are declared exactly as you would expect. To declare such objects, use this syntax:

```
Object_Name : Subtype_Name [range L .. U]
              [:= Initial_Value];
Object_Name : constant Subtype_Name := Initial_Value;
```

For example,

```
VHF_Channel : VHF_Channel_Subtype;
UHF_Channel : UHF_Channel_Subtype;
```

or

```
Summer_Month : Summer_Subtype;
Spring_Month : Spring_Subtype;
```

or

```
PBS : constant VHF_Channel_Subtype := 13;
```

Objects of the base type and objects of any subtype of the base type may be mixed in expressions. For example, suppose the following had been declared and, during execution, had been assigned legal values.

```
Today : Day_Type;
Next_Work_Day : Work_Day_Subtype;
```

The following is then legal.

```
if Today = Next_Work_Day then -- legal comparison
   Go_To_Work;
else
   Sleep_Late;
end if;
```

Objects of different subtypes of the same base type may also be mixed in any expression.

Assignment is permitted between base type and subtype, or between subtypes, as long as the value of the expression is within the range of values allowed for the object being assigned to. For example,

```
Today := Sun;
```

is a legal assignment, but

```
Next_Workday := Sun;  --**ILLEGAL**--
```

is illegal because Sun is not a legal value of Work_Day_Subtype and therefore cannot be assigned to Next_Workday. Similarly, the assignment

```
Next_Workday := Today;
```

will raise Constraint_Error if the value of Today is Sat or Sun. In general, if the value of the expression on the right-hand side of an assignment statement is within the range of values allowed for the type of the object being assigned to, the assignment will take place, but if the value is outside the range of allowed values, Constraint_Error will be raised.

A similar situation occurs when passing objects of one subtype to a formal parameter of another subtype or when passing an actual parameter of a base type to a formal parameter of one of its subtypes. Figure 7-2(a–c) shows Exercise 3.13 recoded using subtypes.

Factorial_of expects a parameter of type Natural, but it is actually passed a parameter of type Positive. As long as the constraints on the formal parameter are satisfied by the actual parameter, there is no problem. Here any actual parameter of type Positive is clearly within the set of values for type Natural. To pass a negative integer value to Factorial_of would raise Constraint_Error, however.

By the way, notice that performing I/O step 2 on the *base type* permits I/O on the base type and its subtypes. Step 2 does not need to be performed for each subtype.

FIGURE 7-2 Factorials with subtypes

```
with Text_IO; use Text_IO;
procedure Compute_Factorials is
   Last_Number : Positive; -- filters negative values and 0
   package Fact_IO is new Integer_IO (Integer);
   use Fact_IO;
   procedure Get_Last(Number : out Positive) is separate;
   function Factorial_of(Number : Natural)
            return Natural is separate;
begin -- Compute_Factorials
   Get_Last (Last_Number);
   for Value in 1 .. Last_Number
   loop
      Put (Factorial_of (Value));
      New_Line;
   end loop;
exception
   when Numeric_Error =>
      Put_Line ("Result too large, terminating...");
end Compute_Factorials;
```

FIGURE 7-2(a) The main program

```
separate (Compute_Factorials)
function Factorial_of (Number : Natural) return Natural is
   -- We have written enough of these.
end Factorial_of;
```

FIGURE 7-2(b) Subunit Factorial_of

```
separate (Compute_Factorials)
procedure Get_Last (Number : out Positive) is
  -- We have written enough of these.
end Get_Last;
```

FIGURE 7-2(c) Subunit Get_Last

EXERCISES

7.6 Recode procedure Compute_Factorials_1_to_10 of Section 5.4 using the following package specification:

```
package Another_Factorial_Package is
   subtype Argument_Subtype is Integer range 0 .. 20;
   subtype Result_Subtype is
           Integer range 0 .. Integer'Last;
   function Factorial_of (Value: Argument_Subtype)
           return Result_Subtype;
end Another_Factorial_Package;
```

a. What modifications were made to the procedure as coded in Section 5.4 and why?
b. Code the function body for Factorial_of. Is type conversion required? Why or why not?

8

CONSTRAINED ARRAY TYPES

CHAPTER OBJECTIVES

- Declare one-dimensional and multidimensional constrained array types.
- Declare objects of constrained array types.
- Access components of single-dimensional and multidimensional constrained arrays.
- Take slices of one-dimensional arrays.
- Write array aggregates in positional or named notation.
- Use the attributes applicable to one-dimensional and multidimensional constrained arrays.
- Perform I/O on constrained arrays.
- Declare anonymous arrays.

Until now we have dealt almost exclusively with types that have a single component, that is, *scalar* types. *Composite* types—types that may have more than one component—are the subject of this and the next few chapters.

There are two composite types in Ada, *arrays* and *records* (see Figure 8-1). Both types provide a mechanism for grouping related data into one structure. Arrays group components of the same type, while records group components of possibly differing types. See Figure 8-2(a,b) for a review of the basic characteristics of an array. Records are the topic of Chapter 11.

Ada has two kinds of arrays, *constrained* and *unconstrained* (see Figure 8-3). Constrained arrays define the lower and upper bounds for each index at type declaration time. Unconstrained arrays do not have their bounds known at type declaration time. Constrained arrays are the subject of this chapter, while unconstrained arrays are addressed in Chapter 10.

FIGURE 8-1 Composite data types

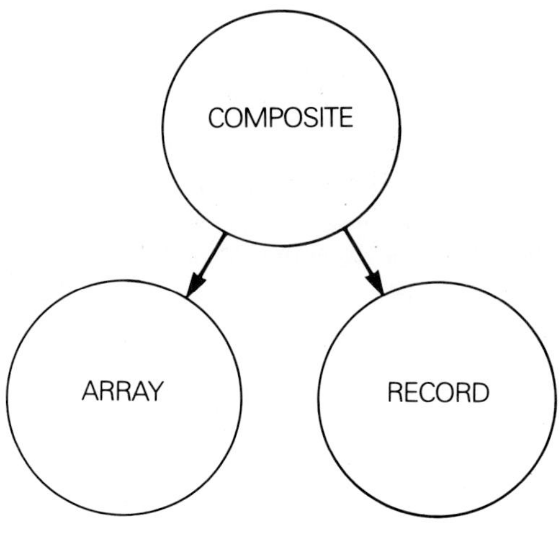

FIGURE 8-2 Array characteristics: dimension, index, component

```
type Point_Type is array (1 .. 2) of Integer;
```

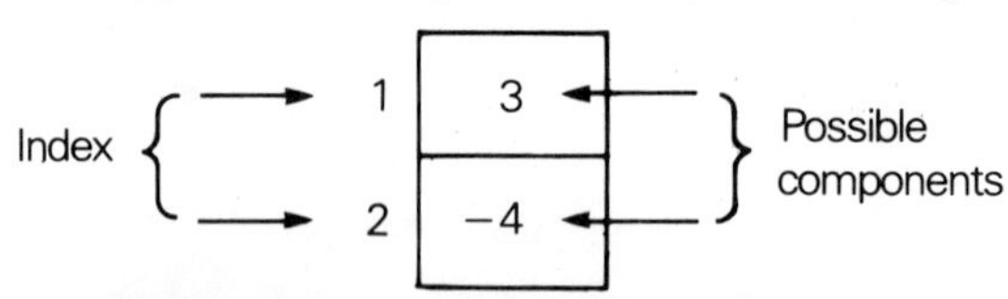

FIGURE 8-2(a) One dimension

FIGURE 8-2(b) Two dimensions

```
type Bit_Type is range 0 .. 1;
type Memory_Type_2 is array (0 .. 255, 0 .. 7) of Bit_Type;
```

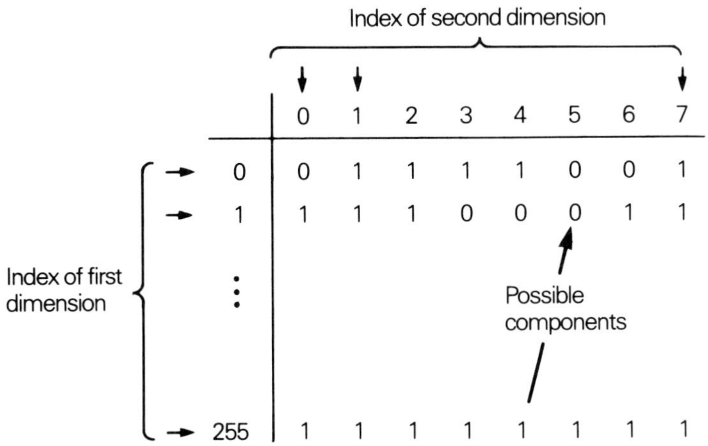

FIGURE 8-3 Composite data types

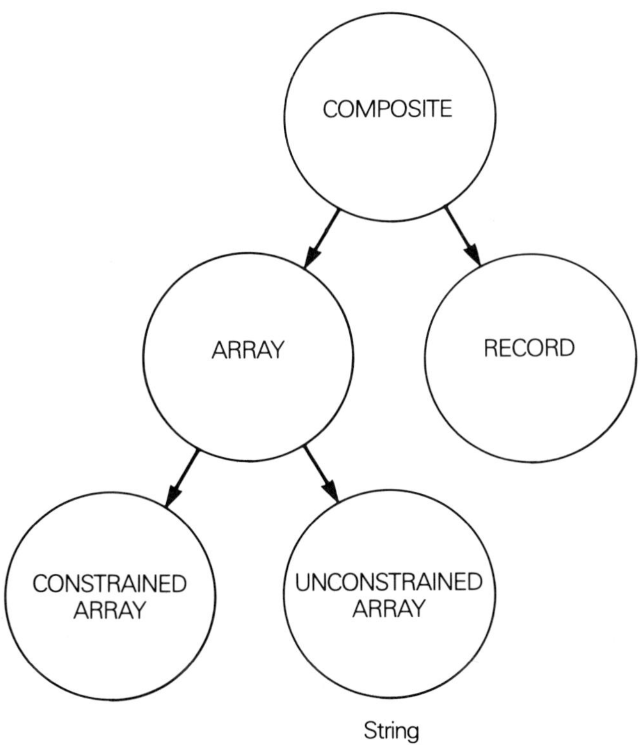

8.1 Type Declarations (LRM 3.6)

Package Simple_Graphics from Chapter 1 contained a declaration for a constrained array named Point_Type.

```
package Simple_Graphics is
   type Point_Type is array (1 .. 2) of Integer;
   procedure Draw_Line (From, To : in Point_Type);
   procedure Draw_Circle (Center : in Point_Type;
                          Radius : in Integer);
end Simple_Graphics;
```

Point_Type is a constrained array type because the bounds of the index, (1 . . 2), are specified in the type declaration.

The syntax of a constrained array type declaration is

```
type Array_Type_Name is array (index {,index})
     of Component_Type_Name;
```

where Array_Type_Name is a legal Ada identifier and index is any discrete range, discrete type (with or without a range constraint), or subtype of a discrete type (with or without a range constraint). *Discrete* means belonging to the class of Integer or Enumeration types. Component_Type_Name specifies the type of the component. Array components in Ada basically may be any type, either scalar or composite. (There are a couple of exceptions, which will be pointed out at the appropriate time.) The number of indices denotes the dimensionality of the array.

One-Dimensional Arrays

The following are legal one-dimensional constrained array type declarations:

```
type Grade_Type is range 0 .. 100;
type List_of_Grades_Type is array (1 .. 25) of Grade_Type;
```

Here a discrete range, 1 . . 25, defines the index. List_of_Grades_Type defines a list of 25 student grades. Each component is of type Grade_Type, specifically an integer in the range 0 to 100.

```
type Rainfall_Type is digits 4 range 0.0 .. 15.0;
type Cumulative_Rainfall_Type
     is array (1 .. 24) of Rainfall_Type;
```

Here again a discrete range, 1 . . 24, is used to specify the index. Cumulative_Rainfall_Type defines an array type containing 24 cumulative rainfall readings, assuming not more than 15.0 inches of rain falls in any 24-hour period.

Consider the declarations

```
type Hours_Worked_Type is digits 3 range 0.0 .. 12.0;
type Day_Type is (Sun, Mon, Tue, Wed, Thu, Fri, Sat);
type Time_Card_Type
     is array (Day_Type) of Hours_Worked_Type;
```

with a discrete type, Day_Type, specifying the index. Time_Card_Type is a list of hours worked, maximum 12.0, for every day of the week. The index is any value in the range Sun through Sat. The components are of the floating point type Hours_Worked_Type and are restricted to the range 0.0 to 12.0 inclusive.

Similarly, one could write

```
type Another_Time_Card_Type is array
        (Day_Type range Mon .. Fri) of Hours_Worked_Type;
```

This declaration uses the discrete type name, Day_Type, with a range constraint, **range** Mon . . Fri, to specify the index. Another_Time_Card_Type defines a list of hours worked during Monday through Friday only.

The following declarations

```
type Bit_Type is range 0 .. 1;
type Byte_Type is array (0 .. 7) of Bit_Type;
```

models an eight-bit byte. An index of 0 is allowed in Ada, as are negative indices. Consider

```
type Fahrenheit_Degrees_Type is range -60 .. 120;
type Count_of_Temps
     is array (Fahrenheit_Degrees_Type) of Natural;
```

which can be used to indicate how many times a particular temperature was recorded.

Finally

```
type Memory_Type_1 is array (0 .. 255) of Byte_Type;
```

uses an array of arrays to model a memory of 256 bytes. As previously stated, the components of an array may be composite. Here a component of an object of Memory_Type_1 is an array of type Byte_Type.

Multidimensional Arrays

Arrays in Ada may have multiple dimensions, as indicated by the appearance of {,index} in the syntax for the type declaration. The following are legal constrained array declarations for multidimensional arrays.

```
type Matrix_Type is array (1 .. 3, 1 .. 3) of Integer;
```

defines 3×3 matrices with integer components.

```
type Inventory_Count_Type is range 0 .. 100;
type Stock_Item_Type is (Izod_Shirts, Izod_Shorts);
type Size_Type is range 1 .. 7;
type Current_Inventory_Type
     is array (Stock_Item_Type, Size_Type)
     of Inventory_Count_Type);
```

declares a two-dimensional array type to maintain an inventory for Izod shirts and shorts in sizes 1 to 7 inclusive. Note that the indices of multidimensional arrays may be of different types.

```
type Bit_Type is range 0 .. 1;
type Memory_Type_2 is array (0 .. 255, 0 .. 7)
     of Bit_Type;
```

uses a two-dimensional array to model a memory of 256 bytes.

Ada places no limit on the number of dimensions in an array type declaration.

8.2 Object Declarations (LRM 3.2)

Objects of an array type are declared as usual. The following

```
A_Point : Point_Type;
```

declares the object A_Point to be an object of type Point_Type. A_Point has this structure:

A_Point

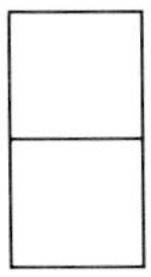

A_Point consists of two components, each of type Integer.

The declaration

```
Small_Memory_1 : Memory_Type_1;
```

declares Small_Memory_1 to be an object of Memory_Type_1. Small_Memory_1 therefore has the following structure:

	0	1	2 3 4 5 6	7
0				
1				
2				
⋮				
255				

The declaration

```
Current_Inventory : Current_Inventory_Type;
```

creates the following structure:

	1	2 3 4 5 6	7
Izod shirts			
Izod shorts			

What structure does the object declaration

```
Small_Memory_2 : Memory_Type_2;
```

create? Is it the same as Small_Memory_1?

constant Objects

Constant array objects may be declared, for example,

```
Mask : constant Byte_Type := (1,1,1,1,1,1,1,1);
```

Mask can now be compared to consecutive bytes of Small_Memory_1.

Constant array objects are declared by writing the reserved word **constant** after the colon, as in

```
Name : constant Array_Type_Name := Aggregate;
```

As with other constants, constant array objects may not have their components changed. *Aggregates* are discussed in the next section.

8.3 Aggregate (LRM 4.3)

Variable array objects may be initialized; constant array objects *must* be initialized. To write a value for an array, list in parentheses a value of the component type for each component in the array. Separate the values by commas like this:

```
A_Point : Point_Type := (3,-4);
A_Byte  : Byte_Type  := (1,1,1,1,0,1,0,1);
```

or like this:

```
A_Point  : Point_Type  := (3,  -4);
A_Byte   : Byte_Type   := (1,  1,  1,  1,  0,  1,  0,  1);
```

The quantities (3, −4) and (1,1,1,1,0,1,0,1), written with or without spaces, are called *aggregates*.

These four aggregates are written in positional notation: the first value in the list is associated with the first index position, the second value in the list is associated with the second index position, and so on. Aggregates may also be written in named notation, where the index position to be associated with a specific value is explicitly named, as in

```
A_Point : Point_Type := (1 => 3, 2 => -4);
A_Byte  : Byte_Type  := (0 => 1, 1 => 1, 2 => 1, 3 => 1,
                         4 => 0, 5 => 1, 6 => 0, 7 => 1);
```

Positional and named notation may not both be used within the *same* dimension, but different notations may be used for *different* dimensions. The following object declaration

```
Current_Inventory : Current_Inventory_Type
      := (Izod_Shirts => (10,15,25,25,25,25,25),
          Izod_Shorts => (20,20,20,35,20,20,5) );
```

is legal and uses named notation for the first dimension and positional notation for the second dimension. The following is an illegal initialization of Current_Inventory.

```
                  --**ILLEGAL**--
Current_Inventory : Current_Inventory_Type
      := (Izod_Shirts => (10,15,25,20,30,5,12),
          (20,20,20,35,12,10,5) );
```

Named notation and positional notation may not both be used to initialize the first dimension.

others Option

When writing an aggregate, you may use an **others** option to name the value to be associated with those index positions not otherwise specified. For example,

```
A_Byte  : Byte_Type  := (4 => 0, 6 => 0, others => 1);
Current_Inventory : Current_Inventory_Type :=
                 (Izod_Shirts =>(1=>10, 2=>15, others=>25),
                  Izod_Shorts =>(4=>35, 7=>5, others=>20) );
Another_Byte : Byte_Type := (0, 0, others => 1);
```

The **others** option may be used with either positional or named notation. When the **others** option is used, it must appear last.

8.4 Accessing Components (LRM 4.1.1)

The identifier A_Point references the entire array object. To reference a single component of an array in Ada, write the array object name directly followed by the index of the specific component desired contained within parentheses—for example, A_Point(1) or A_Point(2). If A_Point had been initialized to (3, −4) like this,

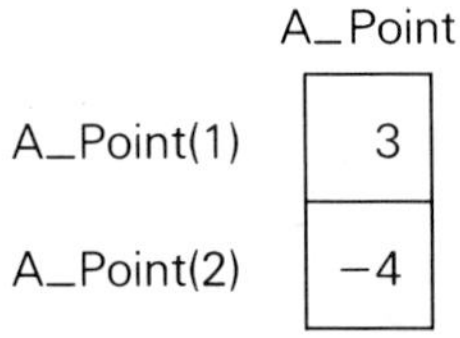

then A_Point(1) equals 3 and A_Point(2) equals −4. A_Point(1) and A_Point(2) are objects of type Integer and may be used in any legal Integer expression, for example,

```
A_Point(1) ** 2 + A_Point(2) ** 2
```

They may also be compared to integer literals, integer constants, or a named number, as in

```
A_Point(1) = 0
```

It is important to remember that A_Point is an *array* object consisting of two components, A_Point(1) and A_Point(2). A_Point(1) and A_Point(2) are objects of type Integer.

Similarly, Small_Memory_1(0) references the first component of Small_Memory_1 and is of type Byte_Type. Therefore Small_Memory_1(0) references an *array*. To access the third bit of the array referenced by Small_Memory_1(0), write Small_Memory_1(0)(2). Again you follow the array object name, Small_Memory_1(0), with the specific index position desired, 2, contained in parentheses [see Figure 8-4(a)].

To access a component of a multidimensional array, follow the name of the object by specific index positions for *each* dimension, separated by a comma, enclosed in parentheses. The following

```
Small_Memory_2(0,2)
```

references the third bit in the first byte [see Figure 8-4(b)].

When choosing a representation for an array type, think about what kind of access to the data will be required. For example, modeling memory as an array of bytes makes both byte and bit access possible, whereas modeling memory as a two-dimensional array of bits permits only bit access.

Slice (LRM 4.1.2)

Consecutive components of an array may be accessed by writing a *slice*. A slice is written as follows:

```
Array_Object_Name (Beginning_Position .. Ending_Position)
```

FIGURE 8-4 Accessing array components

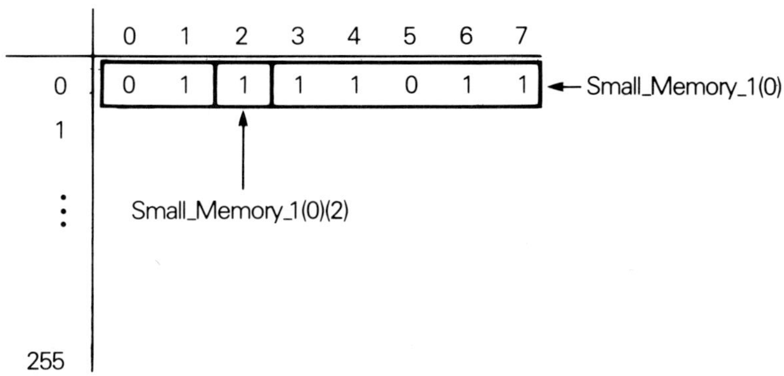

FIGURE 8-4(a) Accessing component of one-dimensional array

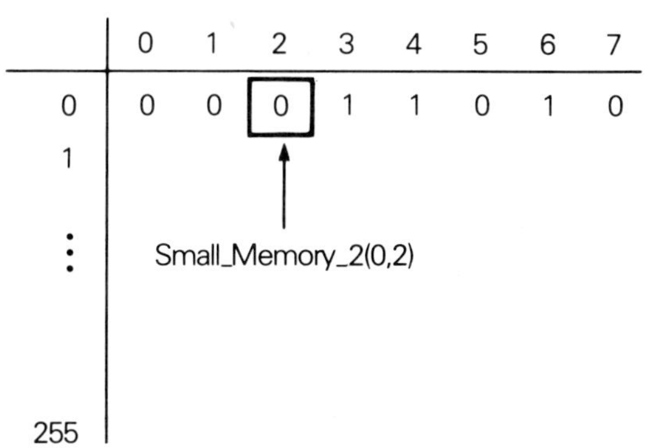

FIGURE 8-4(b) Accessing component of multidimensional array

For example, given the following type and object declarations

```
type Grade_Type is range 0 .. 100;
type List_of_Grades_Type is array (1 .. 25) of Grade_Type;
Ada101 : List_of_Grades_Type;
```

the following slice

```
Ada101(1 .. 10)
```

selects the grades for the first 10 students, while the slice

```
Ada101(5 .. 15)
```

selects the grades for the fifth through fifteenth students. Similarly, the following slice

```
Small_Memory_1(0) (2 .. 5)
```

selects the third through the sixth bits of the array referenced by Small_Memory_1(0).

Slices are applicable to one-dimensional arrays only, including arrays of arrays.

8.5 Array Attributes (LRM 3.6.2)

The four attributes applicable to constrained arrays are

First Last Range Length

Each attribute may be applied to either an array type name or an array object.

First returns the lower bound of the index. Thus, Small_Memory_1'First yields 0.

Last returns the upper bound of the index. Small_Memory_1'Last yields 255.

Range returns the range of the index. Small_Memory_1'Range yields 0 . . 255.

Length returns the number of values in the index range. Small_Memory_1'Length yields 256.

Given the type declarations

```
type Array_Type is array (1 .. 10) of Float;
subtype Position_Subtype is Integer range 1 .. 10;
```

the following procedure inserts an element into an array at the specified position and, starting there, shifts all elements one position to the right. The last element in the array is lost.

```
procedure Insert (X: in out Array_Type;
                  Position : in Position_Subtype;
                  Item     : in Float ) is
begin -- Insert
        for I in reverse Position+1 .. Array_Type'Last
        loop
              X(I) := X(I-1);
        end loop;
        X(Position) := Item;
end Insert;
```

There is a lot of room for coding errors here. The loop must use the **reverse** option to avoid overwriting values. The lower bound of the iteration range starts at Position +1, not Position. Finally, the coder must be careful not to overwrite the inserted value.

In Ada, slices and attributes combined provide a less error-prone solution. Consider

```
procedure Insert (X: in out Array_Type;
                  Position: in Position_Subtype;
                  Item: in Float ) is
begin --Insert
   X(Position+1 .. X'Last):= X(Position .. X'Last-1);
   X(Position)    := Item;
end Insert;
```

For multidimensional arrays, an attribute is applied to a specific dimension by suffixing the attribute name with the specific dimension desired, enclosed within parentheses. Small_Memory_2'First(1) yields the lower bound of the index of the first dimension, 0. Small_Memory_2'First(2) yields the lower bound of the second dimension, 0. Small_Memory_2'Last(1) yields 255, and Small_Memory_2'Last(2) yields 7. Small_Memory_2'Range(1) yields 0. .255, and Small_Memory_2'Range(2) yields 0. .7.

When a dimension is not specified, the first dimension is selected by default. For example, Small_Memory_2'First(1) and Small_Memory_2'First both yield 0. It is a good convention to always explicitly state the dimension desired for a multidimensional array. Doing so guarantees that the maintainer of the code is aware that the code is referencing a multidimensional array.

As stated before, array attributes may be applied to a constrained array type name. For example, Memory_Type_1'First yields 0, Memory_Type_1'Last yields 255, Memory_Type'Range yields 0..255, and Memory_Type_1'Length yields 256. Similarly, Memory_Type_2'First(2) yields 0, and Memory_Type_2'Length(2) yields 8.

8.6 Anonymous Array Objects

An array type declaration defines a type. A type, in turn, defines a set of values and a set of operations that can be performed on objects of that type. There are times, however, when an array structure is appropriate, yet there is no need for multiple objects of that structure; only one object is required.

For example, Exercise 6.1 defined a relationship between D, E, H, L, P, and Q and the commands Debug, Edit, Help, List, Print, and Quit. This is clearly an array structure, with indices D, E, H, L, P, and Q and components Debug, Edit, Help, List, Print, and Quit. Given the following:

```
type Input_Type is (D, E, H, L, P, Q);
type Command_Type is (Debug, Edit, Help, List, Print, Quit);
```

does the following make sense?

```
type Mapping_Type is array (Input_Type) of Command_Type;
     Mapping : Mapping_Type
             := (Debug, Edit, Help, List, Print, Quit);
```

Because the type declaration for Mapping_Type exists, other objects of type Mapping_Type may be declared. However, there is no need for this capability in this problem. We require only one array object to represent the desired mapping from input character to expanded command, and this object really just needs to be read.

Ada provides the capability to create just one array object, which is called an *anonymous array object*. To declare an anonymous array object, write

```
Name : array (index {, index}) of Component_Type
     [:= Aggregate];
```

or

```
Name : constant array (index {, index}) of Component_Type
     [:= Aggregate]:
```

depending on whether you want a variable or a constant object. In either case, the object cannot be passed as an actual parameter because it belongs to an *anonymous* array type.

To express the relationship of the input character to the expanded command in Exercises 6.1–6.3, write

```
Mapping : constant array (Input_Type) of Command_Type
        := (Debug, Edit, Help, List, Print, Quit);
```

By declaring an anonymous array object, the code clearly indicates that there is no firm requirement in the problem to have multiple objects expressing this relationship.

The expanded command problem is now coded as follows:

```
with Text_IO; use Text_IO;
procedure Expand_Command is
   type Input_Type is (D, E, H, L, P, Q);
   type Command_Type is (Debug, Edit, Help, List, Print,
                         Quit);
   Input : Input_Type;
   Expanded_Command : Command_Type;
   Expansion_of
      : constant array (Input_Type) of Command_Type
      := (Debug, Edit, Help, List, Print, Quit);
   package Input_IO is new Enumeration_IO (Input_Type);
   package Command_IO is new Enumeration_IO (Command_Type);
   use Input_IO, Command_IO;
   procedure Get_an (Input : out Input_Type) is separate;
begin -- Expand_Command
   Get_an (Input);
   Expanded_Command := Expansion_of (Input);
   Put (Expanded_Command);
end Expand_Command;
```

8.7 Operations on Array Types (LRM 3.6.2)

Table 8-1 lists the operations, in addition to component selection and attributes, that can be performed on array objects.

Assignment and tests for equality and inequality are defined for both one-dimensional arrays and multidimensional arrays. Catenation, relational operators, and logical operators are defined only for one-dimensional arrays. Furthermore, the logical operators are defined only for those one-dimensional arrays

TABLE 8-1 Array Operations

One-Dimensional Arrays		*Multidimensional Arrays*
:=	Assignment for	array or component of array
= /=	Test for equality/inequality for	array or component of array
&	Catenation	none
< <= > >=	(discrete components only)	none
not xor and or	(Boolean components only)	none

whose components are of type Boolean, and the relational operators are defined only for those one-dimensional arrays with discrete components.

The operations should be self-explanatory, with the possible exception of catenation. Catenation is discussed in Section 10.4.

8.8 Array I/O (LRM 14.3.10)

There are no Text_IO resources applicable to arrays in Ada. Textual I/O on array objects is performed on a component-by-component basis. Each component must be input or output, one at a time. In each case, import Text_IO as usual (step 1), then perform step 2 for the type of the *array component.*

For example, the following inputs two points from the terminal and draws a line between them.

```
with Simple_Graphics; use Simple_Graphics;
with Text_IO; use Text_IO; -- import Text_IO
procedure Illustrate_Array_IO is
   Point_1, Point_2 : Point_Type; -- the two points
   -- Step 2 for the type of the array component,
   -- Integer
   package Int_IO is new Integer_IO (Integer);
   use Int_IO;
   procedure Get_A_Point (Point : out Point_Type)
             is separate;
begin -- Illustrate_Array_IO
   loop
      Get_A_Point (Point_1); -- obtain first point
      Get_A_Point (Point_2); -- obtain second point
      Draw_Line (Point_1, Point_2);
   end loop;
end Illustrate_Array_IO;
```

where Get_A_Point is coded as

```
separate (Illustrate_Array_IO)
procedure Get_A_Point (Point : out Point_Type) is
   procedure Get_A_Coordinate (Coordinate : out Integer)
      is separate;
begin -- Get_A_Point
   -- obtain first component of point
   Get_A_Coordinate (Point(1));
   -- obtain second component of point
   Get_A_Coordinate (Point(2));
end Get_A_Point;
```

and Get_A_Coordinate is coded as

```
separate (Illustrate_Array_IO.Get_A_Point)
procedure Get_A_Coordinate (Coordinate : out Integer) is
begin -- Get_A_Coordinate
   loop
      begin
         Get (Coordinate);
         exit;
      exception
         when Data_Error =>
               Put_Line ("Invalid entry.");
               Put_Line ("Enter only integer values.");
      end;
   end loop;
end Get_A_Coordinate;
```

8.9 Sort

Consider Figure 8-5(a–d), which inputs an array of grades, sorts the array in ascending order, and outputs the sorted array.

The output routine is simpler to code because Output_Sorted is assured of valid values for each component of the array.

If the size of the class were to change to 22 students next year, only the type declaration for Size_of_Class_Type would require modification because the number 25 appears only in the type declaration for Size_of_Class_Type. The type *name,* Size_of_Class_Type, is used to specify the index in Grade_List_Type. The executable code uses attributes.

FIGURE 8-5 Procedure Sort

```
with Text_IO; use Text_IO;
procedure Sort is
  type Size_Type is range 1 .. 25;
  subtype Grade_Subtype is Integer range 0 .. 100;
  type Grade_List_Type is array (Size_Type)
                      of Grade_Subtype;
  Grade_List : Grade_List_Type; -- the array of
                                -- 25 grades
  Sorted      : Boolean := False;
  package Grade_IO is new Integer_IO (Grade_Subtype);
  use Grade_IO;
  -- to get the list of grades and
  -- print the list of grades
  procedure Input ( List : out Grade_List_Type)
            is separate;
  procedure Output_Sorted (List : in Grade_List_Type)
            is separate;
  procedure Swap (Value_1,Value_2: in out Grade_Subtype)
            is separate;
begin -- Sort
   Input (Grade_List);  -- get the list of grades
   while not Sorted  -- a simple bubble sort
   loop
       -- Assume list sorted. If no interchanges
       -- made in the loop,
       -- the list is not examined again.
      Sorted := True;
      for J in Size_Type'First .. Size_Type'Last-1
      loop
         if Grade_List(J) > Grade_List(J + 1) then
            Swap (Grade_List(J), Grade_List(J+1) );
            Sorted := False;
         end if;
      end loop;
   end loop;
   Output_Sorted (Grade_List); -- print the grades
end Sort;
```

FIGURE 8-5(a) The main program

FIGURE 8-5 *(continued)*

```
separate (Sort)
procedure Input ( List : out Grade_List_Type) is
begin -- Input
   for I in Size_Type
   loop   -- outer loop to obtain grade for each student
      loop -- inner loop to ensure valid grade
         begin
            Get ( List(I) );
            exit;
         exception
            when Data_Error =>
               Put_Line ("Invalid entry.");
               Put_Line ("Enter integer value between" &
                         "0 and 100");
         end;
      end loop;
   end loop;
end Input;
```

FIGURE 8-5(b) Subunit Input

```
separate (Sort)
procedure Output_Sorted ( List : in Grade_List_Type) is
begin -- Output_Sorted
   for I in Size_Type
   loop
      Put ( List(I) );
      New_Line;
   end loop;
end Output_Sorted;
```

FIGURE 8-5(c) Subunit Output_Sorted

FIGURE 8-5 *(continued)*

```
separate (Sort)
procedure Swap(Value_1, Value_2 : in out Grade_Subtype) is
      Temp : Grade_Subtype := Value_1;
begin -- Swap
      Value_1 := Value_2;
      Value_2 := Temp;
end Swap;
```

FIGURE 8-5(d) Subunit Swap

EXERCISES

The package specification on p. 219 provides type declarations for a horse show. This horse show has six classes with six ribbons awarded in each class. First place is worth five points, second place is worth 3 points, third place is worth 2 points and fourth place is worth 1 point. There are no points awarded for fifth and sixth places. There are ten riders in the show, each with an entry number from 1 to 10. There are six classes in this show, numbered 1 to 6.

Use the package for Exercises 8.1 through 8.7.

8.1 Write a subprogram to input the winners of a specific class.

8.2 Write a subprogram to output the winners of a specific class.

8.3 Classes in a horse show are grouped into divisions. This show has two divisions, Equitation (Classes 1–3) and Hunter (Classes 4–6). The rider who accumulates the most points in the classes in a division is called the Champion of the division. The rider who accumulates the second highest number of points in a division is called the Reserve Champion of the division. Write a subprogram to determine the Champion and Reserve Champion of each division in the show.

8.4 Make any modifications required to keep track of points for all horse shows in New Jersey. The number of shows in New Jersey varies from year to year, but never exceeds 50.

```
with Text_IO; use Text_IO;
package Horse_Show_Types is
   type Place_Type is (First,Second,Third,Fourth );
   type Class_Type is range 1 .. 6;
   type Entry_Type is range 1 .. 10;
   type Champion_Type is ( Champion,Reserve );
   type Show_Type is range 1 .. 50;
   type Age_13_Type is ( Over, Under );
   subtype Equitation_Division_Subtype
           is Class_Type range 1 .. 3;
   subtype Hunter_Division_Subtype
           is Class_Type range 4 .. 6;
   subtype Total_Score_Subtype is Integer;
   subtype Point_Value_Subtype is Total_Score_Subtype
                       range 1 .. 5;
   type Winner_Array_Type is array(Class_Type,Place_Type)
                       of Entry_Type;
   type Accumulated_Scores_Type is array( Entry_Type )
                       of Total_Score_Subtype;
   type Champion_Array_Type is array( Champion_Type )
                       of Entry_Type;
   type All_Shows_Type is array( Show_Type )
                       of Winner_Array_Type;
   type Age_Array_Type is array( Entry_Type )
                       of Age_13_Type;
   Ribbon_Places_Array
      : constant array(Place_Type) of Point_Value_Subtype
      := ( 5,3,2,1 );
   package Entry_IO is new Integer_IO( Entry_Type );
   package Class_IO is new Integer_IO( Class_Type );
   package Place_IO is new Enumeration_IO( Place_Type );
   package Show_IO is new Integer_IO(Show_Type);
   package Age_13_IO is new Enumeration_IO(Age_13_Type);
end Horse_Show_Types;
```

8.5 Write a subprogram that determines the rider in New Jersey with the highest number of points and the rider with the second highest number of points.

8.6 Modify the system developed so far to categorize riders into two age groups, under 13 and over 13.

8.7 Determine the two riders who have accumulated the most points in both age groups in New Jersey. (This means determine four riders, two in each age group.)

9

FILE I/O

CHAPTER OBJECTIVES

- State the difference between an external file and an internal file.
- Declare file objects.
- Perform normal file I/O operations.
- Define Text_IO exceptions.
- Write handlers for the I/O exceptions.

It is not efficient to sit at a terminal and enter large amounts of data. A far more expedient method of entering and/or displaying data is to work with files. This chapter explains how Ada views a file and describes the subprograms provided by Text_IO for file management and file I/O.

9.1 File Object (LRM 14.1)

Ada considers a file to be an object, just like a variable or a constant. Therefore, for each file in an Ada program, you need to write an object declaration for a file of type File_Type as follows:

```
Internal_Name : File_Type;
```

where Internal_Name is a legal Ada identifier. (Type File_Type is declared in Text_IO.) For the remainder of the program, you will Get and Put to the file, as described below.

You may not read and write to the same Text_IO file at the same time. Text_IO files are either input (read) or output (write) files. We will show you shortly how to specify whether a file is an input file or an output file.

The following sections contain brief discussions of the most commonly used file management operations provided by Text_IO.* As you read these, keep in mind that an *internal file name* is the name by which an Ada program recognizes a file. An *external file name* is the name by which the operating system recognizes a file.

9.2 Text_IO Procedures (LRM 14.2.1,14.3.1)

Create (LRM 14.2.1)

A call to Create has the following form:

* The complete specification for Text_IO is found in Section 14.3.10 of the LRM.

```
Create (Internal_Name, Mode, "External_Name");
```

where Internal_Name is a legal identifier that represents the internal file name. Mode is either In_File or Out_File, to specify that the file is a read or a write file respectively. External_Name is a file name written according to the naming conventions of the operating system. This text follows the conventions of VAX VMS.*

Create is a procedure that creates an external file with the name specified by External_Name, associates that file with the internal file object specified by Internal_Name, sets the file to be either a read file or a write file as indicated by the Mode parameter, and leaves the file open. The exception Status_Error is raised if the file is already open. The exception Name_Error is raised if External_Name is not in conformance with the naming conventions of the operating system.

For example, the call

```
Create(Input_File, In_File, "data.dat");
```

creates a read-only file that will be referred to as Input_File within an Ada program and as data.dat by VAX VMS. The file data.dat is left open. The call

```
Create(Results_File, Out_File, "answer.dat");
```

creates a write-only file, known as Results_File within an Ada program and as answer.dat by VAX VMS, and leaves the file open.

Open (LRM 14.2.1)

A call to Open has the following form:

```
Open (Internal_Name, Mode, "External_Name");
```

Open associates the internal file specified by Internal_Name with the external file specified by External_Name, sets the file to the mode specified by the Mode parameter, and opens the file. The exception Status_Error is raised if

* VAX VMS is a registered trademark of Digital Equipment Corporation.

the file is already open. Name_Error is raised if the name specified by the Name parameter is not in conformance with the naming conventions of the operating system, or if no external file of that name exists.

Close (LRM 14.2.1)

A call to Close has the following form:

```
Close (Internal_Name);
```

Close removes the association between the internal file and the external file. The exception Status_Error is raised if the file is not open.

Delete (LRM 14.2.1)

A call to Delete has the following form:

```
Delete (Internal_Name);
```

Delete closes the named file and then deletes it. The exception Status_Error is raised if the file named is not open. The exception Use_Error is raised if deletion is not supported by the implementation.

Reset (LRM 14.2.1)

A call to Reset may have either of the following forms:

```
Reset (Internal_Name);
        or
Reset (Internal_Name, Mode);
```

The first form resets the named file so that reading or writing will start at the beginning of the file. The second form sets the mode of the named file to the mode specified in the call. For example,

```
Reset (Results_File, Out_File);
```

causes Results_File to become a write-only file, assuming of course that it was a read-only file prior to the call to Reset.

In either form, the exception Status_Error is raised if the file is not open. Some operating systems may not support resetting files. In that case, the exception Use_Error is raised by a call to Reset.

Set_Col (LRM 14.3.4)

A call to Set_Col takes the following form:

```
Set_Col (Internal_Name, Column_Number);
```

If the file named is of mode Out_File, a call to Set_Col causes the next output to start at the specified column number. If the specified column number is less than the current column number, the next output will start on the specified column number of the *next* line.

If the mode of the named file is In_File, a call to Set_Col causes reading to begin at the specified column.

New_Line (LRM 14.3.4)

To output a new line to a file, as opposed to the terminal, simply include Internal_Name as the first parameter and the number of new lines desired as the second parameter in a call to New_Line. If the second parameter is omitted, the next output will start on the first column of the next line. In other words, the default value for the second parameter is 1.

A call to New_Line takes this form:

```
New_Line (Internal_Name, Number);
```

New_Line is defined only for files of mode Out_File. The exception Mode_Error is raised if the file is not an Out_File.

New_Page (LRM 14.3.4)

A call to New_Page takes this form:

```
New_Page (Internal_Name);
```

It does exactly what you would expect it to do: makes the next output start on the first column of the first line of the next page.

New_Page is defined only for files of mode Out_File. The exception Mode_Error is raised if the file named is not an Out_File.

Get and Put for Files (LRM 14.3.6–14.3.9)

To obtain data from a file of mode in (In_File) or to write data to a file of mode out (Out_File), use Get and Put, respectively, with the internal file name as the first parameter.

```
Get (Internal_Name, Item);
Put (Internal_Name, Item);
```

Item represents the value to be input or output. As always, import Text_IO and perform step 2 for the type of the item to be read or written. It should come as no surprise that you may also use Put_Line to write text to a file by writing

```
Put_Line (Internal_Name,"Text to be written to the file");
```

9.3 Text_IO Functions (LRM 14.2.1, 14.3.3)

Is_Open (LRM 14.2.1)

The expression

```
Is_Open (Internal_Name)
```

returns True if the file is currently open, False otherwise.

Mode (LRM 14.2.1)

The expression

```
Mode (Internal_Name)
```

returns either In_File or Out_File, depending on whether the file is a read or a write file respectively.

Status_Error is raised if the named file is not currently open.

End_of_File (LRM 14.3.4)

The expression

```
End_of_File (Internal_Name)
```

returns True if there are no more elements to read, False otherwise.

The function End_of_File is defined only for files of type In_File. The exception Mode_Error is raised if the file is not an In_File.

End_of_Line (LRM 14.3.4)

The expression

```
End_of_Line(Internal_Name)
```

returns True if there are no more elements on the line or if the end of the file has been reached, False otherwise.

The function End_of_Line is only defined for files of mode In_File. The exception Mode_Error is raised if the mode of the file is not In_File.

9.4 Sort

Figure 9-1 shows the Sort program from the last chapter, recoded to obtain inputs from a file and output the sorted list to another file. The two subunits, Input and Output_Sorted, are shown in Figures 9-2(a) and 9-2(b), respectively.

Note that in the exception handlers for Name_Error in both Input and Output_Sorted and in the handler for Data_Error in Input, the exception is propagated to Sort so that Sort can display a message indicating that it is terminating abnormally. Reraising (or propagating) the exception in a handler is a technique that is often used to allow the caller to perform some last minute processing prior to terminating, and is coded by writing **raise;**. The statement

```
raise;
```

may only occur inside an exception handler and reraises the same exception that caused control to pass to the exception handler.

Suppose you want only one file; that is, after reading in the grades, you want to overwrite the input file by returning the sorted list to the same file. Using the Reset procedure, you attempt to recode Output_Sorted as shown in Figure 9-3.

You will find that the subunit does not compile. The file object Data_File was declared within Input and therefore is not accessible to Output_Sorted. (Even if Data_File were accessible, Input closes the file, and the call to Reset in Output_Sorted expects the file to be open. Status_Error therefore would have been raised.) Recode Sort using one file. Because only one file is to be used, the file must be declared within Sort so that it can be accessed by both Input and Output_Sorted. The code for Sort is shown in Figure 9-4.

FIGURE 9-1 Sort recoded using file I/O

```
with Text_IO; use Text_IO;
procedure Sort is
   type Size_Type is range 1 ..25;
   subtype Grade_Subtype is Integer range 0 .. 100;
   type Grade_List_Type is array (Size_Type)
                  of Grade_Subtype;
   Grade_List : Grade_List_Type;
   Sorted     : Boolean := False;
   package Grade_IO is new Integer_IO (Grade_Subtype);
   use Grade_IO;
   procedure Input ( List : out Grade_List_Type)
             is separate;
   procedure Output_Sorted (List : in Grade_List_Type)
             is separate;
   procedure Swap (Value_1,Value_2 : in out Grade_Subtype)
             is separate;
begin -- Sort
   Input (Grade_List);
   while not Sorted -- a simple bubble sort
   loop
      Sorted := True;
      for J in Size_Type'First..Size_Type'Last-1
      loop
         if Grade_List(J)  > Grade_List(J+1) then
            Swap (Grade_List(J), Grade_List(J+1));
            Sorted := False;
         end if;
      end loop;
   end loop;
   Output_Sorted (Grade_List);
exception
   -- handles the exceptions when reraised in the
   -- subunits by displaying a message to the terminal
   when Data_Error | Name_Error =>
      Put_Line ("Terminating main procedure" &
                ". . . . . . . . .");
end Sort;
```

FIGURE 9-2(a) Inputting data from a file

```
separate (Sort)
procedure Input ( List : out Grade_List_Type) is
   Data_File : File_Type; -- internal file declaration
                          -- File_Type declared in
                          -- Text_IO
begin -- Input
   begin
      -- associates internal file name Data_File with
      -- the external file name Data.dat and specifies that
      -- it is a read-only file
      Open (Data_File, In_File, "Data.dat");
   exception
      -- output message to the terminal
      when Status_Error =>
         Put_Line ("File already open, proceeding.");
   end;
   for I in Size_Type
   loop
      -- obtain grade for each student from the file
      Get ( Data_File, List(I) );
   end loop;
   Close (Data_File);
exception
   when Data_Error =>
         Put_Line ("Invalid file entry.");
         Put_Line ("File corrupted, terminating" &
                   "Input procedure.");
         Close (Data_File);
   raise;        -- reraises Data_Error to Sort so
                 -- Sort can terminate
   when Name_Error =>
         Put_Line ("Can't locate external file, check" &
                   "name.");
         Put_Line ("Terminating Input procedure.");
   raise;        -- reraises Name_Error to Sort so Sort
                 -- can terminate
end Input;
```

FIGURE 9-2(b) Outputting data to a file

```
separate (Sort)
procedure Output_Sorted ( List : in Grade_List_Type) is
   Results : File_Type;
begin -- Output_Sorted
   -- create Results.dat and leave it open
   Create (Results, Out_File, "Results.dat");
   for I in Size_Type
   loop   -- outer loop to handle multiple outputs
      -- output to the file
      Put ( Results, List(I) );
      New_Line (Results);
   end loop;
exception
   when Name_Error =>
      -- output message to terminal
      Put_Line ("Either invalid external file" &
                "name or file not present.");
      Put_Line ("Terminating Output procedure.");
   raise;     -- propagate exception to Sort so Sort
              -- can terminate
end Output_Sorted;
```

FIGURE 9-3 A futile attempt at one file

```
separate (Sort)
procedure Output_Sorted ( List : in Grade_List_Type) is
begin -- Output_Sorted
   Reset (Data_File, Out_File);   --**ILLEGAL**--
   for I in Size_Type
   loop
      Put ( Data_File, List(I) ); --**ILLEGAL**--
      New_Line (Data_File);       --**ILLEGAL**--
   end loop;
exception
   -- output messages to the terminal
   when Status_Error =>
      Put_Line ("File not open.");
      Put_Line ("Terminating . . . . . . . . . . .");
   when Use_Error =>
      Put_Line ("This operating system does not" &
                "support resetting.");
      Put_Line ("Terminating . . . . . . . . . . .");
end Output_Sorted;
```

FIGURE 9-4 A successful attempt for one file

```
with Text_IO; use Text_IO;
procedure Sort is
   type Size_Type is range 1 .. 25;
   subtype Grade_Subtype is Integer range 0 .. 100;
   type Grade_List_Type is array (Size_Type)
                    of Grade_Subtype;
   Grade_List  : Grade_List_Type;
   Sorted      : Boolean := False;
   Data_File   : File_Type;
   package Grade_IO is new Integer_IO (Grade_Subtype);
   use Grade_IO;
   procedure Input ( List : out Grade_List_Type)
                      is separate;
   procedure Output_Sorted (List : in Grade_List_Type)
                      is separate;
   procedure Swap(Value_1,Value_2 : in out Grade_Subtype)
                    is separate;
begin -- Sort
    begin
       Open (Data_File, In_File, "Data.dat");
    exception
       when Status_Error =>
          Put_Line ("File already open," &
                    "proceeding.");
          Put_Line ("Data may be corrupted.");
    end;
    Input (Grade_List);
    while not Sorted
    loop
       Sorted := True;
       for J in
       Size_Type'First..Size_Type'Last-1
       loop
          if Grade_List(J) > Grade_List(J + 1) then
          Swap (Grade_List(J), Grade_List(J+1));
          Sorted := False;
          end if;
       end loop;
    end loop;
```

(continued)

FIGURE 9-4 *(continued)*

```
   Output_Sorted (Grade_List);
   Close (Data_File);
exception -- this version of Sort terminates on any
          -- exception
   when Data_Error =>
         Put_Line ("Invalid file entry.");
         Put_Line ("File corrupted, terminating" &
                   "procedure.");
         Close (Data_File);
   when Name_Error =>
         Put_Line ("Incorrect external file name.");
         Put_Line ("Terminating . . . . . . . .");
   when Status_Error =>
         Put_Line ("File not open.");
         Put_Line ("Terminating . . . . . . . . . . .");
   when Use_Error =>
         Put_Line ("This operating system does not" &
                   "support Reset.");
         Put_Line ("Terminating . . . . . . . . . . .");
end Sort;
```

The two subunits for Sort are coded as follows:

```
separate (Sort)
procedure Input ( List : out Grade_List_Type) is
begin -- Input
   -- If Data_Error is raised, it is propagated to Sort
   -- because there is no handler here.
   for I in Size_of_Class_Type
   loop
      Get ( Data_File, List(I) );
   end loop;
end Input;
```

```
separate Sort
procedure Output_Sorted ( List : in Grade_List_Type) is
begin -- Output_Sorted
   -- If Reset raises Status_Error or Use_Error,
   -- the exception is propagated to Sort
   -- and handled in Sort.
   Reset (Data_File, Out_File);
   for I in Size_of_Class_Type
   loop
      Put ( Data_File, List(I) );
      New_Line (Data_File);
   end loop;
end Output_Sorted;
```

9.5 The Data File

Here is one way to construct the input file data.dat. The spaces between values are required.

68 98 75 78 86 99 100 65 57 0 78 88 75 75 75 75 80 88 92 55
94 97 87 88 100

The data could also have been aligned vertically, like this:

68
98
75
.
.
.
100

This can be done using an editor.

EXERCISES

9.1 Recode Exercise 3.13 to obtain *n* from a file and output the factorial table to a different file. Use A_Small_Factorial_Package from Section 5.5.

9.2 Using the following package, write a program to determine the mean of 10 test scores. Each score is between 0 and 100 and is found in a data file named Data_File.

```
package Statistics is
   type Score_Type is range 0 .. 100;
   type List_of_Grades is array (1 .. 10) of Score_Type;
   function Mean_of (Class_Grades : List_of_Grades)
            return Float;
   function Highest_of (Class_Grades : List_of_Grades)
            return Score_Type;
   function Lowest_of (Class_Grades : List_of_Grades)
            return Score_Type;
end Statistics;
```

9.3 Using the following package, obtain two complex numbers from an input file. Add, subtract, multiply, and divide the two numbers and output the results to another file.

```
package Complex_Numbers is
   type Real is digits 4;
   type Component is (Re, Im);
   type Complex_Type is array (Component) of Real;
   function Add (A, B : Complex_Type)
              return Complex_Type;
   function Subtract (A, B : Complex_Type)
              return Complex_Type;
   function Multiply (A, B : Complex_Type)
              return Complex_Type;
   function Divide   (A, B : Complex_Type)
              return Complex_Type;
end Complex_Numbers;
```

9.4 A vector is a $1 \times N$ matrix or an $N \times 1$ matrix. The magnitude of a vector V is defined as

$$\text{Magnitude} = \sqrt{v_1^2 + v_2^2 + v_3^2 + \ldots v_n^2}$$

where $V = (v_1, v_2, v_3, \ldots, v_n)$. A unit vector is a vector with a magnitude of 1.

Write a program to read a vector of 10 integer components from a file and determine whether the vector is a unit vector.

9.5 Using the following package, write a program that reads the entries of two 3 × 3 matrices from a file. Add, subtract, and multiply the two matrices and output the results to another file.

```
package Matrix_Operations is
   type Matrix_Type is array (1..3, 1..3) of Integer;
   function Add (One, Two : Matrix_Type)
              return Matrix_Type;
   function Subtract (One, Two : Matrix_Type)
              return Matrix_Type;
   function Multiply (One, Two : Matrix_Type)
              return Matrix_Type;
end Matrix_Operations;
```

9.6 Write a program to find the transpose of a 3 × 3 matrix.

9.7 Write a program to find the determinant of a 3 × 3 matrix.

9.8 Write a program to solve a system of three simultaneous equations using Cramer's Rule.

9.9 Write a program to search an array of 10 Fahrenheit temperatures for 32 degrees. If 32 degrees is an element of the array, output the position in the array occupied by that temperature. If 32 degrees is not an element of the array, output an appropriate message.

9.10 Write subprograms for each of the resources specified in package Statistics. Write drivers to determine their correctness.

9.11 Write subprograms for each of the resources specified in package Matrix_Operations. Write drivers to determine their correctness, obtaining test data from a file.

9.12 Write a program to sort two distinct lists of 15 integer components and then merge the two lists. In the merge do not discard duplicate entries. Read the two lists from a file and output the merged list to a file.

10

UNCONSTRAINED ARRAY TYPES

CHAPTER OBJECTIVES

- Declare one-dimensional and multidimensional unconstrained array types.
- Declare objects of unconstrained arrays.
- Access components of objects of unconstrained arrays.
- Use the attributes applicable to unconstrained array objects.
- Declare objects of the predefined type String.
- Perform I/O on objects of type String.
- Write String literals.
- Declare objects of the predefined type Character.
- Perform I/O on objects of type Character.
- Write Character literals.
- Code subprograms using unconstrained arrays for more flexible and reusable software.
- State the difference between constrained arrays and unconstrained arrays.

Constrained arrays specify the bounds on an index at type declaration time, as you learned in Chapter 8. Because of this, all objects of a specific constrained array type have the same size. There are situations, however, where objects of different sizes need to be of the same type. *Unconstrained arrays* permit objects of the same array type to have a different size and potentially different index bounds by leaving the specification of the index bounds until object declaration time or subtype declaration time.

10.1 Type Declarations (LRM 3.6)

Given the following constrained array type declaration,

```
type Vector_Type is array (1..10) of Positive;
```

the following object declaration

```
Vector_1, Vector_2 : Vector_Type;
```

declares two vectors of the same size. Both Vector_1 and Vector_2 have 10 components that are indexed by the numbers 1 to 10. In fact, *any* object that is declared to be of type Vector_Type will have exactly 10 components indexed by the numbers 1 to 10.

To declare an unconstrained array type, write

```
type Unconstrained_Array_Name is array
      (Discrete_Type range <>{,Discrete_Type range<>})
      of Constrained_Component_Type;
```

where Unconstrained_Array_Name is a legal Ada identifier, Discrete_Type is the name of a discrete type, and Constrained_Component_Type is the type of the component and, as its name suggests, must be constrained. In other words, you may not have an unconstrained array type as the component type of an unconstrained array. The symbol <> is read as "box" and acts as a placeholder for information that is to be supplied later.

Some examples of unconstrained array declarations follow.

```
type Vector_Type is array (Positive range <>) of Integer;
type Matrix_Type is array
      (Positive range <>, Positive range <>) of Integer;
type List_Type is array (Positive range <>) of Score_Type;
type Time_Sheet_Type is array (Day_Type range <>)
      of Hours_Worked_Type;
```

When declaring multidimensional unconstrained arrays, *each* dimension must be unconstrained.

10.2 Object Declarations (LRM 3.6.1)

When declaring an object of an unconstrained array type, you must specify the index bounds. Write an object declaration as follows:

```
Object_Name : Unconstrained_Array_Type(Index_Constraint)
              [:=Initial_Value];
```

or

```
Object_Name : constant Unconstrained_Array_Type
              := Initial_Value;
```

where Index_Constraint specifies the range of index values and is a discrete type or subtype name followed by an optional range constraint, a range attribute, or L . . U as previously described. Initial_Value is an aggregate written according to the rules of Section 8.3.

You must specify the bounds on the index explicitly when declaring a variable object of an unconstrained array type. When declaring a constant object of an unconstrained array type, however, you need not specify the bounds explicitly because the bounds are derived from the initial value.

10.3 Operations (LRM 3.6.2)

The operations allowed on objects of unconstrained array types are the same as those permitted for arrays in general, with one small exception. Whereas attributes were applicable to either a constrained array type or an object of a constrained array type, attributes are applicable only to *objects* of unconstrained array types. Why? What does List_Type'Range yield? What does Matrix_Type'Last(2) yield?

We will discuss the catenation operator shortly. First, however, we will present a small example to illustrate the use of unconstrained arrays in packages and the technique of declaring objects of an unconstrained array type for a specific problem.

10.4 Obtain_Test_Statistics

Consider the following package specification:

```
package Class_Roster is
   subtype Grade_Subtype is Natural range 0 .. 100;
   subtype Class_List_Type is array (Positive range <>)
            of Grade_Subtype;
   subtype Stats_Type is Float range 0.0 .. 100.0;
   function Mean_of (Class : Class_List_Type)
            return Stats_Type;
   function Median_of (Class : Class_List_Type)
            return Grade_Subtype;
   function Highest_Grade (Class : Class_List_Type)
            return Grade_Subtype;
   function Lowest_Grade (Class : Class_List_Type)
            return Grade_Subtype;
                                          . . .
end Class_Roster;
```

Class_List_Type is an unconstrained array type because the number of students in a class is not restricted to a specific number. Four functions in our package have Class_List_Type as the type of a formal parameter. But how can this be? How can subprograms calculate the mean or median without knowing what the bounds of the array are? The way this is done will become apparent shortly.

Let us now look at a small procedure that uses the resources of this package. Professor Smith is a part-time instructor at Ada Technical Institute. He teaches one Ada class each semester. This semester there are 26 students in his class. Professor Smith has coded the procedure shown in Figure 10-1, that allows him to obtain statistics on the test grades for his class. In the procedure, Ada_101 is declared as an object of Class_List_Type with an index constraint of 1. .26.

FIGURE 10-1 Declaring object of unconstrained array type

```
with Text_IO; use Text_IO;
with Class_Roster; use Class_Roster;
procedure Obtain_Test_Statistics is

   -- index constraint (1..26) for 26 students
   Ada_101 : Class_List_Type (1..26);

   Ada_101_File   : File_Type; -- the file of 26 grades
   Mean_Ada_101   : Stats_Type;
   Median_Ada_101 : Grade_Subtype;
   package Grade_IO is new Integer_IO (Grade_Subtype);
   package Stats_IO is new Float_IO (Float);
   use Grade_IO, Stats_IO;
   procedure Get_a_Grade (Grade_File : in File_Type;
      Grade : out Grade_SubType) is separate;
begin -- Obtain_Test_Statistics
   Open (Ada_101_File, In_File, "Ada_101.dat");
   for Student in Ada_101'Range
   loop
      -- exception handler purposefully not coded
      Get_a_Grade (Ada_101_File, Ada_101 (Student) );
   end loop;
   Mean_Ada_101    := Mean_of (Ada_101);
   Median_Ada_101  := Median_of (Ada_101);
   -- appropriate output statements
   Close (Ada_101_File);
end Obtain_Test_Statistics;
```

The **for** loop is executed 26 times because Ada_101'Range assumes the range 1. .26. When Ada_101 is passed as an actual parameter to the functions Mean_of and Median_of, the bounds of the formal parameter, Class, are taken from the bounds of the actual array object passed, here Ada_101. The bounds of Class for this invocation of Mean_of and Median_of are therefore 1. .26.

Use of the attribute Range creates a more flexible algorithm. Next semester, if Professor Smith has 22 students, he will need to change only the index constraint in the object declaration for Ada_101 and recompile. The executable code for Obtain_Test_Statistics will need no modification.

The coding of the subprograms declared in the package Class_Roster also relies heavily on attributes. For example, the code for Mean_of is as follows:

```
function Mean_of (Class : Class_List_Type)
   return Stats_Type is
   Sum : Natural := 0;
begin -- Mean_of
   for I in Class'Range
   loop
      Sum := Sum + Class(I);
   end loop;
   return Stats_Type(Sum)/Stats_Type(Class'Length);
end Mean_of;
```

The values for Class'Range and Class'Length are obtained from the actual parameter, Ada_101, when it is passed.

Finally, note that the index constraint does not have to be static. For example, the upper bound in the object declaration for Ada_101 could have been written as a function call. Writing the upper bound as a function call eliminates the requirement for modification and recompilation of the procedure. Consider the following function, which obtains the number of students from the terminal.

```
with Text_IO; use Text_IO;
function Number_of_Students return Positive is
   Value : Positive;
   package Int_IO is new Integer_IO (Integer);
   use Int_IO;
begin -- Number_of_Students
   Put_Line ("Enter number of students for this test: ");
   loop
      begin
         Get (Value);
         exit;
      exception
         when Data_Error => Put_Line ("Enter number" &
                               "of students as a value" &
                               "between 0 and 50.");
      end;
   end loop;
   return Value;
end Number_of_Students;
```

The procedure to obtain test statistics for Professor Smith's test is now recoded as in Figure 10-2. Now, for each new test, Professor Smith needs only to update Ada_101_File and re-execute the program.

Catenation Operator

The *catenation operator,* &, joins two one-dimensional arrays, a component and a one-dimensional array, or two components. In each case the result is another one-dimensional array.

Consider the following:

```
type Bit_Type is range 0..1;
type Byte_Type is array (0..7) of Bit_Type;
```

and

```
Byte_1 : Byte_Type := (1,1,0,0,1,1,0,0);
```

To rotate the bits in Byte_1 to the left, write

```
Byte_1 := Byte_1(1..7) & Byte_1(0);
```

FIGURE 10-2 Obtain_Test_Statistics recoded

```
with Text_IO; use Text_IO;
with Class_Roster; use Class_Roster;
with Number_of_Students; -- import the function
procedure Obtain_Test_Statistics is
    -- use a function call to set upper bound
    Ada_101 : Class_List_Type (1..Number_of_Students);
    Ada_101_File   : File_Type;
    Mean_Ada_101   : Stats_Type;
    Median_Ada_101 : Grade_SubType;
    package Grade_IO is new Integer_IO (Grade_SubType);
    package Stats_IO is new Float_IO (Float);
    use Grade_IO, Stats_IO;
    procedure Get_a_Grade (Grade_File : in File_Type;
         Grade : out Grade_SubType) is separate;
begin -- Obtain_Test_Statistics
    Open (Ada_101_File, In_File, "Ada_101.dat");
    for Student in Ada_101'Range
    loop
       Get_a_Grade (Ada_101_File, Ada_101 (Student));
    end loop;
    Mean_Ada_101   := Mean_of (Ada_101);
    Median_Ada_101 := Median_of (Ada_101);
    -- appropriate output statements
    Close (Ada_101_File);
end Obtain_Test_Statistics;
```

To rotate the bits in Byte_1 to the right, write

```
Byte_1 := Byte_1(7) & Byte_1(0..6);
```

The most common uses of catenation are to output strings that are too long for the line, and to output text and nonprintable characters in the same string. The call to Put_Line in the exception handler for Data_Error in function Number_of_Students is an example of the former. The latter is illustrated in Section 10.6.

10.5 Type String (LRM 3.6.3)

There is one predefined unconstrained array type in Ada, type String. The declaration for type String is

```
type String is (Positive range <>) of Character;
```

Type String is an unconstrained array with indices of type Positive and components of type Character. Type Character is discussed in the next section.

Object Declaration

Objects of type String are declared with a constraint, for example,

```
Last_Name : String (1..30);
```

If the object is being declared as a constant, a constraint need not be supplied. The bounds for the object are determined from the value supplied, as in

```
My_Logo : constant String := "AdaTEX";
```

Of course

```
My_Logo : constant String (1..6) := "AdaTEX";
```

is equally correct.

String Literal

A sequence of characters enclosed in quotes is called a *string literal.* Stated another way, a string literal is written by enclosing the desired characters—possibly none—in quotes. If the desired text includes a quotation mark, that quotation mark must be duplicated within the literal, for example,

```
Put_Line ("She said, ""Learning Ada is not that hard.""");
```

The outer quotes bracket the string literal. The double quotation represents the quotation character. The call displays the following:

She said, "Learning Ada is not that hard."

A string literal must not exceed the length of a line. If a string literal exceeds the length of a line, the catenation operator, &, may be used.

String I/O

I/O for type String is provided by Text_IO. There are four Put procedures, with declarations as follows:

```
procedure Put_Line (Item : in String);
procedure Put_Line (File : in File_Type; Item : in String);
procedure Put (Item : in String);
procedure Put (File : in File_Type; Item : in String);
```

There are four Get procedures for String in Text_IO. Their declarations follow:

```
procedure Get_Line (Item : out String; Last out Natural);
procedure Get_Line (File : in File_Type;
                    Item : out String; Last out Natural);
procedure Get (Item : out String);
procedure Get (File : File_Type; Item : out String);
```

The formal parameter named Last in the declaration for Get_Line indicates the index position of the last character read. If no characters are read, a value 1 less than the value of Item'First is returned in Last.

10.6 Type Character

Type Character is also predefined by Ada. The declaration for this type is shown in Figure 10-3. Type Character is an enumeration type, with values consisting of the 128 members of the ASCII character set.

Object Declaration

Objects of type Character are declared as usual. Write

```
Object_Name : Character [range L .. U] [:= Initial_Value];
```

or

```
Object_Name : constant Character := Initial_Value;
```

FIGURE 10-3 Type Character

```
type Character is
(nul,    soh,    stx,    etx,    eot,    enq,    ack,    bel,
 bs,     ht,     lf,     vt,     ff,     cr,     so,     si,
 dle,    dc1,    dc2,    dc3,    dc4,    nak,    syn,    etb,
 can,    em,     sub,    esc,    fs,     gs,     rs,     us,

 ' ',    '!',    '"',    '#',    '$',    '%',    '&',    ''',
 '(',    ')',    '*',    '+',    ',',    '-',    '.',    '/',
 '0',    '1',    '2',    '3',    '4',    '5',    '6',    '7',
 '8',    '9',    ':',    ';',    '<',    '=',    '>',    '?',

 '@',    'A',    'B',    'C',    'D',    'E',    'F',    'G',
 'H',    'I',    'J',    'K',    'L',    'M',    'N',    'O',
 'P',    'Q',    'R',    'S',    'T',    'U',    'V',    'W',
 'X',    'Y',    'Z',    '[',    '\',    ']',    '"',    '_',

 ''',    'a',    'b',    'c',    'd',    'e',    'f',    'g',
 'h',    'i',    'j',    'k',    'l',    'm',    'n',    'o',
 'p',    'q',    'r',    's',    't',    'u',    'v',    'w',
 'x',    'y',    'z',    '{',    '|',    '}',    '~',    del);
```

where Object_Name is a legal Ada identifier and Initial_Value is an expression of type Character.

For example, the following

```
Input_Character : Character range 'A' .. 'Z';
```

declares a variable Input_Character of type Character and restricts the set of values to the capital letters, while

```
Input_Character : Character range 'a' .. 'z';
```

declares Input_Character to be a variable of type Character and restricts its set of values to the lowercase letters of the alphabet.

Character Literal

To write a character literal in Ada, enclose the character within apostrophes. For example, 'B' represents the character B. If the character desired is itself an apostrophe, simply enclose the apostrophe within apostrophes, thus writing ''' .

Nonprintable characters such as carriage return, line feed, or bell are referenced differently. These nonprintable characters are declared in a package called Ascii and are accessed by referencing its *expanded* name.* To reference the carriage return, for example, write Ascii.Cr. To reference the bell, write Ascii.Bel.

The following is a subprogram that rings the bell the number of times indicated by the parameter Length.

```
with Text_IO; use Text_IO;
procedure Sound_Alarm (Length : in Positive) is
begin -- Sound_Alarm
   for I in 1 .. Length
   loop
      Put (Ascii.Bel);
   end loop;
end Sound_Alarm;
```

The operations that may be performed on type Character are the same as the operations applicable to enumeration types in general, as listed in Table 6-1. Attributes applicable to enumeration types, as discussed in Section 6.4, are applicable to type Character.

As previously stated, the catenation operator is often used to output text and nonprintable characters at the same time. For example, the following procedure displays a countdown.

---

* Package Ascii is a resource of another package named Standard. Package Standard is a predefined package that encloses every Ada program. Because package Ascii is nested within package Standard, the expanded name for the resources of package Ascii will be used.

```
with Text_IO; use Text_IO;
with Sound_Alarm;
procedure Display_Countdown (Seconds : in Positive) is
begin -- Display_Countdown
   Sound_Alarm(10);        -- rings the bell for 10 seconds
   Put_Line ("Starting Countdown");
   for I in reverse 1 .. Seconds
   loop  -- displays the seconds and rings the bell
      Put (I);
      Put (" second(s) and counting" & Ascii.Bel);
      New_Line;
   end loop;
   Put_Line ("Liftoff!");
   Sound_Alarm (10);       -- rings the bell for 10 seconds
end Display_Countdown;
```

This procedure displays the following when an actual parameter of 30 is passed to seconds:

```
Starting countdown
30 second(s) and counting
29 second(s) and counting
28 second(s) and counting
  .
  .
  .
 1 second(s) and counting
Liftoff!
```

and rings the bell after each line is displayed. The display is preceded and followed by ringing the bell for 10 seconds.

Character I/O

The following are the declarations of the I/O procedures provided by Text_IO for type Character.

```
procedure Get (Item : out Character);
procedure Get (File : in File_Type; Item : out Character);
procedure Put (Item : in Character);
procedure Put (File : in File_Type; Item : in Character);
```

These subprograms provide read and write capability to the terminal and a file.

10.7 Subtype Declarations (LRM 3.6)

When a subtype of an unconstrained array type is declared, the index constraint must be supplied.

Consider the following subtype declaration:

```
subtype Ten_in_Class_Subtype is Class_List_Type (1..10);
```

All objects of Ten_in_Class_Subtype have 10 components indexed by the integers 1 to 10.

Given the following unconstrained array declaration

```
type Matrix_Type is array
      (Positive range <>, Positive range <>) of Integer;
```

the following subtypes

```
subtype Size_3_x_3_Subtype is Matrix_Type (1..3, 1..3);
subtype Size_2_x_2_Subtype is Matrix_Type (1..2, 1..2);
```

provide for 3 × 3 and 2 × 2 matrices. How nice for evaluating determinants! Remember that objects of subtypes of the same base type may be freely mixed in expressions.

10.8 Pig_Latin

The following Ada program translates an English word into pig Latin. The rules for translation are as follows. If the first letter of the word is a consonant, place the first letter at the end of the word and add "ay." For example, "trout" translates to "routtay," and "hello" translates to "ellohay." If the first letter of the word to be translated is a vowel, simply add "ay" to the end of the word. Thus, "apple" translates to "appleay," and "ever" translates to "everay."

The algorithm used is to first obtain a "word" of 25 characters from a file, english.dat. The actual word to be translated may be embedded between blanks, as in b̸b̸b̸b̸b̸hellob̸b̸b̸b̸b̸b̸b̸b̸b̸b̸b̸b̸b̸b̸b̸. Rotate any beginning blanks to the end of the word, for example, hellob̸b̸b̸b̸b̸b̸b̸b̸b̸b̸b̸b̸b̸b̸b̸b̸b̸b̸b̸b̸. Determine how many characters are in the word to be translated, here 5. Then translate the word to pig Latin, knowing that the first 5 characters of this 25-character string represent the word to be translated.

The code for the main procedure Pig_Latin (see Figure 10-4) loops as long as there are data in the file english.dat. Pig_Latin extracts a 25-character string from the file and passes the string to Rotate_Blanks_to_End, which moves preceding blanks to the end of the string. Pig_Latin then passes the string, which now has a legitimate character as its first component, to Convert_to_Pig_Latin, which converts the word to pig Latin. Finally, Pig_Latin outputs the translated word to the file named pig.dat. The parameter modes for Rotate_Blanks_to_End and Convert_to_Pig_Latin are **in out** because the string is always being modified. Finally, when there are no more data in english.dat, the two files are closed and Pig_Latin terminates.

Procedure Rotate_Blanks_to_End assumes at least one nonblank character. In other words, it is assumed that a file entry does not consist of all blanks. Rotate_Blanks_to_End examines the first component of the string. As long as the first component is a blank, a slice assignment is used to rotate the blank to the end of the string. The word is continually examined until the first character is a nonblank character, at which time Rotate_Blanks_to_End terminates. The code for this procedure is shown in Figure 10-5.

FIGURE 10-4 Procedure Pig_Latin

```
with Text_IO; use Text_IO;
procedure Pig_Latin is
   Word : String (1..25); -- index constraint supplied
   Data_File, Results_File : File_Type;
   procedure Rotate_Blanks_to_End (Word : in out String)
             is separate;
   procedure Convert_to_Pig_Latin (Word : in out String)
             is separate;
begin -- Pig_Latin
   Open (Data_File, In_File, "english.dat");
   Create (Results_File, Out_File, "pig.dat");
   while not End_of_File(Data_File)
   loop
      Get (Data_File, Word);
      Rotate_Blanks_to_End (Word);
      Convert_to_Pig_Latin (Word);
      Put_Line (Results_File, Word);
   end loop;
   Close(Data_File);
   Close(Results_File);
end Pig_Latin;
```

FIGURE 10-5 Procedure Rotate_Blanks_to_End

```
separate (Pig_Latin)
procedure Rotate_Blanks_to_End (Word : in out String) is
   -- This procedure assumes at least one nonblank
   -- character.
begin -- Rotate_Blanks_to_End
   while Word(Word'First) = ' ' -- if a blank
   loop
      -- add blank to end of word
      Word (Word'Range) :=
          Word(Word'First+1. .Word'Last) & ' ';
   end loop;
end Rotate_Blanks_to_End;
```

Procedure Convert_to_Pig_Latin assumes that the first character of the incoming string is a nonblank character. The procedure first counts the number of nonblank characters; the count is required in order to make the proper slice assignment in the translation to pig Latin. Convert_to_Pig_Latin then examines the first character of the string and translates the word to pig Latin according to the rules previously stated. This procedure is coded in Figure 10-6.

Procedure Obtain examines successive characters and counts the number of nonblank characters (see Figure 10-7). The loop in the procedure terminates at the first blank character. Notice the requirement for Temp_Count because Count, an **out** parameter, cannot be read. The statement

```
Count := Count + 1; --**ILLEGAL**--
```

is illegal.

FIGURE 10-6 Procedure Convert_to_Pig_Latin

```
separate (Pig_Latin)
procedure Convert_to_Pig_Latin (Word : in out String) is
   -- This procedure assumes the first character of the
   -- incoming string to be a nonblank character.
   Count : Natural range 1..25;
   -- obtain number of nonblank characters
   procedure Obtain (Count : out Natural) is separate;
begin -- Convert_to_Pig_Latin
   Obtain (Count); -- calculate number of nonblank
                   -- characters
   case Word (Word'First) is
      -- a vowel
      when 'a'|'A'|'e'|'E'|'i'|'I'|'o'|'O'|'u'|'U' =>
         Word (Word'Range) := Word (1..Count) & "ay" &
                              Word (Count+3..Word'Last);
      -- a consonant
      when 'b'..'d'|'B'..'D'|'f'..'h'|'F'..'H'|
           'j'..'n'|'J'..'N'|'p'..'t'|'P'..'T'|
           'v'..'z'|'V'..'Z' =>
           Word (Word'Range) := Word (2..Count) &
                                Word(Word'First) & "ay" &
                                Word(Count+3..Word'Last);
      -- a special character
      when others => Put_Line
          (Results_File, "A special character is" &
          " contained within the input file.");
   end case;
end Convert_to_Pig_Latin;
```

FIGURE 10-7 Procedure Obtain

```
separate (Pig_Latin.Convert_to_Pig_Latin)
procedure Obtain (Count : out Natural) is
   -- Temp_Count required because an out parameter
   -- cannot be read. To write Count := Count + 1;
   -- is illegal, therefore work with Temp_Count.
   Temp_Count : Natural := 0;
   I : Natural :=1;
begin -- Count
   while Word(I) /= ' '
   loop
      Temp_Count := Temp_Count + 1;
      I := I + 1;
   end loop;
   Count := Temp_Count;
end Obtain;
```

EXERCISES

10.1 Recode Exercise 9.4 to accommodate vectors of varying lengths.

10.2 Given the following Matrix_Operations package, recode Exercises 9.5, 9.6, and 9.7.

```
package Matrix_Operations is
   type Matrix_Type is array
       (Positive range <>, Positive range <>) of Integer;
   function Add       (One, Two : Matrix_Type)
                      return Matrix_Type;
   function Subtract (One, Two : Matrix_Type)
                      return Matrix_Type;
   function Multiply (One, Two : Matrix_Type)
                      return Matrix_Type;
end Matrix_Operations;
```

10.3 Write a program to read words from a file and determine whether the word is a palindrome. A palindrome is a word that reads the same forwards and backwards, such as Ada, Anna, or Mum.

10.4 A roman numeral, like MMIX, is composed of a sequence of the roman digits—I, V, X, L, C, D, M. Obtain a legal roman numeral from a file and determine its decimal value.

10.5 What happens in procedure Convert_to_Pig_Latin if the count of non-blank characters in a word is 24 or 25? Modify the code to accommodate this situation.

11

RECORD TYPES

CHAPTER OBJECTIVES

- Declare record types.
- Access components of record objects.
- Write record aggregates in positional or named notation.
- Perform I/O on record objects.

Arrays and records are abstractions of the way data are actually stored. The components of an array are homogeneous, or all of the *same* type. Arrays allow like data to be grouped. *Records,* on the other hand, allow components of possibly *different* types to be grouped into one data structure. In other words, the components of a record may be either heterogeneous or homogeneous.

11.1 Type Declaration (LRM 3.7)

Consider the following package. The boxes represent enhancements to package Calendar_Info introduced in Section 6.6.

```
package Calendar_Info is
   type Month_Type is (Jan, Feb, Mar, Apr, May, Jun,
                       Jul, Aug, Sep, Oct, Nov, Dec);
   type Day_Type is range 1 .. 31;
   type Year_Type is range 1980 .. 2500;

   type Date_Type is
   record
        Month : Month_Type;
        Day   : Day_Type;
        Year  : Year_Type;
   end record;

   function Leap_Year (Year : Year_Type) return Boolean;
   function Last_Day_of (Month : Month_Type)
           return Day_Type;
   procedure Get_a_Date (A_Date : out Date_Type);
   procedure Put_a_Date (A_Date : in Date_Type);
end Calendar_Info;
```

This version of Calendar_Info provides a higher level of abstraction of a date than the version coded in Section 6.6. A date consists of three logically related parts: the month, the day, and the year. Now we can work with a date as a date, rather than having to work with each part independently. By representing the date as a record, we gain the capability of accessing *both* the date and the date's individual parts. Thus two levels of abstraction are provided by one structure.

The logical parts of a record type are called *components* of the record. As shown in Figure 11-1, the record type Date_Type has three components. The first component is named Month and is of type Month_Type. The second component is named Day and is of type Day_Type. The third component is named Year and is of type Year_Type.

As another example, consider the hypothetical driver's license for the state of Colorado that is shown in Figure 11-2. Corresponding type definitions are given in Figure 11-3.

FIGURE 11-1 Conceptual structure of Date_Type

First component: Month	value of Month_Type
Second component: Day	$1 \leq$ value ≤ 31
Third component: Year	value of Year_Type

FIGURE 11-2 A hypothetical driver's license

```
                 STATE OF COLORADO
             Division of Motor Vehicles
                   DRIVER LICENSE

                   B05074318050220

   Expiration Date                      Issue Date
   Mar 30 1986                          Mar 30 1985

   AUTO
   Richard Edward Bettencourt
   511 Boxer St.
   Sometown, CO 80122

Sex  Model  Restrictions  Month  Year  Fee
 M   Buick      None       May   1943  8.00
```

FIGURE 11-3

```
type License_Number_Type is
record
   First_Letter   : Character;
   Digit_Sequence : String(1..14);
end record;
type Month_Type is (Jan, Feb, Mar, Apr, May, Jun,
                    Jul, Aug, Sep, Oct, Nov, Dec);
type Year_Type is range 1900 .. 2000;
type Date_Type is
record
   Month : Month_Type;
   Day   : Positive range 1..31;
   Year  : Year_Type;
end record;
type Name_Type is
record
   Last_Name        : String(1..20);
   First_Name       : String(1..20);
   Middle_Initial   : Character;
end record;
subtype Street_Type is String(1..30);
subtype City_Type is String(1..30);
subtype State_Type is String(1..2);
type Zip_Code_Type is range 80001 .. 81658;
type Sex_Type is (Male, Female);
type Restrictions_Type is (Glasses, Handicapped, None);
type Car_Type is (Buick, Oldsmobile, Chevrolet, Mercedes,
                  Porsche, Ford, Ferrari, Volkswagen);
```

The following is a record declaration for a driver's license that might be used in a program to maintain a data base of Colorado licenses.

```
type Drivers_License_Type is
record
   License_Number  : License_Number_Type;
   Issue_Date      : Date_Type;
   Expiration_Date : Date_Type;
   Name            : Name_Type;
   Street          : Street_Type;
   City            : City_Type;
   State           : State_Type;
   Zip_Code        : Zip_Code_Type;
   Birth_Date      : Date_Type;
   Car             : Car_Type;
   Restrictions    : Restrictions_Type;
   Sex             : Sex_Type;
   Points          : Natural range 0..12;
end record;
```

We leave it to you as an exercise to make any modifications to this record type declaration that you think might improve it—for example, a way to accommodate additional kinds of vehicles such as motorcycles and trucks. At this point, licenses can be issued only for cars.

A record declaration in Ada is written as follows:

```
type Record_Type_Name is
record
   component declaration {component declaration}
end record;
```

where each component declaration is written as

```
Component_Name : Component_Type [:= Initial_Value];
```

Component_Name is a legal Ada identifier. Component_Type is basically any legal Ada type or subtype (with two exceptions that will be covered in a moment). For example, in the declaration for Drivers_License_Type the Sex component in our example is an enumeration type. The Points component is basically an integer type. The Street component is of type Street_Type, which is an array type, specifically String. The Name component is a record type, specifically Name_Type.

The first exception previously mentioned is that when a component of a record is a composite type, the composite type must be constrained. This means that the component of a record cannot be, for example, an unconstrained array type. To declare type Name_Type as

```
type Name_Type is
record
   Last_Name      : String;   --**ILLEGAL**--
   First_Name     : String;   --**ILLEGAL**--
   Middle_Initial : Character;
end record;
```

is illegal because String is an unconstrained array type. To make the declaration legal, just add a constraint, such as (1. .20), as in

```
type Name_Type is
record
   Last_Name      : String(1..20); -- constraint supplied
   First_Name     : String(1..20); -- constraint supplied
   Middle_Initial : Character;
end record;
```

Finally, a record component may not be an anonymous array. For example, the following declaration

```
type Illegal_Record_Type is
record
   First_Component : Integer range 1..45;
   Second_Component: array(1..6) of Boolean; --**ILLEGAL**--
end record;
```

is illegal.

11.2 Object Declaration (LRM 3.2)

Objects of a record type are declared as usual. The following:

```
Today : Date_Type;
```

declares an object named Today of type Date_Type, with the following conceptual structure:

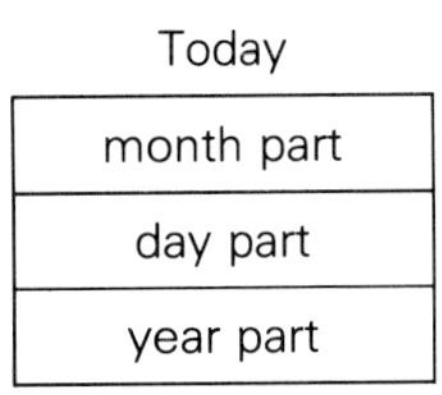

This line

```
Dick_B : Drivers_License_Type;
```

declares Dick_B to be an object of type Drivers_License_Type. Dick_B has the following conceptual structure:

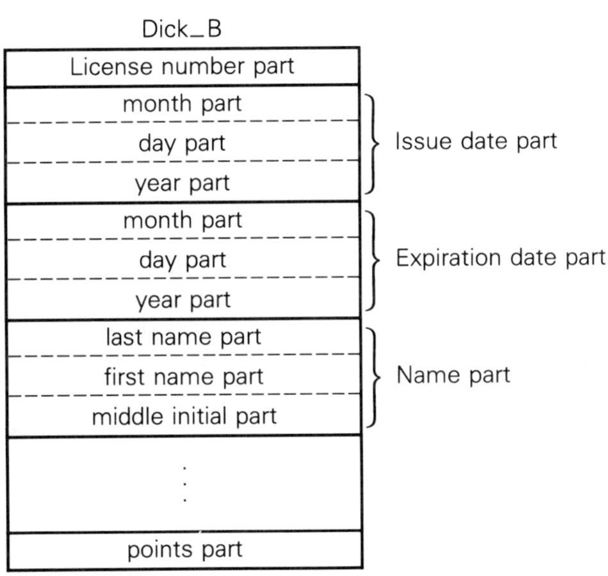

Constant Record Objects (LRM 3.2.1)

Constant record objects may be declared. Consider the following:

```
Christmas : constant Date_Type := (Dec, 25, 1986);
```

Constant record objects are declared by writing the reserved word **constant** after the colon, as in

```
Object_Name : constant Type_Name := Aggregate;
```

Constants may not have their values changed. Constants are read only.

Record Aggregate (LRM 4.3, 4.3.1)

Variable record objects *may* be initialized, and constant record objects *must* be initialized. To write a value for a record, list in parentheses a value of the component type for each component in the record. If you think that sounds familiar, you are right. It is just like writing the value of an aggregate for an array.

Record aggregates may be written in positional notation, named notation, or a mixture of the two. Here is an object declaration for Today with an initial value written in positional notation.

```
Today : Date_Type := (Mar, 7, 1985);
```

Here is the same declaration with the initial value written in named notation.

```
Today : Date_Type := (Month => Mar, Day => 7, Year => 1985);
```

As with array aggregates, order is significant when writing a record aggregate in positional notation. Order is *not* significant when writing an aggregate in named notation. The following declaration achieves the same effect as the preceding declaration for Today.

```
Today : Date_Type := (Day => 7, Month => Mar, Year => 1985);
```

As a matter of style, note that it is much easier on the eye to see the associations aligned vertically, as in

```
Today   : Date_Type := (Day     => 7,
                        Month   => Mar,
                        Year    => 1985);
```

rather than horizontally, as in

```
Today : Date_Type := (Day => 7, Month => Mar, Year => 1985);
```

Finally, Today can be initialized using a mixture of positional and named notation. Of course, positional must come first and in the correct order. Once named notation is introduced, named notation must be used for the remainder of the aggregate. Both of the following declarations are perfectly legal and represent the same value.

```
Today : Date_Type := (Mar, 7, Year => 1985);
Today : Date_Type := (Mar, Year => 1985, Day => 7);
```

As with array aggregates, an **others** option may be used in writing record aggregates. However, it is not used very often because the components of a record are usually of different types.

What does the following mean?

```
--**ILLEGAL**--
Today   : Date_Type := (Mar, others => 7);
```

Depending on the implementation, the declaration may not compile because 7 is not a legal value for the Year component. In any case, Constraint_Error will be raised at run time.

Consider the following object declaration:

```
Dick_B : Drivers_License_Type
       := ( License_Number   => ('B', "05074318050220"),
            Issue_Date       => (Mar, 30, 1985),
            Expiration_Date  => (Mar, 30, 1986),
            Name             => ("Bettencourt         ",
                                  "Richard            ", 'E'),
            Street  => ("511 Boxer St.                 "),
            City    => ("Sometown                      "),
            State   => ("CO"),
            Zip_Code         => 80122,
            Birth_Date       => (May, 7, 1943),
            Car              => Buick,
            Restrictions     => None,
            Sex              => Male,
            Points           => 0);
```

Because the component License_Number is itself a record, its value must be written as a record aggregate and enclosed in parentheses. The same is true for the Issue_Date, Expiration_Date, Name, and Birth_Date components.

Street, City, and State are arrays (type String), so their values must be written as array aggregates and enclosed in parentheses.

11.3 Accessing Components (LRM 4.1.3)

Arrays and records differ in the way their components are accessed. Index notation is used to select a specific component of an array, whereas *dot notation* is used to select a component of a record. In this form of notation, the name of the record object is followed by a dot and then by the name of the component desired. For example, to select the month component of Today, write

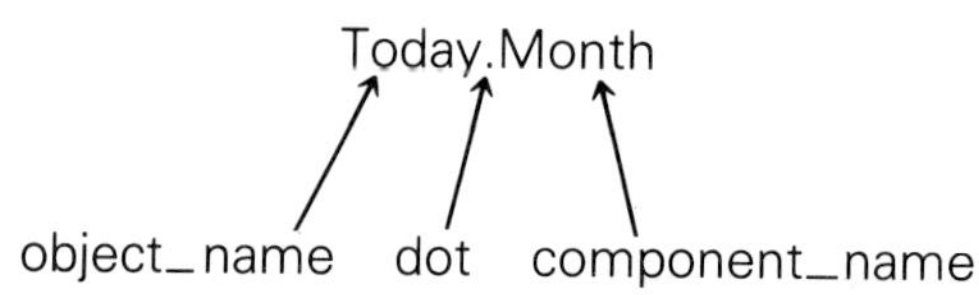

Figure 11-4 shows that Today is an object of Date_Type and has three components. The first component is named Month, has the value Mar of type Month_Type, and is accessed by writing Today.Month. The second component is named Day, has the value 7 (which is between 1 and 31), and is accessed by writing Today.Day. The third component is named Year, has the value 1985 (which is between 1980 and 2000 inclusive), and is accessed by writing Today.Year.*

---

* Ada has a facility, like Pascal's "with," that permits the programmer to eliminate the name of the record and the dot and thus reference the component by writing only the component name. This facility in Ada is called renaming. Renaming permits the programmer to declare a shorter name to be used in place of the full name. Renaming is discussed briefly in Section 11.6.

FIGURE 11-4 Conceptual structure of Today

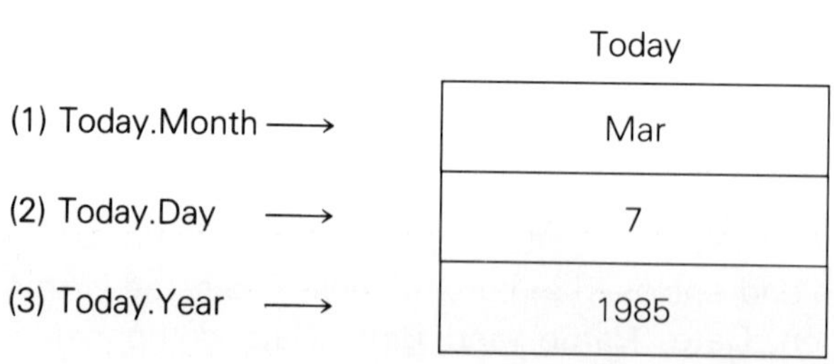

Figure 11-5 shows the conceptual structure of Dick_B, an object of Drivers_License_Type that has the value described in the previous section. Note the dot notation used to name the record's components. As you saw in the last section, Dick_B has 13 components. The first component is named License_Number and is of type License_Number_Type. The second component is named Issue_Date and is of type Date_Type. The third component, Expiration_Date, is also of type Date_Type, and so on.

The identifier

```
Dick_B.License_Number
```

FIGURE 11-5 Conceptual structure of Dick_B

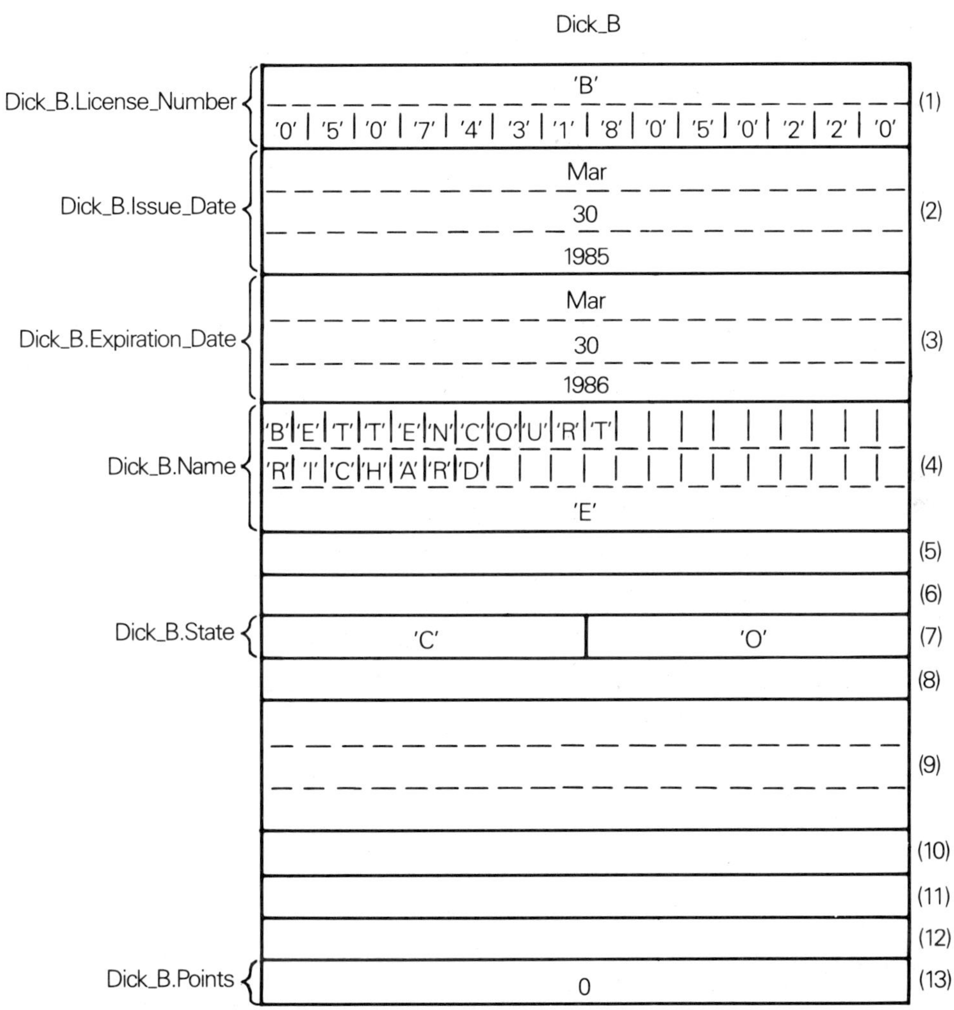

references the entire first component of Dick_B. The value of Dick_B. License_Number is ('B', "05074318050220"). License_Number_Type, the type of this component, is a record type that in turn is made up of the components First_Letter (with the value 'B') and Digits_Sequence (with the value "05074318050220"). See Figure 11-6.

This identifier

```
Dick_B.License_Number.First_Letter
```

references just the first component of the License_Number_Type record. This component is of type Character. See Figure 11-7. Similarly,

```
Dick_B.License_Number.Digits_Sequence
```

references the sequence of digits, stored as a string, that follows the first letter in the driver's license number and makes up the second component of License_Number_Type. See Figure 11-8.

FIGURE 11-6 Dick_B.License_Number is a record

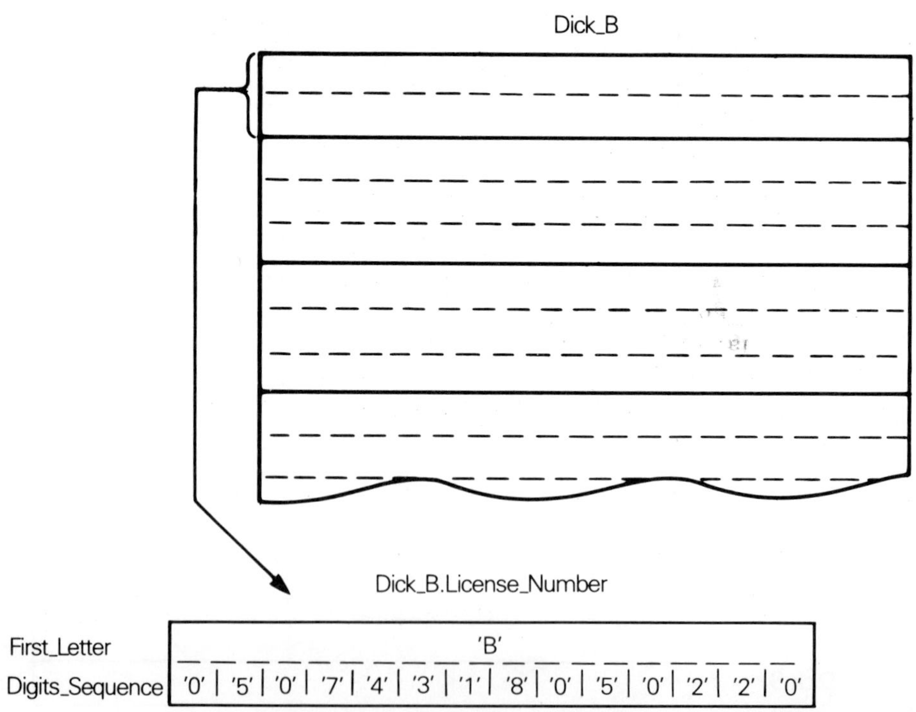

As we have noted, Dick_B.License_Number.Digits_Sequence has a value of "05074318050220". Can we access individual components of this string? Sure! The string is just a kind of array, so we use index notation to access the array's individual components, as in

```
Dick_B.License_Number.Digits_Sequence(1..2)
```

This identifier references the slice indexed by 1. .2 in the string.

Have you figured out the code for the driver's license number? The first letter of the license is the first letter of the driver's last name. The next six digits represent the month, day, and year of birth. Therefore

```
Dick_B.License_Number.Digits_Sequence(1..2)
```

actually represents the month of birth, "05".* See Figure 11-9.

The general point to be noted here is that by careful representation of data, one can work at a very high level of abstraction and still gain access to details whenever the need arises.

* Yes, this identifier is rather long. You will see very soon how to provide a shorter name that references the same entity.

FIGURE 11-7 Record component access

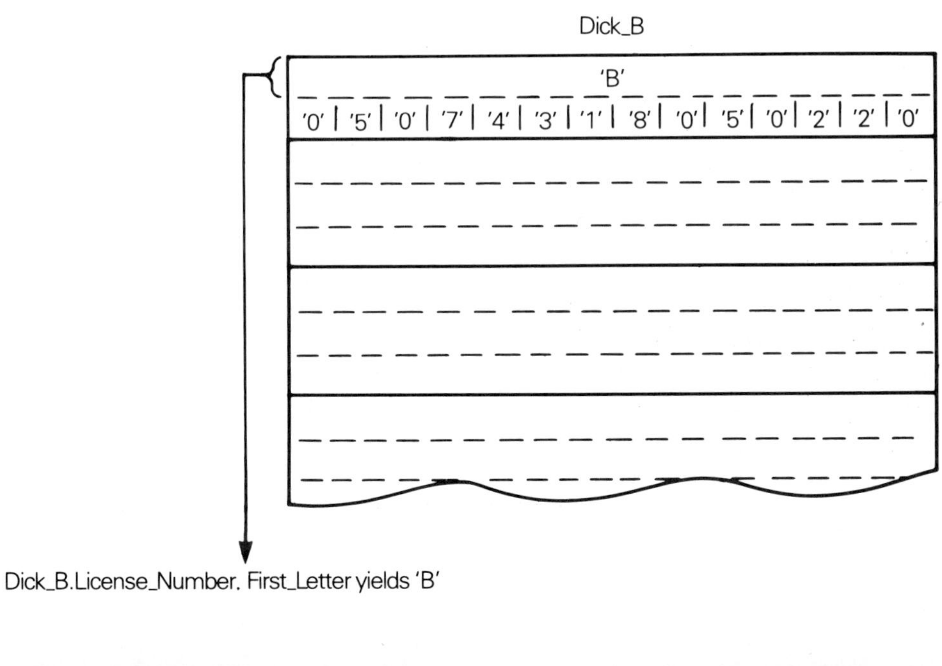

FIGURE 11-8 Array component access

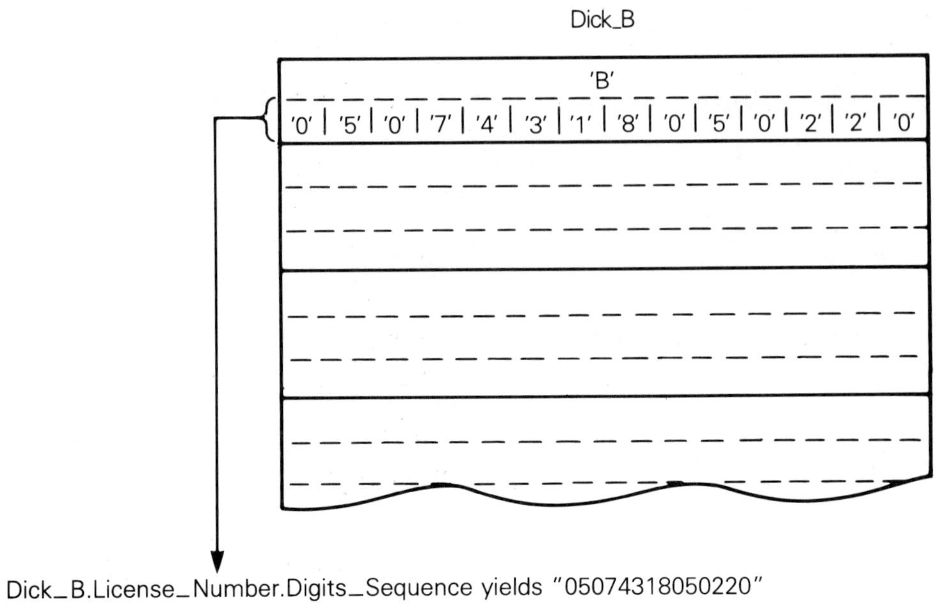

FIGURE 11-9 A more complicated component access

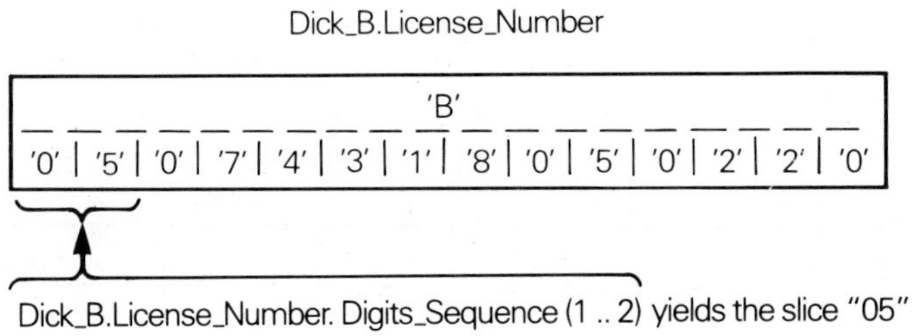

11.4 Attributes (LRM 3.7.4)

Ada supplies some attributes for records that are beyond the scope of this text.* For our purposes, therefore, there are no attributes applicable to record types or record objects.

* Discriminated records will be covered in the next text in this series.

Of course, attributes may be applied to record *components*, as long as each attribute is appropriate for the component to which it is applied. For example, to obtain the successor month for the Month component of an object Date of type Date_Type, write

```
Month_Type'Succ (Date.Month)
```

11.5 Operations on Record Types (LRM 3.7.4)

The only operations provided by Ada itself that can be performed on whole records are assignment (:=) tests for equality or inequality (=, /=) and component selection. However, packages will almost always provide subprograms that have the record type as a parameter, like Get_a_Date of package Calendar_Info or the subprograms in the package Finite_Sequence, which will be discussed next.

An Example: Sequences

An *arithmetic sequence* is a sequence in which each term after the first term is the sum of the preceding term plus some constant. For example, in the sequence

2, 6, 10, 14, 18

each term is the sum of the preceding term plus the constant 4. The constant 4 is called the *common difference* in the sequence.

A *geometric sequence* is one in which each term after the first is the product of the preceding term multiplied by some constant. For example, in the sequence

3, 6, 12, 24

each term is the product of the preceding term and the constant 2. The constant 2 is again called the common difference.

Now consider the package shown in Figure 11-10.

This package provides a record type, Sequence_Description_Type, to describe a sequence in terms of the kind of sequence it is (arithmetic or geometric), the first and last terms of the sequence, and the common difference. (The package is limited because is permits only integer terms in the sequence.) Additionally, the package provides functions that

- calculate the sum of the terms of a sequence
- provide the value of a term given the term number
- provide the term number given the value of the term

and procedures to

- get a sequence description from a file
- put a sequence description to a file
- put all terms of a sequence to a file

FIGURE 11-10

```
package Finite_Sequence is
   type Sequence_Type is (Arithmetic, Geometric);
   type Sequence_Description_Type is
   record
      Kind          : Sequence_Type;
      First_Term    : Integer;
      Last_Term     : Integer;
      Common_Diff   : Integer;
   end record;
   function
      Sum_of (Sequence : Sequence_Description_Type)
      return Integer;
   function
      Value_of (Sequence : Sequence_Description_Type;
             Term_Number : Positive)
      return Integer;
   function N_th_Term_of
       (Sequence : Sequence_Description_Type;
        Value : Integer)
      return Positive;
   procedure Get_a_Sequence
       (Sequence : out Sequence_Description_Type;
        Seq_File : in out File_Type);
   procedure Put_a_Sequence
       (Sequence : in Sequence_Description_Type;
        Seq_File : in out File_Type);
   procedure Display_Terms
       (Sequence : in Sequence_Description_Type;
        Seq_File : in out File_Type);
   Bad_Sequence : exception;  -- raised by Display_Terms
end Finite_Sequence;
```

Finally, the package provides an exception, Bad_Sequence, that is raised by Display_Terms if Display_Terms determines that the terms generated do not conform to the sequence description. For example, if the sequence generated using the first term and the common difference does not yield a last term whose value equals the value of the Last_Term component read from the file, Bad_Sequence is raised.

Figure 11-11 shows a program that gets two sequences from a file named "seq.dat" and determines whether they represent the same sequence. A message is then printed to an output file indicating equality or inequality. If the sequences are the same, Display_Terms is called to output the sequence of terms to the file.

Determine_Equality_of_Sequences shows how simple it is to test for equality of records in Ada. The program also shows how packages provide "operations," in the form of subprograms, that operate on record types.

Another Example: Calculate_Next_Day

Figure 11-12 contains a recoding of the program in Chapter 7 that, given a date, returns the next day. This context clause imports the updated Calendar_Info that appeared in Section 11.1.

Remember that Date references the entire record object that consists of three components. The operations that can be performed on a record such as Date are assignment and test for equality and inequality, plus the operations (subprograms) that are imported with the package, like Get_a_Date and Put_a_Date.

Date.Month references only the month component of the object Date. The operations that can be performed on Date.Month are the ones defined for enumeration types because Date.Month is of Month_Type, which is an enumeration type. The operations that can be performed on Date.Day are those defined for the class of integer types because Date.Day is of Day_Type, which is a user-defined integer type.

Always keep clear whether an operation is being performed on the entire record or on a component of a record, because components may be of different types and thus may have different allowable operations performed on them.

11.6 Renaming Components (LRM 8.5)

You may have noted that the preceding recoding of Calculate_Next_Day is at a higher level of abstraction in terms of getting and putting the dates, but it is at the same level of abstraction in terms of working on the components of the

FIGURE 11-11

```
with Text_IO; use Text_IO;
with Finite_Sequence; use Finite_Sequence;
procedure Determine_Equality_of_Sequences is
   Data_File, Results_File : File_Type;
   Sequence_1, Sequence_2  : Sequence_Description_Type;
begin -- Determine_Equality_of_Sequences
   Open (Data_File, In_File, "seq.dat");
   Create (Results_File, Out_File, "ans.dat");
   while not End_of_File (Data_File)
   loop
      -- get two sequence descriptions
      Get_a_Sequence (Sequence_1,Data_File);
      Get_a_Sequence (Sequence_2,Data_File);
      -- output two sequence descriptions
      Put_a_Sequence (Sequence_1,Results_File);
      Put_a_Sequence (Sequence_2,Results_File);
      if Sequence_1 = Sequence_2 then -- test for =
         Put_Line (Results_File, "The sequences are" &
                                 "equal");
         Display_Terms (Sequence_1,Results_File);
      else
         Put_Line (Results_File, "The sequences are not" &
                                 "equal");
      end if;
   end loop;
   Close (Data_File);
   Close (Results_File);
exception
   when Bad_Sequence =>
    Put_Line ("Cannot generate a sequence with last" &
              "term the same as Last_Term component" &
              "of the sequence description record read" &
              "from the file.");
      Close (Data_File);
      Close (Results_File);
end Determine_Equality_of_Sequences;
```

FIGURE 11-12

```
with Text_IO; use Text_IO;
with Calendar_Info; use Calendar_Info;
procedure Calculate_Next_Day is
   Date : Date_Type;
begin -- Calculate_Next_Day
   loop
      Get_a_Date (Date);
      case Date.Month is
         when Feb =>
            if Date.Day < 28 or
               (Date.Day = 28 and Leap_Year(Date.Year))
            then
               Date.Day := Date.Day + 1;
            else
               Date.Day := 1;
               Date.Month := Mar;
               -- Date.Year stays the same
            end if;
         when Dec =>
            if Date.Day = 31 then -- Dec 31
               Date := (Jan, 1, Date.Year + 1);
            else
               Date.Day := Date.Day + 1;
               -- Date.Month and Date.Year stay the same
            end if;
         when others =>
            if Date.Day = Last_Day_of (Date.Month) then
               Date.Day := 1;
               Date.Month := Month_Type'Succ (Date.Month);
               --Date.Year stays the same
            else
               Date.Day := Date.Day + 1;
               -- Date.Month and Date.Year stay the same
            end if;
      end case;
      Put ("The new date is: "); -- Text_IO.Put
      Put_a_Date (Date);
   end loop;
end Calculate_Next_Day;
```

date. Additionally, all the occurrences of Date.Month, Date.Day, and Date.Year are fairly cumbersome.

Ada permits renaming of certain entities, one of which is an object. Consider the code in Figure 11-13 that provides shorter, yet meaningful, names for the components of Date. Note that the executable code refers to Month, Day, and Year instead of Date.Month, Date.Day, and Date.Year.

Renaming can be used to provide a shorter name for an object and thus provide more readable code. A renaming declaration for objects is written as

```
New_Name : Type_Name renames Old_Name;
```

where Old_Name is the identifier to be renamed, New_Name is the new name to be associated with Old_Name, and Type_Name is the type of Old_Name. The new name is only usable within the procedure.

11.7 Default Values (LRM 3.7)

In Ada, default values may be supplied for components of a record type at type declaration time. When objects of that type are declared, the default value is assigned to those components.

For example, new drivers start out with no points. The record type declaration for Drivers_License_Type thus can be written as follows, with a default value of 0 for the Points component.

```
type Drivers_License_Type is
record
   License_Number  : License_Number_Type;
   Issue_Date      : Date_Type;
   Expiration_Date : Date_Type
   Name            : Name_Type;
   Street          : Street_Type;
   City            : City_Type;
   State           : State_Type;
   Zip_Code        : Zip_Code_Type;
   Birth_Date      : Date_Type;
   Car             : Car_Type;
   Restrictions    : Restrictions_Type;
   Sex             : Sex_Type;
   Points          : Natural range 0..12 := 0;
end record;
```

FIGURE 11-13

```
with Text_IO; use Text_IO;
with Calendar_Info; use Calender_Info;
procedure Calculate_Next_Day is
   Date : Date_Type;
   Month : Month_Type renames Date.Month;
   Day   : Day_Type   renames Date.Day;
   Year  : Year_Type  renames Date.Year;
begin -- Calculate_Next_Day
   loop
      Get_a_Date (Date);
      case Month is
         when Feb =>
            if Day < 28 or
               (Day = 28 and Leap_Year(Year)) then
               Day := Day + 1;
            else
               Day := 1;
               Month := Mar;
               -- Year stays the same
            end if;
         when Dec =>
            if Day = 31 then
               Date := (Jan, 1, Year + 1);
            else
               Day := Day + 1;
               -- Month and Year stay the same
            end if;
         when others =>
            if Day = Last_Day_of (Month) then
               Day := 1;
               Month := Month_Type'Succ (Month);
               -- Year stays the same
            else
               Day := Day + 1;
               -- Month and Year stay the same
            end if;
      end case;
      Put ("The new date is: ") ;  -- Text_IO.Put
      Put_a_Date (Date);
   end loop;
end Calculate_Next_Day;
```

Now, when an object of Drivers_License Type is declared, as in

```
Dick_B : Drivers_License_Type;
```

the default value, 0, is automatically assigned to the Points component of Dick_B. In other words, Dick_B.Points will have the value 0.

Remember, however, that record aggregates must supply a value for each and every component. This is true even if the component has a default value specified in the type declaration. When assigning a value to Dick_B, therefore, if you desire the default value for Points, you must supply that value for the Points component, like this:

```
Dick_B := ( License_Number => ('B', "05074318050220"),
            Issue_Date     => (Mar, 30, 1985),
            Expiration_Date=> (Mar, 30, 1986),
            Name           => ("Bettencourt         ",
                                "Richard             ",'E'),
            Street => ("511 Boxer St         "),
            City   => ("Sometown             "),
            State  => ("CO"),
            Zip_Code       => 80122,
            Birth_Date     => (May, 7, 1943),
            Car            => Buick,
            Restrictions   => None,
            Sex            => Male,
            Points         => 0); -- value 0 supplied
```

Suppose that Dick B. is given a ticket for speeding on the way to the Motor Vehicle Registration Bureau, *before* his license information is entered in the data base. Speeding (less than 15 mph over the speed limit) adds two points to Dick B's record. To make the necessary change, simply supply that value in the aggregate, as in

```
Dick_B := ( License_Number => ('B', "05074318050220"),
            Issue_Date     => (Mar, 30, 1985),
            Expiration_Date=> (Mar, 30, 1986),
            Name           => ("Bettencourt      ",
                               "Richard          ",'E'),
            Street => ("511 Boxer St        "),
            City   => ("Sometown            "),
            State  => ("CO"),
            Zip_Code      => 80122,
            Birth_Date    => (May, 7, 1943),
            Car           => Buick,
            Restrictions  => None,
            Sex           => Male,
            Points        => 2);
```

The value 2 will replace, or override, the default value of 0.

If Dick B's record is already in the data base, then of course only Dick_B.Points needs to be reassigned, which you would do like this:

```
Dick_B.Points := 2;
```

11.8 Record I/O (LRM 14.3.10)

There are no I/O routines supplied by Text_IO for records. As with arrays, I/O for records must be done component by component. For example, the following represents the code for Get_a_Date in the package Calendar_Info.

```
separate (Calendar_Info)
procedure Get_a_Date (A_Date : out Date_Type) is
   procedure Get_a_Month (A_Month : out Month_Type)
             is separate;
   procedure Get_a_Day (A_Day : out Day_Type)
             is separate;
   procedure Get_a_Year (A_Year : out Year_Type)
             is separate;
begin -- Get_a_Date
   Get_a_Month  (A_Date.Month); -- get month component
   Get_a_Day    (A_Date.Day);   -- get day component
   Get_a_Year   (A_Date.Year);  -- get year component
end Get_a_Date;
```

The code for one subunit, Get_a_Month, follows. It is assumed that Text_IO has been imported to Calendar_Info.

```
separate (Calendar_Info.Get_a_Date)
procedure Get_a_Month (A_Month : out Month_Type) is
   -- STEP 2 for enumeration type Month_Type
   package Month_IO is new Enumeration_IO (Month_Type);
   use Month_IO;
begin -- Get_a_Month
   loop
      begin
         Get (A_Month);
         exit;
      exception
         when Data_Error =>
            Put_Line ("Invalid entry-Try again");
            Put_Line ("Enter first three letters of" &
                      "month. ");
      end;
   end loop;
end Get_a_Month;
```

The other subunits are coded similarly. The point to keep in mind is that I/O for records must be performed component by component. To get a date requires three Gets, one each for the month, day, and year. I/O Step 2 is provided in the subunit Get_a_Month to permit I/O on values of the enumeration type Month_Type.

EXERCISES

11.1 Modify the record declaration for Drivers_License_Type so that the type declaration contains one component for the whole address.

11.2 Modify the record declaration for Drivers_License_Type to accommodate trucks, both under two tons and over two tons, and motorcycles. Accommodate different registration fees for cars, trucks, and motorcycles. The fee for a car is $8.00; for a truck under two tons, $10.00; and for a truck over two tons, $15.00. The cost to register a motorcycle is the same as that for a car, $8.00.

11.3 Write a record type declaration for each of the following items in a car:

a. the radio
b. the clock
c. the climate control
d. the headlight control
e. the windshield washer control

11.4 Write a record type declaration for the car's entire dashboard.

Use the following package specification for Exercises 11.5 and 11.6.

```
package Complex_Numbers is
   type Real_Type is digits 4;
   type Complex_Type is
   record
      Re, Im : Real_Type;
   end record;
   function Add        (A, B : Complex_Type) return
                       Complex_Type;
   function Subtract   (A, B : Complex_Type) return
                       Complex_Type;
   function Multiply   (A, B : Complex_Type) return
                       Complex_Type;
   function Divide     (A, B : Complex_Type) return
                       Complex_Type;
end Complex_Numbers;
```

11.5 Write a program to obtain two complex numbers from a file. Add, subtract, multiply, and divide the two numbers and output the results to another file.

11.6 Write a program to obtain the conjugate of a complex number. The conjugate of a + bi is a − bi.

11.7 Write a program to read a sequence of values from a file and determine whether the sequence is arithmetic or geometric.

11.8 A package specification for a data base management system for drivers' licenses is shown in the accompanying figure. Write a main procedure that updates the data base in this way:

1. prompts the user for the kind of action required: add, delete, update, or quit;

2. inputs the required data;
3. calls the correct routine in the package to update the data base accordingly.

Figure for Exercise 11.8

```
package Drivers_License_DBMS is
   type License_Number_Type is
   record
      First_Letter     : Character;
      Digit_Sequence   : String (1..14);
   end record;
   type Month_Type is ( Jan, Feb, Mar, Apr, May, Jun,
                        Jul, Aug, Sep, Oct, Nov, Dec);
   type Year_Type is range 1900..2000;
   type Date_Type is
   record
      Month    : Month_Type;
      Day      : Positive range 1..31;
      Year     : Year_Type;
   end record;
   type Name_Type is
   record
      Last_Name        : String (1..20);
      First_Name       : String (1..20);
      Middle_Initial   : Character;
   end record;
   subtype   Street_Type is String (1..30);
   subtype     City_Type is String (1..30);
   subtype    State_Type is String (1.. 2);
   type Zip_Code_Type is range 07000..88999;
   type Sex_Type is (Male, Female);
   type Restrictions_Type is (Glasses, Handicapped, None);
   type Car_Type is (Buick, Oldsmobile, Chevrolet, Mercedes,
                     Porsche, Ford, Ferrari, Volkswagen);
   type Drivers_License_Type is
   record
      License_Number   : License_Number_Type;
      Issue_Date       :           Date_Type;
      Expiration_Date  :           Date_Type;
      Name             :           Name_Type;
      Street           :         Street_Type;
      City             :           City_Type;
```

Figure for Exercise 11.8 (*continued*)

```
      State              :           State_Type;
      Zip_Code           :        Zip_Code_Type;
      Birth_Date         :            Date_Type;
      Car                :             Car_Type;
      Restrictions       :    Restrictions_Type;
      Sex                :             Sex_Type;
      Points             : Natural range 0..12 := 0;
   end record;
   -- adds drivers license record to database
   -- License_Number_Exists exception raised
   -- if license number already in database
   -- Database_Full exception raised if database is full
   procedure Add_Drivers_License
    (Drivers_License : in Drivers_License_Type);

   -- deletes drivers license record from database
   -- License_Number_Not_Found exception raised
   -- if license number is not in the database
   procedure Delete_Drivers_License
    (License_Number : in License_Number_Type);

   -- adds new points to points total for specified
   -- license number
   -- License_Number_Not_Found exception raised
   -- if license number is not in the database
   -- Driver_Suspended exception raised if points total
   -- exceeds maximum
   procedure Update_Points
    (License_Number : in License_Number_Type;
     New_Points     : in Natural);

   License_Number_Exists,     Database_Full     : exception;
   License_Number_Not_Found,  License_Suspended : exception;
end Drivers_License_DBMS;
```

12

PACKAGES REVISITED

CHAPTER OBJECTIVES

- Code a simple package body.
- Code a package body with local data.
- Import to the package body.
- Use private types to enforce abstraction.
- Overload operators.
- Design packages to model abstract state machines.
- Design packages to model abstract data types.

The basic constructs of Ada have now been presented, so you should have a clear understanding of how to *use* packages. It is therefore time to examine packages in more detail. Specifically, it is time to describe the way package bodies are coded.

12.1 Basic Package Structure

As you know, packages are a major component of the Ada language. We explained in Chapter 1 how the two parts of a package, the package specification and the package body, support abstraction and information hiding. A package specification supports abstraction because it presents to the external world one level of detail, omitting the lower levels of detail. A package body supports information hiding because all code in the body is inacessible to the external world and is thus protected from accidental corruption. Theoretically, a package specification should give you sufficient information to decide whether the package contains the resources that you need; you should not need the package body to make this decision.*

You probably recall that a package specification merely states what resources the package provides to a potential user. The implementation of each algorithm declared in the package specification is contained in the package body. You have been using many packages throughout this text, yet so far you have been exposed only to package specifications.

Figure 12-1 shows the basic structure of a package body. In the coding of a package body, the reserved words **package body** are followed by the name of the package and then by the reserved word **is**. The implementation of the

* Actually, the package specification needs to be annotated with additional information, such as which algorithm is used for a subprogram, which exceptions are raised by each subprogram, and so on.

FIGURE 12-1 Package body structure

```
package body Package_Name is
   --
   -- How it is implemented
   --
end [Package_Name];
```

package comes next, followed by the closing structure.

```
end [Package_Name];
```

The name of the package body must correspond exactly to the name of the package specification. The use of Package_Name after the word **end** is optional but strongly recommended.

A_Small_Factorial_Package

Let us reexamine A_Small_Factorial_Package, originally presented in Section 5.5. The specification for this package is as follows:

```
package A_Small_Factorial_Package is
   subtype Argument_Subtype is Integer
           range 1 .. Integer'Last;
   subtype Result_Subtype is Integer
           range 1 .. Integer'Last;
   function Factorial_of (Value : Argument_Subtype)
           return Result_Subtype;
end A_Small_Factorial_Package;
```

The specification states that the resources provided by the package are two subtypes of type Integer, Argument_SubType and Result_SubType, and a function, Factorial_of, that, given a value of type Argument_SubType, returns a value of type Result_SubType. Any unit that imports this package can declare objects of the two subtypes, create subtypes of the two types, call the function Factorial_of (just as was done in Compute_Factorials_1_to_10 in Section 5.5), and so on.

When we wrote Compute_Factorials_1_to_10, we had no knowledge of the way Factorial_of is coded. Is it coded as a recursive function (that is, does it call itself)? Is it coded such that repeated multiplication is done in a loop? As we have noted, the exact form of the coding will not matter to the user under most circumstances. It is enough to know that he or she has the capability to get the factorial of any number as long as neither the number nor the factorial of the number exceeds the capacity of the hardware (in which case the user of the package should code an exception handler for Numeric_Error).

A package body contains the implementation of the algorithm(s) declared in the package specification, so the code for Factorial_of must be in the package body for A_Small_Factorial_Package. The body for A_Small_Factorial_Package is coded as follows:

```
package body A_Small_Factorial_Package is
   function Factorial_of (Value : Argument_Subtype)
            return Result_Subtype is
   begin -- Factorial_of
      if Value = 1 then
         return 1;
      else
            return Value * Factorial_of (Value-1);
      end if;
   end Factorial_of;
end A_Small_Factorial_Package;
```

Binary_Operations

Recall package Binary_Operations from Section 2.4, whose specification is as follows:

```
package Binary_Operations is
   procedure Interchange (First, Second : in out Integer);
     ...
end Binary_Operations;
```

The code for the package body for Binary_Operations is

```
package body Binary_Operations is
   procedure Interchange (First,Second : in out Integer) is
      Temp : Integer := First;
   begin -- Interchange
      First := Second;
      Second := Temp;
   end Interchange;
end Binary_Operations;
```

Figure 12-2 shows the code for Math_Library of Section 7.6. This package contains multiple algorithms. As you can see, the algorithms are simply coded in the package body one after the other.

Stub for Readability

When a package contains many algorithms, the code for these algorithms may extend over many pages and make the basic structure of a package body difficult to see. In this case, stub out the individual algorithms for better readability.

FIGURE 12-2 Math_Library

```
package Math_Library is
   function Power (A_Power, Number : Integer)
                  return Integer;
   function Square_Root (Number : Float) return Float;
   function Cube_Root (Number : Float) return Float;
end Math_Library;

package body Math_Library is
   function Power (A_Power, Number : Integer)
                  return Integer is
   begin -- Power
      return Number ** A_Power;
   end Power;
   function Square_Root (Number : Float) return Float is
      Epsilon : constant := 0.000001;
      Root    : Float;
   begin -- Square_Root
      if Number = 0.0 then
         return 0.0;
      else
         Root := 1.0;
         Root := (Number / Root + Root) / 2.0;
         while abs (Number / Root**2 -1.0) >= Epsilon
            loop
               Root := (Number / Root + Root) / 2.0;
            end loop;
         return Root;
      end if;
   end Square_Root;
```

(continued)

FIGURE 12-2 *(continued)*

```
      function Cube_Root (Number : Float) return Float is
         Epsilon : constant := 0.0000001;
         Old_Guess, New_Guess   : Float;
      begin -- Cube_Root
         if Number = 0.0 then
            return 0.0;
         else
            Old_Guess := 1.0;
            New_Guess := (2.0 * Old_Guess +
                             Number/Old_Guess**2)/3.0;
            while abs (New_Guess - Old_Guess) >= Epsilon
               loop
                  Old_Guess := New_Guess;
                  New_Guess := (2.0 * Old_Guess +
                                   Number/Old_Guess**2)/3.0;
               end loop;
         end if;
         return New_Guess;
      end Cube_Root;
   end Math_Library;
```

Figure 12-3(a–e) shows the package body for Math_Library with the algorithms stubbed out. Now it is easy to see that the package body contains three subprograms. Although the degree of benefit gained by stubbing is perhaps questionable here, we will see very shortly how useful stubbing can be with larger packages.

FIGURE 12-3 Math_Library with subunits

```
package Math_Library is
   function Power (A_Power, Number : Integer)
                  return Integer;
   function Square_Root (Number : Float) return Float;
   function Cube_Root   (Number : Float) return Float;
end Math_Library;
```

FIGURE 12-3(a) Math_Library specification

```
package body Math_Library is
   function Power (A_Power, Number : Integer)
                  return Integer is separate;
   function Square_Root (Number : Float)
                  return Float is separate;
   function Cube_Root (Number : Float)
                  return Float is separate;
end Math_Library;
```

FIGURE 12-3(b) Math_Library body

```
separate (Math_Library)
function Power (A_Power, Number : Integer)
               return Integer is
begin -- Power
   return Number ** A_Power;
end Power;
```

FIGURE 12-3(c) Subunit Power

```
separate (Math_Library)
function Square_Root (Number : Float) return Float is
   Epsilon : constant := 0.000001;
   Root    : Float;
begin -- Square_Root
      if Number = 0.0 then
         return 0.0;
      else
         Root := 1.0;
         Root := (Number / Root + Root) / 2.0;
         while abs(Number / Root**2 -1.0) >= Epsilon
            loop
               Root := (Number / Root + Root) / 2.0;
            end loop;
         return Root;
      end if;
end Square_Root;
```

FIGURE 12-3(d) Subunit Square_Root

```
separate (Math_Library)
function Cube_Root (Number : Float) return Float is
   Epsilon : constant := 0.0000001;
   Old_Guess, New_Guess   : Float;
begin -- Cube_Root
   if Number = 0.0 then
      return 0.0;
   else
      Old_Guess := 1.0;
      New_Guess := (2.0 * Old_Guess +
                   Number/Old_Guess**2)/3.0;
      while abs (New_Guess - Old_Guess) >= Epsilon
         loop
            Old_Guess := New_Guess;
            New_Guess := (2.0 * Old_Guess +
                         Number/Old_Guess**2)/3.0;
         end loop;
   end if;
   return New_Guess;
end Cube_Root;
```

FIGURE 12-3(e) Subunit Cube_Root

12.2 Local Data

Very often local data are required to implement the algorithms in a package body. These local data appear only in the coding of the package *body*; they are not part of the interface to the user and therefore do not appear in the package specification.

Statistics

For example, consider package Statistics from Chapter 2. Its package specification is as follows:

```
package Statistics is
   type List_of_Grades is array (1..10) of Integer;
   function Mean_of     (Class_Grades : List_of_Grades)
                         return Float;
   function Highest_of (Class_Grades : List_of_Grades)
                         return Integer;
   function Lowest_of   (Class_Grades  : List_of_Grades)
                         return Integer;
end Statistics;
```

The code for the package body of Statistics is shown in Figure 12-4.

FIGURE 12-4 Package body with local data

```
package body Statistics is
  -- Temp_List holds list of grades once sorted
  Temp_List : List_of_Grades;
  -- indicates whether list is Sorted
  Sorted : Boolean := False;
  -- the bubble sort from Chapter 8
  procedure Sort (List : in out List_of_Grades) is
     Sorted : Boolean := False;
  begin -- Sort
     while not Sorted
        loop
           Sorted := True;
           for J in List'First .. List'Last-1
           loop
              if List(J) > List (J+1) then
                 Temp := List(J);
                 List(J) := List(J+1);
                 List(J+1) := Temp;
                 Sorted := False;
              end if;
           end loop;
        end loop;
     Temp_List := List;
  end Sort;
```

Local data

(continued)

FIGURE 12-4 *(continued)*

```
      function Mean_of (Class_Grades : in List_of_Grades)
               return Float is
         Sum : Integer := 0;
      begin -- Mean_of
         for I in Class_Grades'Range
         loop
            Sum := Sum + Class_Grades(I);
         end loop;
         return Float(Sum)/Float(Class_Grades'Length);
      end Mean_of;
      function Highest_of (Class_Grades : in List_of_Grades)
               return Integer is
         Hold_List : List_of_Grades := Class_Grades;
      begin -- Highest_of
         if not Sorted then
            Sort (Hold_List);
            Temp_List := Hold_List;
         end if;
         return Temp_List(Temp_List'Last);
      end Highest_of;
      function Lowest_of (Class_Grades : in List_of_Grades)
               return Integer is
         Hold_List : List_of_Grades := Class_Grades;
      begin -- Lowest_of
         if not Sorted then
            Sort (Hold_List);
            Temp_List := Hold_List;
         end if;
         return Temp_List(Temp_List'First);
      end Lowest_of;
   end Statistics;
```

The variable Temp_List holds the sorted list of grades and is used by Lowest_of and Highest_of. Temp_List is local data; it *cannot* be accessed outside of the package body.

The variable Sorted indicates whether the list is sorted or not and is examined by Lowest_of and Highest_of. Sorted cannot be accessed outside the package body.

The procedure Sort is used to sort the list of grades so that Highest _of and Lowest_of can simply select the first and last elements in the sorted list

```
package Statistics is
        . . .
end Statistics
```

External view

```
package body Statistics is
     Temp_List: List_of_Grades;
     Sorted : Boolean := False;
     procedure Sort (List : in out List_of_Grades) is
               .
               .
               .
     end Sort;
     .
     .
     .
end Statistics;
```

FIGURE 12-5 External view of statistics

respectively. This procedure is needed only by the package body and is not intended as a resource to be supplied to the external world. Sort therefore cannot be called outside of the package body. Figure 12-5 illustrates this point.

Calendar_Info

Sometimes local data require additional resources. Recall package Calendar_Info from Chapter 11, whose specification follows:

```
package Calendar_Info is
   type Month_Type is (Jan, Feb, Mar, Apr, May, Jun,
                       Jul, Aug, Sep, Oct, Nov, Dec);
   type Day_Type is range 1 .. 31;
   type Year_Type is range 1980 .. 2500;
   type Date_Type is
   record
        Month : Month_Type;
        Day   : Day_Type;
        Year  : Year_Type;
   end record;
   function Leap_Year (Year : Year_Type) return Boolean;
   function Last_Day_of (Month : Month_Type)
           return Day_Type;
   procedure Get_a_Date (A_Date : out Date_Type);
   procedure Put_a_Date (A_Date : in Date_Type);
end Calendar_Info;
```

The body for package Calendar_Info is coded as follows. Not all subunits are shown.

The context clause for the package body imports Text_IO so that Step 2 can be performed for each of the data types that require I/O.

```
with Text_IO; use Text_IO:
package body Calendar_Info is
   package Day_IO is new Integer_IO (Day_Type);
   package Month_IO is new Enumeration_IO (Month_Type);
   package Year_IO is new Integer_IO (Year_Type);
   use Day_IO, Month_IO, Year_IO;
   function Leap_Year (Year : Year_Type) return Boolean
            is separate;
   function Last_Day_of (Month : Month_Type)
            return Day_Type is separate;
   procedure Get_a_Date (A_Date : out Date_Type)
             is separate;
   procedure Put_a_Date (A_Date : in Date_Type)
             is separate;
end Calendar_Info;
```

```
separate (Calendar_Info)
function Leap_Year (Year : Year_Type) return Boolean is
begin -- Leap_Year
   if Year mod 400 = 0 or
      (Year mod 4 = 0 and Year mod 100 /= 0) then
      return True;
   else
      return False;
   end if;
end Leap_Year;
```

```
separate (Calendar_Info)
function Last_Day_of (Month : Month_Type)
         return Day_Type is
begin -- Last_Day_of
   if Month = Apr or Month = Sep or Month = Jun or
      Month = Nov then
      return 30;
   elsif Month = Feb then
      return 28;
   else
      return 31;
   end if;
end Last_Day_of;
```

```
separate (Calendar_Info)
procedure Get_a_Date (A_Date : out Date_Type) is
   procedure Get_a_Month (A_Month : out Month_Type)
             is separate;
   procedure Get_a_Day (A_Day : out Day_Type)
             is separate;
   procedure Get_a_Year (A_Year : out Year_Type)
             is separate;
begin -- Get_a_Date
   Get_a_Month (A_Date.Month); -- get month component
   Get_a_Day   (A_Date.Day);   -- get day component
   Get_a_Year  (A_Date.Year);  -- get year component
end Get_a_Date;
```

```
separate (Calendar_Info)
procedure Put_a_Date (A_Date : in Date_Type) is
          -- similar to Get_a_Date
end Put_a_Date;
```

```
separate (Calendar_Info.Get_a_Date)
procedure Get_a_Month (A_Month : out Month_Type) is
begin -- Get_a_Month
   loop
      begin
         Get (A_Month);
   exit;
      exception
         when Data_Error =>
            Put_Line ("Invalid entry-try again.");
            Put_Line ("Enter first three letters of" &
                      "month.");
      end;
   end loop;
end Get_a_Month;
```

As you can see, there is no problem with importing library units to just the package body. Those resources, however, are not accessible to the package specification. By contrast when a context clause imports units to a package specification, the resources of the imported units are accessible throughout the entire package—both its specification and its body. Figure 12-6 illustrates this point.

Ordering the Resources

The specific order of appearance of the subprograms in the package body depends upon the relationship, if any, of the subprograms. For example, the subprograms in Math_Library have no relationship to each other: Cube_Root does not call Square_Root, Square_Root does not call Cube_Root. The order in which you physically place these subprograms in the package body is irrelevant.

When the package body requires local data, that local data must be placed prior to the implementation of the resources. For example, in the body for Statistics_Services the local data (Temp_List, Sorted, and Sort) precede the implementation of the resources that require them.

Finally, if the implementation of a specific resource requires another resource of the *same* package, the *resource required* must be placed *before* the resource that uses it in the package body.

FIGURE 12-6 Resource availability

```
package X is
    --resources
end X;
```

with X; use X;
package A is
    --resources of X
    --accessible here
end A;
	package specification	package B is
		    --resources of X
		    --not accessible
		    here
		end B;

package body A is
    --resources of X
    --accessible here
end A;
	package body	with X; use X;
		package body B is
		    --resources of X
		    --accessible here
		    --but not in the
		    --specification.
		end B;

12.3 Coin_Changer

Imagine a bus driver with a coin changer on his or her belt. The coin changer accepts a coin and dispenses a coin. The changer holds nickels, dimes, and quarters. In this section we will attempt to model such a coin changer.

We will use the following package specification:

```
with Text_IO; use Text_IO;
package Coin_Changer is
   type Coin_Type is (Nickel, Dime, Quarter);
   -- raises Bucket_Full if slot for the coin is full
   procedure Add_Coin (Coin : in Coin_Type);
   -- raises No_Coins if the slot for the coin is empty
   procedure Dispense_Coin (Coin : in Coin_Type);
   Bucket_Full : exception;
   No_Coins    : exception;
end Coin_Changer;
```

The package body for Coin_Changer is as follows:

```
package body Coin_Changer is
      -- define capacity of the coin changer
      Max_Quarter  : constant := 20;
      Max_Dime     : constant := 50;
      Max_Nickel   : constant := 20;
      -- define data structure for the coin changer
      The_Changer : array (Coin_Type) of Natural;
      -- I/O for coins
      package Coin_IO is new Enumeration_IO (Coin_Type);
      use Coin_IO;
      -- stub out the procedures
      -- raises Bucket_Full if slot for the coin is full
      procedure Add_Coin (Coin : in Coin_Type)
                is separate;
      -- raises No_Coins if the slot for the coin is empty
      procedure Dispense_Coin (Coin : in Coin_Type)
                is separate;
end Coin_Changer;
```

Figure 12-7 shows a main procedure that tests the coin changer. Note the exception handlers that are coded to handle the exceptions raised by the package subprograms.

FIGURE 12-7 Procedure Test_the_Changer

```
with Coin_Changer, Text_IO;
use Coin_Changer, Text_IO;
procedure Test_the_Changer is
   -- This procedure will simply insert coins
   -- into and extract coins from the coin changer.
   package Coin_IO is new Enumeration_IO (Coin_Type);
   use Coin_IO;
   Coin_to_Deposit, Coin_to_Dispense : Coin_Type;
   Command : Character;
begin -- Test_the_Changer
   loop
      begin -- to form a frame for the handlers
         Put_Line("Kind of transaction : Add, Dispense," &
                  "Quit?");
         New_Line;
         Put_Line ("Enter: A, D, or Q: ");
         Get (Command);
         case Command is
            when 'Q' | 'q' =>
   exit;
            when 'A' | 'a' =>
                 Put_Line ("Adding nickel, dime, or" &
                           "quarter? ");
                 Get (Coin_to_Deposit); -- no handler for
                                        -- lack of space
                 Add_Coin (Coin_to_Deposit);
            when 'D' | 'd' =>
                 Put_Line ("Do you need a nickel, dime," &
                           "or quarter?");
                 Get (Coin_to_Dispense); -- no handler
                                         -- no space
                 Dispense_Coin (Coin_to_Dispense);
            when others => Put_Line ("Illegal command");
         end case;
      exception
         when Bucket_Full => Put ("The ");
                             Put (Coin_to_Deposit);
                             Put (" slot is full.");
                             New_Line;
```

(*continued*)

FIGURE 12-7 *(continued)*

```
            when No_Coins     => Put ("The ");
                                 Put (Coin_to_Dispense);
                                 Put (" slot is empty.");
                                 New_Line;
        end;
    end loop;
end Test_the_Changer;
```

The code for the subunits Add_Coin and Dispense_Coin is shown in Figures 12-8(a) and 12-8(b), respectively. Note here that we are raising a *specific* exception, either Bucket_Full or No_Coins. Because there is no exception handler in either Add_Coin or Dispense_Coin, the user of the package will have to code appropriate handlers, as was shown in Figure 12-7.

FIGURE 12-8 Coin_Changer subunits

```
separate (Coin_Changer)
procedure Add_Coin (Coin : in Coin_Type) is
begin -- Add_Coin
    case Coin is
        when Quarter =>
             if The_Changer (Coin) + 1 <= Max_Quarter
             then
                 The_Changer (Quarter) :=
                 The_Changer(Quarter) + 1:
             else
                 raise Bucket_Full;
             end if;
        when Dime =>
             if The_Changer (Coin) + 1 <= Max_Dime
             then
                 The_Changer (Dime) :=
                 The_Changer(Dime) + 1:
             else
                 raise Bucket_Full;
             end if;
```

(continued)

FIGURE 12-8 *(continued)*

```
        when Nickel =>
            if The_Changer (Coin) + 1 <= Max_Nickel
            then
               The_Changer(Nickel):=The_Changer(Nickel)+1;
            else
               raise Bucket_Full;
            end if;
      end case;
   end Add_Coin;
```

FIGURE 12-8(a) Subunit Add_Coin

```
separate (Coin_Changer)
procedure Dispense_Coin (Coin : in Coin_Type) is
begin -- Dispense_Coin
   if The_Changer (Coin) = 0 then
      raise No_Coins;
   else
      The_Changer (Coin) := The_Changer (Coin) - 1;
      Put (Coin);
      Put_Line (" dispensed ");
   end if;
end Dispense_Coin;
```

FIGURE 12-8(b) Subunit Dispense_Coin

EXERCISES

12.1 Code the package body for package Outdoor_Thermometer from Chapter 7.

12.2 Code the package body for package Complex_Numbers introduced in the Exercises for Chapter 11.

12.3 Code the package body for package Trig_Package from Chapter 7.

12.4 Our coin changer model is fairly simple. What modifications would be required to make the package model a smart coin changer? A smart coin changer dispenses two nickels for a dime, two dimes and a nickel for a quarter, or five nickels for a quarter if there are no dimes. Code the modifications, and test the new package.

12.4 Soda Machine

In this section we seek to model a soda vending machine. A soda machine takes in money and dispenses change and/or soda cans. To be attractive to customers, the soda machine must offer a variety of soft drinks and must work reliably. Our machine is equipped with soda selection buttons, a coin return button, and a variety of sodas. Only nickels, dimes, and quarters are accepted. For now, assume that the machine has an infinite supply of change. (We leave it to you as an exercise to modify the code to keep track of the number and kind of coins in the machine and issue a "Use Correct Change" warning when there are not sufficient coins in the machine to accommodate the change required.)

Soda Machine Package Specifications

As you know, packages group logically related data. Consider the following package specifications, which we will use to model the soda machine. Each package specification is *preceded* by a *block comment* or *prologue* that describes the package.

package Money The block comment and package specification for Money are shown here.

```
-----------------------------------------------------------------
--    PROGRAMMER        : P. Texel/P. Smeton                    --
--    DATE              : 10/25/1984                            --
--    PROGRAM UNIT      : package specification                 --
--    LIBRARY           : soda                                  --
--    DEPENDENCIES      : none                                  --
--                                                              --
--    DEPENDENT UNITS   : package Machine_Description           --
--                        package Soda_Machine_Operations       --
--                        procedure Plug_It_In                  --
--                                                              --
```

```
--    MAIN SUBPROGRAM : procedure Plug_It_In                      --
--                                                                --
--                                                                --
--    DESCRIPTION:                                                --
--                                                                --
--    This package contains resources that relate to the         --
--    currency used for the soda machine. If the machine         --
--    were to be installed in a foreign country, changes         --
--    with respect to currency would be made in this             --
--    package.                                                    --
--                                                                --
--------------------------------------------------------------------

package Money is
   subtype Change_Type is Integer range 0 .. 100;
   Cost_of_Can : constant Change_Type := 50;
   type Coin_Type is (Nickel, Dime, Quarter);
   type Coin_Value_Type is array (Coin_Type) of Change_Type;
   Value_of    : constant Coin_Value_Type := (5, 10, 25);
end Money;
```

The subtype Change_Type represents monetary values, for example, 50 cents or 10 cents. The monetary unit for the American implementation of the soda machine is cents.

Cost_of_Can is a constant of type Change_Type that is used to represent the cost of a can of soda. It is declared as a constant because the value should not be alterable. Should the price of a can of soda increase, the only change required will be in this declaration. All references, in the implementation of our soda machine, to the cost of a can of soda are in terms of this constant.

Coin_Type is an enumeration type that allows us to represent our coins by their name. The type Coin_Value_Type is an array, indexed by the coin's name, whose components represent the monetary value of the coin.

Value_of is declared to be a constant of type Coin_Value_Type and is initialized so that the value of a nickel is 5, the value of a dime is 10, and the value of a quarter is 25 cents. In other words, if we should write Value_of(Dime), the result will be the monetary value of a dime in cents, which is 10.

package Machine_Description Following is the block comment and package specification for Machine_Description.

```
-----------------------------------------------------------------
--   PROGRAMMER       : P. Texel/P. Smeton                      --
--   DATE             : 10/26/1984                              --
--   PROGRAM UNIT     : package specification                   --
--   LIBRARY          : soda                                    --
--   DEPENDENCIES     : package Money                           --
--                                                              --
--   DEPENDENT UNITS  : package Soda_Machine_Operations         --
--                    : procedure Plug_It_In                    --
--                                                              --
--   MAIN SUBPROGRAM  : procedure Plug_It_In                    --
--                                                              --
-----------------------------------------------------------------
--   DESCRIPTION:                                               --
--                                                              --
--   This package contains the resources required to            --
--   describe the soda machine as it is viewed by the           --
--   user. This machine has seven possible selections,          --
--   which are indicated in the type declaration for            --
--   Soda_Can_Type. The declaration for Soda_Machine            --
--   indicates that button 1 on the machine will dispense       --
--   Coke, button 2 will dispense Pepsi, and so on.             --
--                                                              --
--   Any changes to the machine, for example adding more        --
--   selections or changing the kind of soda offered, will      --
--   require changes in only this program unit. All other       --
--   program units refer to these declarations.                 --
--                                                              --
-----------------------------------------------------------------

with Money; use Money;
package Machine_Description is
   type Soda_Selection_Button_Type is range 1 .. 7;
   type Soda_Can_Type is (Coke, Pepsi, Diet_Coke, Diet_Pepsi,
        Caffeine_Free_Coke, Caffeine_Free_Diet_Coke,
        Ginger_Ale);
   type Soda_Machine_Type is array
        (Soda_Selection_Button_Type) of Soda_Can_Type;
   Soda_Machine : Soda_Machine_Type :=
        (Coke, Pepsi, Diet_Coke, Diet_Pepsi,
        Caffeine_Free_Coke, Caffeine_Free_Diet_Coke,
        Ginger_Ale);
end Machine_Description;
```

Type Soda_Selection_Button_Type indicates that seven possible buttons are available for selection.

Type Soda_Can_Type defines the kinds of soda that are carried by the machine.

Type Soda_Machine_Type is an array indexed by user selections. This array's components are of Soda_Can_Type.

The object Soda_Machine is our soda machine. This declaration specifies that the first button will dispense a Coke, the second button a Pepsi, and so on.

package Soda_Machine_Operations The block comment and package specification for Soda_Machine_Operations are shown here.

```
---------------------------------------------------------------
--                                                          --
--    PROGRAMMER       : P.Texel/P. Smeton                  --
--    DATE             : 10/27/1984                         --
--    PROGRAM UNIT     : package specification              --
--    LIBRARY          : soda                               --
--    DEPENDENCIES     : package Money                      --
--                       package Machine_Description        --
--                                                          --
--    DEPENDENT UNITS  : package body                       --
--                       procedure Plug_It_In               --
--                                                          --
--    MAIN SUBPROGRAM  : procedure Plug_It_In               --
--                                                          --
---------------------------------------------------------------
--    DESCRIPTION:                                          --
--                                                          --
--    This package contains the operations that are performed --
--    by the soda machine. Our soda machine performs the   --
--    following operations:                                 --
--                                                          --
--        - accepts coins                                   --
--        - returns the coins, if the user depresses the    --
--          coin return button                              --
--        - releases the appropriate change, if necessary   --
--        - dispenses a can of soda dependent upon the      --
--          specific button selected.                       --
--                                                          --
---------------------------------------------------------------
```

```
with Money; use Money;
with Machine_Description; use Machine_Description;
package Soda_Machine_Operations is
   procedure Accept_Coins
      (Total_Inserted   : out Change_Type;
       Money_Returned   : out Boolean);
   procedure Accept_Soda
      (Button_Selection : out Soda_Selection_Button_Type);
   procedure Release_Change
      (Coins_Inserted   : in Change_Type);
   procedure Release_Can
      (Selection        : in Soda_Selection_Button_Type);
end Soda_Machine_Operations;
```

Accept_Coins gets the coins inserted and sums the values of the coins in order to determine the total amount of money inserted. Accept_Coins returns to the caller the total amount of money inserted (Total_Inserted) and whether or not the user depressed the coin return button to get his/her money back (Money_Returned).

Accept_Soda gets the number of the button selected.

Release_Change releases the amount of change when Total_Inserted is more than the cost of a can of soda.

Release_Can releases the can of soda indicated by the specific button depressed by the user.

The Main Routine

The main routine for our soda machine is shown in Figure 12-9. This routine is called, oddly enough, Plug_It_In.

The dependency diagram for Plug_It_In is shown in Figure 12-10.

FIGURE 12-9 Soda machine main procedure

```
-------------------------------------------------------------------
--                                                               --
--    PROGRAMMER        : P. Texel/P. Smeton                     --
--    DATE              : 10/28/1984                             --
--    PROGRAM UNIT      : procedure main                         --
--    LIBRARY           : soda                                   --
--    DEPENDENCIES      : package Money                          --
--                        package Machine_Description            --
--                        package Soda_Machine_Operations        --
--                                                               --
```

(continued)

FIGURE 12-9 *(continued)*

```
--    DEPENDENT UNITS : none                                   --
--                                                             --
--    MAIN SUBPROGRAM : Plug_It_In                             --
--                                                             --
-----------------------------------------------------------------
--                                                             --
--    DESCRIPTION:                                             --
--                                                             --
--    This main procedure represents the soda machine. It      --
--    gets the coins inserted, and, as long as the money       --
--    was not returned, accepts the soda selection from        --
--    the user, releases the appropriate change, and           --
--    finally dispenses the can of soda.                       --
--                                                             --
-----------------------------------------------------------------

with Money; use Money;
with Machine_Description; use Machine_Description;
with Text_IO; use Text_IO;
with Soda_Machine_Operations; use Soda_Machine_Operations;
procedure Plug_It_In is
   --
   -- The machine needs to know the total amount of money
   -- inserted, the button selected by the user, and whether
   -- the money was returned or not.
   --
   Coins_Inserted   : Change_Type;
   Button_Selection : Soda_Selection_Button_Type;
   Money_Returned   : Boolean;
begin -- Plug_It_In
    loop
       Accept_Coins (Coins_Inserted, Money_Returned);
       if not Money_Returned then
          Accept_Soda    (Button_Selection);
          Release_Change (Coins_Inserted);
          Release_Can    (Button_Selection);
       end if;
    end loop;
end Plug_It_In;
```

FIGURE 12-10 Soda machine dependency diagram

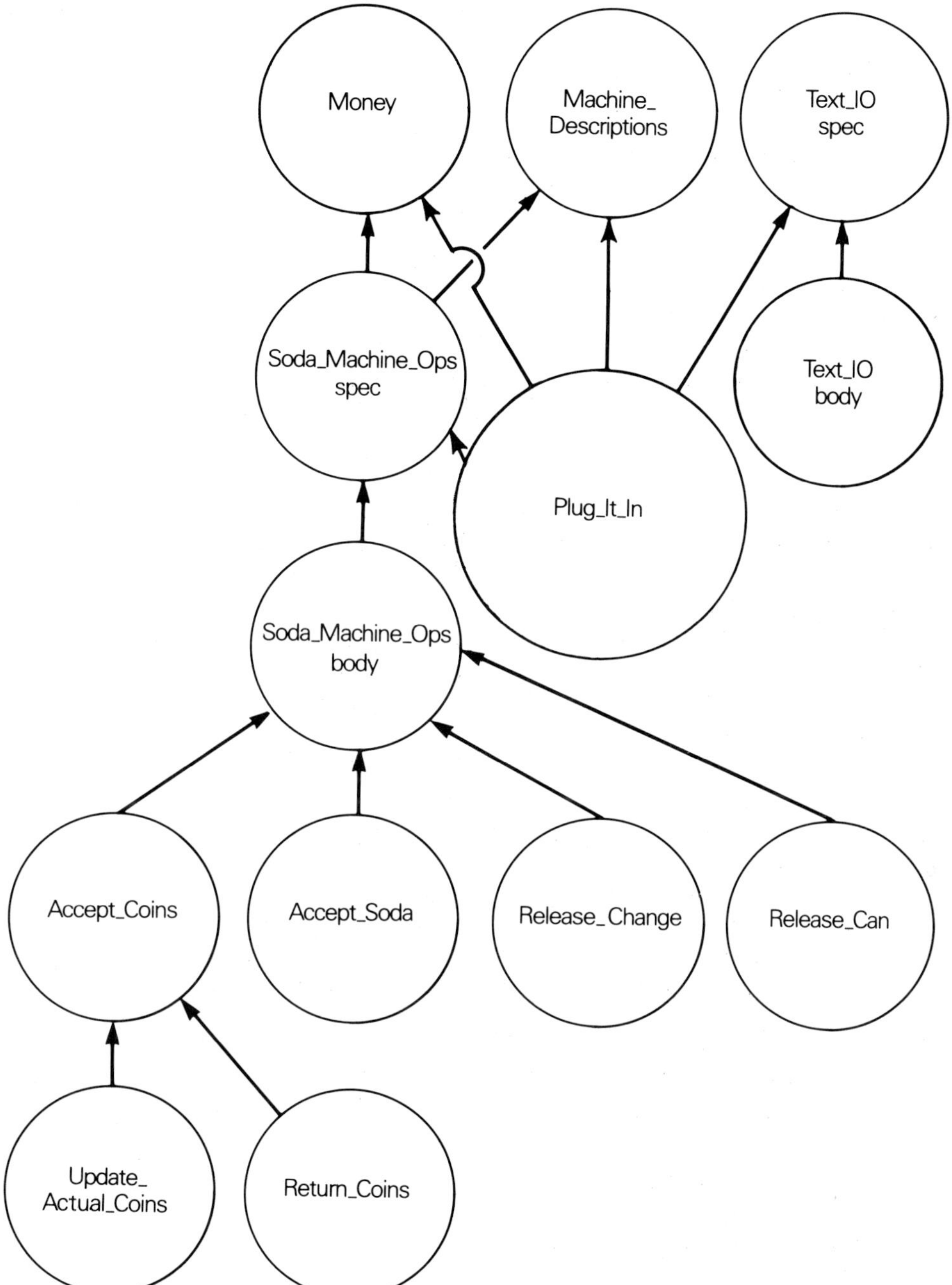

Soda Machine Package Body

Figure 12-11 shows the code for the body of package Soda_Machine_Operations. Figures 12-12 (a) through 12-12 (d) show the code for the subunits Accept_Coins, Accept_Soda, Release_Change and Release_Can, respectively. Finally, Figure 12-13 shows the subunit Return_Coins that is stubbed out of Accept_Coins.

FIGURE 12-11 Soda_Machine_Operations body

```
----------------------------------------------------------------
--                                                            --
--    PROGRAMMER       : P. Texel/ P. Smeton                  --
--    DATE             : 5/20/1985                            --
--    PROGRAM UNIT     : package body                         --
--    LIBRARY          : soda                                 --
--    DEPENDENCIES     : package spec                         --
--                       package Money                        --
--                       package Machine_Description          --
--                       package Text_IO                      --
--                                                            --
--    DEPENDENT UNITS  : none                                 --
--                                                            --
--    MAIN SUBPROGRAM  : procedure Plug_It_In                 --
--                                                            --
----------------------------------------------------------------
--                                                            --
--    DESCRIPTION      :                                      --
--                                                            --
--    This package body contains the algorithms for the       --
--    operations specified in the package specification.      --
--    Additionally it contains a procedure local to the       --
--    body, specifically:                                     --
--                                                            --
--         - Return_Coins which returns the actual coins      --
--           inserted when the coin return button is de-      --
--           pressed.                                         --
--                                                            --
--    All I/O is embedded within this body.                   --
--                                                            --
----------------------------------------------------------------
```

(continued)

FIGURE 12-11 *(continued)*

```
with Text_IO; use Text_IO;
package body Soda_Machine_Operations is
   -- I/O for the nickels, dimes and quarters
   package Coin_IO is new Enumeration_IO (Coin_Type);
   use Coin_IO;
   -- I/O for the soda button selections
   package Soda_Selection_Button_IO is new Integer_IO
           (Soda_Selection_Button_Type);
   use Soda_Selection_Button_IO;
   -- I/O for the cans of soda
   package Soda_Can_IO is new Enumeration_IO (Soda_Can_Type);
   use Soda_Can_IO;
   procedure Accept_Coins
      (Total_Inserted : out Change_Type;
       Money_Returned : out Boolean) is separate;
   procedure Accept_Soda
      (Button_Selection : out Soda_Selection_Button_Type)
      is separate;
   procedure Release_Change
      (Coins_Inserted   : in Change_Type) is separate;
   procedure Release_Can
      (Selection : in Soda_Selection_Button_Type)
      is separate;
end Soda_Machine_Operations;
```

FIGURE 12-12(a) Subunit Accept_Coins

```
--
-- This procedure accepts the coins inserted and keeps
-- track of them in the array Actual_Coins_Inserted.
-- Actual_Coins_Inserted is an array indexed by coin type,
-- whose components are the number of that particular coin
-- inserted.
--
-- This procedure returns the coins if the coin return button
-- is depressed.

separate (Soda_Machine_Operations)
procedure Accept_Coins (Total_Inserted : out Change_Type;
                        Money_Returned : out Boolean) is
   type Actual_Coins_Inserted_Type is array (Coin_Type)
        of Natural;
   type  Coin_Return_Desired_Type is (Yes, No);
   -- I/O for coin return button
```

(continued)

FIGURE 12-12(a) Subunit Accept_Coins (*continued*)

```
   package Coin_Return_Desired_IO is new Enumeration_IO
          (Coin_Return_Desired_Type);
   use Coin_Return_Desired_IO;
   Actual_Coins_Inserted : Actual_Coins_Inserted_Type
                         := (0, 0, 0);
   Coin_Inserted         : Coin_Type;
   Coins_Returned        : Coin_Return_Desired_Type;
   procedure Return_Coins
       (Actual_Coins_Inserted: in Actual_Coins_Inserted_Type)
       is separate;
begin -- Accept_Coins
   Total_Inserted := 0;
   FIFTY_CENTS_LOOP: -- obtain at least 50 cents
   while Total_Inserted < 50
   loop
      Put ("Enter coin: ");
      COIN_INPUT_LOOP: -- get one coin at a time
      loop
         begin
            Get (Coin_Inserted);
      exit;
         exception
            when Data_Error | Constraint_Error =>
               Put ("Invalid entry," &
                    "enter only nickel, dime or quarter: ");
         end;
      end loop COIN_INPUT_LOOP;
      -- update actual list of coins and update total
      -- amount inserted
      Actual_Coins_Inserted(Coin_Inserted) :=
       Actual_Coins_Inserted(Coin_Inserted) + 1;
      Total_Inserted := Total_Inserted + Value_of
      (Coin_Inserted);
      --Coin return option
      Put ("Do you want your coins returned: ");
      loop
         begin
            Get (Coins_Returned);
      exit;
         exception
            when Data_Error | Constraint_Error =>
               Put ("Invalid entry, enter either yes or no: ");
         end;
      end loop;
```

FIGURE 12-12(a) Subunit Accept_Coins (*continued*)

```
      case Coins_Returned is
         when Yes =>
            Return_Coins (Actual_Coins_Inserted);
            Money_Returned := True;
   exit;
         when No =>
            Money_Returned := False;
      end case;
   end loop FIFTY_CENTS_LOOP;
end Accept_Coins;
```

FIGURE 12-12(b) Subunit Accept_Soda

```
-- This procedure accepts the user's soda selection.

separate (Soda_Machine_Operations)
procedure Accept_Soda
  (Button_Selection : out Soda_Selection_Button_Type) is
begin -- Accept_Soda
   -- display possible selections
   for Soda_Selection_Button in Soda_Selection_Button_Type
   loop
      Put ("For ");
      Put (Soda_Machine(Soda_Selection_Button));
      Put (", select ");
      Put (Soda_Selection_Button);
      New_Line;
   end loop;
   -- input selection
   Put ("Enter soda selection: ");
   loop
      begin
         Get (Button_Selection);
   exit;
      exception
         when Data_Error | Constraint_Error =>
            Put ("Invalid entry, enter only 1 through ");
            Put (Soda_Selection_Button_Type'Last);
            Put (": ");
      end;
   end loop;
end Accept_Soda;
```

FIGURE 12-12(c) Subunit Release_Change

```
-- This procedure releases the correct change if the total
-- amount of money inserted exceeds the cost of the can.

separate (Soda_Machine_Operations)
procedure Release_Change (Coins_Inserted : in Change_Type) is
   Remaining_Change : Change_Type
      := Coins_Inserted - Cost_of_Can;
   Coin_Released    : Coin_Type;
begin -- Release_Change
   while Remaining_Change > 0
   loop
      if    Remaining_Change in 25..50 then
         Coin_Released := Quarter;
      elsif Remaining_Change in 10..24 then
         Coin_Released := Dime;
      elsif Remaining_Change in 5..9 then
         Coin_Released := Nickel;
      end if;
      Remaining_Change
         := Remaining_Change - Value_of (Coin_Released);
      Put ("Releasing a ");
      Put (Coin_Released);
      New_Line;
   end loop;
end Release_Change;
```

FIGURE 12-12(d) Subunit Release_Can

```
-- This procedure releases the soda, given the user button
-- selection.
separate (Soda_Machine_Operations)
procedure Release_Can
   (Selection : in Soda_Selection_Button_Type) is
begin -- Release_Can
   Put      (Soda_Machine(Selection));
   Put_Line (" can released");
end Release_Can;
```

FIGURE 12-13 Return_Coins

```
separate (Soda_Machine_Operations.Accept_Coins)
procedure Return_Coins
   (Actual_Coins_Inserted : in Actual_Coins_Inserted_Type) is
begin -- Return_Coins
   for Coin in Coin_Type
   loop
      for I in 1..Actual_Coins_Inserted(Coin)
      loop
         Put ("Dispensing a ");
         Put (Coin);
         New_Line;
      end loop;
   end loop;
end Return_Coins;
```

EXERCISES

12.5 Why do packages Money and Machine_Description not have package bodies?

12.6 Discuss how the specifications for our soda machine support abstraction.

12.7 Discuss how the package body for Soda_Machine_Operations supports information hiding.

12.8 Modify the model for the soda machine so that the machine keeps track of what coins are available for making change. Start with 25 coins for each coin type in the machine. Have the machine issue a message that says "Use Exact Change Only" at some predetermined point.

12.9 Modify the model for the soda machine so that the machine turns a selection light on when the machine is out of that particular soda.

12.10 As currently coded, the algorithm for Release_Change is applicable to U.S. coins only.

a. Recode Release_Change to make it a more general-purpose change routine that can release change for any currency.
b. Modify package Money to accommodate Japanese currency.

12.11 Code the package body for the Drivers_License_DBMS of Chapter 11.

a. Modify the Drivers_License_DBMS package. Add a new subprogram to the package to determine if a driver's license has expired, given the current date and the license number.
b. Modify the Drivers_License_DBMS package. Add a new subprogram to the package to determine the number of drivers' licenses in the database system issued for a specific car type (e.g. Ford).
c. Modify the Drivers_License_DBMS package, adding a new subprogram to the package to determine the number of drivers' licenses in the database system issued to senior citizens (i.e. anyone 65 years or older).
d. Modify part c to determine the number of drivers' licenses issued to drivers in a specified age range.

e. Write a program (Query_Drivers_License_DBMS) similar to Update_Drivers_License_DBMS of Chapter 11 to utilize the new package. (Note: the user should only be asked once to enter the current date.)

12.12 Design an interactive Telephone Exchange data base for the ABC Corp. Permit the user to add, delete, and modify employees' four-digit telephone exchanges and print out a new directory every six months. Test the package.

12.5 Private Types

As you have seen, an Ada package supports abstraction. However, a package does not *enforce* abstraction. Recall package Complex_Numbers from the Exercises for Chapter 11. The specification for that package is as follows:

```
package Complex_Numbers is
   type Real_Type is digits 4;
   type Complex_Type is
   record
      Re, Im : Real_Type;
   end record;
   function Add        (A, B : Complex_Type)
                       return Complex_Type;
   function Subtract   (A, B : Complex_Type)
                       return Complex_Type;
   function Multiply   (A, B : Complex_Type)
                       return Complex_Type;
   function Divide     (A, B : Complex_Type)
                       return Complex_Type;
end Complex_Numbers;
```

The user of this package knows that a complex number is implemented as a record. To Get values of a complex number, Z, let us say from a file, the user writes:

```
Get (Input_File, Z.Re);
Get (Input_File, Z.Im);
```

The user cannot write

```
Get (Input_File, Z);
```

because a Get procedure, with a formal parameter of type Complex_Type, has not been defined.

The present coding permits the user to work at too low a level of detail. It is preferable that the user think of a complex number as a complex number, not as a record with two components, Re and Im. Furthermore, if a package designer has gone to a great deal of effort to provide a Complex_Numbers package with operations that can be performed on these complex numbers, the designer may want to *enforce* the abstraction by *not* allowing the user to access the components of the complex number. This can be accomplished by coding type Complex_Type as a *private* type, as follows:

```
package Complex_Numbers is
   type Real_Type is digits 4;
   type Complex_Type is private;
   function Add (A,B: Complex_Type) return Complex_Type;
   function Subtract (A,B: Complex_Type)
                 return Complex_Type;
   function Multiply (A,B: Complex_Type)
                 return Complex_Type;
   function Divide (A,B: Complex_Type)
                 return Complex_Type;
private
   type Complex_Type
   is record
      Re:Real_Type;
      Im:Real_Type;
   end record;
end Complex_Numbers;
```

The package body for Complex_Numbers is shown in Figure 12-14.

By coding Complex_Type as a private type, the package hides the implementation of Complex_Type from the user. Because the implementation is hidden, the user does not know Complex_Type is a record and therefore does not have access to the components of Complex_Type. It is as if type Complex_Type were coded in the package body: the structure of the data type is inaccessible. For example, the following code would *not* compile:

```
with Complex_Numbers; use Complex_Numbers;
with Text_IO; use Text_IO;
procedure Try_It_Out is
   -- Step 2 to allow I/O on type Real_Type, thus
   -- enabling I/O on individual components
   package Real_IO is new Float_IO (Real_Type);
   use Real_IO;
   Z: Complex_Type;
begin -- Try_It_Out
   Get (Z.Re); --**ILLEGAL**--
   . . .
   -- other statements
end Try_It_Out;
```

The diagnostic issued should be something akin to "Incompatible operation for the type."

Operations on Private Types

As you know, every type is described by a set of values and a set of operations permissible on those values. The set of legal values for a private type is the set of legal values for the type that is declared in the private portion of the package specification. For example the set of legal values for Complex_Type is the set of record aggregates with components of type Real_Type.

The set of operations applicable to private types depends upon whether the operation is being performed inside or outside the package body. *Inside* the package body, the operations applicable to the private type are those that are applicable to the type as declared in the private part of the package specification. For example, the operations that are applicable to objects of type Complex_Type *inside* the package body are those operations that are legal for

FIGURE 12-14 Complex_Numbers package body

```
package body Complex_Numbers is
   function Add (A,B: Complex_Type)
                 return Complex_Type is
      Ans:Complex_Type;
   begin -- Add
      Ans.Re:= A.Re+B.Re;
      Ans.Im:= A.Im+B.Im;
      return Ans;
   end Add;
   function Subtract (A,B: Complex_Type)
                      return Complex_Type is
      Ans:Complex_Type;
   begin -- Subtract
      Ans.Re:=A.Re-B.Re;
      Ans.Im:=A.Im-B.Im;
      return Ans;
   end Subtract;
   function Multiply (A,B:Complex_Type)
                      return Complex_Type is
      Ans:Complex_Type;
   begin -- Multiply
      Ans.Re:=A.Re*B.Re-A.Im*B.Im;
      Ans.Im:=A.Im*B.Re+A.Re+B.Im;
      return Ans;
   end Multiply;
   function Divide (A,B:Complex_Type)
                    return Complex_Type is
      Denom:Real;
      Ans:Complex_Type;
   begin -- Divide
      Denom:=B.Re*B.Re-B.Im*(-B.Im);
      Ans.Re:=A.Re*B.Re+A.Im*B.Im;
      Ans.Im:=A.Im*B.Re-A.Re*B.Im;
      Ans.Re:=Ans.Re/Denom;
      Ans.Im:=Ans.Im/Denom;
      return Ans;
   end Divide;
end Complex_Numbers;
```

record types in general: component selection, assignment, and test for equality and inequality.

Outside the package body, the *only* operations applicable to private types are assignment (:=)* and test for equality and inequality. Component selection is no longer available outside the package. The fact that in this case the two sets of operations are almost the same is purely coincidental. If Complex_Type had been declared in the private part of the package specification as an array type, as in

```
package Complex_Numbers is
   type Real_Type is digits 4;
   type Complex_Type is private;
   function Add (A,B: Complex_Type) return Complex_Type;
   function Subtract (A,B: Complex_Type)
                      return Complex_Type;
   function Multiply (A,B: Complex_Type)
                      return Complex_Type;
   function Divide (A,B: Complex_Type)
                      return Complex_Type;
private
   type Complex_Type is array (1..2) of Real_Type;
end Complex_Numbers;
```

then the set of operations applicable *inside* the package body would include catenation, slicing, component selection, attributes, and so on, but the set of operations outside the package body would still be simply copy and tests for equality and inequality.

Finally, note that the subprograms provided by the package specification are viewed as operations applicable to the private type both inside *and* outside the package. These subprograms are available to both the package body and the external world. For example, Add, Subtract, and so on can be called both from within the package body and from outside the package body.

Figure 12-15 summarizes the two views of private types.

---

* Assignment cannot be made to an object of a private type because the object's structure is not known outside the package. For example, to write Z:=(6.0,3.0) is illegal. The use of the assignment operator outside the package body is limited to *copying* the value of one object to the value of another object of the same type.

Complex_Numbers Improved

If we can't use literal assignment outside the package, how can we get any values for complex numbers so that we can add or subtract them? In order to let us do this, the package must either provide a subprogram that "constructs" a value of the required type from individual components or inputs a value of the type. Here is the package specification for Complex_Numbers with a new function called Make_Complex added.

```
package Complex_Numbers is
   type Real_Type is digits 4;
   type Complex_Type is private;
   function Add (A,B: Complex_Type) return Complex_Type;
   function Subtract (A,B: Complex_Type)
                      return Complex_Type;
   function Multiply (A,B: Complex_Type)
                      return Complex_Type;
   function Divide (A,B: Complex_Type)
                      return Complex_Type;
   function Make_Complex (A,B : Real_Type)
                      return Complex_Type;
private
   type Complex_Type is
   record
      Re:Real_Type;
      Im:Real_Type;
   end record;
end Complex_Numbers;
```

The revised package body is shown in Figure 12-16.

Now, if you send Make_Complex two values of type Real_Type, it will construct a value of type Complex_Type. Figure 12-17 shows Try_It_Out recoded to reflect the usage of Make_Complex.

As the final comment indicates, there is a problem with outputting the results. To write

```
Put(Ans_Add.Re); --**ILLEGAL**--
```

is illegal because component access is not permitted for private types outside the package body.

This final modification to package Complex_Numbers supplies output capability.

```
package Complex_Numbers is
   type Real_Type is digits 4;
   type Complex_Type is private;
   function Add (A,B: Complex_Type) return Complex_Type;
   function Subtract (A,B: Complex_Type)
                    return Complex_Type;
   function Multiply (A,B: Complex_Type)
                    return Complex_Type;
   function Divide (A,B: Complex_Type)
                    return Complex_Type;
   function Make_Complex (A,B : Real_Type)
                    return Complex_Type;
   procedure Output (Answer : in Complex_Type);
private
   type Complex_Type is
   record
      Re: Real_Type;
      Im: Real_Type;
   end record;
end Complex_Numbers;
```

FIGURE 12-15 Two views of a private type

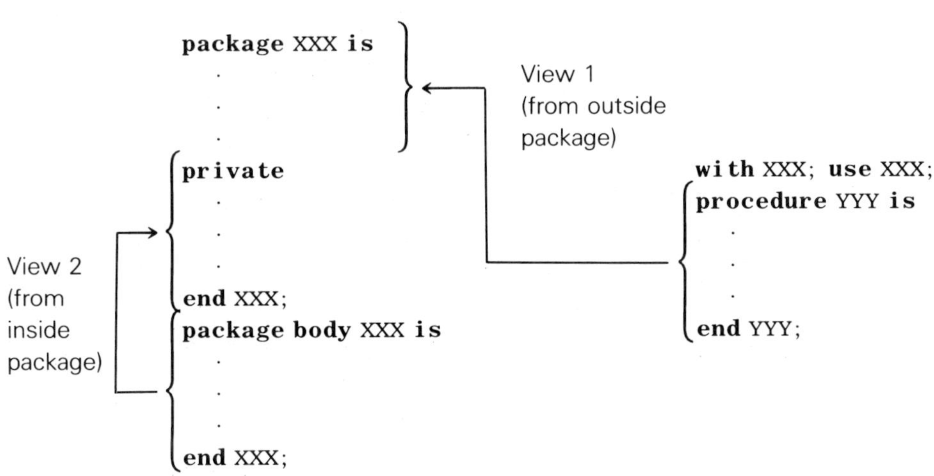

FIGURE 12-16 Complex_Numbers with Make_Complex added

```
package body Complex_Numbers is
   function Add (A,B: Complex) return Complex_Type is
      Ans:Complex_Type;
   begin -- Add
      Ans.Re:= A.Re+B.Re;
      Ans.Im:= A.Im+B.Im;
      return Ans;
   end Add;
   function Subtract (A,B: Complex_Type)
                      return Complex_Type is
      Ans:Complex_Type;
   begin -- Subtract
      Ans.Re:=A.Re-B.Re;
      Ans.Im:=A.Im-B.Im;
      return Ans;
   end Subtract;
   function Multiply (A,B: Complex_Type)
                      return Complex_Type is
      Ans:Complex_Type;
   begin -- Multiply
      Ans.Re:=A.Re*B.Re-A.Im*B.Im;
      Ans.Im:=A.Im*B.Re+A.Re+B.Im;
      return Ans;
   end Multiply;
   function Divide   (A,B: Complex_Type)
                      return Complex_Type is
      Denom:Real;
      Ans:Complex_Type;
   begin -- Divide
      Denom:=B.Re*B.Re-B.Im*(-B.Im);
      Ans.Re:=A.Re*B.Re+A.Im*B.Im;
      Ans.Im:=A.Im*B.Re-A.Re*B.Im;
      Ans.Re:=Ans.Re/Denom;
      Ans.Im:=Ans.Im/Denom;
      return Ans;
   end Divide;
   function Make_Complex (A,B : Real_Type)
                      return Complex_Type is
      Z : Complex_Type;
   begin -- Make_Complex
      Z.Re  := A;
      Z.Im  := B;
      return Z;
   end Make_Complex;
end Complex_Numbers;
```

FIGURE 12-17 Try_It_Out using Make_Complex

```
with Complex_Numbers; use Complex_Numbers;
with Text_IO; use Text_IO;
procedure Try_It_Out is
   Real_Component, Imaginary_Component : Real_Type;
   X : Complex_Type;
   Y : Complex_Type;
   Ans_Add, Ans_Sub, Ans_Mult, Ans_Div : Complex_Type;
   package My_Float_IO is new Float_IO(Real_Type);
   use My_Float_IO;
begin -- Try_It_Out
   Put ("Enter X components. . . . .");
   Get (Real_Component);
   Get (Imaginary_Component);
   X := Make_Complex (Real_Component,
                      Imaginary_Component);
   Put ("Enter Y components. . . .");
   Get (Real_Component);
   Get (Imaginary_Component);
   Y := Make_Complex (Real_Component,
                      Imaginary_Component);
   Ans_Add  := Add (X,Y);
   Ans_Sub  := Subtract (X,Y);
   Ans_Mult := Multiply (X,Y);
   Ans_Div  := Divide (X,Y);
   --
   -- How to output results?
   --
end Try_It_Out;
```

The package body now has the following structure:

```
with Text_IO; use Text_IO;
package body Complex_Numbers is
   -- required by Output procedure
   package My_Float_IO is new Float_IO(Real_Type);
   use My_Float_IO;
   --
   -- the five functions Add, Subtract, Multiply,
   -- Divide, and Make_Complex as before
   --
   --
   -- the new output procedure
   --
   procedure Output (Answer : in Complex_Type) is
   begin -- Output
     Put    (Answer.Re);
     Put    ("   +");
     Put    (Answer.Im);
     Put    ("I");
     New_Line   (2);
   end Output;
end Complex_Numbers;
```

Finally, Figure 12-18 shows procedure Try_It_Out with the results now displayed.

12.6 Limited Private Types

If the designer of a package wants to restrict the operations applicable to a private type to just those subprograms provided by the package specification, the type is declared as a *limited private type.* When a type is declared as **limited private,** the set of operations applicable to objects of the limited private type *within* the package is not affected, but the set of operations *outside* the package is further restricted to only those subprograms provided by the package specification. Copy and test for equality and inequality are no longer permissible operations on objects of the limited private type *outside* the package.

Figures 12-19(a) and 12-19(b) show the specification and body for package Complex_Numbers with type Complex_Type coded as a limited private type. You should note two distinct changes from the previous version of Complex_Numbers. They are 1.) the addition of the word **limited** in the type declaration for Complex_Type and 2.) the subprograms have changed from functions to procedures.

The addition of the word **limited** is required by the language. The fact that the subprograms have been recoded as procedures is a consequence of the

FIGURE 12-18 Try_It_Out displaying results

```
with Complex_Numbers; use Complex_Numbers;
with Text_IO; use Text_IO;
procedure Try_It_Out is
   Real_Component, Imaginary_Component : Real_Type;
   X : Complex_Type;
   Y : Complex_Type;
   Ans_Add, Ans_Sub, Ans_Mult, Ans_Div : Complex_Type;
   package My_Float_IO is new Float_IO (Real_Type);
   use My_Float_IO;
begin -- Try_It_Out
   Put ("Enter X components. . . . .");
   Get (Real_Component);
   Get (Imaginary_Component);
   X := Make_Complex (Real_Component,
                      Imaginary_Component);
   Put ("Enter Y components. . . .");
   Get (Real_Component);
   Get (Imaginary_Component);
   Y := Make_Complex (Real_Component,
                      Imaginary_Component);
   Ans_Add  := Add (X,Y);
   Ans_Sub  := Subtract (X,Y);
   Ans_Mult := Multiply (X,Y);
   Ans_Div  := Divide (X,Y);
   Output (Ans_Add);
   Output (Ans_Sub);
   Output (Ans_Mult);
   Output (Ans_Div);
end Try_It_Out;
```

FIGURE 12-19(a) Complex_Type as limited private type

```
package Complex_Numbers is
   type Real_Type is digits 4;
   type Complex_Type is limited private;
   procedure Add        (A,B : in Complex_Type;
                         Ans : out Complex_Type);
   procedure Subtract   (A,B : in Complex_Type;
                         Ans : out Complex_Type);
   procedure Multiply   (A,B : in Complex_Type;
                         Ans : out Complex_Type);
   procedure Divide     (A,B : in Complex_Type;
                         Ans : out Complex_Type);

   procedure Make_Complex (A,B : in Real_Type;
                   Complex_Num : out Complex_Type);
   procedure Output (Answer : in Complex_Type);
private
   type Complex_Type is
   record
      Re:Real_Type;
      Im:Real_Type;
   end record;
end Complex_Numbers;
```

FIGURE 12-19(b) Functions recoded as procedures

```
package body Complex_Numbers is
   procedure Add (A,B: in Complex_Type;
                  Ans : out Complex_Type) is
   begin -- Add
      Ans.Re:= A.Re+B.Re;
      Ans.Im:= A.Im+B.Im;
   end Add;
```

(continued)

FIGURE 12-19(b) *(continued)*

```
      procedure Subtract (A,B: in Complex_Type;
                          Ans : out Complex_Type) is
      begin -- Subtract
         Ans.Re:=A.Re-B.Re:
         Ans.Im:=A.Im-B.Im;
      end Subtract;
      procedure Multiply (A,B: in Complex_Type;
                          Ans : out Complex_Type) is
      begin -- Multiply
         Ans.Re:=A.Re*B.Re-A.Im*B.Im;
         Ans. Im:=A.Im*B.Re+A.Re+B.Im;
      end Multiply;
      procedure Divide (A,B: in Complex_Type;
                        Ans : out Complex_Type) is
         Denom:Real_Type;
      begin -- Divide
         Denom:=B.Re*B.Re-B.Im*(-B.Im);
         Ans.Re:=A.Re*B.Re+A.Im*B.Im;
         Ans.Im:=A.Im*B.Re-A.Re*B.Im;
         Ans.Re:=Ans.Re/Denom;
         Ans.Im:=Ans.Im/Denom;
      end Divide;
      procedure Make_Complex (A,B : in Real_Type;
                     Complex_Num : out Complex_Type) is
      begin -- Make_Complex
         Complex_Num.Re := A;
         Complex_Num.Im := B;
      end Make_Complex;
      procedure Output (Answer : in Complex_Type) is
      begin -- Output
         Put (Answer.Re);
         Put ("  +");
         Put (Answer.Im);
         Put ("I");
         New_Line (2);
      end Output;
   end Complex_Numbers;
```

fact that assignment is not permitted on objects of limited private types outside the package. This means that there is no way to capture the result of a call to any of the functions, so the results must be passed back via procedure calls with **out** parameters.

Procedure Try_It_Out, recoded to output the results, is shown in Figure 12-20.

FIGURE 12-20 Try_It_Out recoded

```
with Complex_Numbers; use Complex_Numbers;
with Text_IO; use Text_IO;
procedure Try_It_Out is
   Real_Component, Imaginary_Component : Real_Type;
   X,Y : Complex_Type;
   Ans_Add, Ans_Sub, Ans_Mult, Ans_Div : Complex_Type;
   package My_Float_IO is new Float_IO(Real_Type);
   use My_Float_IO;
begin -- Try_It_Out
   Put_Line ("Enter X components.....");
   Get (Real_Component);
   Get (Imaginary_Component);
   Make_Complex (Real_Component,
                 Imaginary_Component, X);
   Put_Line ("Enter Y components....");
   Get (Real_Component);
   Get (Imaginary_Component);
   Make_Complex (Real_Component,
                 Imaginary_Component, Y);
   Add (X,Y, Ans_Add);
   Subtract (X,Y, Ans_Sub);
   Multiply (X,Y, Ans_Mult);
   Divide (X,Y, Ans_Div);
   Output (Ans_Add);
   Output (Ans_Sub);
   Output (Ans_Mult);
   Output (Ans_Div);
end Try_It_Out;
```

Deciding Between Private and Limited Private Types

How do you decide whether a type should be limited private or private? Make the decision based on the answer to the following question: *Do assignment and test for equality make sense for the type as fully declared in the private part of the package?* If the answer is yes, code the type as a private type. If the answer is no, code the type as a limited private type.

For example, consider the following implementation of a list for lower case characters whose maximum length is 50.

```
package List_Package is
   subtype Item_Type is Character range 'a'..'z';
   Max_Length: constant := 50;
   type List_Type is private;
   ...
private
   type Actual_List_Type is array (1..Max_Length)
                               of Item_Type;
   type List_Type is
   record
      Current_Length : Natural range 0..Max_Length;
      The_List : Actual_List_Type;
   end record;
end List_Package;
```

A list is implemented as a record with two components, Current_Length and The_List. The_List is the actual list of characters implemented as an array. The Current_Length component contains the index position of the last character of the list. Remember that when the user declares lists, the fact that the list is implemented as a record with two components is hidden.

```
with List_Package; use List_Package;
with Text_IO; use Text_IO;
procedure My_List is
   List_1, List_2 : List_Type; --List_Type structure
   ...                          --not visible to user
begin -- My_List
   ...
end My_List;
```

Now ask yourself the question posed earlier. Do assignment and test for equality make sense for lists implemented as we have done here? The answer to the question is no. Asking if List_1 = List_2 will most likely yield false, even if the values of List_1 and List_2 are as follows:

List_1

10

'a'	'b'	'c'	'd'	'e'	'f'	'g'	'h'	'i'	'j'	. . .

List_2

10

'a'	'b'	'c'	'd'	'e'	'f'	'g'	'h'	'i'	'j'	. . .

In essence the lists are the same, "abcdefghij", but equality for records checks both components. The Current_Length component of the two records are the same, ten. Yet when the two array components are compared, *all* index positions are compared, and the chance that the contents of positions 11 through 50 in the two arrays are identical is remote.

In summary the equality test does *not* make sense here. Equality compares the *entire* array component of the record when all equality needs to do is to compare the number of elements indicated by the Current_Length component. Therefore code List_Type as a limited private type, prohibit the user from using these operations, and provide subprograms in the package, named Equal and Copy, to perform those operations for you. Code Equal so that the Current_Length components are compared first. If they are not equal, they return False. If the Current_Length components are equal, then compare only the number of elements in the array indicated by the Current_Length component and return the appropriate Boolean value.

12.7 Overloading of Operators

How strange to have to write

```
Add (X, Y);
```

Whether the quantities are integers, complex numbers, matrices, or vectors, it is much more natural to write

```
X + Y
```

Before showing you how to accomplish this more natural technique in Ada, a definition of overloaded subprograms is necessary.

Overloaded subprograms in Ada have the same identifier but different parameter types. Consider

```
Put ("Enter a value between 1 and 10: ");
```

and

```
Put (Letter); -- Letter is an object of type Character
```

Each call invokes a distinct procedure. The first call invokes the Put procedure in Text_IO for type String. The second call invokes the Put procedure in Text_IO for type Character. Text_IO has several subprograms that have the same name, Put, and different parameter types. These subprograms are therefore overloaded. There is no problem in determining which procedure is referenced in a call because the parameter types are different.

The names of the I/O subprograms are identifiers, for example Put, Get, and so on. The names of some of the arithmetic operators in Ada are not identifiers, but rather the operator symbol itself enclosed in quotation marks, for example "+", "−", and so on, and these operators are implemented as functions. In Ada, some arithmetic operators are overloaded functions. That is, there are multiple functions of the name "+"; one for integers, one for floating point types, one for unary plus for integers, one for unary plus for floating point types, and so on. Which "+" is being invoked in a given case is determined by the actual parameters in the call. For example,

```
Integer_1 + Integer_2     -- invokes integer +
+ Integer_Value_1         -- invokes unary + for integer
Float_1 + Float_2         -- invokes + for floating point types
```

Table 12-1 lists those operators that may be legally overloaded in Ada. Figure 12-21 shows the specification and body, respectively, of package Complex_Numbers recoded with the operators overloaded.

TABLE 12-1 Overloadable operators

and	**or**	**xor**	**not**
=	/= <	>	<= >=
+	−	**abs**	&
*	/	**mod**	**rem** **

FIGURE 12-21 Overloaded operators

```
package Complex_Numbers is
   type Real_Type is digits 4;
   type Complex_Type is private;
   function "+" (A, B : Complex_Type)
                 return Complex_Type;
   function "-" (A, B : Complex_Type)
                 return Complex_Type;
   function "*" (A, B : Complex_Type)
                 return Complex_Type;
   function "/" (A, B : Complex_Type)
                 return Complex_Type;
   function Make_Complex (A, B : Real_Type)
                 return Complex_Type;
   procedure Output (Answer : in Complex_Type);
private
   type Complex_Type is
   record
      Re, Im : Real_Type;
   end record;
end Complex_Numbers;
package body Complex_Numbers is
   function "+" (A, B : Complex_Type)
                 return Complex_Type is
      Ans : Complex_Type;
   begin -- "+"
      Ans.Re := A.Re + B.Re;
      Ans.Im := A.Im + B.Im;
      return Ans;
   end "+";
   function "-" (A, B : Complex_Type)
                 return Complex_Type is
      Ans : Complex_Type;
   begin -- "-"
      Ans.Re := A.Re - B.Re;
      Ans.Im := A.Im - B.Im;
      return Ans;
   end "-";
   function "*" (A, B : Complex_Type)
                return Complex_Type is separate;
   function "/" (A, B : Complex_Type)
                return Complex_Type is separate;
   function Make_Complex (A, B : Real_Type)
                return Complex_Type is separate;
   procedure Output (Answer : in Complex_Type)
                is separate;
end Complex_Numbers;
```

Try_It_Out, recoded with calls to the overloaded operators, is shown in Figure 12-22. As a final comment, Complex_Type is coded as a private type because copy and test for equality and inequality make sense here. For example one complex number equals another complex number if their real and imaginary components are equal.

FIGURE 12-22 Try_It_Out with calls to overloaded operators

```
with Complex_Numbers; use Complex_Numbers;
with Text_IO; use Text_IO;
procedure Try_It_Out is
   X, Y : Complex_Type;
   Ans_Add, Ans_Sub, Ans_Mul, Ans_Div : Complex_Type;
   Real, Imag : Real_Type;
   package Real_IO is new Float_IO (Real_Type);
   use Real_IO;
begin -- Try_It_Out
   Put_Line ("Enter X Components.....");
   Get (Real); -- no room for exception handlers
   Get (Imag);
   X := Make_Complex (Real, Imag);
   Put_Line ("Enter Y Components ....");
   Get (Real);  -- no room for exception handlers
   Get (Imag);
   Y := Make_Complex (Real, Imag);
   Ans_Add := X + Y; -- calls the "+" in Complex_Numbers
   Ans_Sub := X - Y; -- calls the "-" in Complex_Numbers
   Ans_Mul := X * Y; -- calls the "*" in Complex_Numbers
   Ans_Div := X / Y; -- calls the "/" in Complex_Numbers
   Output (Ans_Add);
   Output (Ans_Sub);
   -- output remaining results
end Try_It_Out;
```

EXERCISES

12.13 Recode package Complex_Numbers with type Complex_Type coded as a private type and implemented as an array. Provide Make_Complex and Output as resources of the package.

12.14 As a result of recoding package Complex_Numbers in Exercise 12.13, does Try_It_Out, as coded at the end 12.5, change? Why or why not?

12.15 Write a package that provides a type for Matrices and operations that are applicable to matrices, such as add, subtract, multiply, and determinant.

12.16 Write a package that provides a type for Vectors and operations that are applicable to vectors, such as add, subtract, dot product, and cross product.

12.17 Let your imagination be your guide. Model an airline reservation system, an air traffic control system, a snack vending machine, toll booth, rational numbers...whatever. Most of all, *have fun.* Ada makes it easy!

A

SIMPLE_GRAPHICS FOR THE VAX 11/780*

In a real-life situation, when trying to implement Simple_Graphics on, say, a VAX 11/780*, it is necessary to provide more capability for overcoming implementation-dependent problems. For example, the ReGIS (Remote Graphics Instruction Set) graphics routines provide two cursors—one for text and one for graphics. When you leave the text mode, the graphics cursor appears, and you can draw lines and circles at will or enter graphics text.

In order to use Text_IO, you must re-enter the text mode. When you re-enter text mode, the text cursor appears where you last left it in the previous *text mode* session, not where the graphics cursor was prior to entering text mode. Obviously, this can create problems.

This Appendix contains code for a modified Simple_Graphics package that runs on a VAX 11/780 (with the ReGIS graphics routines) and a VT-125 (or equivalent) terminal.

The routines included are

- Simple_Graphics specification
- Simple_Graphics body
- VT-125 specification
- VT-125 body
- procedure Test (to test the packages)

They were coded by John K. Cannella and Thomas Heaney.

The dependency diagram for these units is shown in Figure A-1.

---

* VAX is a registered trademark of Digital Equipment Corporation.

FIGURE A-1

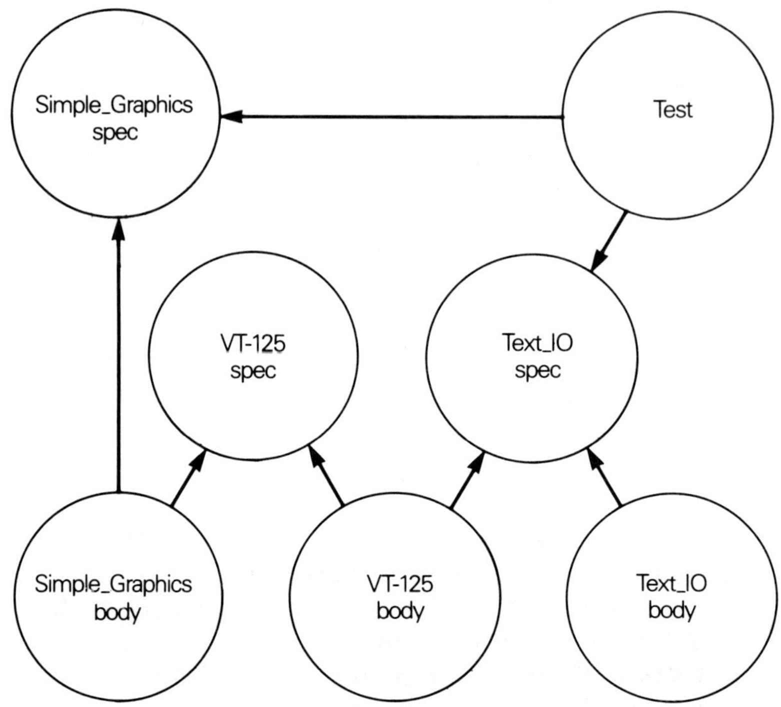


```
package Simple_Graphics is
   type Point_Type is array (1..2) of Integer;
-- This procedure will clear the text screen, put you in
-- graphics mode, and clear the graphics screen. It will
-- also set the coordinate space to 100,100.
   procedure Initialize_Graphics;
   procedure Clear_Text_Screen;
   procedure Clear_Graphics_Screen;
-- These procedures will put you into the mode described
-- but not erase any screens.
   procedure Graphics_Mode;
   procedure Text_Mode;
   procedure Draw_Line ( From, To : Point_Type );
   procedure Draw_Circle ( Center : Point_Type;
                           Radius : Integer );
```

```
-- This procedure must be used to write a string to
-- specific coordinates on the screen. A Text_IO.Put will
-- write to the last place the TEXT cursor, was, not the
-- graphics cursor position. The procedure Move_Cursor
-- will only move the graphics cursor.
   procedure Graphics_Put_Line ( Text : String );
   procedure Move_Cursor ( To : Point_Type );
end Simple_Graphics;

with VT_125; use VT_125;
package body Simple_Graphics is
   procedure Initialize_Graphics is
   begin -- Initialize_Graphics
      Erase_Text_Screen;
      Enter_Graphics_Mode;
      Erase_Graphics_Screen;
      Set_Coordinate_Space ( Max_X => 100, Max_Y => 100 );
   end Initialize_Graphics;
   procedure Clear_Text_Screen is
   begin -- Clear_Text_Screen
      Erase_Text_Screen;
   end Clear_Text_Screen;
   procedure Clear_Graphics_Screen is
   begin -- Clear_Graphics_Screen
      Erase_Graphics_Screen;
   end Clear_Graphics_Screen;
   procedure Graphics_Mode is
   begin -- Graphics_Mode
      Enter_Graphics_Mode;
   end Graphics_Mode;
   procedure Text_Mode is
   begin -- Text_Mode
      Exit_Graphics_Mode;
   end Text_Mode;
   procedure Draw_Line ( From,To : Point_Type ) is
   begin -- Draw_Line
      Draw_Line ( From_X => From(1), From_Y => From(2),
                  To_X   => To(1)  , To_Y   => To(2) );
   end Draw_Line;
   procedure Draw_Circle ( Center : Point_Type;
                           Radius : Integer ) is
   begin -- Draw_Circle
      Draw_Circle ( Center_X => Center(1),
                    Center_Y => Center(2),
                    Radius => Radius );
```

```
   end Draw_Circle;
   procedure Graphics_Put_Line ( Text : String ) is
   begin -- Graphics_Put_Line
      Graphics_Text_Write ( Text => Text );
   end Graphics_Put_Line;
   procedure Move_Cursor ( To : Point_Type ) is
   begin -- Move_Cursor
      Move_Cursor_Absolute ( X_Pos => To(1),
                             Y_Pos => To(2) );
   end Move_Cursor;
end Simple_Graphics;

package VT_125 is
   procedure Enter_Graphics_Mode;
   procedure Exit_Graphics_Mode;
   procedure Erase_Text_Screen;
   procedure Erase_Graphics_Screen;
   procedure Set_Coordinate_Space
             ( Max_X : Integer := 767;
               Max_Y : Integer := 479 );
   procedure Draw_Line
             ( From_X, From_Y, To_X, To_Y : Integer );
   procedure Draw_Circle
             ( Center_X, Center_Y, Radius : Integer );
   procedure Move_Cursor_Absolute
             ( X_Pos, Y_Pos : Integer );
   procedure Graphics_Text_Write ( Text : String );
end VT_125;

with Text_IO; use Text_IO;
package body VT_125 is
   package VT_125_Int_IO is new Integer_IO( Integer );
   use VT_125_Int_IO;
   Graphics_Off : Boolean := True;
   procedure Enter_Graphics_Mode is
   begin -- Enter_Graphics_Mode
      Put ( Ascii.Esc );        -- go into VT125
      Put_Line ( "P1p" );       -- ReGIS
      Graphics_Off := false;
      Set_Coordinate_Space;
   end Enter_Graphics_Mode;
   procedure Exit_Graphics_Mode is
   begin -- Exit_Graphics_Mode
      Put ( Ascii.Esc );        -- leave VT125
      Put_Line ( "\" );         -- ReGIS
      Graphics_Off := true;
```

```
end Exit_Graphics_Mode;
procedure Erase_Text_Screen is
begin -- Erase_Text_Screen
   Put ( Ascii.Esc );          -- Erase all of text
   Put_Line ( "[2J" );         -- on the display.
end Erase_Text_Screen;
procedure Erase_Graphics_Screen is
begin -- Erase_Graphics_Screen
   if Graphics_Off then
      Enter_Graphics_Mode;
      Put ( "S(E)" );          -- erase screen
      Exit_Graphics_Mode;
   else
      Put ( "S(E)" );          -- erase screen
   end if;
end Erase_Graphics_Screen;
procedure Set_Coordinate_Space
          ( Max_X : Integer := 767;
            Max_Y : Integer := 479 ) is
begin -- Set_Coordinate_Space
   if Graphics_Off then
      Enter_Graphics_Mode;
   end if;
   Put ( "S(A[" );             -- Set screen
   Put ( 0 );                  -- coordinate origin
   Put ( "," );                -- to lower left-hand
   Put ( Max_Y );              -- corner.
   Put ( "]" );
   Put ( "[" );
   Put ( Max_X );
   Put ( "," );
   Put ( 0 );
   Put_Line ( "])" );
end Set_Coordinate_Space;
procedure Draw_Line
          ( From_X,From_Y,To_X,To_Y : Integer ) is
begin -- Draw_Line
   if Graphics_Off then
      Enter_Graphics_Mode;
   end if;
   Put ( "P[" );
   Put ( From_X );    -- Change graphics cursor absolute
   Put ( "," );
   Put ( From_Y );    -- position to point From.
   Put ( "]" );
```

```
      Put ( "V" );          -- Put dot at From.
      Put ( "V[" );         -- Draw line from first pixel after From
      Put ( To_X );
      Put ( "," );
      Put ( To_Y );         -- to To.
      Put_Line ( "]" );
   end Draw_Line;
   procedure Draw_Circle
            ( Center_X,Center_Y,Radius : Integer ) is
   begin -- Draw_Circle
      if Graphics_Off then
         Enter_Graphics_Mode;
      end if;
      Put ( "P[" );
      Put ( Center_X ); -- Change graphics cursor absolute
      Put ( "," );
      Put ( Center_Y ); -- position to point From.
      Put ( "]" );
      Put ( "C[+" );        -- Draw line from first pixel after From.
      Put ( Radius );
      Put_Line ( "]" );
   end Draw_Circle;
   procedure Move_Cursor_Absolute
            ( X_Pos,Y_Pos : Integer ) is
   begin -- Move_Cursor_Absolute
      if Graphics_Off then
         Enter_Graphics_Mode;
      end if;
      Put ( "P[" );
      Put ( X_Pos );         -- Change graphics cursor absolute
      Put ( "," );
      Put ( Y_Pos );         -- position to (X_Pos,Y_Pos).
      Put_Line ( "]" );
   end Move_Cursor_Absolute;
   procedure Graphics_Text_Write ( Text : String ) is
   begin -- Graphics_Text_Write
      if Graphics_Off then
         Enter_Graphics_Mode;
      end if;
      Put ( "t" );
      Put ( "'" );
      Put ( Text );
      Put_Line ( "'" );
   end Graphics_Text_Write;
end VT_125;
```

```
with Simple_Graphics; use Simple_Graphics;
with Text_IO; use Text_IO;
procedure Test is
   Coord1 : Point_Type;
   Coord2 : Point_Type;
   Radius : Integer;
   Char   : Character;
begin -- Test
   Initialize_Graphics;  -- described in Simple-Graphics spec
   Coord1(1) := 10;
   Coord1(2) := 10;
   Coord2(1) := 10;
   Coord2(2) := 50;
   Draw_Line ( Coord1,Coord2 );       -- connects (10,10) to
                                      -- (10,50)
   Coord1 := Coord2;
   Coord2(1) := 50;
   Coord2(2) := 50;
   Draw_Line ( Coord1,Coord2 );       -- connects (10,50) to
                                      -- (50,50)
   Coord1 := Coord2;
   Coord2(1) := 50;
   Coord2(2) := 10;
   Draw_Line ( Coord1,Coord2 );       -- connects (50,50) to
                                      -- (50,10)
   Coord1 := Coord2;
   Coord2(1) := 10;
   Coord2(2) := 10;
   Draw_Line ( Coord1,Coord2 );       -- connects (50,10) to
                                      -- (10,10)
   Coord1(1) := 80;
   Coord1(2) := 30;
   Radius    := 10;
   Draw_Circle ( Coord1,Radius );     -- draw circle at (80,30),
                                      -- radius = 10
   Coord1(1) := 28;
   Coord1(2) := 5;
   Move_Cursor ( Coord1 );            -- Uses ReGIS text mode to
   Graphics_Put_Line ( "box" );       -- label the box as a box.
   Coord1(1) := 78;
   Coord1(2) := 5;
   Move_Cursor ( Coord1 );            -- Uses ReGIS text mode to
   Graphics_Put_Line ( "circle" );    -- label the circle as a
                                      -- circle.
   Coord1(1) := 18;
   Coord1(2) := 52;
```

```
   Move_Cursor ( Coord1 );                   -- moves graphics cursor
                                             -- to (18,52)
   Text_Mode;                                -- enter text mode
   Put ( "this is a box" );                  -- Text_IO.Put at bottom
                                             -- of screen,
                                             -- not at (18,52).
   Graphics_Mode;                            -- enter graphics mode
   Coord1(1) := 72;
   Coord1(2) := 52;
   Move_Cursor ( Coord1);                    -- move graphics cursor to
                                             -- (72,52)
   Text_Mode;                                -- enter text mode
   Put ( "this is a circle" );               -- Text_IO.Put at bottom
                                             -- of screen,
                                             -- not at (72,52).
   for i in 1..2
   loop
      Graphics_Mode;
      Coord1(1) := 0;
      Coord1(2) := 98;
      Move_Cursor ( Coord1 );
      Text_Mode;   -- permit use of Text_IO
                   -- Permits user to clear either graphics or
                   -- Text_IO text from the screen.
      Put ("enter A to clear graphics or B to clear text > ");
      Get ( Char );
      if Char = 'a' then
         Clear_Graphics_Screen;
      else
         Clear_Text_Screen;
      end if;
   end loop;
end Test;
```

B

LITERALS WITH BASE OTHER THAN 10

B.1 Based 10 Literals

Numeric literals are of two classes: integer literals and real literals. Integer literals are exact numbers, while real literals are approximations. Integer literals are entered without a decimal point (see Section 5.1) while real literals are entered with a decimal point (see Section 7.1). The number 3 is an example of an integer literal, while 3.5 is an example of a real literal. All numeric literals in Ada may be written in exponential notation. All numeric literals in Ada are considered to be decimal (base 10) unless written as a based literal. Based literals are the subject of this appendix.

B.2 Based Literals

Ada does permit literals to be expressed in bases other than 10. Specifically, Ada permits literals to be expressed in any base between 2 and 16 inclusive.

The following is an example of a based literal.

```
2#11011#e3
↑  ↑     ↖
base  based number  exponent
```

The above based literal represents the following value in base 10.

$$(1 \times 2^4 + 1 \times 2^3 + 0 \times 2^2 + 1 \times 2^1 + 1 \times 2^0) \times 2^3$$

or

$$(16 + 8 + 0 + 2 + 1) \times 8$$

or

$$(27) \times 8$$

B.3 How to Write Based Literals

The rules for writing a based numeric literal are as follows:

- The digits that represent the based number must be enclosed between sharp characters, (#)*.
- The characters A through F may be used in representing the based number.
- The base, written in base 10, precedes the first # character.
- An optional exponent, written in base 10, may follow the based number, after the second # character.

Both the base and the exponent are written in base 10. The exponent indicates the power of the base that the based number must be multiplied by to obtain the value of the literal.

B.4 Examples

The following are legal based integer literals:

2#101#	represents $1 \times 2^2 + 1 \times 2^0$ or 5
16#11#	represents $1 \times 16^1 + 1 \times 16^0$ or 17
16#11#e2	represents 17×16^2 or 4,352
16#aa#	represents 170

The following is a legal based real literal:

2#101.1# represents $4 + 1 + \frac{1}{2}$ or 5.5

---

* An allowable replacement for the # character is the colon, (:), provided the colon is used for both occurrences of the character. See LRM 2.10.

C

LEXICAL STYLE

Chapter 1 introduces a small Ada program, Draw_Specific_Line, that draws a line between two points. The program needs to be discussed from another point of view, that of lexical style.

C.1 Free Format

Ada is a free-format language. There are no requirements to start a line on a specific column. Blank spaces, as well as blank lines, may be freely used to enhance readability and program structure.

The code for Draw_Specific_Line appears in Chapter 1 as

```
with Simple_Graphics; use Simple_Graphics;
procedure Draw_Specific_Line is
   --
   -- Two hyphens indicate a comment line in Ada.
   --
begin -- Draw_Specific_Line
   --
   -- This procedure draws a line
   -- from the point (1,5) to the point (2,7).
   --
   Draw_Line ( (1, 5), (2, 7) );
end Draw_Specific_Line;
```

Blank spaces are used to indent the code enclosed by the **begin–end** structure of the procedure. Blank spaces are used to make the call to Draw_Line more readable. Without spaces, the call is written as

```
Draw_Line((1,5),(2,7));
```

and is rather messy and difficult to read.

Blank lines could surround the call to Draw_Line to help the eye separate the comment lines from the executable code. Because of space limitations, blank lines have not been used in this text but should be used by the programmer.

C.2 Continuation

There are no continuation marks in Ada. Ada code may freely cross line boundaries. There are two exceptions to this rule that will be addressed shortly.

Consider

```
with Simple_Graphics; use Simple_Graphics;
procedure
   Draw_Specific_Line
      is -- using three lines instead of one line
   --
   -- Two hyphens indicate a comment line in Ada.
   --
begin -- Draw_Specific_Line
   --
   -- This procedure draws a line
   -- from the point (1, 5) to the point (2, 7).
   --
   Draw_Line ( (1, 5),
      (2, 7) );; -- uses two lines instead of one line.
end Draw_Specific_Line;
```

This is perfectly legal, although somewhat difficult to read. Extend a line over the line boundary only when absolutely necessary.

As previously stated, there are two exceptions to this rule. The first exception is that a call to Put_Line to output a string longer than a line needs the catenation operator, as described in Section 3.1. The second exception is a comment line. A comment may not cross line boundaries.* When continuing a comment onto another line, make sure that two hyphens precede the continuation of the comment, as in

```
with Simple_Graphics; use Simple_Graphics;
procedure Draw_Specific_Line is
   --
   -- Two hyphens indicate a comment line in Ada. If
   -- the comment is very, very long, each line of
   -- the comment must be preceded by the two
   -- hyphens (--).
   --
begin -- Draw_Specific_Line
   --
   -- This procedure draws a line
   -- from the point (1, 5) to the point (2, 7).
   --
   Draw_Line ( (1, 5), (2, 7) );
end Draw_Specific_Line;
```

To write

```
   --
   -- Two hyphens indicate a comment line in Ada. If
      the comment is very, very long, each line of
      the comment must be
      preceded by the two hyphens (--).
```

is illegal.

* No lexical element may cross line boundaries.

C.3 Multiple Statements per Line

One line may contain more than one Ada statement, as in

```
with Simple_Graphics; use Simple_Graphics;
procedure Draw_Specific_Line is
   --
   -- Two hyphens indicate a comment line in Ada.
   --
begin -- Draw_Specific_Line
   --
   -- This procedure draws a line
   -- from the point (1,5) to the point (2, 7).
   --
   Draw_Line ((1, 5), (2, 7)); Draw_Line ((1, 8), (3, 10));
end Draw_Specific_Line;
```

which draws two lines.

C.4 Summary

To summarize, an Ada program should be written in such a fashion that the physical appearance of the code makes the code easier to read. Write one statement per line. Separate like statements by blank lines. Use spaces within parentheses to make the arguments readable. Use spaces to create indentation levels for the control constructs **if, case,** and **loop.** The end goal is to make Ada code more readable so that the code can be more easily maintained by someone other than the original coder (although the original coder will be helped by improved readability, too!).

D

ADA QUICK-REFERENCE CARD*

Program Structure

Compilation

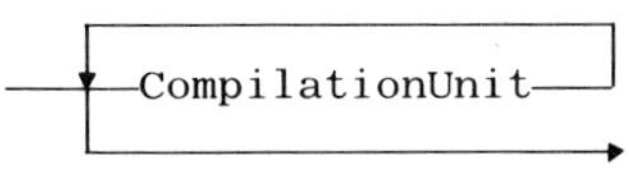

CompilationUnit

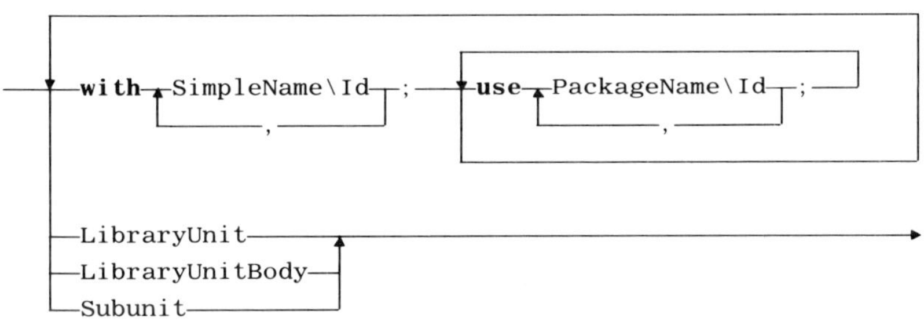

LibraryUnit

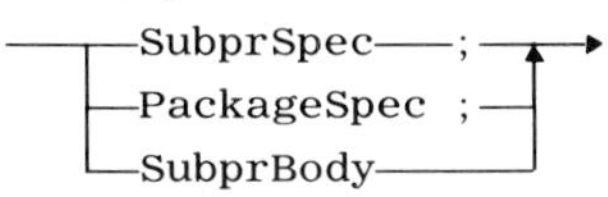

LibraryUnitBody

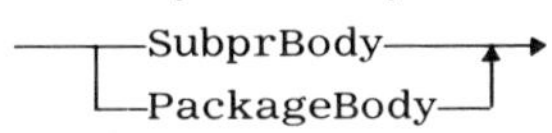

Subunit

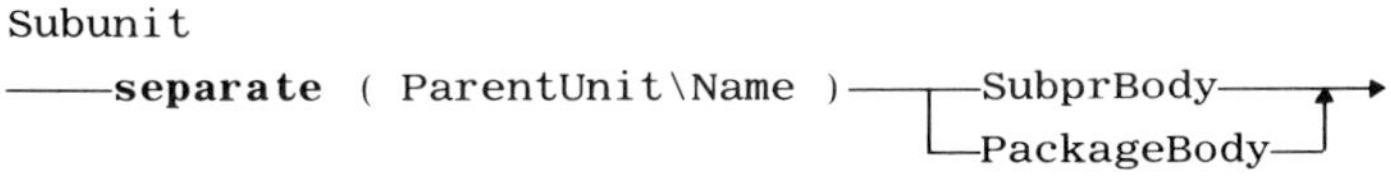

SubprSpec

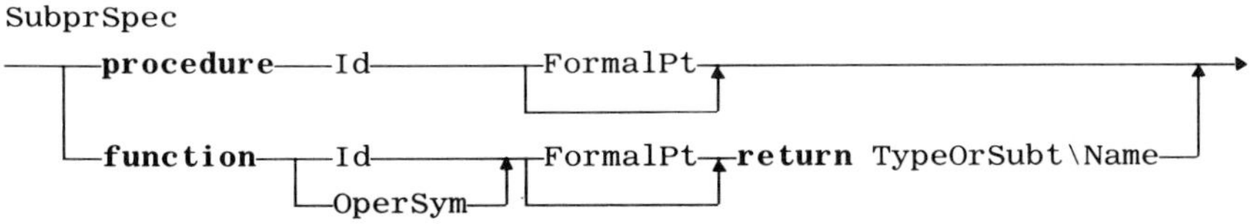

---

* Prepared by and reprinted courtesy of David A. Smith, Hughes Aircraft Company, Denver Engineering Laboratories.

FormalPt

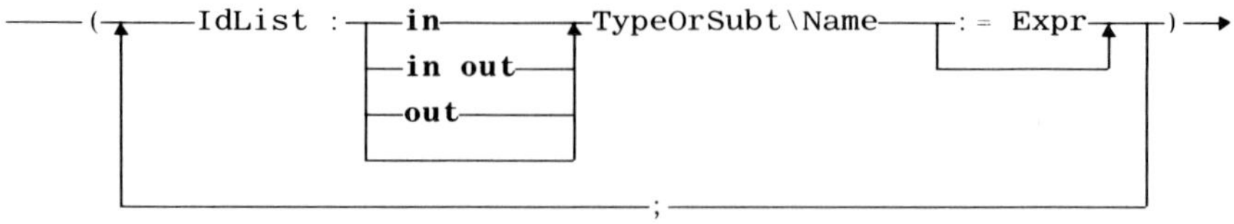

SubprBody

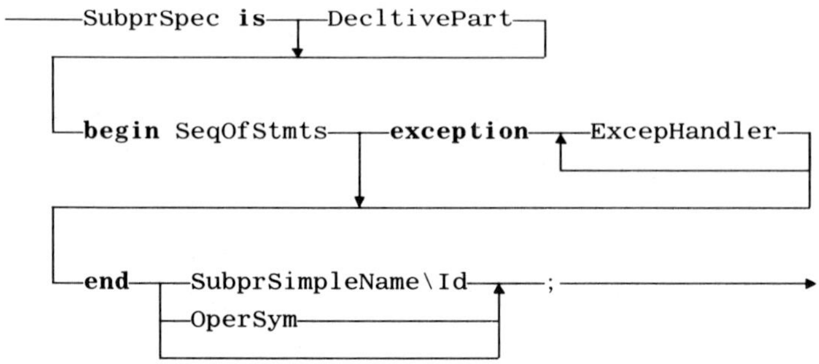

PackageSpec

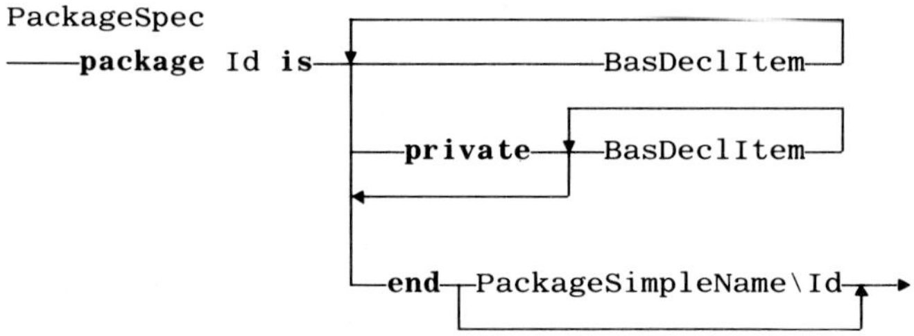

PackageBody

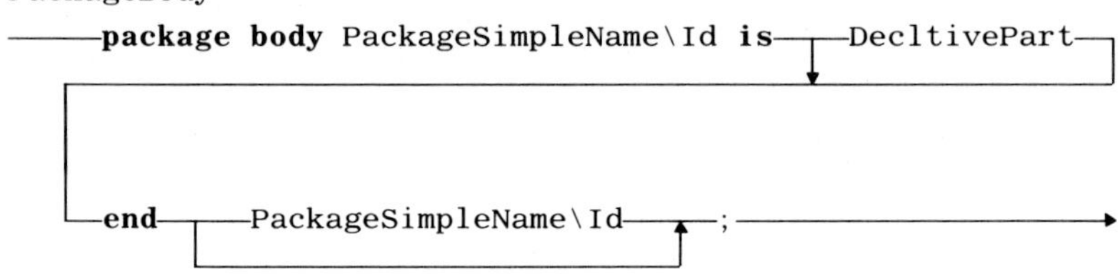

ExcepHandler

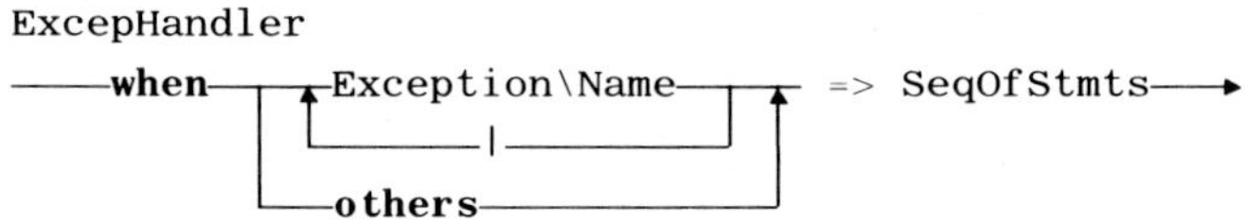

---------------------------- Declarations ----------------------------

DecltivePart

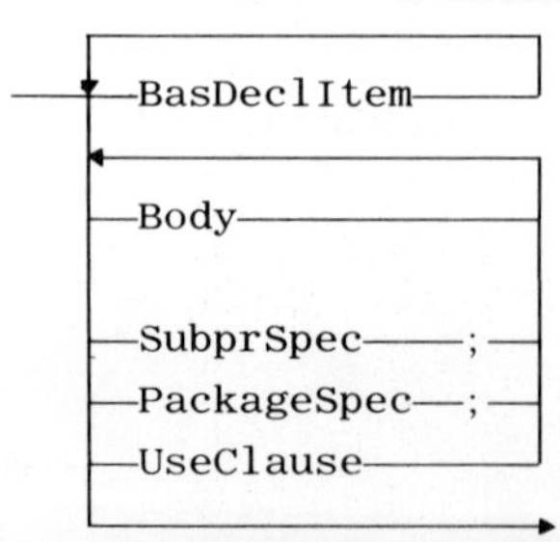

UseClause

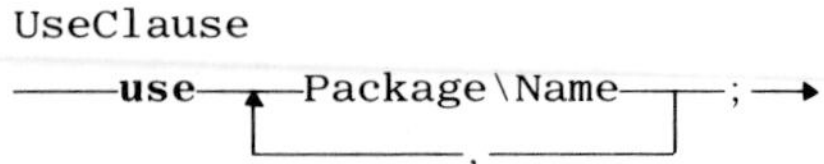

IdList

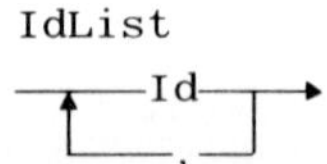

BasDeclItem

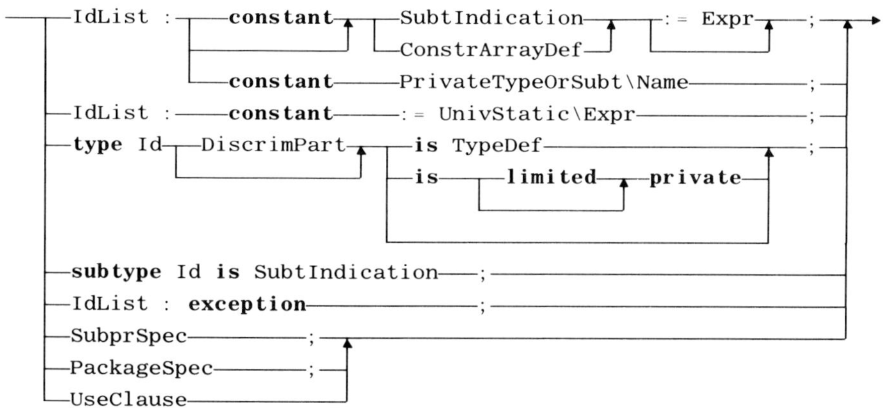

Body

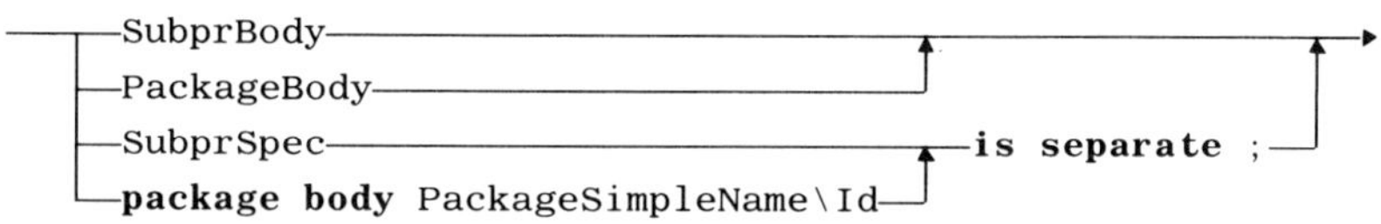

TypeDef

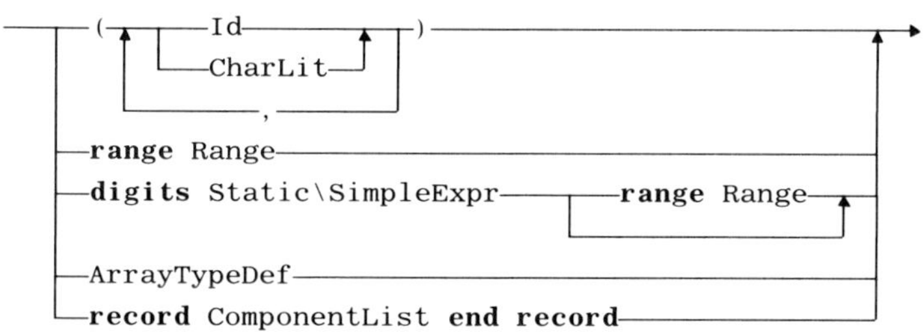

SubtIndication

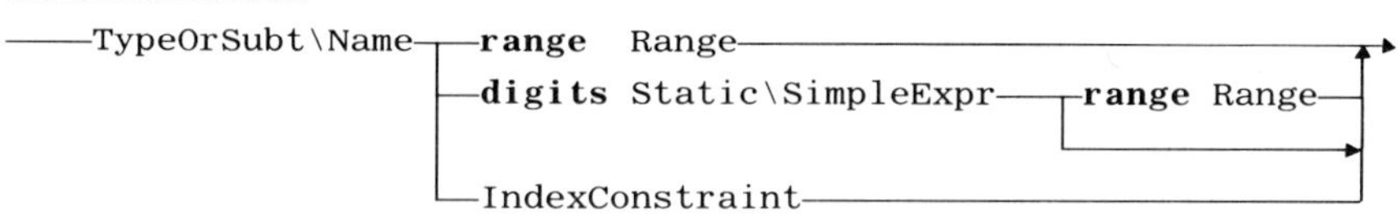

IndexConstraint

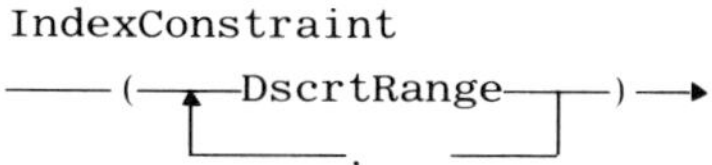

ArrayTypeDef

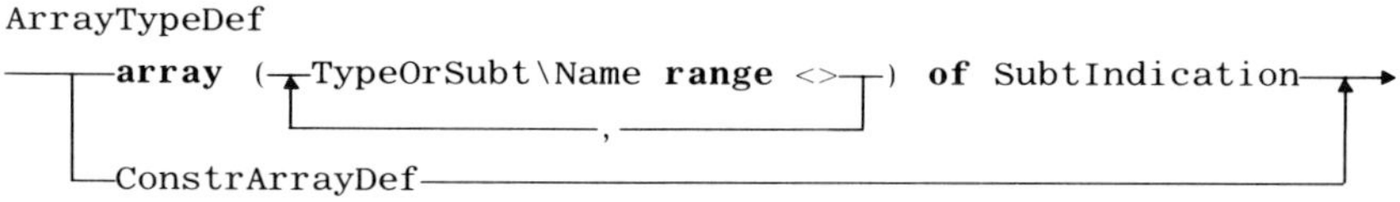

ConstrArrayDef

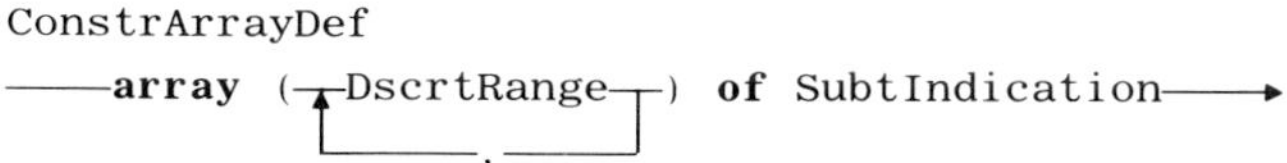

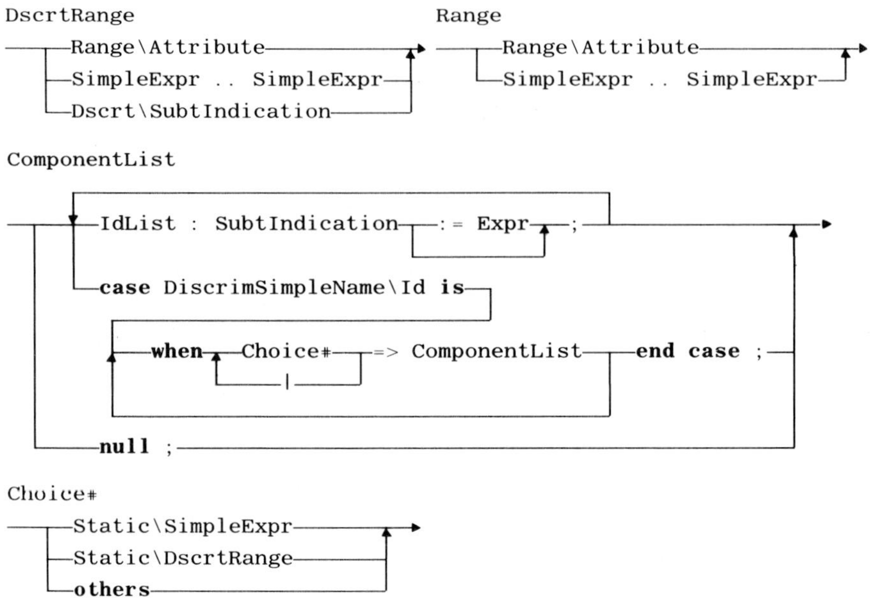
DscrtRange
Range\Attribute
SimpleExpr .. SimpleExpr
Dscrt\SubtIndication
Range
Range\Attribute
SimpleExpr .. SimpleExpr
ComponentList
IdList : SubtIndication
:= Expr
;
case DiscrimSimpleName\Id is
when
Choice#
|
=> ComponentList
end case ;
null ;
Choice#
Static\SimpleExpr
Static\DscrtRange
others

Lexemes

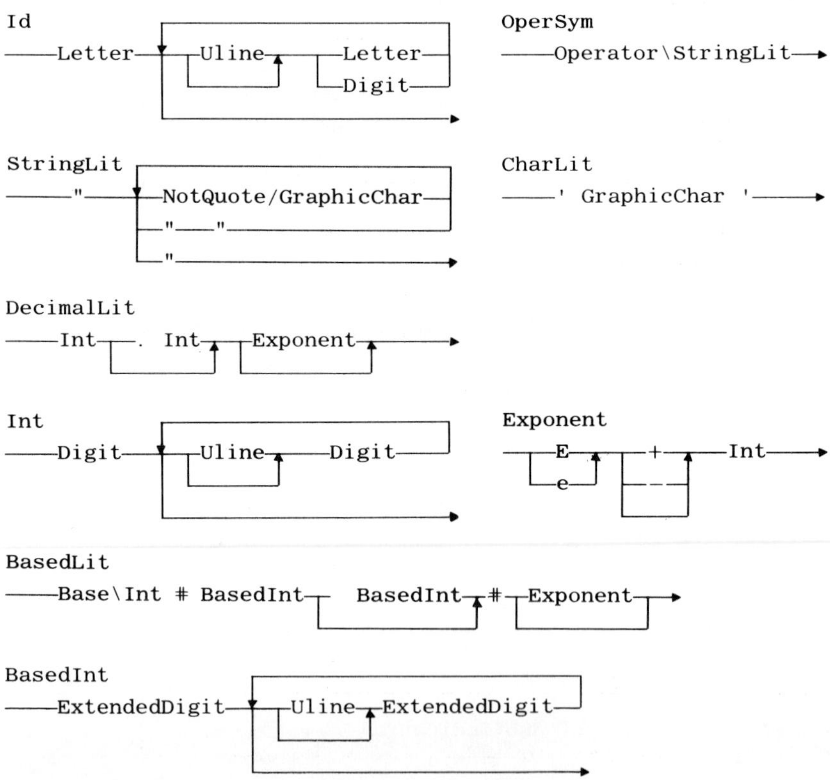
Id
Letter
Uline
Letter
Digit
OperSym
Operator\StringLit
StringLit
"
NotQuote/GraphicChar
"   "
"
CharLit
' GraphicChar '
DecimalLit
Int
. Int
Exponent
Int
Digit
Uline
Digit
Exponent
E
e
+
-
Int
BasedLit
Base\Int # BasedInt
BasedInt
#
Exponent
BasedInt
ExtendedDigit
Uline
ExtendedDigit

Characters

Letter	A..Z, a..z	Uline	Underline
Digit	0..9	ExtendedDigit	0..9, A..F, a..f
GraphicChar	Space..Tilde		

Statements

SeqOfStmts

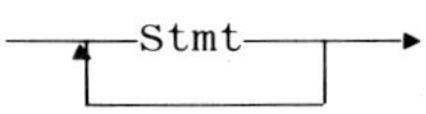

Stmt

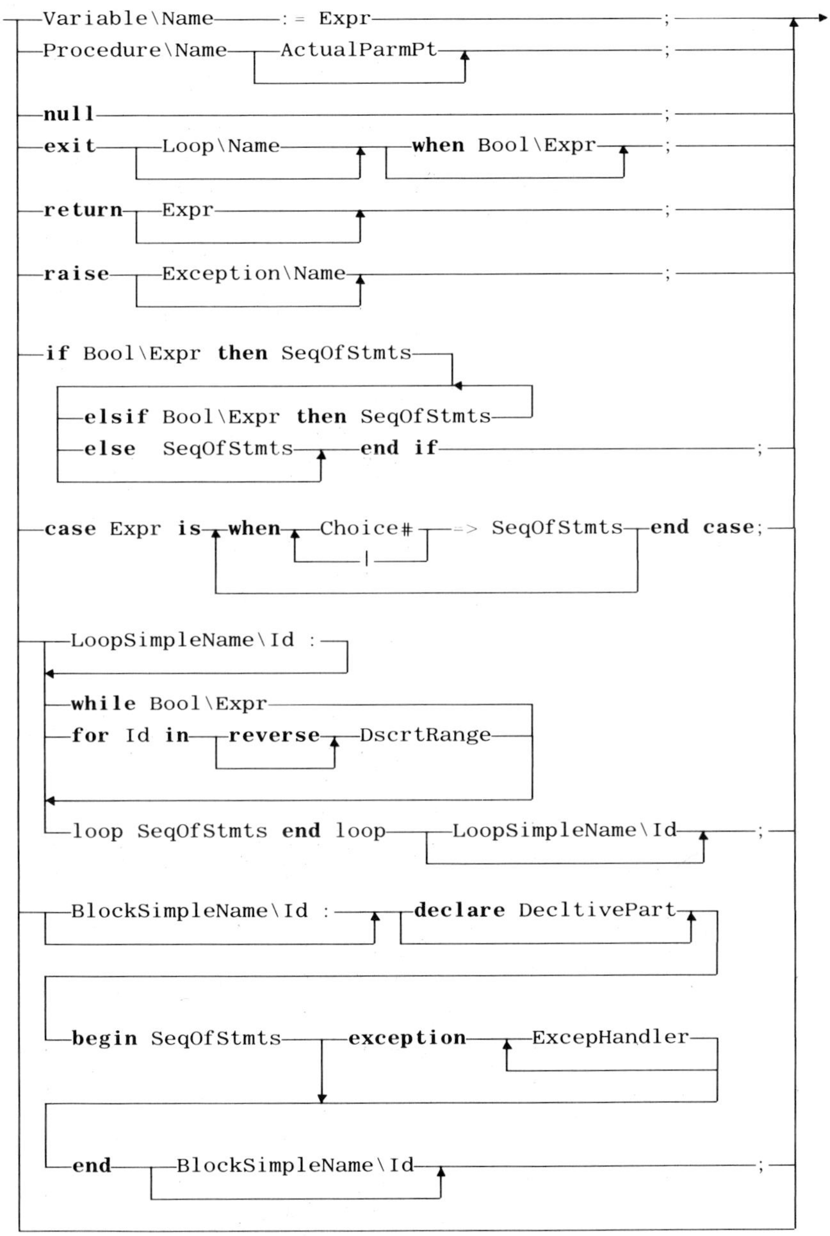

Expressions

Expr

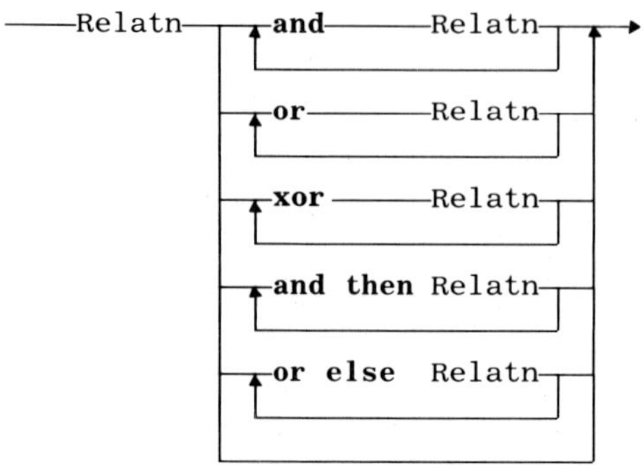

Relatn

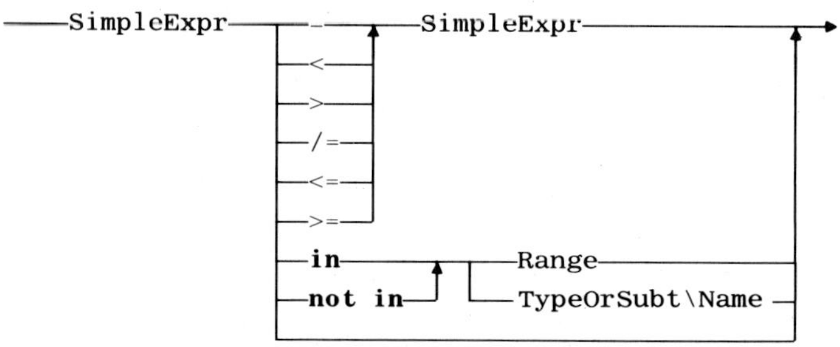

SimpleExpr

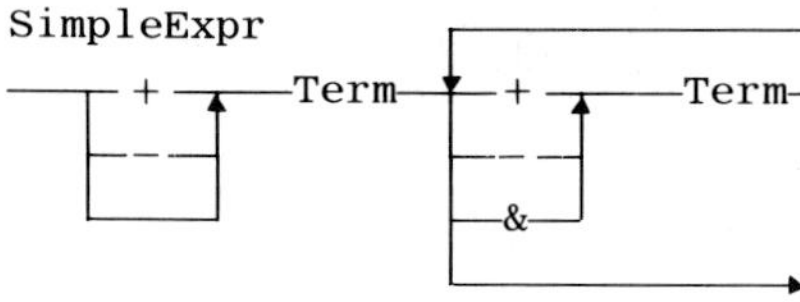

Term

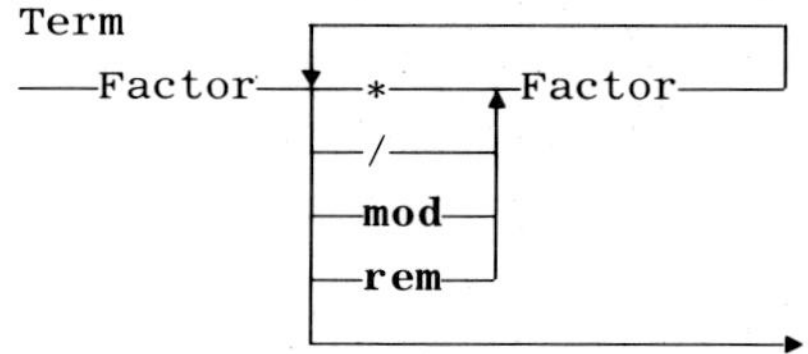

Factor

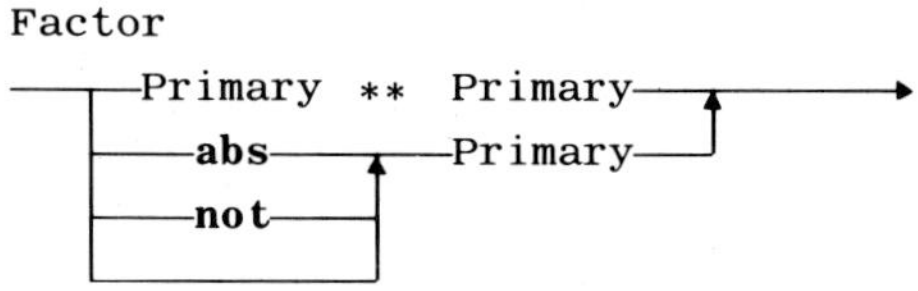

Primary

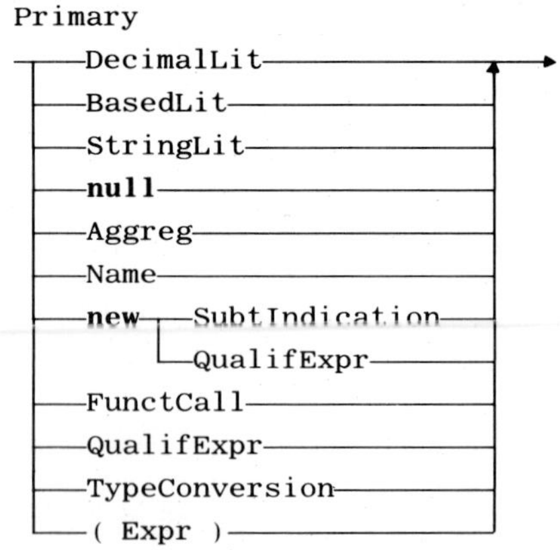

QualifExpr

TypeConversion

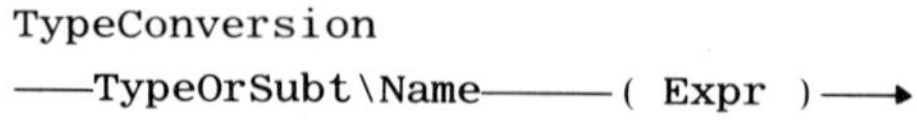

FunctCall

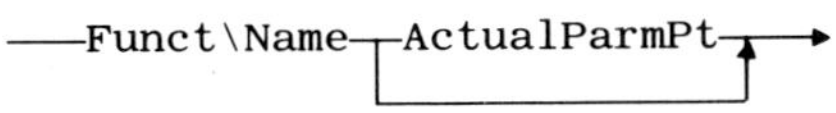

ActualParmPt

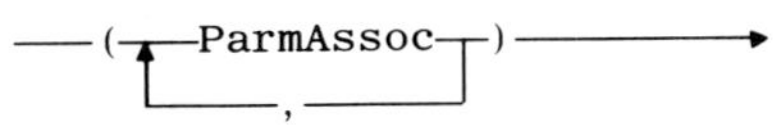

ParmAssoc

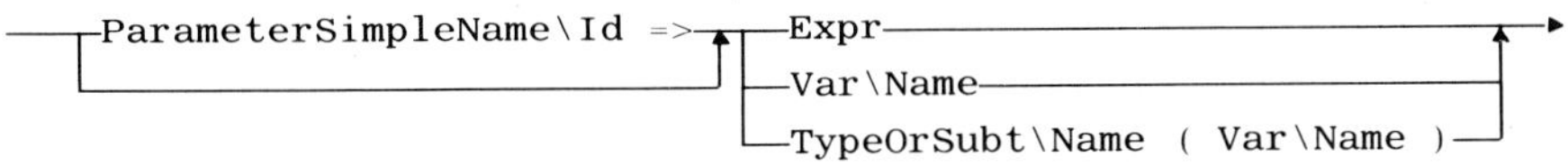

Aggreg

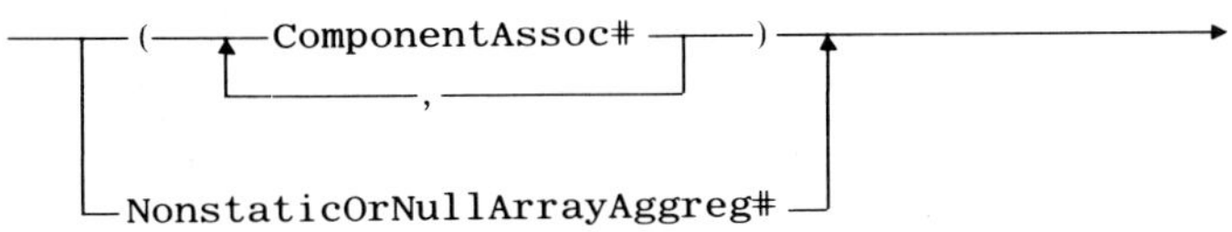

ComponentAssoc#

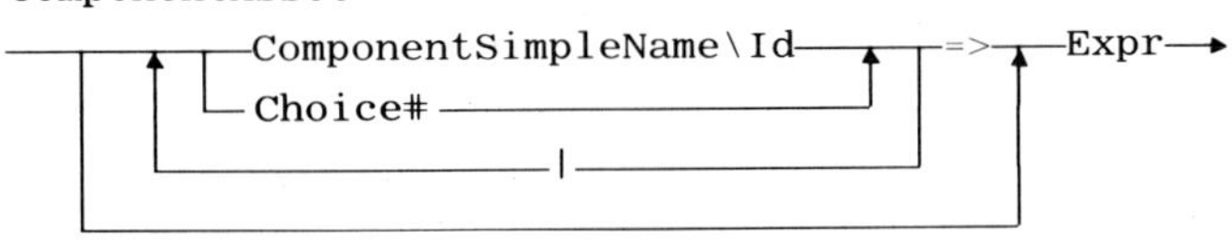

NonstaticOrNullArrayAggreg#

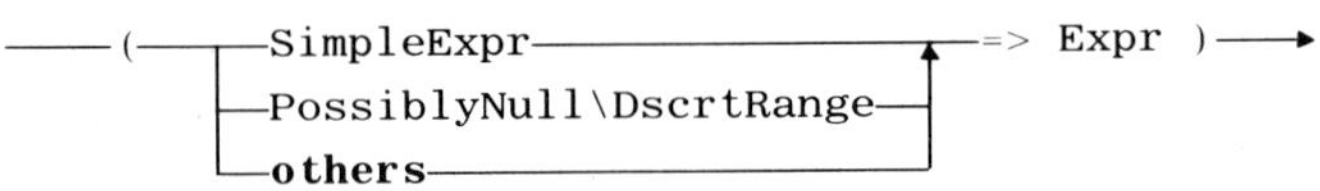

Name

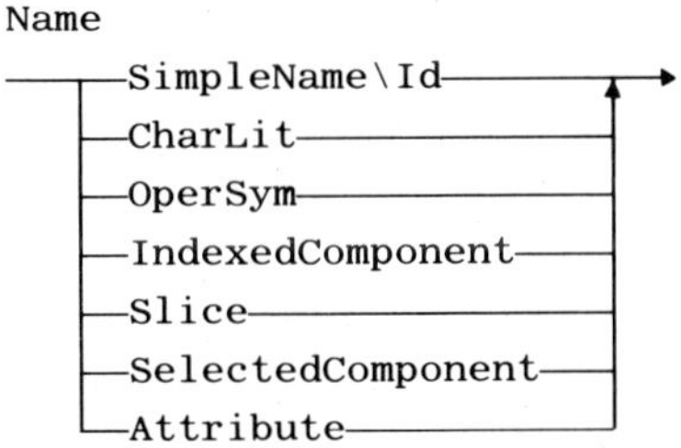

IndexedComponent

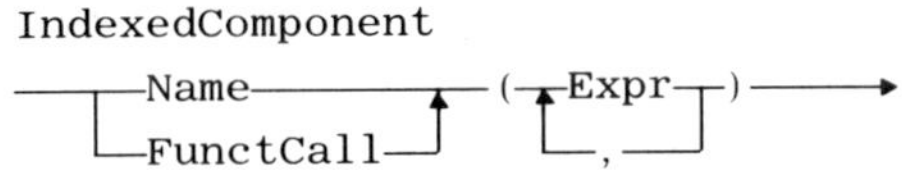

Slice

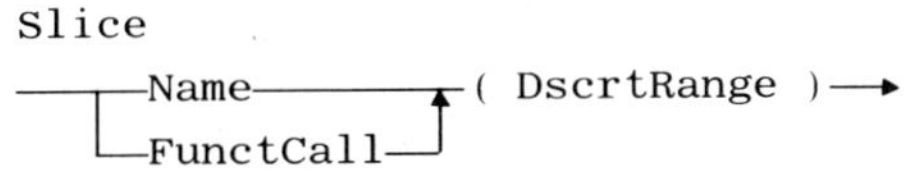

SelectedComponent

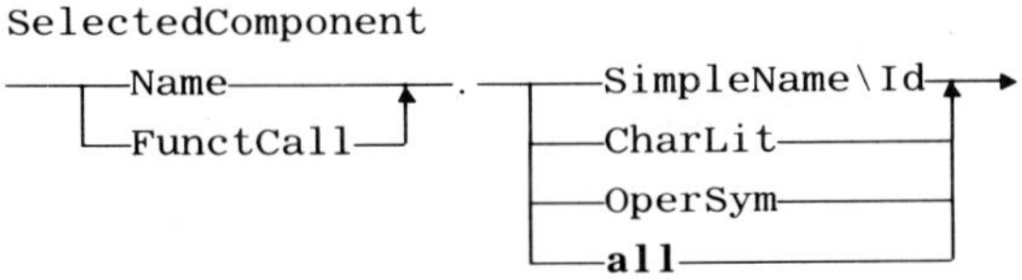

Attribute

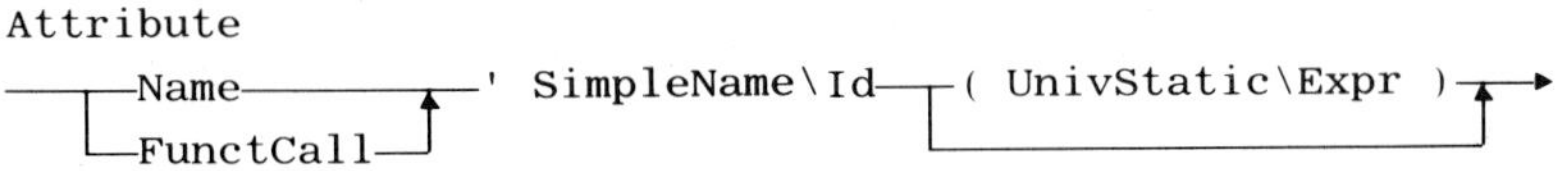

Reserved Words

abort	body	elsif	if	of	range	task
abs	case	end	in	or	record	terminate
accept	constant	entry	is	others	rem	then
access	declare	exception	limited	out	renames	type
all	delay	exit	loop	package	return	use
and	delta	for	mod	pragma	reverse	when
array	digits	function	new	private	select	while
at	do	generic	not	procedure	separate	with
begin	else	goto	null	raise	subtype	xor

------------------------ Predefined Packages ------------------------

```
package Standard is  --------------------------Standard-------------
 type     Boolean    is (False, True);
 type     Integer    is range  [ImplDef];
 type     Float      is digits [ImplDef];
 type     Character  is [EnumerationTypeOfAsciiCharSet];
 subtype  Natural    is Integer range 0 .. Integer'Last;
 subtype  Positive   is Integer range 1 .. Integer'Last;
 type     String     is array (Positive range <>) of Character;
 type     Duration   is delta [ImplDef] range [ImplDef];
   for      Character use (0, 1, 2, ..., 126, 127);
   pragma   Pack(String);

 package Ascii is                                 ----- Ascii -----
  -- Nul Soh Stx Etx Eot Eng Ack Bel Bs  Ht Lf  Vt  Ff Cr So Si
  -- Dle Dc1 Dc2 Dc3 Dc4 Nak Syn Etb Can Em Sub Esc Fs Gs Rs Us Del
  -- ! Exclam      & Ampersand  [ L_Bracket   ` Grave     a Lc_P
  -- " Quotation   : Colon      \ Back_Slash  { L_Brace   : :
  -- # Sharp       ; Semicolon  ] R_Bracket   | Bar       z Lc_Z
  -- $ Dollar      ? Query      ^ Circumflex  } R_Brace
  -- % Percent     @ At_Sign    _ Underline   ~ Tilde
 end Ascii;

 Constraint_Error, Numeric_Error, Program_Error : exception;
 Storage_Error,    Tasking_Error                : exception;

end Standard;
```

```
package System is  ------------------------ System ---------------
 type    Address  is [ImplDef];
 type    Name     is [ImplDefEnumType];
 subtype Priority is Integer range [ImplDefined];
 System_Name   : constant Name := [ImplDef];
 Storage_Unit  : constant := [ImplDef]; --Bits Per Storage Unit
 Memory_Size   : constant := [ImplDef]; --Mem Size In Storage Units
 Min_Int       : constant := [ImplDef]; --MostNeg Val Of Any IntType
 Max_Int       : constant := [ImplDef]; --Largest Val Of Any IntType
 Max_Digits    : constant := [ImplDef]; --Largest Possible "digits"
 Max_Mantissa  : constant := [ImplDef]; --Max Bits For Fixed Pt type
 Fine_Delta    : constant := [ImplDef]; --Min Delta For -1.0 .. 1.0
 Tick          : constant := [ImplDef]; --Clock Period In Seconds
end System;


with IO_Exceptions;
package Text_IO is  ----------------------- Text_IO ---------------

 type    File_Type      is limited private;
 type    File_Mode      is (In_File, Out_File);
 type    Count          is range 0 .. [ImplDefined];
 subtype Positive_Count is Count range 1 Count'Last;
 Unbounded: constant Count := 0

 subtype Field       is Integer range 0 .. [ImplDefined];
 subtype Number_Base is Integer range 2 .. 16;
 type    Type_Set    is (Lower_Case, Upper_Case);

 procedure Create(File: in out File_Type; Mode: File_Mode:=Out File;
                  Name: String:="";        Form: String:="" );
 procedure Open  (File: in out File_Type; Mode:  File_Mode;
                  Name: String;            Form: String:="" );
 procedure Close (File: in out File_Type);
 procedure Delete(File: in out File_Type);
 procedure Reset (File: in out File_Type; Mode: File_Mode);
 procedure Reset (File: in out File_Type);

 function  Mode    (File: File_Type) return File_Mode;
 function  Name    (File: File_Type) return String;
 function  Form    (File: File_Type) return String;
 function  Is_Open (File: File_Type) return Boolean;
```

```
procedure Set_Input  (File: File_Type);
procedure Set_Output (File: File_Type);
function  Standard_Input  return File_Type;
function  Standard_Output return File_Type;
function  Current_Input   return File_Type;
function  Current_Output  return File_Type;

--An underlined parameter denotes two subprograms, one with a file
--parameter and one using the current default input or output file.

procedure Set_Line_Length (File: File_Type;  To: Count);
procedure Set_Page_Length (File: File_Type;  To: Count);
function  Line_Length     (File: File_Type)   return Count;
function  Page_Length     (File: File_Type)   return Count;

procedure New_Line   (File: File_Type; Spacing: Positive_Count:=1);
procedure Skip_Line  (File: File_Type; Spacing: Positive_Count:=1);
function  End_Of_Line(File: File_Type)    return Boolean;
procedure New_Page   (File: File_Type);
procedure Skip_Page  (File: File_Type);
function  End_Of_Page(File: File_Type)    return Boolean;
function  End_of_File(File: File_Type)    return Boolean;
procedure Set_Col    (File: File_Type; To: Positive_Count);
procedure Set_Line   (File: File_Type; To: Positive_Count);
function  Col        (File: File_Type)    return Positive_Count;
function  Line       (File: File_Type)    return Positive_Count;
function  Page       (File: File_type)    return Positive_Count;

procedure Get      (File: File_Type; Item: out Character);
procedure Put      (File: File_Type; Item: in  Character);
procedure Get      (File: File_Type; Item: out String);
procedure Put      (File: File_Type; Item: in  String);
procedure Get_Line (File: File_Type; Item: out String;
                    Last: out Natural );
procedure Put_Line (File: File_Type; Item: in  String);

generic type Num is range <>;              ----- Integer_IO -----
package Integer_IO is
 Default_Width  : Field       := Num'Width;
 Default_Base   : Number_Base := 10;
 procedure Get(File : File_Type; Item: out Num;  Width: Field:=0);
 procedure Put(File : File_Type; Item: in  Num;
              Width: Field       :=Default_Width;
              Base : Number_Base :=Default_Base );
 procedure Get(From: in  String;  Item: out Num;
              Last: out Positive );
```

```
  procedure Put(To  : out String;  Item: in  Num;
                Base: Number_Base:=Default_Base );
 end Integer_IO;

 generic type Num is digits <>;                   ----- Float_IO -----
 package Float_IO is
   Default_Fore : Field := 2;
   Default_Aft  : Field := Num'Digits-1;
   Default_Exp  : Field := 3;
   procedure Get(File: File_Type;  Item: out Num;  Width: Field:=0);
   procedure Put(File: File_Type;  Item: in  Num;
                 Fore: Field:=Default_Fore;
                 Aft : Field:=Default_Aft;
                 Exp : Field:=Default_Exp );
   procedure Get(From: in  String;  Item: out Num;
                 Last: out Positive );
   procedure Put(To  : out String;  Item: in Num;
                 Aft : Field:=Default_Aft;     -- Fore fills string
                 Exp : Field:=Default_Exp );
 end Float_IO;

 generic type Num is delta <>;                    ----- Fixed_IO -----
 package Fixed_IO is
   Default_Fore : Field := Num'Fore;
   Default_Aft  : Field := Num'Aft;
   Default_Exp  : Field := 0;
   -- Same subprogram definitions as in "Float_IO"
 end Fixed_IO;

 generic type Enum is (<>);             ----- Enumeration_IO -----
 package Enumeration_IO is
   Default_Width   : Field    := 0;
   Default_Setting : Type_Set := Upper_Case;
   procedure Get (File : File_Type;  Item: out Enum );
   procedure Put (File : File_Type;  Item: in  Enum;
                  Width: Field    :=Default_Width;
                  Set  : Type_Set :=Default_Setting );
   procedure Get (From: in  String;  Item: out Enum;
                  Last: out Positive );
   procedure Put (To  : out String;  Item: in  Enum;
                  Set : Type_Set:=Default_Setting );
 end Enumeration_IO;
 --  IO_Exceptions renamed here: Status_Error, Mode_Error, Name_Error,
 --  Use_Error, Device_Error, End_Error, Data_Error, Layout_Error
private
  -- implementation dependent
end Text_IO;
```

Attributes

Prefix P	Attribute	Result Type	Meaning
[1]	P'Address	System.Address	Address of item
TySb:X	P'Aft	UInt	# chars after
TySb:Any	P'Base'...	<BT>	Base type of type P
Objt:AppTsk	P'Callable	Bool	Task is callable
Objt:W/Dscr	P'Constrained	Bool	Obj is constrained
TySb:Privat	P'Constrained	Bool	Subt is constrained
Entry	P'Count	UInt	# waiting calls
TySb:X	P'Delta	UReal	Spec'd delta
TySb:L	P'Digits	UInt	Spec'd digits
TySb:L	P'Emax	UInt	Max exponent in Mn
TySb:L	P'Epsilon	UReal	(Next Mn>1.0) - 1.0
TySb:IELX	P'First	<BT> [2]	First val in subtype
ObSb:Array	P'First	<IxTy>	Lo bound of 1st indx
ObSb:Array	P'First(N)	<IxTy>	Lo bound of Nth indx
Objt:RecCmp	P'First-Bit	UInt	Bit dspl from 1st Su
TySb:X	P'Fore	UInt	# chars before .
TySb:IE	P'Image(...)	<BT> -> Str	Printed form of ...
TySb:LX	P'Large	UReal	Maximum Mn
TySb:IELX	P'Last	<BT> [2]	Last val in subtype
ObSb:Array	P'Last	<IxTy>	Hi bound of 1st indx
ObSb:Array	P'Last(N)	<IxTy>	Hi bound of Nth indx
Objt:RecCmp	P'Last-Bit	UInt	Bit dspl from 1st Su
ObSb:Array	P'Length	UInt	# values of 1st indx
ObSb:Array	P'Length(N)	UInt	# values of Nth indx
TySb:L	P'Machine-Emax	UInt	Max exponent in Mr
TySb:L	P'Machine-Emin	UInt	Most neg exp in Mr
TySb:L	P'Machine-Mantissa	UInt	# radix dgts in Mr
TySb:LX	P'Machine-Overflows	Bool	Exception if oflo
TySb:L	P'Machine-Radix	UInt	Radix used in Mr
TySb:LX	P'Machine-Rounds	Bool	Ops exact or rounded
TySb:LX	P'Mantissa	UInt	# bits in Mn ("B")
TySb:IE	P'Pos(...)	<BT> -> UInt	Position num of ...
Objt:RecCmp	P'Position	UInt	Dspl of field (Su's)
TySb:IE	P'Pred(...)	<BT> -> <BT>	Predecessor of ...
ObSb:Array	P'Range	<IxTy>..<IxTy>	Range of 1st index
ObSb:Array	P'Range(N)	<IxTy>..<IxTy>	Range of Nth index
TySb:L	P'Safe-Emax	UInt	Max exponent in Sn
TySb:LX	P'Safe-Large	UReal	Maximum Sn
TySb:LX	P'Safe-Small	UReal	Minimum Sn > 0
ObTy:Any	P'Size	UInt	Size of obj (bits)

Prefix P	Attribute	Result Type	Meaning
TySb: LX	P'Small	UReal	Minimum Mn > 0
TySb: Access	P'Storage-Size	UInt	Space for objs (Su's)
ObTy: Task	P'Storage-Size	UInt	ActivationSize (Su's)
TySb: IE	P'Succ(...)	<BT> -> <BT>	Successor of ...
Objt: AppTsk	P'Terminated	Bool	Task is terminated
TySb: IE	P'Val(...)	AnyInt -> <BT>	Inverse of "Pos"
TySb: IE	P'Value(...)	Str -> <BT>	Inverse of "Image"
TySb: IE	P'Width	UInt	Max of "Image(...)"

Nature of Prefix

[1] Program Unit (subpr, package, or task), Label, or Entry.
(Function name refers to function itself, not call.)

TySb: Type or subtype, including the following abbreviations:
I=Integer type or subt L=Floating-pt type or subt
E=Enumeration type or subt X=Fixed-point type or subt

Objt: Object.
"Objt: RecCmp" = Component of a record object.

ObSb: Object or constrained subtype
"ObSb: Array" = AppArrayObject, or ConstrainedArraySubtype

ObTy: Object, type, or subtype.
"ObTy: Any" = AnyObject, or AnyTypeOrSubtype
"ObTy: Task" = TaskObject, or TaskType

Note--"AppXxx" means "appropriate to type Xxx" -- ie, the prefix is an object of type Xxx or a pointer object to type Xxx.

Result Type

<BT> : Base type of prefix
<IxTy> : Base type of array index position
[2] : P'First and P'Last for a floating point (sub) type need not yield model or safe numbers.

Abbreviations

Mn=ModelNumber, Sn=SafeNumber, Mr=MachineRepr, Su=StorageUnit

------------ Relationships among Floating-Point Attributes ------------

```
P'Digits  = D            P'Mantissa = B = Ceil(D*log(10)/log(2)+1)
P'Emax    = 4*B          P'Small    = 2 ** (-4*B - 1)
P'Epsilon = 2 ** (1-B)   P'Large    = 2 ** (4*B)  *  (1 - 2**(-B))
   D = 1  2  3  4  5  6  7  8  9 10 11 12 13 14 15 16 17 18 19 20
   B = 5  8 11 15 18 21 25 28 31 35 38 41 45 48 51 55 58 61 65 68
-- Safe numbers have the same (binary) mantissa as model numbers but
-- possibly larger expon.  The machine rep may have more precision.
```

Pragmas

—pragma Controlled (AccessTypeSimpleName\Id) ;→

After the type declaration and in the same DecltivePart or PackageSpec. (Not allowed for a derived type.)

Suppresses garbage collection.

```
—pragma Elaborate (─┬─LibraryUnitSimpleName\Id─┬─) ;→
                    └────────────,─────────────┘
```

Between a context clause and the subsequent LibraryUnit, LibraryUnitBody, or SubUnit. Each name must be mentioned in the context clause.

Requires prior elaboration of each named LibraryUnit<u>Body</u>.

```
—pragma Inline (─┬─SubprOrGenericSubpr\Name─┬─) ; →
                 └────────────,────────────┘
```

1) After the declaration(s) of the named subprogram and in the same DecltivePart or PackageSpec, or

2) After the named LibraryUnit (1 name only).

This pragma may be ignored, on a per-call basis.

—pragma Interface (Language\Name , Subpr\Name) ;→

1) After the named SubprSpec in the same DecltivePart or PackageSpec, or

2) After the named LibraryUnit.

```
—pragma List (─┬─On──┬─) ;→
               └─Off─┘
```

Anywhere a pragma is allowed. Turns compiler listing on/off.

—pragma Memory-Size (NumericLiteral)→

Before the 1st CompilationUnit. Sets "System.Memory-Size".

```
—pragma Optimize (─┬─Time──┬─) ;→
                   └─Space─┘
```

In a DecltivePart. Applies to the associated body or block.

—pragma Pack (RecordOrArrayTypeSimpleName\Id) ;→

Same places as a ReprClause, and before use of a representation attribute of the packed entity.

Storage minimization is preferred for the data type.

—pragma Page ;→

Anywhere a pragma is allowed. Ejects page in compiler listing.

—pragma Priority (Static\Expression)→

1) In a TaskSpec, or 2) In the DecltivePart of a main subpr.

Value must be in Integer subtype "System.Priority"; larger value means greater urgency. Don't use for synchronization.

```
—pragma Shared ( VariableSimpleName\Id )—▸
```

After the variable declaration and in the same DecltivePart or PackageSpec and before any other use of the variable name (except Address ReprClause). Variable type must be access or scalar with indivisible machine operations.

Causes all reads\writes of the variable to be done to memory.

```
—pragma Storage-Unit ( NumericLiteral )—▸
```

Before 1st CompilationUnit. Sets "System.Storage-Unit".

```
—pragma Suppress (——Check\Id—┬—,—┬—On =>—▲—Name—▲—)—▸
                             │    └─────────┘      │
                             └──────────────────────┘
```

1) With or without the name, in a DecltivePart; or

2) With the name, in the PackageSpec where the name is declared.

Suppresses checking for the specified exception from this point on. If name is given, checking is only suppressed for the named entity. (This pragma need not have any effect.)

Check\Id	Exception	Name denotes (if present);
Discriminant-Check, Access-Check, Index-Check, Length-Check, Range-Check	Constraint-Error	Object, Type
Division-Check, Overflow-Check	Numeric-Error	NumericType
Elaboration-Check	Program-Error	TaskUnit, GenericUnit, Subpr
Storage-Check	Storage-Error	AccessType, TaskUnit, Subpr

```
—pragma System-Name (—┬——EnumerationLiteral\Id————————▲—)—▸
                      └—EnumerationLiteral\CharLit————┘
```

Before 1st CompilationUnit. Sets "System.System-Name".

- -

1) A pragma may only appear after a semicolon delimiter (but not in a formal part or discriminant part).

2) If a pragma name is undefined or pragma argument is incorrect, then the program is still legal but the pragma is ignored.

3) These predefined pragmas must be provided in every implementation, but not all are required to have an effect.

SOLUTIONS FOR ODD-NUMBERED EXERCISES*

CHAPTER 1

The package Simple_ Graphics as coded in the text is a simplified version of a graphics package. The solutions for 1.1 and 1.3 are coded with respect to this simple package. Appendix A contains a Simple_Graphics package modified to run on a VAX 11/780† with a VT-125 terminal.

1.1

```
with Simple_Graphics;
procedure Draw_Square is
begin -- Draw_Square
   Simple_Graphics.Draw_Line ( (1,2), (3,2) );
   Simple_Graphics.Draw_Line ( (3,2), (3,0) );
   Simple_Graphics.Draw_Line ( (3,0), (1,0) );
   Simple_Graphics.Draw_Line ( (1,0), (1,2) );
end Draw_Square;
```

1.3

```
with Simple_Graphics; use Simple_Graphics;
procedure Draw_Flag is
begin -- Draw_Flag
   Draw_Line ( (1,2), (3,2) );
   Draw_Line ( (3,2), (3,0) );
   Draw_Line ( (3,0), (1,0) );
   --
```

* and selected even-numbered exercises

† VAX 11/780 is a registered trademark of Digital Equipment Corporation.

```
   -- Draw the entire pole.
   --
   Draw_Line ( (1,2), (1, -2) );
   --
   -- Draw one diagonal.
   --
   Draw_Line ( (1,2), (3,0) );
   --
   -- Draw second diagonal.
   --
   Draw_Line ( (3,2), (1,0) );
end Draw_Flag;
```

1.5

```
with Math_Library;
procedure Sine_of_30 is
begin -- Sine_of_30
   Math_Library.Trigonometric_Functions.Print_Sine_of (30);
end Sine_of_30;
```

1.7

Main advantages are as follows:

—Removes any chance for ambiguity (the compiler will not be confused).

—When importing multiple packages, the prefix clearly shows *which* package supplied a specific resource.

CHAPTER 2

2.1

a. Legal.
b. Legal.
c. Illegal. Trailing underlines are not permitted. An underline is permitted only between adjacent legal characters.
   Correction: Front_40 as in part b, or Front_40_Acres.
d. Legal.
e. Illegal. The character $ is not allowed in identifiers.
   Correction: Amount_in_Dollars.
f. Illegal. Accept is a reserved word. See Table 2-1.
   Correction: Add what is to be accepted, for example, Accept_the_Check or Accept_the_Message.
g. Legal.
h. Illegal. Underlines must be *isolated* and embedded. Only one underline is permitted at a time.
   Correction: First_Value.
i. Illegal. Spaces are not permissible in identifiers.
   Correction: Simple_Graphics or SimpleGraphics.
j. Illegal. Leading underlines are illegal.
   Correction: Silly_Name.

k. Illegal. Identifiers must start with a letter.
   Correction: One_to_One.
l. Illegal. Range is a reserved word. See Table 2-1.
   Correction: Add descriptive information, e.g. Range_of_Values or Frequency_Range.

2.3

1. the word "procedure"
2. the name of the procedure
3. the formal parameter list

No. Parameterless procedures do not have a formal parameter list.

2.5

Procedure	*Formals*	*Type of Formals*
Accept_Deposit	Account_Number Amount	Integer Float
Accept_Withdrawal	Account_Number Amount	Integer Float
Accept_Order_etc.	Account_Number Quantity	Integer Integer

2.7

Resource	*Actuals*	*Type of Actuals*
Balance_of	none	none
Accept_Deposit	12369 50.00	Integer Float
Accept_Withdrawal	none	none
Accept_Order_etc.	12369 300	Integer Integer

2.9

```
with Simple_Graphics; use Simple_Graphics;
procedure Draw_Flag is
    --
    --  This procedure draws the flag by first drawing
    --  the square. Then it draws the two diagonal lines
```

```
    --  and finally draws the remainder of the pole.
    --
    --  This procedure does not label the points.
    --
   procedure Draw_Square (Top_Left    : Point_Type;
                          Side_Length : Integer) is
       --
       -- Three data items are introduced to represent
       -- the three other corners of the square. This is
       -- done to improve the readability of the executable code.
       --
       Top_Right    : Point_Type := (Top_Left(1) + Side_Length,
                                     Top_Left(2));
       Bottom_Right : Point_Type := (Top_Left(1) + Side_Length,
                                     Top_Left(2) - Side_Length);
       Bottom_Left  : Point_Type := (Top_Left (1),
                                     Top_Left(2) - Side_Length);
   begin -- Draw_Square
       Draw_Line ( Top_Left, Top_Right );        -- the top
       Draw_Line ( Top_Right, Bottom_Right);     -- the right side
       Draw_Line ( Bottom_Right, Bottom_Left);   -- the bottom
       Draw_Line ( Bottom_Left, Top_Left) ;      -- the left side
   end Draw_Square;
   procedure Draw_Diagonals (Top_Left    : Point_Type;
                             Side_Length : Integer) is
       --
       -- Local data introduced to improve readability
       -- of the executable code.
       --
       Top_Right    : Point_Type := (Top_Left(1) + Side_Length,
                                     Top_Left(2));
       Bottom_Right : Point_Type := (Top_Left(1) + Side Length,
                                     Top_Left(2) - Side_Length);
       Bottom_Left  : Point_Type := (Top_Left (1),
                                     Top_Left(2) - Side_Length);
   begin -- Draw_Diagonals
      Draw_Line (Top_Left, Bottom_Right); -- draw diagonal \
      Draw_Line (Top_Right, Bottom_Left); -- draw diagonal /
   end Draw_Diagonals;
begin -- Draw_Flag
   Draw_Square ( (1,2), 2 );          -- draw the square
   Draw_Diagonals ( (1,2), 2);        -- draw diagonals
   Draw_Line ( (1, 0), (1, -2));      -- draw rest of pole
end Draw_Flag;
--
```

```
-- NOTE:  This is sloppy code. The local declarations for the three
-- other points of the square are repeated twice, once in each nested
-- procedure. This is also inefficient because it causes them to
-- be initialized twice.
-- There are two reasons for this situation. The first is that
-- Simple_Graphics is very simple and is so for pedagogical
-- reasons. The second is that we haven't learned enough Ada yet to
-- code this in a more Ada-like style.
--
```

2.11

1. the word function
2. the name of the function
3. the formal parameter list
4. the reserved word return
5. the type of the result to be returned to the caller

No. A function such as

```
function Hour return Integer;
```

returns the hour when called. It does not require any parameters.

2.13

Resource	*Formals*	*Type of Formals*	*Type Returned*
Balance_of	Account_Number	Integer	Float
Deposit_into	Account_Number Amount	Integer Float	Float
Withdrawal_from	Account_Number Amount	Integer Float	Float

2.15

Resource	*Actuals*	*Type of Actuals*
Balance_of	none	none
Deposit_into	12369 50.00	Integer Float
Withdrawal_from	none	none
Accept_Order_etc.	12369 300	Integer Integer

2.17

```
with Simple_Graphics; use Simple_Graphics;
procedure Draw_Rectangle is
   Area : Integer;
   function Area_of_Rectangle (Length, Width : Integer) return Integer is
      -- No local data required.
   begin -- Area_of_Rectangle
      return Length * Width;
   end Area_of_Rectangle;
begin -- Draw_Rectangle
   Draw_Line ( (3,0), (7,0) );
   Draw_Line ( (7,0), (7,-2) );
   Draw_Line ( (7, -2), (3, -2) );
   Draw_Line ( (3, -2), (3, 0) );
   Area := Area_of_Rectangle (4, 2);
end Draw_Rectangle;
--
-- NOTE:  Again - we will learn how to output results in Chapter 3.
--
```

2.19

```
with Simple_Graphics; use Simple_Graphics;
procedure Draw_Two_Rectangles is
   procedure Draw_Rectangle (Top_Left : Point_Type := (0,0);
                             Length, Width : Integer) is
      Top_Right    : Point_Type := (Top_Left(1) + Length, Top_Left(2));
      Bottom_Right : Point_Type := (Top_Left(1) + Length,
                                   Top_Left(2) - Width);
      Bottom_Left  : Point_Type := (Top_Left(1), Top_Left(2) - Width);
   begin -- Draw_Rectangle
      Draw_Line ( Top_Left, Top_Right );
      Draw_Line ( Top_Right, Bottom_Right);
      Draw_Line ( Bottom_Right, Bottom_Left);
      Draw_Line ( Bottom_Left, Top_Left);
   end Draw_Rectangle;
begin -- Draw_Two_Rectangles
   Draw_Rectangle (Length => 6, Width => 2);
   Draw_Rectangle ( (3, 4), 2, 4);
end Draw_Two_Rectangles;
```

2.21

```
with Statistics; use Statistics;
procedure Sort_Ascending (Array_In  : in  List_of_Grades;
                          Array_Out : out List_of_Grades) is
   -- local data
begin -- Sort_Ascending
   -- code
end Sort_Ascending;
```

```
with Statistics; use Statistics;
procedure Sort_Descending (Array_In  : in  List_of_Grades;
                           Array_Out : out List_of_Grades) is
   -- local data
begin -- Sort_Descending
   -- code
end Sort_Descending;

with Statistics; use Statistics;
with Sort_Ascending, Sort_Descending;
procedure A_Contrived_Example is
   Grades,
   Grades_in_Ascending_Order,
   Grades_in_Descending_Order : List_of_Grades;
   procedure Sort_Both_Ways
     (Array_to_be_Sorted : in  List_of_Grades,
      Ascending_Array,
      Descending_Array   : out List_of_Grades) is separate;
begin -- A_Contrived_Example
   -- Statements to input the list
   Sort_Both_Ways (Array_to_be_Sorted => Grades,
                   Ascending_Array    => Grades_in_Ascending_Order,
                   Descending_Array   => Grades_in_Descending_Order);
   -- Statements to output the two lists
end A_Contrived_Example;

separate (A_Contrived_Example)
procedure Sort_Both_Ways
 (Array_to_be_Sorted : in  List_of_Grades,
  Ascending_Array,
  Descending_Array   : out List_of_Grades) is
begin -- Sort_Both_Ways
   Sort_Ascending  (Array_In  => Array_to_be_Sorted,
                    Array_Out => Ascending_Array);
   Sort_Descending (Array_In  => Array_to_be_Sorted,
                    Array_Out => Descending_Array);
end Sort_Both_Ways;
```

2.23

Compilation Units (text):

A.	Statistics	(package specification)
B.	Statistics	(package body)
C.	A_Contrived_Example	(procedure)
D.	Sort_Both_Ways	(subunit)
E.	Sort_Ascending	(subunit)
F.	Sort_Descending	(subunit)

Legal Compilation Orders (text)

1. A, B, C, D, E, F
2. A, C, B, D, E, F
3. A, C, D, B, E, F
4. A, C, D, E, B, F
5. A, C, D, E, F, B
6. A, B, C, D, F, E
7. A, C, B, D, F, E
8. A, C, D, B, F, E
9. A, C, D, F, B, E
10. A, C, D, F, E, B

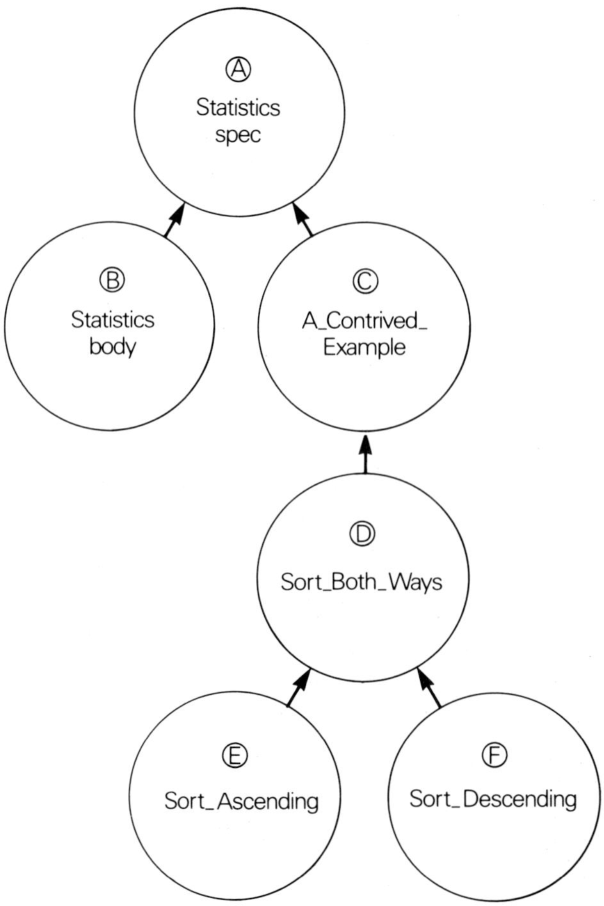

Dependency diagram

2.25

↓
Illegal Order of Compilation (text): BACDEF
(package body compiled before package specification)

↓
Illegal Order of Compilation (exercise 2.21): ABECDF
(main procedure compiled before "withed" procedures compiled)

2.27
The following units need to be recompiled (text):
Sort_Ascending
Sort_Descending

The following units need to be recompiled (exercise 2.21):
None

CHAPTER 3

3.1

```
with Text_IO, Simple_Graphics;
use Text_IO, Simple_Graphics;
procedure Draw_Two_Rectangles is
   Area_1, Area_2 : Integer;
   function Area_of_Rectangle (Length, Width : Integer) return Integer is
      -- No local data required.
   begin -- Area_of_Rectangle
      return Length * Width;
   end Area_of_Rectangle;
   procedure Draw_Rectangle (Top_Left : in Point_Type := (0,0);
                             Length, Width : in Integer) is
      Top_Right    : Point_Type := (Top_Left(1) + Length, Top_Left(2));
      Bottom_Right : Point_Type := (Top_Left(1) + Length,
                                    Top_Left(2) - Width);
      Bottom_Left  : Point_Type := (Top_Left(1), Top_Left(2) - Width);
   begin -- Draw_Rectangle
      Draw_Line ( Top_Left, Top_Right );
      Draw_Line ( Top_Right, Bottom_Right);
      Draw_Line ( Bottom_Right, Bottom_Left);
      Draw_Line ( Bottom_Left, Top_Left);
   end Draw_Rectangle;
   package IntIO is new Integer_IO (Integer);
   use Int_IO;
begin -- Draw_Two_Rectangles
   -- The first rectangle
   Draw_Rectangle (Length => 6, Width => 2);
```

```
   Area_1 := Area_of_Rectangle (Length => 6, Width => 2);
   Put_Line ("The area of the first rectangle is: ");
   Put (Area_1);
   New_Line;
   -- The second rectangle
   Draw_Rectangle ( (3,4), 2, 4);
   Area_2 := Area_of_Rectangle (Length => 2, Width => 1);
   Put_Line ("The area of the second rectangle is: ");
   Put (Area_2);
end Draw_Two_Rectangles;
```

3.3

```
with Metric_Conversions; use Metric_Conversions;
with Text_IO; use Text_IO;
procedure Conversion_Routine is
   An_Inch : Float;
   package Flt_IO is new Float_IO (Float);
   use Flt_IO;
begin -- Conversion_Routine
   Put_Line ("Enter the inches to be converted: ");
   Get (An_Inch);
   Put ("The value in centimeters is: ");
   Put ( Inches_to_Centimeters (An_Inch) );
end Conversion_Routine;
```

3.5

```
with Metric_Conversions; use Metric_Conversions;
with Text_IO; use Text_IO;
procedure Convert_Gallons is
   Gallons : Integer;
   Liters  : Float;
   package Int_IO is new Integer_IO (Integer);
   package Flt_IO is new Float_IO (Float);
   use Int_IO, Flt_IO;
begin -- Convert_Gallons
   Put_Line ("Enter the gallons to be converted: ");
   Get (Gallons);
   Liters := Gallons_to_Liters (Gallons);
   Put (Gallons);
   Put (" gallons is ");
   Put (Liters);
   Put (" liters");
end Convert_Gallons;
```

3.7

a. Compile time error. When a loop is named, the name must appear after the end loop. The correct code is

```
OBTAIN_FIRST_VALUE:
   loop
       ...
   end loop OBTAIN_FIRST_VALUE;
```

b. Run time error. The exception Numeric_Error is raised.
c. Compile time error. Parts of an expression must be of the same type. Here Value is of type Integer and 0.0 is of type Float.
d. Run time error. The exception Numeric_Error is raised.
e. Run time error. The exception raised is Constraint_Error.
f. Run time error. The exception raised is Constraint_Error. The compiler finds nothing wrong with

```
GET (I);
   ...
Center(I) := I;
```

but the run time system will raise Constraint_Error upon an attempt to assign to Center (3) when 3 is input for I.

3.9

block

3.11a

```
with Factorial_Operations; use Factorial_Operations;
with Text_IO; use Text_IO;
procedure Compute_Factorial is
   Number : Integer;
   package Int_IO is new Integer_IO (Integer);
   use Int_IO;
begin -- Compute_Factorial
   loop
      begin
         Get (Number);
         exit;
      exception
         when Data_Error => Put ("Invalid entry.");
                            Put ("Enter only integer values");
      end;
   end loop;
   Put ("The factorial of ");
   Put (Number);
   Put (" is ");
   Put ( Factorial_of(Number) );
end Compute_Factorial;
```

3.11b

```
-- The exception Numeric_Error is raised. The following represents 3.11a
-- recoded to handle this situation.
with Factorial_Operations; use Factorial_Operations;
with Text_IO; use Text_IO;
procedure Compute_Factorial is
   Number : Integer;
   package Int_IO is new Integer_IO (Integer);
   use Int_IO;
begin -- Compute_Factorial
   loop
      begin
         Get (Number);
         exit;
      exception
         when Data_Error => Put ("Invalid entry.");
                            Put ("Enter only integer values");
      end;
   end loop;
   Put ("The factorial of ");
   Put (Number);
   Put (" is ");
   Put ( Factorial_of(Number) );
exception
   when Numeric_Error => Put ("too large for the system to handle.");
end Compute_Factorial;
```

3.11c

```
-- The following represents 3.11b recoded to handle the exception
-- Negative_Number.
--
with Factorial_Operations; use Factorial_Operations;
with Text_IO; use Text_IO;
procedure Compute_Factorial is
begin
   NEGATIVE_NUMBER :
   loop
      INPUT :
      loop
         begin
            Get (Number);
            exit;
         exception
            when Data_Error =>
               Put ("Invalid Entry.");
```

```
               Put ("Enter integer values only.");
            end;
         end loop INPUT;
         begin
            Put (Factorial_of (Number));
         exception
            when Negative_Number =>
               Put_Line ("Factorials can only be computed for values > 0".);
         end;
      end loop NEGATIVE_NUMBER;
exception
   when Numeric_Error =>
      Put ("Too large for the system to handle.");
end Compute_Factorial;
```

3.13

```
with Factorial_Operations; use Factorial_Operations;
with Text_IO; use Text_IO;
procedure Table is
   Last_Number : Integer;
   package Int_IO is new Integer_IO (Integer);
   use Int_IO;
begin -- Table
   Put_Line ("Enter last number: ");
INPUT_LOOP:
   loop
      begin
         Get (Last_Number);
         exit;
      exception
         when Data_Error => Put_Line ("Invalid entry, try again.");
      end;
   end loop INPUT_LOOP;
   for Number in 1..Last_Number
   loop
      Put (Number);
      begin
         Put ( Factorial_of(Number) );
         New_Line;
      exception
         when Numeric_Error =>
            Put_Line ("Result too large, terminating the procedure.");
         exit;
      end;
   end loop;
end Table;
```

CHAPTER 4

4.1

```
with Text_IO; use Text_IO;
procedure Exercise_4_1 is
   package Bool_IO is new Enumeration_IO (Boolean);
   use Bool_IO;
   Value : Boolean;
begin -- Exercise_4_1
   loop
      begin
         Get (Value);
         exit;
      exception
         when Data_Error => Put ("Invalid entry, enter True or False");
      end;
   end loop;
   Put (not Value);
end Exercise_4_1;
```

4.3

```
with Text_IO;  use Text_IO;
procedure Table_4_1 is
   package Boolean_IO is new Enumeration_IO (Boolean);
   use Boolean_IO;
   procedure Print_NOT_Table is separate;
   procedure Print_AND_Table is separate;
   procedure Print_OR_Table is separate;
   procedure Print_XOR_Table is separate;
begin   -- Table_4_1
   Print_NOT_Table;
   Print_AND_Table;
   Print_OR_Table;
   Print_XOR_Table;
end Table_4_1;

separate (Table_4_1)
procedure Print_NOT_Table is
begin -- Print_NOT_Table
    New_Line (5);
    Put ("Logic table for the boolean function NOT.");
    New_Line (3);
    Put ("        |     NOT");
    New_Line;
    Put ("-------------------");
    New_Line;
    Put ("True    |    ");
```

```
    Put (not True);
    New_Line;
    Put ("False  |    ");
    Put (not False);
end Print_NOT_Table;

separate (Table_4_1)
procedure Print_AND_Table is
begin -- Print_AND_Table
   New_Line (5);
   Put ("Logic table for the boolean function AND.");
   New_Line (3);
   Put ("AND    |      True      False");
   New_Line;
   Put ("--------------------------");
   New_Line;
   Put ("True   |     ");
   Put (True and True, 5);
   Put ("     ");
   Put (True and False);
   New_Line;
   Put ("False  |     ");
   Put (False and True, 5);
   Put ("     ");
   Put (False and False);
end Print_AND_Table;

separate (Table_4_1)
procedure Print_OR_Table is
begin -- Print_OR_Table
   New_Line (5);
   Put ("Logic table for the boolean function OR.");
   New_Line (3);
   Put ("OR     |      True      False");
   New_Line;
   Put ("--------------------------");
   New_Line;
   Put ("True   |     ");
   Put (True or True, 5);
   Put ("     ");
   Put (True or False);
   New_Line;
   Put ("False  |     ");
   Put (False or True, 5);
```

```
   Put ("     ");
   Put ("False or False);
end Print_OR_Table;

separate (Table_4_1)
procedure Print_XOR_Table is
begin -- Print_XOR_Table
   New_Line (5);
   Put ("Logic table for the boolean function XOR.");
   New_Line (3);
   Put ("XOR    |     True      False");
   New_Line;
   Put ("--------------------------");
   New_Line;
   Put ("True   |     ");
   Put (True xor True, 5);
   Put ("     ");
   Put (True xor False);
   New_Line;
   Put ("False  |     ");
   Put (False xor True, 5);
   Put ("     ");
   Put (False xor False);
end Print_XOR_Table;
```

4.5

```
with Text_IO; use Text_IO;
with Simple_Graphics; use Simple_Graphics;
procedure Determine_Zero_Component is
   Point : Point_Type;
   procedure Display_0_Present is separate;
   procedure Display_0_not_Present is separate;
   procedure Get_A_Point (A_Point : out Point_Type) is separate;
begin -- Determine_Zero_Component
   Get_A_Point (Point);
   if Point(1) = 0 and then Point(2) = 0 then
      Put_Line ("The point is the origin.");
   elsif Point(1) = 0 then
      Display_0_Present;
      Put_Line ("The point is on the x-axis.");
   elsif Point(2) = 0 then
      Display_0_Present;
      Put_Line ("The point is on the y-axis.");
   else
      Display_0_not_Present;
   end if;
end Determine_Zero_Component;
```

```
separate (Determine_Zero_Component)
procedure Get_A_Point (A_Point : Out Point_Type) is
   package Int_IO is new Integer_IO (Integer);
   use Int_IO;
begin -- Get_A_Point
   for I in 1 .. 2
   loop
      loop
         begin
            Get (Point(I));
            exit;
         exception
            when Data_Error =>
               Put_Line ("Enter only integer values.");
         end;
      end loop;
   end loop;
end Get_A_Point;

separate (Determine_Zero_Component)
procedure Display_0_Present is
begin -- Display_0_Present
   Put_Line ("A zero component is present.");
end Display_0_Present;

separate (Determine_Zero_Component)
procedure Display_0_not_Present is
begin -- Display_0_not_Present
   Put_Line ("A zero component is not present.");
end Display_0_not_Present;
```

4.7

```
package Math_Library is
   --
   -- This package has been modified from the Math_Library
   -- of Chapter 1.
   --
   function Power ( Power, Number : Integer) return Integer;
   function Square_Root (Number : Float) return Float;
   function Cube_Root   (Number : Integer) return Float;
end Math_Library;

with Math_Library; use Math_Library;
with Text_IO; use Text_IO;
```

```
procedure Determine_Triangle_Construction is
   Side_A, Side_B, Side_C : Integer;
   package Int_IO is new Integer_IO (Integer);
   use Int_IO;
   package Flt_IO is new Float_IO (Float);
   use Flt_IO;
   procedure Get_A_Side (Side : out Integer) is separate;
   function  Area_of_Triangle (A,B,C : Integer) return Float is separate;
begin -- Determine_Triangle_Construction
   Get_A_Side (Side_A);
   Get_A_Side (Side_B);
   Get_A_Side (Side_C);
   if Side_A + Side_B > Side_C and
      Side_B + Side_C > Side_A and
      Side_A + Side_C > Side_B then
      Put_Line ("A triangle may be constructed.");
      Put ("The area of the triangle is: ");
      Put (Area_of_Triangle (Side_A, Side_B, Side_C) );
      New_Line;
   else
      Put_Line ("A triangle may not be constructed.");
   end if;
end Determine_Triangle_Construction;

separate (Determine_Triangle_Construction)
procedure Get_A_Side (Side : out Integer) is
begin -- Get_A_Side
   loop
      begin
         Put_Line ("Enter a triangle side: ");
         Get (Side);
         exit;
      exception
         when Data_Error =>
            Put_Line ("Invalid entry, enter only positive integer" &
                      "values.");
      end;
   end loop;
end Get_A_Side;

separate ( Determine_Triangle_Construction)
function  Area_of_Triangle (A,B,C : Integer) return Float is
   S : Float := Float(A+B+C)/2.0;
begin -- Area_of_Triangle
```

```
   return Square_Root  (S*(S-Float(A))*(S-Float(B))*(S-Float(C))  );
end Area_of_Triangle;
```

4.9

```
with Text_IO; use Text_IO;
procedure Determine_Quadrant is
-- 1 = Quadrant 1              6 = Negative X
-- 2 = Quadrant 2              7 = Positive Y
-- 3 = Quadrant 3              8 = Negative Y
-- 4 = Quadrant 4              9 = Origin
-- 5 = Positive X
   type Quadrant_Type is range 1..9;
   type Point_Type is array (1..2) of Integer;
   Point : Point_Type;
   package Int_IO is new Integer_IO (Integer);
   use Int_IO;
   procedure Display_Which_Quadrant (Quadrant : in Quadrant_Type) is
       separate;
   function  Quadrant_of (Point: in Point_Type) return Quadrant_Type is
       separate;
   function  Get_Point return Point_Type is separate;
begin --  Determine_Quadrant
   Display_Which_Quadrant ( Quadrant_of( Get_Point ) );
end Determine_Quadrant;

separate (Determine_Quadrant)
procedure Display_Which_Quadrant (Quadrant : in Quadrant_Type) is
begin -- Display_Which_Quadrant
   if Quadrant = 1 then
      Put_Line ("The point lies in Quadrant 1");
   elsif Quadrant = 2 then
      Put_Line ("The point lies in Quadrant 2");
   elsif Quadrant = 3 then
      Put_Line ("The point lies in Quadrant 3");
   elsif Quadrant = 4 then
      Put_Line ("The point lies in Quadrant 4");
   elsif Quadrant = 5 then
      Put_Line ("The point lies on the positive x axis");
   elsif Quadrant = 6 then
      Put_Line ("The point lies on the negative x axis");
   elsif Quadrant = 7 then
      Put_Line ("The point lies on the positive y axis");
   elsif Quadrant = 8 then
      Put_Line ("The point lies on the negative y axis");
```

```
   elsif Quadrant = 9 then
      Put_Line ("The point lies at the Origin");
   else
      Put_Line ("Don't know where the point is");
   end if;
end Display_Which_Quadrant;

separate (Determine_Quadrant)
function Quadrant_of (Point : in Point_Type) return Quadrant_Type is
begin -- Quadrant_of
   if Point(1) > 0 then
      -- First or Fourth Quadrant
      if Point(2) > 0 then
         return 1;
      elsif Point(2) < 0 then
         return 4;
      else
         return 5;
      end if;
   elsif Point(1) < 0 then
      -- Second or Third Quadrant
      if Point(2) > 0 then
         return 2;
      elsif Point(2) < 0 then
         return 3;
      else
         return 6;
      end if;
   else
      -- Y-axis or Origin
      if Point(2) > 0 then
         return 7;
      elsif Point(2) < 0 then
         return 8;
      else
         return 9;
      end if;
   end if;
end Quadrant_of;

separate (Determine_Quadrant)
function Get_Point return Point_Type is
   Point : Point_Type;
   Have_X_Coordinate : Boolean := False;
```

```
begin -- Get_Point
   loop
      begin
          if not Have_X_Coordinate then
             Put ("Enter x coordinate:  ");
             Get (Point(1));
             Have_X_Coordinate := True;
          end if;
          Put ("Enter y coordinate:  ");
          Get (Point(2));
          exit;
      exception
         when Data_Error =>
            Put_Line ("Invalid entry, enter only integer values.");
            Skip_Line;
      end;
   end loop;
   return Point;
end Get_Point;
```

4.11

```
with Text_IO; use Text_IO;
procedure Print_Square_Root_Table is
   Value : Float;
   package Table_Entry_IO is new Float_IO (Float);
   use Table_Entry_IO;
   function Square_Root ( Number : Float) return Float is separate;
   function Number (Units, Tenths : Integer) return Float is separate;
begin -- Print_Square_Root_Table
   for Units in 1 .. 9
   loop
      for Tenths in 0 .. 9
      loop
         Value := Number(Units, Tenths);
         Put ( Value );
         Put ( Square_Root(Value) );
         New_Line;
      end loop;
   end loop;
   --
   -- A last calculation for 10.0
   --
   Put (10.0);
   Put ( Square_Root(10.0) );
end Print_Square_Root_Table ;
```

```
separate (Print_Square_Root_Table)
function Square_Root ( Number : Float) return Float is
   Epsilon : constant Float := 0.000001;
   Root    : Float;
begin -- Square_Root
   if Number = 0.0 then
      return 0.0;
   else
      Root := 1.0;
      Root := (Number / Root + Root) / 2.0;
      while abs (Number / Root**2 -1.0) >= Epsilon
         loop
            Root := (Number / Root + Root) / 2.0;
         end loop;
      return Root;
   end if;
end Square_Root;

separate (Print_Square_Root_Table)
function Number (Units, Tenths : Integer) return Float is
begin -- Number
   return Float (Units) + Float(Tenths)/10.0;
end Number;
```

CHAPTER 5

5.1

a. Decimal point not allowed
b. Negative exponent not allowed
c. Adjacent underlines not allowed
d. Spaces not allowed
e. Spaces not allowed
f. Trailing underline not allowed
g. Commas not allowed

5.3

The three values for the constants are in error.

```
package Some_Conversion_Constants is
   Meter_to_Decimeter : constant Integer := 10;
   Meter_to_Centimeter: constant Integer := 100;
   Meter_to_Kilometer : constant Integer := 1000;
end Some_Conversion_Constants;
```

5.5

```
with Text_IO; use Text_IO;
procedure Output_Leap_Years is
```

```
   type Years_to_Test is range 1850 .. 2500;
   package Year_IO is new Integer_IO (Years_to_Test);
   use Year_IO;
begin -- Output_Leap_Years
   for Year in Years_to_Test
   loop
      if Year mod 400 = 0 or (Year mod 4 = 0 and Year mod 100 /= 0) then
         Put (Year);
         New_Line;
      end if;
   end loop;
end Output_Leap_Years;
```

Note: Any year divisible by 4 is a leap year, except certain century years. The only century years that are leap years are those century years divisible by 400.

For example, 1964 and 1988 are leap years. So are 1200, 1600, and 2400. The years 1100, 1300, and 2300 are not leap years.

CHAPTER 6

6.1

```
with Text_IO; use Text_IO;
procedure Expand_Command is
   type Input_Character_Type is (D, E, H, L, P, Q);
   Input   : Input_Character_Type;
   package Input_IO is new Enumeration_IO (Input_Character_Type);
   use Input_IO;
   procedure Get_an_Input (Character : out Input_Character_Type) is
             separate;
begin -- Expand_Command
   Get_an_Input (Input);
   if Input = D then
      Put_Line ("Debug");
   elsif Input = E then
      Put_Line ("Edit");
   elsif Input = H then
      Put_Line ("Help");
   elsif Input = L then
      Put_Line ("List");
   elsif Input = P then
      Put_Line ("Print");
   elsif Input = Q then
      Put_Line ("Quit");
   end if;
end Expand_Command;

separate (Expand_Command)
procedure Get_an_Input (Character : out Input_Character_Type) is
```

```
begin -- Get_an_Input
   loop
      begin
         Get (Character);
         exit;
      exception
         when Data_Error =>
              Put_Line ("Invalid entry.");
              Put_Line ("Enter one of D, E, H, L, P, Q");
      end;
   end loop;
end Get_an_Input;
```

6.3

```
with Text_IO; use Text_IO;
procedure Expand_Command is
   type Input_Type is (D, E, H, L, P, Q);
   type Expanded_Command_Type is (Debug, Edit, Help, List, Print, Quit);
   package Input_IO is new Enumeration_IO (Input_Type);
   package Expanded_Command_IO is new Enumeration_IO
      (Expanded_Command_Type);
   use Input_IO;
   use Expanded_Command_IO;
   Input             : Input_Type;
   Expanded_Command  : Expanded_Command_Type;
   Position          : Integer;
   procedure Get_an_Input (Character : out Input_Type) is separate;
begin -- Expand_Command
   Get_an_Input (Input);
   Position := Input_Type'Pos(Input);
   Expanded_Command := Expanded_Command_Type'Val(Position);
   Put (Expanded_Command);
end Expand_Command;

separate (Expand_Command)
procedure Get_an_Input (Character : out Input_Type) is
begin -- Get_an_Input
   loop
      begin
         Get (Character);
         exit;
      exception
         when Data_Error =>
         Put_Line("Invalid entry.");
         Put_Line ("Enter one of D, E, H, L, P, Q");
      end;
   end loop;
end Get_an_Input;
```

6.5

```
package Toll_Structure is
   type Vehicle_Type is ( Car, Car_and_Trailer, Motorcycle, Truck, Bus);
   type Weight_in_Tons_Type is range 0 .. 50;
end Toll_Structure;

with Toll_Structure; use Toll_Structure;
with Text_IO; use Text_IO;
procedure Calculate_Toll is
   Toll    : Float;
   Vehicle : Vehicle_Type;
   Weight  : Weight_in_Tons_Type;
   procedure Get_a_Vehicle (Vehicle : out Vehicle_Type) is separate;
   procedure Get_a_Weight  (Weight  : out Weight_in_Tons_Type)  is
      separate;
   procedure Display (Toll : Float) is separate;
begin -- Calculate_Toll
   loop
      Get_a_Vehicle (Vehicle);
      case Vehicle is
         when Car             => Toll := 0.25;
         when Car_and_Trailer => Toll := 0.50;
         when Truck           => Get_a_Weight  (Weight);
                                 if Weight < 5 then
                                    Toll := 1.00;
                                 else
                                    Toll := 1.50;
                                 end if;
         when Motorcycle      => Toll := 0.20;
         when Bus             => Toll := 2.00;
      end case;
      Display (Toll);
   end loop;
end Calculate_Toll;

separate (Calculate_Toll)
procedure Get_a_Vehicle (Vehicle : out Vehicle_Type) is
   package Vehicle_IO is new Enumeration_IO (Vehicle_Type);
   use Vehicle_IO;
begin -- Get_a_Vehicle
   loop
      begin
         Put_Line ("Enter vehicle type.");
         Get (Vehicle);
         exit;
      exception
         when Data_Error =>
```

```
            Put_Line ("Invalid entry.");
            Put_Line ("Enter Car, Car_and_Trailer, Motorcycle, Bus, or" &
                      "Truck");
         end;
      end loop;

separate (Calculate_Toll)
procedure Get_a_Weight (Weight : out Weight_in_Tons_Type) is
   package Weight_IO is new Integer_IO (Weight_in_Tons_Type);
   use Weight_IO;
begin -- Get_a_Weight
   loop
      begin
         Put_Line ("Enter weight.");
         Get (Weight);
         exit;
      exception
         when Data_Error =>
         Put_Line ("Invalid entry.");
         Put_Line ("Enter integer value between 0 and 50.");
      end;
   end loop;
end Get_a_Weight;

separate (Calculate_Toll)
procedure Display (Toll : Float) is
   package Vehicle_IO is new Enumeration_IO (Vehicle_Type);
   package Toll_IO is new Float_IO (Float);
   use Vehicle_IO;
   use Toll_IO;
begin -- Display
      Put ("The toll for a ");
      Put (Vehicle);
      Put (" is ");
      Put (Toll);
      New_Line;
end Display;
```

6.7

```
with Text_IO; use Text_IO;
procedure Determine_Quadrant is
   type Location_Type is ( Quadrant_1, Quadrant_2, Quadrant_3, Quadrant 4,
                           Positive_X, Negative_X, Positive_Y, Negative_Y,
                           Origin );
   type Point_Type is array (1..2) of Integer;
   Point : Point_Type;
```

```
   package Int_IO is new Integer_IO (Integer);
   use Int_IO;
   procedure Display_Which_Location (Location : in Location_Type) is
      separate;
   function  Location_of (Point: in Point_Type) return Location_Type is
      separate;
   function  Get_Point return Point_Type is separate;
begin -- Determine_Quadrant
   Display_Which_Location( Location_of( Get_Point ) );
end Determine_Quadrant;

separate (Determine_Quadrant)
function Get_Point return Point_Type is
   Point : Point_Type;
   Have_X_Coordinate : Boolean := False;
begin -- Get_Point
   loop
      begin
          if not Have_X_Coordinate then
             Put ("Enter x coordinate:  ");
             Get (Point(1));
             Have_X_Coordinate := True;
          end if;
          Put ("Enter y coordinate:  ");
          Get (Point(2));
          exit;
      exception
          when Data_Error =>
             Put_Line ("Invalid entry, enter only integer values.");
             Skip_Line;
      end;
   end loop;
   return Point;
end Get_Point;

separate (Determine_Quadrant)
function Location_of (Point : in Point_Type) return Location_Type is
begin -- Location_of
   if Point(1) > 0 then
      -- First or Fourth Quadrant
      if Point(2) > 0 then
         return Quadrant_1;
      elsif Point(2) < 0 then
         return Quadrant_4;
      else
         return Positive_X;
```

```
      end if;
   elsif Point(1) < 0 then
      -- Second or Third Quadrant
      if Point(2) > 0 then
         return Quadrant_2;
      elsif Point(2) < 0 then
         return Quadrant_3;
      else
         return Negative_X;
      end if;
   else
      -- Y-axis or Origin
      if Point(2) > 0 then
         return Positive_Y;
      elsif Point(2) < 0 then
         return Negative_Y;
      else
         return Origin;
      end if;
   end if;
end Location_of;

separate (Determine_Quadrant)
procedure Display_Which_Location (Location : in Location_Type) is
begin -- Display_Which_Location
   if Location = Quadrant_1 then
      Put_Line ("The point lies in Quadrant 1");
   elsif Location = Quadrant_2 then
      Put_Line ("The point lies in Quadrant 2");
   elsif Location = Quadrant_3 then
      Put_Line ("The point lies in Quadrant 3");
   elsif Location = Quadrant_4 then
      Put_Line ("The point lies in Quadrant 4");
   elsif Location = Positive_X then
      Put_Line ("The point lies on the positive x axis");
   elsif Location = Negative_X then
      Put_Line ("The point lies on the negative x axis");
   elsif Location = Positive_Y then
      Put_Line ("The point lies on the positive y axis");
   elsif Location = Negative_Y then
      Put_Line ("The point lies on the negative y axis");
   elsif Location = Origin then
      Put_Line ("The point lies at the Origin");
   else
      Put_Line ("Don't know where the point is");
   end if;
end Display_Which_Location;
```

CHAPTER 7

7.1

a. no commas allowed
b. no spaces allowed
c. adjacent underlines not allowed
d. trailing underline not allowed
e. decimal point missing
f. digit missing before decimal point
g. digit missing after decimal point
h. underline may appear only between digits
i. real exponent not allowed

7.3

```
with Trig_Package; use Trig_Package;
with Text_IO; use Text_IO;
with Conversion_Degrees_to_Radians;
procedure Ex_3 is
   Distance : Float;
   Angle_1 : Radians_Type := Conversion_Degrees_to_Radians (68.0);
   Angle_2 : Radians_Type := Conversion_Degrees_to_Radians (46.0);
   package Distance_IO is new Float_IO(Float);
   use Distance_IO;
begin -- Ex_3
   Distance := Float ( Sin (Angle_1) * 48.0 / Sin (Angle_2) );
   Put ("The distance between the two transmitting antennas is :");
   Put (Distance);
   New_Line;
end Ex_3;
```

7.5

```
with Simple_Graphics; use Simple_Graphics;
with Trig_Package; use Trig_Package;
with Math_Library; use Math_Library;
with Text_IO; use Text_IO;
with Invsin;
with Conversion_Degrees_to_Radians; -- as coded in Section 7.3
procedure Ex_5 is
     type Conversion_Type is (Polar_to_Cartesian, Cartesian_to_Polar);
     Choice : Conversion_Type;
     Point : Point_Type;
     R     : Float range 0.0 .. Float'Last;
     Theta : Degrees_Type;
     X,Y   : Float;
     package Cartesian_IO is new Integer_IO (Integer);
     package R_IO is new Float_IO (Float);
     package Theta_IO is new Float_IO (Degrees_Type);
     package Choice_IO is new Enumeration_IO (Conversion_Type);
     use Cartesian_IO, R_IO, Theta_IO, Choice_IO;
```

```
     procedure  Get_a_Point (Point: out Point_Type) is separate;
     procedure  Get_a_R     (R : out Float) is separate;
     procedure  Get_a_Theta (Theta : out Degrees_Type) is separate;
     procedure  Get_the_Choice (Choice : out Conversion_Type) is separate;
begin -- Ex_5
   loop
     Put_Line ("Enter conversion required: ");
     Get_the_Choice (Choice);
     case Choice is
         when Cartesian_to_Polar =>
            Get_a_Point (Point);
            R := Square_Root ( Float(Point(1)**2 + Point (2)**2) );
            Theta := Invsin (Answer_Type(Point(2))/Answer_Type(R) );
            Put_Line ("The polar coordinates are :");
            Put ( '(' );   Put(R); Put (','); Put (Theta); Put ( ')' );
         when Polar_to_Cartesian =>
            Get_a_R (R);
            Get_a_Theta (Theta);
            Y := R * Float(Sin (Conversion_Degrees_to_Radians(Theta)));
            X := R * Float(Cos (Conversion_Degrees_to_Radians(Theta)));
            Put_Line ("The Cartesian Coordinates are: ");
            Put ( '(' ); Put (X); Put (','); Put (Y); Put (')');
         end case;
         New_Line;
   end loop;
end Ex_5;

separate (Ex_5)
procedure Get_a_Point (Point : out Point_Type) is
begin -- Get_a_Point
   Put_Line ("Enter the x and y coordinates for the point: ");
   for I in 1..2
   loop
      begin
         Get (Point(I));
         exit;
      exception
         when Data_Error =>
              Put_Line("Invalid entry.");
              Put_Line ("Enter only integer values.");
      end;
   end loop;
end Get_a_Point;

separate (Ex_5)
procedure  Get_a_R    (R : out Float) is
```

```
begin -- Get_a_R
   Put_Line ("Enter R; ");
   loop
      begin
         Get (R);
         exit;
      exception
         when Data_Error =>
              Put_Line ("Invalid entry.");
              Put_Line ("Enter distance with a decimal point.");
      end;
   end loop;
end Get_a_R;

separate (Ex_5)
procedure Get_a_Theta (Theta : out Degrees_Type) is
begin  -- Get_a_Theta
   Put_Line ("Enter theta in degrees: ");
   loop
      begin
         Get (Theta);
         exit;
      exception
         when Data_Error =>
              Put_Line ("Invalid entry.");
              Put_Line ("Enter only degrees between 0.0 and 360.0.");
      end;
   end loop;
end Get_a_Theta;

separate (Ex_5)
procedure Get_the_Choice (Choice: out Conversion_Type) is
begin -- Get_the_Choice
   Put_Line ("Which way are you converting?");
   loop
      begin
         Get (Choice);
         exit;
      exception
         when Data_Error =>
            Put_Line ("Invalid entry.");
            Put_Line ("Enter only Polar_to_Cartesian or" &
                      "Cartesian_to_Polar.");
      end;
   end loop;
end Get_the_Choice;
```

```
with Trig_Package; use Trig_Package;
with Conversion_Radians_to_Degrees; -- as coded in Section 7.3
function Invsin (Value : in Answer_Type) return Degrees_Type is
   Sum : Float := Float(Value);
   function Next_Term (K : Natural) return Float is
      Coefficient  : Answer_Type;
      Numerator    : Integer := 1;
      Denominator : Float   := 2.0;
   begin -- Next_Term
      for I in 1..K-1
      loop
         Numerator := Numerator * (Numerator+2);
         Denominator := Denominator * (Denominator + 2.0);
      end loop;
      Coefficient := Answer_Type(Numerator)/Answer_Type(Denominator);
      return Float(Coefficient *
         Answer_Type(Value**(2*K+1))/Answer_Type(2*K));
   end Next_Term;
begin -- Invsin
   for K in 1 .. 4
   loop
      Sum := Sum + Next_Term(K);
   end loop;
   return Conversion_Radians_to_Degrees (Radians_Type(Sum) );
end Invsin;
```

CHAPTER 8

8.1

```
with Horse_Show_Types; use Horse_Show_Types;
with Text_IO; use Text_IO;
procedure Input_a_Winner( Winner_Array : in out Winner_Array_Type ) is
   Class : Class_Type;
begin -- Input_a_Winner
loop
   begin
      Put ( "Enter Class --> " );
      Class_IO.Get( Class );
      New_Line;
      exit;
   exception
      when others =>
         New_Line;
         Put_Line ( "illegal input...please try again" );
   end;
end loop;
for i in Place_Type
```

```
loop
   loop
      begin
         Put ( "Enter entry number of " );
         Place_IO.Put ( i );
         Put( " place --> " );
         Entry_IO.Get ( Winner_Array( Class,i ));
         New_Line;
         exit;
      exception
         when others =>
            New_Line;
            Put_Line ( "illegal input...please try again" );
      end;
   end loop;
end loop;
end Input_a_Winner;
```

8.3

```
with Horse_Show_Types; use Horse_Show_Types;
with Text_IO; use Text_IO;
procedure Determine_Champion ( Winner_Array : in Winner_Array_Type) is
   Champions          : Champion_Array_Type;
   Accumulated_Scores : Accumulated_Scores_Type := ( others => 0 );
   procedure Find_Champions(Score     : in out Accumulated_Scores_Type;
                            Champions : in out Champion_Array_Type) is
                            separate;
begin -- Determine_Champions
   for j in Equitation_Division_Subtype
   loop
      for k in Place_Type
      loop
         Accumulated_Scores(Winner_Array(j,k)) :=
            Accumulated_Scores(Winner_Array(j,k)) +
            Ribbon_Places_Array(k);
      end loop;
   end loop;
   Find_Champions ( Accumulated_Scores,Champions );
   Put ( "Grand Champion of Equitation Division is " );
   Entry_IO.Put ( Champions(Champion) );
   New_Line;
   Put ( "Reserve Champion of Equitation Division is " );
   Entry_IO.Put ( Champions(Reserve) );
   New_Line( 2 );
```

```
   for j in Hunter_Division_Subtype
   loop
      for k in Place_Type
      loop
         Accumulated_Scores(Winner_Array(j,k)) :=
            Accumulated_Scores(Winner_Array(j,k)) +
            Ribbon_Places_Array(k);
      end loop;
   end loop;
   Find_Champions ( Accumulated_Scores,Champions );
   Put ( "Grand Champion of Hunter Division is " );
   Entry_IO.Put ( Champions(Champion) );
   New_Line;
   Put ( "Reserved Champion of Hunter Division is " );
   Entry_IO.Put ( Champions(Reserve) );
   New_Line ( 2 );
end Determine_Champion;

separate( Determine_Champion )
procedure Find_Champions( Score     : in out Accumulated_Scores_Type;
                          Champions : in out Champion_Array_Type ) is
begin  -- Find_Champions
   Champions(Champion) := Entry_Type'First;
   for i in Entry_Type'First + 1..Entry_Type'Last
   loop
      if Score(Champions(Champion)) < Score(i) then
         Champions(Champion) := i;
      end if;
   end loop;
   if Champions(Champion) = Entry_Type'First then
      Champions(Reserve) := Entry_Type'First;
      for i in Entry_Type'First + 2..Entry_Type'Last
      loop
         if Score(Champions(Reserve)) < Score(i) then
            Champions(Reserve) := i;
         end if;
      end loop;
   else
      Champions(Reserve) := Entry_Type'First;
      for i in Entry_Type'First + 1..Entry_Type'Last
      loop
         if i /= Champions(Champion) and then
            Score(Champions(Reserve)) < Score(i) then
            Champions(Reserve) := i;
         end if;
      end loop;
   end if;
end Find_Champions;
```

8.5

```
with Horse_Show_Types; use Horse_Show_Types;
with Text_IO; use Text_IO;
procedure Determine_Overall_Champion ( NJ_Shows : in All_Shows_Type ) is
   Champions : Champion_Array_Type;
   Accumulated_Scores : Accumulated_Scores_Type;
procedure Find_Champions ( Score     : in out Accumulated_Scores_Type;
                           Champions : in out Champion_Array_Type )
                           is separate;
begin -- Determine_Overall_Champion
   for i in Show_Type
   loop
      for j in Class_Type
      loop
         for k in Place_Type
         loop
            Accumulated_Scores(NJ_Shows(i)(j,k)) :=
               Accumulated_Scores(NJ_Shows(i)(j,k)) +
               Ribbon_Places_Array(k);
         end loop;
      end loop;
   end loop;
   Find_Champions ( Accumulated_Scores,Champions );
   Put ( "Grand Champion of New Jersey is " );
   Entry_IO.Put ( Champions(Champion) );
   New_Line;
   Put ( "Reserved Champion of New Jersey is " );
   Entry_IO.Put ( Champions(Reserve) );
   New_Line;
end Determine_Overall_Champion;
```

8.7

```
with Horse_Show_Types; use Horse_Show_Types;
with Text_IO; use Text_IO;
procedure Determine_Age_Group_Champion ( NJ_Shows  : in All_Shows_Type;
                                         Age_Array : in Age_Array_Type ) is
   Champions : Champion_Array_Type;
   Accumulated_Scores : Accumulated_Scores_Type;
   procedure Find_Champions_of_Age_Group
             ( Score     : in out Accumulated_Scores_Type;
               Champions : in out Champion_Array_Type;
               Age_Array : in     Age_Array_Type;
               Age_Group : in     Age_13_Type ) is separate;
```

```
begin -- Determine_Age_Group_Champion
   for i in Show_Type
   loop
      for j in Class_Type
      loop
         for k in Place_Type
         loop
            Accumulated_Scores(NJ_Shows(i)(j,k)) :=
               Accumulated_Scores(NJ_Shows(i)(j,k)) +
               Ribbon_Places_Array(k);
         end loop;
      end loop;
   end loop;
   for i in 1..2
   loop
      Find_Champions_of_Age_Group
            (Accumulated_Scores,Champions,Age_Array,Age_13_Type'Val(i));
      Put ( "Grand Champion of New Jersey in " );
      Age_13_IO.Put ( Age_13_Type'Val( i ) );
      Put ( " 13 is " );
      Entry_IO.Put ( Champions(Champion) );
      New_Line;
      Put ( "Reserved Champion of New Jersey in " );
      Age_13_IO.Put ( Age_13_Type'Val( i ) );
      Put ( " 13 is " );
      Entry_IO.Put ( Champions(Reserve) );
      New_Line;
   end loop;
end Determine_Age_Group_Champion;

separate( Determine_Age_Group_Champion)
procedure Find_Champions_of_Age_Group
          ( Score     : in out Accumulated_Scores_Type;
            Champions : in out Champion_Array_Type;
            Age_Array : in     Age_Array_Type;
            Age_Group : in     Age_13 Type ) is
   Start : Entry_Type;
begin -- Find_Champions_of_Age_Group
   for i in Entry_Type
   loop
      if Age_Array(i) = Age_Group then
         Start := i;
         exit;
      end if;
   end loop;
```

```
   Champions(Champion) := Start;
   for i in Start + 1..Entry_Type'Last
   loop
      if Age_Array(i) = Age_Group and then
         Score(Champions(Champion)) < Score(i) then
         Champions(Champion) := i;
      end if;
   end loop;
   if Champions(Champion) = Start then
      for i in Start + 1..Entry_Type'Last
      loop
         if Age_Array(i) = Age_Group then
            Start := i;
            exit;
         end if;
      end loop;
      Champions(Reserve) := Start + 1;
      for i in Start + 2..Entry_Type'Last
      loop
         if Age_Array(i) = Age_Group and then
            Score(Champions(Reserve)) < Score(i) then
            Champions(Reserve) := i;
         end if;
      end loop;
   else
   Champions(Reserve) := Start;
      for i in Start + 1..Entry_Type'Last
      loop
         if Age_Array(i) = Age_Group and then
            i /= Champions(Champion) and then
            Score(Champions(Reserve)) < Score(i) then
            Champions(Reserve) := i;
         end if;
      end loop;
   end if;
end Find_Champions_of_Age_Group;
```

CHAPTER 9

9.1

```
with Text_IO; use Text_IO;
with A_Small_Factorial_Package; use A_Small_Factorial_Package;
procedure Factorial is
   Input_File, Output_File : File_Type;
   Input_Number : Argument_Type;
   package Argument_IO is new Integer_IO (Argument_Type);
   use Argument_IO;
```

```
   package Result_IO is new Integer_IO (Result_Type);
   use Result_IO;
begin -- Factorial
   Open   ( Input_File, In_File, "Factorial.in" );
   Create ( Output_File, Out_File, "Factorial.out" );
   while not End_of_File ( Input_File )
   loop
      begin
      Get ( Input_File, Input_Number );
      for I in 1..Input_Number
      loop
         Put ( Output_File, "The factorial of " );
         Put ( Output_File, I );
         Put ( Output_File, " is " );
         Put ( Output_File, Factorial_of ( I ) );
         New_Line ( Output_File, 2 );
      end loop;
      exception
         when Data_Error =>
            New_Line ( Output_File );
            Put_Line ( Output_File, "Data_Error exception raised" );
            New_Line ( Output_File );
         when Numeric_Error =>
            Put ( Output_File, "XXXXXXX" );
            Put_Line ( Output_File, "     Numeric_Error: Overflow" );
            New_Line ( Output_File );
      end;
   end loop;
   Close ( Input_File );
   Close ( Output_File );
end Factorial;
```

9.3

```
with Complex_Numbers; use Complex_Numbers;
with Text_IO; use Text_IO;
procedure Complex_Math is
   Num_Char        : Natural;
   Input_File      : File_Type;
   Output_File     : File_Type;
   Input_Filename  : String(1..20);
   Output_Filename : String(1..20);
   Answer          : Complex_Type;
   Complex_1       : Complex_Type;
   Complex_2       : Complex_Type;
   function  Read_Complex  ( File    : In File_Type ) return Complex_Type
                                                        is separate;
   procedure Write_Complex ( File    : in File_Type;
                             Complex : in Complex_Type ) is separate;
```

```
begin   -- Complex_Math
   Put ( "Enter Input Filename --> " );
   loop
      begin
         Get_Line ( Input_Filename, Num_Char );
         Open ( Input_File, In_File, Input_Filename(1..Num_Char) );
         exit;
      exception
         when others =>
            Put ( "File Not Opened..Please Re_Enter Name --> " );
      end;
   end loop;
   Put ( "Enter Output Filename --> " );
   loop
      begin
         Get_Line ( Output_Filename, Num_Char );
         Create ( Output_File, Out_File, Output_Filename(1..Num_Char) );
         exit;
      exception
         when others =>
            Put ( "File Not Opened..Please Re_Enter Name --> " );
      end;
   end loop;
   Complex_1 := Read_Complex ( Input_File );
   Complex_2 := Read_Complex ( Input_File );
   Answer := Add ( Complex_1, Complex_2 );
   Write_Complex ( Output_File, Answer );
   Answer := Subtract ( Complex_1, Complex_2 );
   Write_Complex ( Output_File, Answer );
   Answer := Multiply ( Complex_1, Complex_2 );
   Write_Complex ( Output_File, Answer );
   Answer := Divide ( Complex_1, Complex_2 );
   Write_Complex ( Output_File, Answer );
   exception
      when Numeric_Error =>
         Put_Line( "Problem with Numbers...Numeric_Error...Stop" );
      when Data_Error =>
         Put_Line( "Problem with File...Data_Error...Stop" );
end Complex_Math;

separate ( Complex_Math )
function Read_Complex( File : in File_Type ) return Complex_Type is
   package Real_IO is new Float_IO( Real );
   use Real_IO;
   Complex  : Complex_Type;
```

```
   Line     : String(1..80);
   Num_Char : Natural;
begin  -- Read_Complex
   Get_Line( File, Line, Num_Char );
   Get( Line, Complex(Re), Num_Char );
   Get( Line(Num_Char + 1..80), Complex(Im), Num_Char );
   return Complex;
end Read_Complex;

separate ( Complex_Math )
procedure Write_Complex ( File    : in File_Type;
                          Complex : in Complex_Type ) is
   package Real_IO is new Float_IO( Real );
   use Real_IO;
begin  -- Write_Complex
   Put ( File, Complex(Re), 3, 3, 0 );
   if Complex(Im) > 0.0 then
      Put (File, "+" );
   end if;
   Put ( File, Complex(Im), 3, 3, 0 );
   Put_Line ( File, "i" );
end Write_Complex;
```

9.5

```
with Matrix_Operations; use Matrix_Operations;
with Text_IO; use Text_IO;
procedure Matrix_Math is
   Matrix_A,Matrix_B,Matrix_C : Matrix_Type;
   Infile,Outfile             : File_Type;
   package Int_IO is new Integer_IO( Integer );
   use Int_IO;
   procedure Read_Matrix ( File   : in out File_Type ;
                           Matrix :    out Matrix_Type ) is separate;
   procedure Write_Matrix ( File   : in out File_Type ;
                            Matrix : in     Matrix_Type ) is separate;
begin  -- Matrix_Math
   Open ( Infile, In_File, "Matrix.Dat" );
   Create ( Outfile, Out_File, "Matrix.out" );
   Read_Matrix ( Infile, Matrix_A );
   Read_Matrix ( Infile, Matrix_B );
   Matrix_C := Add ( Matrix_A, Matrix_B );
   Write_Matrix ( Outfile, Matrix_C );
   New_Line ( Outfile );
   Matrix_C := Subtract ( Matrix_A, Matrix_B );
   Write_Matrix ( Outfile, Matrix_C );
```

```
   New_Line ( Outfile );
   Matrix_C := Multiply ( Matrix_A, Matrix_B );
   Write_Matrix ( Outfile, Matrix_C );
   New_Line ( Outfile );
   Close ( Infile ) ;
   Close ( Outfile );
end Matrix_Math;

separate ( Matrix_Math )
procedure Read_Matrix ( File   : in out File_Type;
                        Matrix :    out Matrix_Type ) is
begin -- Read_Matrix
   for i in 1..3
   loop
      for j in 1..3
      loop
         Get ( File, Matrix(i,j) );
      end loop;
   end loop;
end Read_Matrix;

separate ( Matrix_Math )
procedure Write_Matrix ( File   : in out File_Type;
                         Matrix : in     Matrix_Type ) is
begin -- Write_Matrix
   for i in 1..3
   loop
      for j in 1..3
      loop
         Put ( File, Matrix(i,j) );
         Put ( File, ' ' );
      end loop;
      New_Line ( File );
   end loop;
end Write_Matrix;
```

9.7

```
separate ( Solve_System.Cramers_Rule )
function Determinant ( Matrix : Matrix_Type ) return Integer is
   A,B,C,D,E,F : Integer;
begin  -- Determinant
   A := Matrix(1,1) * Matrix(2,2) * Matrix(3,3);
   B := Matrix(1,2) * Matrix(2,3) * Matrix(3,1);
   C := Matrix(1,3) * Matrix(2,1) * Matrix(3,2);
   D := Matrix(1,3) * Matrix(2,2) * Matrix(3,1);
```

```
   E := Matrix(1,1) * Matrix(2,3) * Matrix(3,2);
   F := Matrix(1,2) * Matrix(2,1) * Matrix(3,3);
   return ( A + B + C ) - ( D + E + F );
end Determinant;
```

9.9

```
with Text_IO; use Text_IO;
procedure Is_Freezing is
   Input_File              : File_Type;
   Temperature             : array(1..10) of Integer;
   Freezing_Found          : Boolean := False;
   package Int_IO is new Integer_IO( Integer );
   use Int_IO
begin -- Is_Freezing
   Open ( Input_File, In_File, "Is_Freezing.In" );
   for I in 1 .. 10
   loop
      Get ( Input_File, Temperature(I) );
   end loop;
   for I in 1 .. 10
   loop
      if Temperature(I) = 32 then
         Freezing_Found := True;
         Put ( "Freezing temperature ( 32 deg ) was found at location " );
         Put ( I, Width => 2 );
         New_Line;
      end if;
   end loop;
   if not Freezing_Found then
      New_Line;
      Put ( "A Freezing temperature was not found in the input file" );
      New_Line;
   end if;
   Close ( Input_File );
end Is_Freezing;
```

9.11a

```
with Matrix_Operations; use Matrix_Operations;
function Add ( One,Two : Matrix_Type ) return Matrix_Type is
   Three : Matrix_Type;
begin  -- Add
   for i in 1..3
   loop
      for j in 1..3
      loop
```

```
         Three(i,j) := One (i,j) + Two(i,j);
      end loop;
   end loop;
   return Three;
end Add;

-- A driver to test Add
with Matrix_Operations; use Matrix_Operations;
with Text_IO; use Text_IO;
with Add;
procedure Add_Driver is
   package Int_IO is new Integer_IO( Integer );
   use Int_IO;
   Matrix_A : Matrix_Type := ( ( 1,2,3 ),
                               ( 4,5,6 ),
                               ( 7,8,9 ) );
   Matrix_B : Matrix_Type := ( ( 8,1,5 ),
                               ( 9,3,4 ),
                               ( 2,6,7 ) );
   Matrix_C : Matrix_Type;
begin -- Add_Driver
   Matrix_C := Add( Matrix_A,Matrix_B );
   for i in 1..3
   loop
      for j in 1..3
      loop
         Put ( Matrix_C(i,j) );
         Put ( ' ' );
      end loop;
      New_Line;
   end loop;
end Add_Driver;
```

9.11b

```
with Matrix_Operations; use Matrix_Operations;
function Subtract ( One,Two : Matrix_Type ) return Matrix_Type is
   Three : Matrix_Type;
begin  -- Subtract
   for i in 1..3
   loop
      for j in 1..3
      loop
         Three(i,j) := One(i,j) - Two(i,j);
   end loop;
```

```
   end loop;
   return Three;
end Subtract;

-- A driver to test Subtract
with Matrix_Operations; use Matrix_Operations;
with Text_IO; use Text_IO;
with Subtract;
procedure Subtract_Driver is
   package Int_IO is new Integer_IO( Integer );
   use Int_IO;
   Matrix_A : Matrix_Type := ( ( 1, 2, 3 ),
                               ( 4,5,6 ),
                               ( 7,8,9 ) );
   Matrix_B : Matrix_Type := ( ( 8,1,5 ),
                               ( 9,3,4 ),
                               ( 2,6,7 ) );
   Matrix_C : Matrix_Type;
begin -- Subtract_Driver
   Matrix_C := Subtract( Matrix_A,Matrix_B );
   for i in 1..3
   loop
      for j in 1..3
      loop
         Put ( Matrix_C(i,j) );
         Put ( ' ' );
      end loop;
      New_Line;
   end loop;
end Subtract_Driver;
```

9.11c

```
with Matrix_Operations; use Matrix_Operations;
function Multiply ( One,Two : Matrix_Type ) return Matrix_Type is
   Three : Matrix_Type := ( others => ( others => 0 ) );
begin  -- Multiply
   for i in 1..3
   loop
      for j in 1..3
      loop
         for k in 1..3
         loop
            Three(i,j) := Three (i,j) + One(i,k) * Two(k,j);
         end loop;
      end loop;
```

```
   end loop;
   return Three;
end Multiply;

-- A driver to test Multiply
with Matrix_Operations; use Matrix_Operations;
with Text_IO; use Text_IO;
with Multiply;
procedure Multiply_Driver is
   package Int_IO is new Integer_IO( Integer );
   use Int_IO;
   Matrix_A : Matrix_Type := ( ( 1,2,3 ),
                               ( 3,2,1 ),
                               ( 2,3,1 ) );
   Matrix_B : Matrix_Type := ( ( 4,3,1 ),
                               ( 1,3,4 ),
                               ( 2,3,1 ) );
Matrix_C : Matrix_Type;
begin -- Multiply_Driver
   Matrix_C := Multiply ( Matrix_A, Matrix_B );
   for i in 1..3
   loop
      for j in 1..3
      loop
         Put ( Matrix_C(i,j) );
         Put ( ' ' );
      end loop;
      New_Line;
   end loop;
end Multiply_Driver;
```

CHAPTER 10

10.1

```
with Text_IO; use Text_IO;
with Float_Math_Lib; use Float_Math_Lib;
procedure Is_Unit_Vector is
   type Vector_Type is array (Positive Range <>) of Integer;
   Input_File              : File_Type;
   Vector                  : Vector_Type(1..10);
   Sum_Squared_Components  : Integer := 0;
   Magnitude               : Float;
   package Int_IO is new Integer_IO( Integer );
   use Int_IO;
   package Flt_IO is new Float_IO( Float );
   use Flt_IO;
```

```
begin -- Is_Unit_Vector
   Open ( Input_File, In_File, "Is_Unit_Vector.In" );
   for I in Vector'Range
   loop
      Get ( Input_File, Vector(I) );
   end loop;
   for I in Vector'Range
   loop
      Sum_Squared_Components := Sum_Squared_Components + Vector(I) ** 2;
   end loop;
   Magnitude := Sqrt ( Float ( Sum_Squared_Components ) );
   New_Line;
   Put ( "The magnitude of the vector is: " );
   Put ( Magnitude );
   New_Line;
   if Magnitude = 1.0 then
      Put ( "The vector is a unit vector" );
   else
      Put ( "The vector is not a unit vector" );
   end if;
   Close (Input_File);
end Is_Unit_Vector;
```

10.3

```
with Text_IO; use Text_IO;
procedure Palindrome is
   Word : String (1..25); -- index constraint supplied
   Data_File, Results_File : File_Type;
   Answer : Boolean;
   function See_if_Same_Forward_Backward ( Word : String ) return Boolean
            is separate;
   procedure Rotate_Blanks_to_End ( Word : in out String ) is separate;
   package Bool_IO is new Enumeration_IO( Boolean );
   use Bool_IO;
begin -- Palindrome
   Open (Data_File, In_File, "in.dat");
   Create (Results_File, Out_File, "out.dat");
   while not End_of_File (Data_File)
   loop
      Get (Data_File, Word);
      Rotate_Blanks_to_End (Word);
      Answer := See_if_Same_Forward_Backward ( Word );
      Put (Results_File, Answer);
      New_Line (Results_File );
   end loop;
```

```
   Close (Data_File);
   Close (Results_File);
end Palindrome;

separate ( Palindrome )
function See_if_Same_Forward_Backward ( Word : String ) return Boolean is
   Count : Natural;
   function Reverse_String (In_String: String) return String is separate;
   procedure Obtain ( Count : out Natural ) is separate;
begin  -- See_if_Same_Forward_Backward
   Obtain ( Count );
   declare
      Reverse_Word : String(1..Count);
   begin
      Reverse_Word := Reverse_String( Word(1..Count) );
      if Reverse_Word = Word(1..Count) then
         return True;
      else
         return False;
      end if;
   end;
end See_if_Same_Forward_Backward;

separate (Palindrome.See_if_Same_Forward_Backward)
procedure Obtain (Count : out Natural) is
   -- Temp_Count required because an out parameter
   -- cannot be read. To write Count := Count + 1;
   -- is illegal, therefore work with Temp_Count.
   Temp_Count : Natural := 0;
   I : Natural :=1;
begin -- Count
   while Word(I) /= ' '
   loop
      Temp_Count := Temp_Count + 1;
      I := I + 1;
   end loop;
   Count := Temp_Count;
end Obtain;

separate ( Palindrome.See_if_Same_Forward_Backward )
function Reverse_String ( In_String : in String ) return String is
   Out_String : String (In_String'Range);
begin  -- Reverse_String
   for i in In_String'Range
```

```
   loop
      Out_String(In_String'Last - ( i - 1 ) ) := In_String(i);
   end loop;
   return Out_String;
end Reverse_String;

separate (Palindrome)
procedure Rotate_Blanks_to_End (Word : in out String) is
   -- This procedure assumes at least one nonblank character.
begin -- Rotate_Blanks_to_End
   while Word(Word'First) = ' ' -- if a blank
   loop
      -- Add blank to end of word.
      Word(Word'Range) :=
         Word(Word'First+1..Word'Last) & ' ';
   end loop;
end Rotate_Blanks_to_End;
```

10.5

```
with Text_IO; use Text_IO;
procedure Pig_Latin is
   subtype My_Natural_Subtype is Natural range 1..28;
   Word : String (1..25); -- index constraint supplied
   Data_File, Results_File : File_Type;
   Count : My_Natural_Subtype;
   procedure Obtain ( Count : out My_Natural_Subtype ) is separate;
   procedure Rotate_Blanks_to_End (Word : in out String) is separate;
   procedure Convert_to_Pig_Latin (Word  : in out String;
                                   Count : in     My_Natural_Subtype )
                                   is separate;
begin -- Pig_Latin
   Open (Data_File, In_File, "English.dat");
   Create (Results_File, Out_File, "pig.dat");
   while not End_of_File(Data_File)
   loop
      Get (Data_File, Word);
      Rotate_Blanks_To_End (Word);
      Obtain (Count);
      if Count > 22 then
         declare
            Big_Word : String(1..27) := Word & "  ";
            begin
               Convert_to_Pig_Latin (Big_Word, Count);
               Put_Line (Results_File, Big_Word);
            end;
```

```
      else
         Convert_to_Pig_Latin (Word, Count);
         Put_Line (Results_File, Word);
      end if;
   end loop;
   Close (Data_File);
   Close (Results_File);
end Pig_Latin;

separate (Pig_Latin)
procedure Obtain (Count : out My_Natural_Subtype) is
   -- Temp_Count required because an out parameter
   -- cannot be read.  To write Count := Count + 1;
   -- is illegal, therefore work with Temp_Count.
   Temp_Count : Natural := 0;
   I : Natural :=1;
begin -- Count
   while I <= 25 and then Word(I) /= ' '
   loop
      Temp_Count := Temp_Count + 1;
      I := I + 1;
   end loop;
   Count := Temp_Count;
end Obtain;

separate (Pig_Latin)
procedure Convert_to_Pig_Latin (Word  : in out String;
                                Count : in     My_Natural_Subtype) is
   -- This procedure assumes the first character of the
   -- incoming string is a non-blank character.
begin -- Convert_to_Pig_Latin
   case Word (Word'First) is
      -- a vowel
      when 'a'|'A'|'e'|'E'|'i'|'I'|'o'|'O'|'u'|'U' =>
              if Count >= 25 then
                 Word (Word'Range) := Word (1..Count) & "ay" ;
              else
                 Word (Word'Range) := Word (1..Count) & "ay" &
                                      Word (Count+3..Word'Last);
              end if;
      -- a consonant
      when 'b'..'d'|'B'..'D'|'f'..'h'| 'F'..'H'|
           'j'..'n'|'J'..'N'|'p'..'t'|'P'..'T'|
           'v'..'z'|'V'..'Z' =>
```

```
            if Count >= 25 then
               Word (Word'Range) := Word (2..Count) & Word(Word'First) &
                                     "ay";
            else
               Word (Word'Range) := Word (2..Count) & Word(Word'First) &
                                     "ay" & Word(Count+3..Word'Last);
            end if;
      -- a special character
      when others => Put_Line (Results_File, "A special character is" &
                               "contained within the input file.");
   end case;
end Convert_to_Pig_Latin;
```

CHAPTER 11

11.1

```
type Address_Type is
record
   Street   : Street_Type;
   City     : City_Type;
   State    : State_Type;
   Zip_Code : Zip_Code_Type;
end record;
type Drivers_License_Type is
record
   License_Number  : License_Number_Type;
   Issue_Date      : Date_Type;
   Expiration_Date : Date_Type;
   Name            : Name_Type;
   Address         : Address_Type;
   Birth_Date      : Date_Type;
   Car             : Car_Type;
   Restrictions    : Restrictions_Type;
   Sex             : Sex_Type;
   Points          : Natural range 0..12;
end record;
```

11.2

```
type Registration_Fee_Type is digits 4 range 0.0..99.99;
type Vehicle_Type is ( Buick,Oldsmobile,Chevrolet,Mercedes,Porsche,
                       Ford,Ferrari,Volkswagen,Truck_1_Ton,
                       Truck_2_Ton,Motorcycle );
Registration_Fee_Array : constant array( Vehicle_Type ) of
                          Registration_Fee_Type := ( Buick..Volkswagen |
                          Motorcycle => 8.00, Truck_1_Ton => 10.00,
                          Truck_2_Ton => 15.00 );
```

```
type Drivers_License_Type is
record
   License_Number   : License_Number_Type;
   Issue_Date       : Date_Type;
   Expiration_Date  : Date_Type;
   Name             : Name_Type;
   Address          : Address_Type;
   Birth_Date       : Date_Type;
   Vehicle          : Vehicle_Type;
   Restrictions     : Restrictions_Type;
   Sex              : Sex_Type;
   Points           : Natural range 0..12;
   Registration_Fee: Registration_Fee_Type;
end record;
```

11.3a

```
type Setting_Type is ( On,Off );
type Station_Type is digits 6 range 50.0..1600.00;
type Frequency_Type is ( AM,FM );
type Speaker_Type is ( Front,Back,Both );
type Radio_Type is
record
   Switch         : Setting_Type;
   Station        : Station_Type;
   Frequency      : Frequency_Type;
   Speakers       : Speaker_Type;
end record;
```

11.3b

```
type Hour_Type is range 1..12;
type Minute_Type is range 1..60;
type Second_Type is range 1..60;
type Am_Pm_Type is ( Am,Pm );
type Time_Type is
record
   Hours   : Hour_Type := 0;
   Minutes : Minute_Type := 0;
   Seconds : Second_Type := 0;
   Am_Pm   : Am_Pm_Type := Am;
end record;
type Year_Type is range 1980..2050;
type Month_Type is range 1..12;
type Day_Type is range 1..31;
type Date_Type is
```

```
record
   Year  : Year_Type;
   Month : Month_Type;
   Day   : Day_Type;
end record;
type Clock_Type is
record
   Time : Time_Type;
   Date : Date_Type;
end record;
```

11.3c

```
type Temp_Type is ( Hot,Cold );
type Control_Type is ( Off,Low,High );
type Vent_Type is ( Open,Closed );
type Climate_Control_Type is
record
   Temp         : Temp_Type;
   Defroster    : Setting_Type;
   AC           : Control_Type;
   Vent         : Vent_Type;
   Heat_Control : Control_Type;
end record;
```

11.3d

```
type Headlight_Control_Type is
record
   Lights  : Setting_Type;
   Brights : Setting_Type;
end record;
```

11.3e

```
type Wiper_Type is ( Off,Delayed,Slow,Fast );
type Windshield_Wiper_Control_Type is
record
   Wipers : Wiper_Type;
   Washer : Setting_Type;
end record;
```

11.4

```
type Dashboard_Type is
record
   Radio           : Radio_Type;
   Clock           : Clock_Type;
   Climate_Control : Climate_Control_Type;
```

```
   Headlight_Control : Headlight_Control_Type;
   Windshield_Wiper_Control : Windshield_Wiper_Control_Type;
end record;
```

11.5

```
with Complex_Numbers; use Complex_Numbers;
with Text_IO; use Text_IO;
procedure Complex_Math is
   Num_Char         : Natural;
   Input_File       : File_Type;
   Output_File      : File_Type;
   Input_Filename   : String(1..20);
   Output_Filename  : String(1..20);
   Answer           : Complex_Type;
   Complex_1        : Complex_Type;
   Complex_2        : Complex_Type;
   function  Read_Complex ( File    : in File_Type ) return Complex_Type
                                                           is separate;
   procedure Write_Complex( File    : in File_Type;
                            Complex : in Complex_Type ) is separate;
begin   -- Complex_Math
   Put ( "Enter Input Filename --> " );
   loop
      begin
         Get_Line ( Input_Filename, Num_Char );
         Open ( Input_File, In_File, Input_Filename(1..Num_Char) );
         exit;
      exception
         when others =>
            Put ( "File Not Opened..Please Re_Enter Name --> " );
      end;
   end loop;
   Put( "Enter Output Filename --> " );
   loop
      begin
         Get_Line ( Output_Filename, Num_Char );
         Create ( Output_File, Out_File, Output_Filename(1..Num_Char) );
         exit;
      exception
         when others =>
            Put ( "File Not Opened..Please Re_Enter Name --> " );
      end;
   end loop;
   Complex_1 := Read_Complex ( Input_File );
   Complex_2 := Read_Complex ( Input_File );
```

```
   Answer := Add ( Complex_1, Complex_2 );
   Write_Complex ( Output_File, Answer );
   Answer := Subtract ( Complex_1, Complex_2 );
   Write_Complex ( Output_File, Answer );
   Answer := Multiply ( Complex_1, Complex_2 );
   Write_Complex ( Output_File, Answer );
   Answer := Divide ( Complex_1, Complex_2 );
   Write_Complex ( Output_File, Answer );
   Close (Input_File); Close (Output_File);
exception
   when Numeric_Error =>
      Put_Line( "Problem with Numbers...Numeric_Error...Stop" );
      Close (Input_File); Close (Output_File);
   when Data_Error =>
      Put_Line( "Problem with File...Data_Error...Stop" );
      Close (Input_File); Close (Output_File);
end Complex_Math;

separate ( Complex_Math )
function Read_Complex ( File : in File_Type ) return Complex_Type is
   package Real_IO is new Float_IO( Real );
   use Real_IO;
   Complex  : Complex_Type;
   Line     : String(1..80);
   Num_Char : Natural;
begin  -- Read_Complex
   Get_Line ( File,Line, Num_Char );
   Get ( Line, Complex.Re, Num_Char );
   Get ( Line(Num_Char + 1..80), Complex.Im,Num_Char );
   return Complex;
end Read_Complex;
```

11.6

```
function Get_Conjugate (A : in Complex_Type ) return Complex_Type is
   Answer : Complex_Type;
begin  -- Get_Conjugate
   Answer.Re := A.Re;
   Answer.Im := -A.Im;
   return Answer;
end Get_Conjugate;

separate ( Complex_Math )
procedure Write_Complex( File    : in File_Type;
                         Complex : in Complex_Type ) is
   package Real_IO is new Float_IO( Real );
   use Real_IO;
```

```
begin  -- Write_Complex
   Put ( File, Complex.Re, 3, 3, 0 );
   if Complex.Im > 0.0 then
      Put ( File,"+" );
   end if;
   Put ( File,Complex.Im, 3, 3, 0 );
   Put_Line ( File, "i" );
end Write_Complex;
```

11.7

```
with Text_IO; use Text_IO;
package body Finite_Sequence is
   procedure Get_a_Sequence ( Sequence : out Sequence_Description_Type;
                              Seq_File : in out File_Type ) is
      Value         : Integer;
      First_Value   : Integer;
      Next_Value    : Integer;
      Diff          : Float;
      New_Diff      : Float
      Comma         : Character;
      Quotient      : Float;
      New_Quotient  : Float;
      package Int_IO is new Integer_IO( Integer );
      use Int_IO;
   begin  -- Get_a_Sequence
      Get ( Seq_File,First_Value );
      Sequence.First_Term := First_Value;
      Get ( Seq_File,Comma );
      Get ( Seq_File,Value );
      Diff := Float( Value - First_Value );
      Quotient := Float( Value) / Float( First_Value );
      for i in 1..2
      loop
         Get ( Seq_File, Comma );
         Get ( Seq_File, Next_Value );
         New_Quotient := Float( Next_Value ) / Float( Value );
         if Quotient = New_Quotient then
            Sequence.Kind := Geometric;
            Sequence.Common_Diff := Quotient;
         else
            Sequence.Kind := Arithmetic;
            Sequence.Common_Diff := Diff;
            exit;
         end if;
         if End_of_File( Seq_File ) then
            exit;
```

```
         else
            Value := Next_Value;
         end if;
      end loop;
      while not End_of_File( Seq_File )
      loop
         Get ( Seq_File,Comma );
         Get ( Seq_File,Next_Value );
      end loop;
      Sequence.Last_Term := Next_Value;
   exception
      when Data_Error =>
         Put ( "Error in Sequence" );
   end Get_a_Sequence;
end Finite_Sequence;
```

11.8

```
with Drivers_License_DBMS; use Drivers_License_DBMS;
with Text_IO; use Text_IO;
procedure Update_Drivers_License_DBMS is
   type Action_Type is (A, D, U, Q);
   package Action_IO is new Enumeration_IO (Action_Type);
   use     Action_IO;
   Action : Action_Type;
   Points : Natural;
   function A_License_Number return License_Number_Type is
      License_Number  : License_Number_Type;
      Non_Digit_Found : Boolean;
   begin -- A_License_Number
      Put ("Enter first (capital) letter of license number: ");
      loop
         Get (License_Number.First_Letter);
         if License_Number.First_Letter not in 'A'..'Z'
         then
            Put ("Invalid, re-enter: ");
         else
            exit;
         end if;
      end loop;
      Put ("Enter remaining fifteen digits of license number: ");
      loop
         Get (License_Number.Digit_Sequence);
         Non_Digit_Found := False;
         for I in License_Number.Digit_Sequence'Range
         loop
```

```
            if License_Number.Digit_Sequence(I) not in '0'..'9'
            then
               Non_Digit_Found := True;
               exit;
            end if;
         end loop;

         if Non_Digit_Found
         then
            Put ("Invalid, re-enter: ");
         else
            exit;
         end if;
      end loop;
      return License_Number;
   end A_License_Number;
   function A_Drivers_License return Drivers_License_Type is
      -- code for I/O instantiations
      Drivers_License : Drivers_License_Type;
   begin -- A_Drivers_License
      Drivers_License.License_Number := A_License_Number;
      -- code to get rest of drivers license data
      return Drivers_License;
   end A_Drivers_License;
   function Number_of_Points return Natural is
      package Nat_IO is new Integer_IO (Natural); use Nat_IO;
      Number : Natural;
   begin -- Number_of_Points
      Put ("Enter number of points: ");
      loop
         begin
            Get (Number);
            exit;
         exception
            when Constraint_Error => Put ("Invalid, re-enter: ");
         end;
      end loop;
      return Number;
   end Number_of_Points;
begin -- Update_Drivers_License_DBMS
   Put_Line
    ("The New Jersey Drivers License Bureau is open for business");
   loop
      Put_Line ("A = add new drivers license to system,");
      Put_Line ("D = delete existing drivers license from system,");
```

```
      Put_Line ("U = update drivers license points total,");
      Put_Line ("Q = quit");
      Put      ("Enter next action: ");
      begin
         loop
            Get (Action);
            exit;
         end loop;
      exception
         when Constraint_Error => Put ("Invalid, re-enter: ");
      end;
      begin
         case Action is
         when A => Add_Drivers_License (A_Drivers_License);
         when D => Delete_Drivers_License (A_License_Number);
         when U => Update_Points (A_License_Number, Number_of_Points);
         when Q => exit;
         end case;
      exception
         when License_Number_Exists    =>
            Put_Line ("Duplicate license number already in system");
         when License_Number_Not_Found =>
            Put_Line ("License number not found in system");
         when Database_Full            =>
            Put_Line ("System is full, notify supervisor");
         when License_Suspended        =>
            Put_Line ("License suspended, issue official notification");
      end;
   end loop;
end Update_Drivers_License_DBMS;
```

CHAPTER 12

12.1

```
package body Outdoor_Thermometer is
   function Conversion_to_Celsius   (Temp : Fahrenheit_Temp_Type)
            return   Celsius_Temp_Type is
   begin -- Conversion_to_Celsius
      return Celsius_Temp_Type((Temp - 32.0) * 5.0 / 9.0);
   end Conversion_to_Celsius;
   function Conversion_to_Fahrenheit (Temp :   Celsius_Temp_Type)
            return Fahrenheit_Temp_Type is
   begin -- Conversion_to_Fahrenheit
      return Fahrenheit_Temp_Type((Temp * 9.0 / 5.0) + 32.0);
   end Conversion_to_Fahrenheit;
end Outdoor_Thermometer;
```

12.3

```
package body Trig_Package is
   Terms : constant := 9;
   function Fac (Value : Positive) return Positive is
   begin -- Fac (recursive method)
      if Value = 1
      then
         return 1;
      else
         return Value * Fac (Value - 1);
      end if;
   end Fac;
   function Sin (Angle : Radians_Type) return Answer_Type is
      Answer : Float := Float(Angle);
      Power  : Integer;
   begin -- Sin (Taylor expansion method)
      for I in 1..Terms
      loop
         Power := (I * 2) + 1;
         if (I mod 2) = 0
         then
            Answer := Answer +
             Float(Angle) ** Power / Float (Fac (Power));
         else
            Answer := Answer -
             Float(Angle) ** Power / Float (Fac (Power));
         end if;
      end loop;
      return Answer_Type(Answer);
   end Sin;
   function Cos (Angle : Radians_Type) return Answer_Type is
      Answer : Float := 1.0;
      power  : Integer;
   begin -- Cos (Taylor expansion method)
      for I in 1..Terms
      loop
         Power := I * 2;
         if (I mod 2) = 0
         then
            Answer := Answer +
             Float (Angle) ** Power / Float (Fac (Power));
         else
            Answer := Answer -
             Float (Angle) ** Power / Float (Fac (Power));
         end if;
```

```
      end loop;
      return Answer_Type(Answer);
   end Cos;
   function Tan (Angle : Radians_Type) return Float is
   begin -- Tan
      return Float (Sin (Angle) / Cos (Angle));
   end Tan;
   function Cot (Angle : Radians_Type) return Float is
   begin -- Cot
      return Float (Cos (Angle) / Sin (Angle));
   end Cot;
   function Sec (Angle : Radians_Type) return Float is
   begin -- Sec
      return 1.0 / Float (Cos (Angle));
   end Sec;
   function Csc (Angle : Radians_Type) return Float is
   begin -- Csc
      return 1.0 / Float (Sin (Angle));
   end Csc;
end Trig_Package;
```

12.5
Because the packages export only types and/or objects. The packages *do not* contain any resources that require implementation in a package body.

12.7
The details concerning *how* the soda machine implements its operations are protected from the user. The external world therefore cannot inadvertently modify the activity of the soda machine.

```
with Text_IO; use Text_IO;
package body Soda_Machine_Operations is
   -- I/O for the nickels, dimes and quarters
   package Coin_IO is new Enumeration_IO (Coin_Type);
   use     Coin_IO;
   -- I/O for the soda button selections
   package Soda_Selection_Button_IO is new Integer_IO
          (Soda_Selection_Button_Type);
   use     Soda_Selection_Button_IO;
   -- I/O for the cans of soda
   package Soda_Can_IO is new Enumeration_IO (Soda_Can_Type);
   use     Soda_Can_IO;
   -- global object to hold exact change required status
   Exact_Change_Required : Boolean;                  := False;
   -- global object to hold exact change required status
   Change_Return          : array (Coin_Type) of Natural := (25, 25, 25);
   -- global object to hold amount of cans available for each soda
   Soda_Stock             : array (Soda_Selection_Button_Type) of Natural
                          := (20, 20, 20, 20, 20, 20, 20);
```

```
      procedure Accept_Coins
        (Total_Inserted : out Change_Type;
         Money_Returned : out Boolean) is separate;
      procedure Accept_Soda
        (Button_Selection : out Soda_Selection_Button_Type) is separate;
      procedure Release_Change
        (Coins_Inserted   : in Change_Type) is separate;
      procedure Release_Can
        (Selection        : in Soda_Selection_Button_Type) is separate;
end Soda_Machine_Operations;

-- This procedure accepts the coins inserted and keeps track of them in
-- the array Actual_Coins_Inserted.  Actual_Coins_Inserted is an array
-- indexed by coin type and whose component is the number of that
-- particular coin inserted.
--
-- This procedure returns the coins if the coin return button is
-- depressed.
separate (Soda_Machine_Operations)
procedure Accept_Coins (Total_Inserted : out Change_Type;
                        Money_Returned : out Boolean) is
   type Actual_Coins_Inserted_Type is array (Coin_Type) of Natural;
   type   Coin_Return_Desired_Type is (Yes, No);
   -- I/O for coin return button
   package Coin_Return_Desired_IO is new Enumeration_IO
          (Coin_Return_Desired_Type);
   use Coin_Return_Desired_IO;
   Actual_Coins_Inserted : Actual_Coins_Inserted_Type := (0, 0, 0);
   Coin_Inserted         : Coin_Type;
   Coins_Returned        : Coin_Return_Desired_Type;
   -- now nested instead of stubbed out
   procedure Return_Coins
    (Actual_Coins_Inserted : in Actual_Coins_Inserted_Type) is
   begin -- Return_Coins
      for Coin In Coin_Type
      loop
         for I in 1..Actual_Coins_Inserted(Coin)
         loop
            Put ("Dispensing a ");
            Put (Coin);
            New_Line;
         end loop;
      end loop;
   end Return_Coins;
begin -- Accept_Coins
```

```
   Total_Inserted := 0;
   while Total_Inserted < 50
   loop
      if Exact_Change_Required
      then
         Put ("Enter coin (exact change required) : ");
      else
         Put ("Enter coin: ");
      end if;
      loop
         begin
            Get (Coin_Inserted);
            exit;
         exception
            when Data_Error | Constraint_Error =>
               Put ("Invalid entry, " &
                    "enter only nickel, dime or quarter: ");
         end;
      end loop;
      Actual_Coins_Inserted(Coin_Inserted) :=
       Actual_Coins_Inserted(Coin_Inserted) + 1;
      Total_Inserted := Total_Inserted + Value_of (Coin_Inserted);
      Put ("Do you want your coins returned: ");
      loop
         begin
            Get (Coins_Returned);
            exit;
         exception
            when Data_Error |  Constraint_Error =>
               Put ("Invalid entry, enter either yes or no: ");
         end;
      end loop;
      case Coins_Returned is
      when Yes =>
         Return_Coins (Actual_Coins_Inserted);
         Money_Returned := True;
         exit;
      when No  =>
         Money_Returned := False;
      end case;
   end loop;
end Accept_Coins;

-- This procedure accepts the user's soda selection.
separate (Soda_Machine_Operations)
```

```
procedure Accept_Soda
 (Button_Selection : out Soda_Selection_Button_Type) is
begin -- Accept_Soda
   for Soda_Selection_Button in Soda_Selection_Button_Type
   loop
      Put ("For ");
      Put (Soda_Machine(Soda_Selection_Button));
      Put (", Select ");
      Put (Soda_Selection_Button);
      New_Line;
   end loop;
   Put ("Enter soda selection: ");
   loop
      begin
         Get (Button_Selection);
         if Soda_Stock(Button_Selection) = 0
         then
            Put ("Out of stock, enter another selection:");
         else
            exit;
         end if;
      exception
         when Data_Error | Constraint_Error =>
            Put ("Invalid entry, enter only 1 through ");
            Put (Soda_Selection_Button_Type'Last);
            Put (": ");
      end;
   end loop;
end Accept_Soda;

-- This procedure releases the correct change if the total amount of
-- money inserted exceeds the cost of the can.
separate (Soda_Machine_Operations)
procedure Release_Change (Coins_Inserted : in Change_Type) is
   Remaining_Change : Change_Type := Coins_Inserted - Cost_of_Can;
   Coin_Released    : Coin_Type;
begin -- Release_Change
   while not Exact_Change_Required and Remaining_Change > 0
   loop
      if    Remaining_Change in 25..50
      then
         Coin_Released := Quarter;
      elsif Remaining_Change in 10..24
      then
         Coin_Released := Dime;
```

```
      elsif Remaining_Change in  5..9
      then
         Coin_Released := Nickel;
      end if;
      Remaining_Change := Remaining_Change - Value_of (Coin_Released);
      Change_Return(Coin_Released) := Change_Return(Coin_Released) - 1;
      Put ("Releasing a ");
      Put (Coin_Released);
      New_Line;
   end loop;
   Exact_Change_Required := Change_Return(Nickel) < 1 or
                            Change_Return(Dime   ) < 2;
end Release_Change;

-- This procedure releases the soda, given the user button selection.
separate (Soda_Machine_Operations)
procedure Release_Can (Selection : in Soda_Selection_Button_Type) is
begin -- Release_Can
   Soda_Stock(Selection) := Soda_Stock(Selection) - 1;
   Put       (Soda_Machine(Selection));
   Put_Line (" can released");
end Release_Can;
```

12.11

```
package body Drivers_License_DBMS is
   Database_Limit : constant := 10;
   type Database_Count_Type is range 0..Database_Limit;
   subtype Database_Range_Type is
           Database_Count_Type    range 1..Database_Limit;
   Database_Count :         Database_Count_Type := 0;
   Database       : array (Database_Range_Type) of Drivers_License_Type;
   function Index_of
    (License_Number : License_Number_Type) return Database_Range_Type is
   begin -- Index_of
      for Index in 1..Database_Count
      loop
         if License_Number = Database(Index).License_Number
         then
            return Index;
         end if;
      end loop;
      raise License_Number_Not_Found;
   end Index_of;
   procedure Add_Drivers_License
    (Drivers_License : in Drivers_License_Type) is
      Index : Database_Range_Type;
```

```
  begin -- Add_Drivers_License
     -- check if record already exists in database
     begin
        Index := Index_of (Drivers_License.License_Number);
        raise License_Number_Exists)
     exception
        when License_Number_Not_Found => null;
     end;
     -- check if database full
     if Database_Count = Database_Limit
     then
        raise Database_Full;
     else
        -- update database count
        Database_Count := Databasc_Count + 1;
        -- store record in next available position
        Database(Database_Count) := Drivers_License;
     end if;
  end Add_Drivers_License;
  procedure Delete_Drivers_License
   (License_Number : in License_Number_Type) is
  begin -- Delete_Drivers_License
     -- swap last record in database
     -- into position of record to be deleted
     Database(Index_of (License_Number)) := Database(Database_Count);
     -- update database count
     Database_Count := Database_Count - 1;
  end Delete_Drivers_License;
  procedure Update_Points
   (License_Number : in License_Number_Type;
    New_Points     : in                Natural) is
     Index : Database_Range_Type := Index_of (License_Number);
  begin -- Update_Points
     -- update points total
     Database(Index).Points := Database(Index).Points + New_Points;
  exception
     when Constraint_Error =>
        -- set points total to maximum
        Database(Index).Points := 12;
        raise License_Suspended;
  end Update_Points;
end Drivers_License_DBMS;
```

12.11a

```
-- function declaration in package specification
-- License_Number_Not_Found exception raised
--  if license number is not in the database.
function Expired
 (License_Number : License_Number_Type;
  Current_Date   :            Date_Type) return Boolean;
-- function body (in package body) uses the two subprograms
-- Leap_Year and Date_Number
function Leap_Year (Year : Year_Type) return Boolean is
begin -- Leap_Year
   return Year rem 400 = 0 or (Year rem 100 /= 0 and Year rem 4 = 0);
end Leap_Year;
function Date_Number (Input : Date_Type) return Natural is
   -- Returns a date number for the input date record.
   -- e.g. (Apr, 15, 1985) returns 1985105.
   -- This is useful for date comparisons.
   Number_of_Days_Before : constant array (Month_Type) of Natural :=
    (  0,  31,  59,  90,  120, 151, 181, 212, 243, 273, 304, 334);
   Date : Natural := Natural(Input.Year) * 1000
    + Number_of_Days_Before (Input.Month) + Natural(Input.Day);
begin -- Date_Number
   if Input.Month > Feb and Leap_Year (Input.Year)
   then
      Date := Date + 1; -- Add Leap Day
   end if;
   return Date;
end Date_Number;
function Expired
 (License_Number : License_Number_Type;
  Current_Date   :            Date_Type) return Boolean is
begin -- Expired
   return Date_Number (Current_Date) >
    Date_Number (Database(Index_of (License_Number)).Expiration_Date);
end Expired;
```

12.11b

```
-- function declaration in package specification
function Number_of_Licenses_Issued_for
 (Car : Car_Type) return Natural;
-- function body (in package body)
function Number_of_Licenses_Issued_for
 (Car : Car_Type) return Natural is
   Number : Natural := 0;
```

```
begin -- Number_of_Licenses_Issued_for
   for Index in 1..Database_Count
   loop
      if Car = Database(Index).Car
      then
         Number := Number + 1;
      end if;
   end loop;
   return Number;
end Number_of_Licenses_Issued_for;
```

12.11c

```
-- function declaration in package specification
function Number_of_Licenses_Issued_for_Senior_Citizens
 (Current_Date : Date_Type) return Natural;
-- function body (in package body)
-- This function also uses Date_Number as coded in exercise 12.11a.
function Number_of_Licenses_Issued_for_Senior_Citizens
 (Current_Date : Date_Type) return Natural is
   Date   : Date_Type := (Current_Date.Month,
                          Current_Date.Day,
                          Current_Date.Year - 65);
   Number : Natural   := 0;
begin -- Number_of_Licenses_Issued_for_Senior_Citizens
   for Index in 1..Database_Count
   loop
      -- If driver born on or before current date - 65 years, increment.
      if Date_Number (Database(Index).Birth_Date) <= Date_Number (Date)
      then
         Number := Number + 1;
      end if;
   end loop;
   return Number;
end Number_of_Licenses_Issued_for_Senior_Citizens;
```

12.11d

```
-- function declaration in package specification
function Number_of_Licenses_Issued_for
 (Lower_Age, Upper_Age : Year_Type;
  Current_Date         : Date_Type) return Natural;
-- function body (in package body)
-- this function also uses Date_Number as coded in Exercise 12.11a
function Number_of_Licenses_Issued_for
 (Lower_Age, Upper_Age : Year_Type;
  Current_Date         : Date_Type) return Natural is
```

```
   Lower_Date : Date_Type := (Current_Date.Month,
                              Current_Date.Day,
                              Current_Date.Year - Lower_Age);
   Upper_Date : Date_Type := (Current_Date.Month,
                              Current_Date.Day,
                              Current_Date.Year - Upper_Age);
   Number     : Natural   := 0;
begin -- Number_of_Licenses_Issued_for
   for Index in 1..Database_Count
   loop
      -- If driver born on or after  current date - upper age and
      --    driver born on or before current date - lower age, increment.
      if  Date_Number (Database(Index).Birth_Date) >=
          Date_Number (Lower_Date)
      and Date_Number (Database(Index).Birth_Date) <=
          Date_Number (Upper_Date)
      then
         Number := Number + 1;
      end if;
   end loop;
   return Number;
end Number_of_Licenses_Issued_for;
```

12.11e

```
with Drivers_License_DBMS; use Drivers_License_DBMS;
with Text_IO; use Text_IO;
procedure Query_Drivers_License_DBMS is
   type Action_Type is (E, C, S, R, Q);
   package Action_IO is new Enumeration_IO (Action_Type);
   use     Action_IO;
   package Natural_IO is new Integer_IO (Natural);
   use     Natural_IO;
   Current_Date : Date_Type;
   Action       : Action_Type;
   function The_Current_Date return Date_Type is separate;
   function A_License_Number return License_Number_Type is separate;
   function A_Car return Car_Type is separate;
   function An_Age (Kind : String) return Natural is separate;
begin -- Query_Drivers_License_DBMS
   Put_Line
    ("The New Jersey Drivers License Bureau is open for information");
   Current_Date := The_Current_Date;
   loop
      Put_Line ("E = check if a driver's license has expired,");
```

```
Put_Line ("C = check number of licenses issued for " &
          "a specific car,");
Put_Line ("S = check number of licenses issued for " &
          "senior citizens,");
Put_Line ("R = check number of licenses issued for " &
          "drivers in specific age range,");
Put_Line ("Q = quit");
Put      ("Enter next action: ");
begin
   loop
      Get (Action);
      exit;
   end loop;
exception
   when Constraint_Error => Put ("Invalid, re-enter: ");
end;
begin
   case Action is
      when E =>
         if Expired (A_License_Number, Current_Date)
         then
            Put_Line ("License expired");
         else
            Put_Line ("License not expired");
         end if;
      when C =>
         Put ("Number of licenses issued = ");
         Put (Number_of_Licenses_Issued_for (A_Car));
         New_Line;
      when S =>
         Put ("Number of licenses issued = ");
         Put (Number_of_Licenses_Issued_for_Senior_Citizens
             (Current_Date));
         New_Line;
      when R =>
         Put ("Number of licenses issued = ");
         Put (Number_of_Licenses_Issued_for
             (An_Age("lower"), An_Age("upper"), Current_Date)); New_Line;
      when Q =>
         exit;
   end case;
```

```
      exception
         when License_Number_Not_Found =>
            Put_Line ("License number not found in system");
      end;
   end loop;
end Query_Drivers_License_DBMS;
```

Solutions to exercises 12.13, 12.15, and 12.17 are not supplied.

INDEX